Quest for More

A One Year Devotional Through the Bible

Whispers & Fringes

WESTBOW
PRESS®
A DIVISION OF THOMAS NELSON
& ZONDERVAN

WestBow Press books may be ordered through booksellers or by contacting:

WestBow Press
A Division of Thomas Nelson & Zondervan
1663 Liberty Drive
Bloomington, IN 47403
www.westbowpress.com
1 (866) 928-1240

ISBN: 978-1-9736-7304-0 (sc)
ISBN: 978-1-9736-7306-4 (hc)
ISBN: 978-1-9736-7305-7 (e)

Library of Congress Control Number: 2019914407

Print information available on the last page.

WestBow Press rev. date: 02/19/2020

To those who taught us to
love the Word of God...
our parents, pastors,
teachers, and mentors.

See, we really were listening.
Thank you.

Just in case you were wondering ...

In 2011, Whispers & Fringes started as a small Bible study in the Dallas area. Over the years, we continued meeting monthly but then expanded our territory on-line through a website, social media (including Facebook Live meetings) and YouVersion devotionals.

In 2017, we hosted a discipleship program for women in our local area. The goal was to read through the entire Bible in one-year, following the chronological reading plan.

For many, it was their first time to read through the entire Bible. When asked how they felt after accomplishing this, the common response was, *"I'm so glad I did this."* They had an understanding of scripture that they never had before ... because now, they knew the whole story.

A few months later, after a "random" conversation with a family friend (Janet), a seed for a devotional book was planted. In 2018, the team embarked on this project and the result is what you are now holding in your hands.

We believe what scripture says:

"There's nothing like the written Word of God for showing you the way to salvation through faith in Christ Jesus. Every part of Scripture is God-breathed and useful one way or another—showing us truth, exposing our rebellion, correcting our mistakes, training us to live God's way. Through the Word we are put together and shaped up for the tasks God has for us." (2 Timothy 3:16b-17 MSG)

We are not theologians so our thoughts may be simple. Our prayer is that women would understand the Bible more - from Genesis to Revelation - and learn how to apply God's truths to their everyday lives.

With love,
Anu, Binu, Betsy, Joyce, Shiney and Vijoy

The Whispers & Fringes Team (Left to Right): Joyce George, Elizabeth Thomas, Binu Samuel, Vijoy Joseph, Anu Abraham, Shiney Thomas

The Ministry

The name "Whispers & Fringes" is taken from Job 26:14. As he was describing the incredible majesty and power of God, Job concludes his remarks with this telling statement - *"And these are but the outer fringe of His works; how faint the whisper we hear of Him!"* The pursuit of God must be constant because what we have seen is just a glimpse.

The Writers

Anu ~ Growing up in a Christian home, Anu (Anitha) was saved at an early age. For years, she served in the worship ministry and eventually married the cute piano player on the team. In 2011, God called her to step out of her comfort zone and start a women's Bible study and from there, Whispers & Fringes was born. Her heart is to encourage and empower women through speaking, writing and community study. She continues to serve alongside her husband, Lance, as elders in the marriage ministry at Covenant Church. If she isn't at work or church, she is probably napping or cheering on the Dallas Cowboys.

Binu ~ Binu is probably a lot like you. A woman who relies upon God for everything. She was born and raised in Texas, graduated from the University of Houston and is grateful for her job as a retail pharmacist. Her favorite place to be is at home with her husband and her two basketball-loving teenage sons. Binu considers it an honor to serve on the leadership team of Whispers & Fringes. Her sincere prayer is that God would use her to encourage and impart hope and practical wisdom into the lives of women. She wants women to know, they are not alone.

Elizabeth ~ Elizabeth Thomas, "Betsy", is a woman who is passionate to serve Christ and share her faith with the lost. She was born in Houston, Texas and is the first child of a Chaplain and a Registered Nurse. Her love for kids came from her role as the oldest of four children. Elizabeth considers it an honor to serve as a pediatrician for children in south Dallas and loves to be a part of their families. She is married to a wonderful husband and has three beautiful children.

Joyce ~Joyce is a native New Yorker and enjoys having breakfast and "caw-fee" at any time of day. Since her teen years, she has felt a tug to leap out of her comfort zone. Such adventures have included teaching Sunday School to young children and pursuing a career as a social worker. Joyce and her husband Shibu share a passion for marriages and seeing couples walk in oneness with God. To round out the fun, Joyce has become a stay at home mom to their three great kids whom she also home schools.

Shiney ~ Shiney is a wife, mom, sister and friend. She has been married for 15 years and is mom to one four-legged child and two, two legged children. She loves Jesus and coffee, both of which fuel her day. She is a physical therapist and uses her skills as a means to spread God's love and joy to her patients. Being a part of Whispers & Fringes has been life changing for her and she loves the opportunity to share that with others.

Vijoy ~ Vijoy grew up in the church and gave her life to Christ at a very young age. She considers it such a joy to be a follower of Christ, as she daily experiences God's love and sovereignty in her life. Her desire is to encourage women to trust God and His plan, even when their life takes an unexpected turn. She hopes that God will use her life and her story to bring glory to His name. She is a proud Texan and has a career as a CPA in the Dallas area. Outside of work, she loves to spend time at home with her family, or with the wonderful lifelong friends that she has been blessed with. She also loves to cook and bake and can always find an occasion to whip up a sweet treat to share with family and friends.

Follow us on Facebook, Instagram, YouTube, and our website: www. whispersandfringes.com

Cover Design by Kayla George
Photography by Just Inspired Visuals

How to use this devotional

This devotional book follows the one-year chronological reading plan which takes the reader through the Bible in the order in which things happened.

For example, the stories of David in Kings and Chronicles are often paired together along with the Psalm he wrote during that time. In the New Testament, a story that is repeated in each Gospel will be typically be in one day's reading. The beauty of this method is that you read the story from different perspectives at one time.

Each devotional includes the daily reading assignment at the top along with a key verse. These devotions do not typically provide a complete explanation of the scripture passage for the day. Instead, it offers one particular thought/application that encouraged us in some way ... and we hope it does the same for you.

We strongly encourage you to read the assigned passages and formulate your own thoughts first using the SITT^C method:

SUMMARIZE - *What did I just read?*
IMPLEMENT - *How can I apply this to my daily life?*
TREASURE - *What verse stood out to me?*
TRAIT - *What character trait of God do I see in this passage?*

Then, you can read the devotion for additional insight!

Even after you've read through the Bible, read it again...and again. And then again. It amazes us that no matter how many times we may have read a particular passage, God will reveal something new.

What we know now is just the faintest *whisper* & outer *fringe* of who He is. There is always more.

Enjoy the journey.

January 1 ~ Genesis 1-3
"Then the Lord God said, 'It is not good that the man should be alone; I will make him a helper fit for him.'" Genesis 2:18 (ESV)

There's a phrase you may have heard in a marriage class... *"What if God designed marriage to make us holy more than to make us happy?"*

I understand the sentiment behind it but I feel like it is missing something.

Recently, I attended my cousin's wedding. Everything was beautiful, especially the bride. As she walked in, I couldn't help but look at my cousin too ... the groom.

He couldn't contain his emotions as he waited for his bride.

I am pretty sure his thought wasn't *"My wife is going to make me so holy!"* We choose our life partner because there is something about them that makes us happy ... and that's not a bad thing.

In Genesis, the first marriage was formed not because God was trying to make Adam holy. Adam had not sinned yet. God wanted a companion...a helper...for Adam. Since the animals didn't seem to fit what He had in mind, God created a woman for that purpose. Interestingly and unfortunately, Eve influenced Adam in a way that actually caused him to be further away from holiness.

Of course, we know that was never God's intent when He created Eve. She made her choice and her husband did too.

Don't get me wrong. Marriage is a great refiner (aka holiness maker). Unfortunately, my husband sees my very human, emotional, and irrational side that no one else may see. As I recognize what is actually in me, I am led to repentance and asking God to mold me into who He wants me to be.

The other side is that often what my husband does for me doesn't contribute to my holiness, it enhances my happiness.

Paul called the believers in Philippi his *"joy and crown" (Philippians 4:1 ESV).* This is the same man who counted everything as loss compared to knowing Jesus but he also recognized the place certain people have in our lives.

My husband is not THE source of my happiness but he is a RESOURCE used by God to make my journey of life a lot more fun...and happy. I want to be the same for him.

If you are married, you have a powerful place in your husband's life. What you do can certainly draw him closer to God and closer to you. That's a happy place to be.

~Anu

January 2 ~ Genesis 4-7

*"In the course of time Cain brought to the Lord an offering of
the fruit of the ground, and Abel also brought of the firstborn of
his flock and of their fat portions." Genesis 4:3-4 (ESV)*

The story of the first pair of brothers is a familiar one. God was pleased with Abel's offering but not Cain's.

This is before the Levitical law of sacrifices had been established ... so, what was going on?

Notice the words used to describe each of their sacrifices: *"In the course of time Cain brought to the Lord an offering of the fruit of the ground, and Abel also brought of the firstborn of his flock and of their fat portions." (Genesis 4:3-4 ESV)*

What happens to fruit in the course of time? If I could show you the strawberries I have now in my fridge, it would make this point even better. Let's just say, it is not at its best.

While their sacrifices were obviously different, there is a key indicator when it comes to Abel's sacrifice... *firstborn.* Cain's sacrifice feels like an afterthought. His response to God when the sacrifice was disregarded confirms there was a heart issue as well. On the other hand, Abel's offering was intentional. He didn't just bring any animal; Abel brought the first of his flock. Scripture later affirms that his sacrifice was given, *"by faith" (Hebrews 11:4 ESV).*

As we continue reading through Genesis, we encounter a man named Enoch. The Amplified version describes his life as one *"who walked in habitual fellowship with God ... in reverent fear and obedience." (Genesis 5:22,24)*

With our busy lives, time with God can become one more item on our to-do list. So, being intentional doesn't mean *"I have to do this",* it means *"I get to do this".* Then, once you are there, engage your heart and mind in the process. We may not get to hear the audible voice of God like they did in Old Testament times but this is still a chance for us to have an encounter with the Most High.

God told Cain, *"If you do well [believing Me and doing what is acceptable and pleasing to Me], will you not be accepted?" (Genesis 4:7a AMP).* The lives of Abel and Enoch were pleasing to God. A heart of faith and obedience is what God wants from us too.

~Anu

January 3 ~ Genesis 8-11
"But God remembered Noah..." Genesis 8:1a (NIV)

We had just sat down for family prayer when out of the mouth of my thirteen-year-old came these words, *"Mama, you are so lucky. We all have issues. I've got eczema, Josh has feet issues (don't ask) and Daddy has a cough, but you don't have anything. You are so lucky."*

Lucky? Is he kidding me? That's when it hit me. He just didn't get it. Anything he carries, I carry. As his mother, I feel the weight of his struggles even more than he does.

At that moment, the Holy Spirit spoke to me, *"That's how I feel about you. I carry your burdens. What you go through, I feel. You don't ever leave my mind.'*

There is a story in the Bible I am sure you are familiar with. It's the story of Noah, the ark and the flood. Forty days of rain had come and gone, and *"The waters flooded the earth for a hundred and fifty days." (Genesis 7:24 NIV)*

Genesis 8:1a tells us, *"But God remembered Noah..." (NIV)* Another translation says it this way, *"God kept Noah in mind." (ISV)*

All along, throughout the rain and the flood, Noah was on God's mind. After 150 days, God, in His sovereignty, knew it was time to act. He *"sent a wind over the earth and the waters receded." (Genesis 8:1b NIV)*

The word *"wind"* is the Hebrew word, *"ru-ah."* It's the same word we see in scripture for Spirit. God sent His Spirit so that the flood waters would subside. He does the same for us.

Maybe you feel forgotten. You've been dealing with your situation for way over 150 days and it seems no one understands or cares about what you are going through.

As I told my son that evening, what concerns him, concerns me....and it concerns the heart of our Heavenly Father even more. God is not detached from our cares. You, my friend, are never alone. God carries our burdens so that we don't have to.

I pray that whatever surrounds you, may you feel His Spirit, His Wind, His Ru-ah... and may God's sweet presence hover over you and cause the cares of this world within you to subside.

~Binu

January 4 ~ Job 1-5

"Then his wife said to him, 'Do you still hold fast your integrity? Curse God and die.' But he said to her, 'You speak as one of the foolish women would speak. Shall we receive good from God, and shall we not receive evil?' In all this Job did not sin with his lips." Job 2:9-10 (ESV)

If your husband was asked who his biggest cheerleader is, what would his answer be? Would it be you? (And not because he knows you'll get mad if he doesn't say you.)

In the midst of all that happened in their lives, the one line we hear from Job's wife is, *"... Are you still trying to maintain your integrity? Curse God and die." (Job 2:9 NLT)* I'm guessing her love language was not words of affirmation.

Our words are sure to make an impact, either positively or negatively.

When my husband and I were first married, I asked him if he felt like our home was a haven. His delayed response told me everything. It wasn't.

It broke my heart and convicted my spirit. God began to show me things that contributed to his response. My high expectations and lack of tolerance for anything less were making our home a place my husband didn't like to be.

As wives, we should be very intentional about showing respect and offering encouragement. If your husband does something you appreciate, tell him. If he's looking good, tell him that too! Unfortunately, at times we can be nicer to strangers than we are to our own spouses.

God created men and women differently so scripture guides us accordingly. Men are told to love their wives. Wives, on the other hand, are told to respect their husbands.

Unfortunately, we, as women, often have a double standard on this. On those days when our emotions are running wild, we still expect our husbands to love us through that. In turn, if our husbands aren't acting very "respect worthy", we conclude that we don't have to put up with that! Then, it's all downhill from there.

There is something about how a woman treats her man. 1 Peter 3:1 (NIV) even goes so far to say that a husband can be *"won over without words by the behavior of their wives."*

Whether it is in word or deed, we contribute to the environment in our home. If someone were to have recorded the last interaction you had with your husband, what story would it tell? The wife who has won her husband over or Job's wife?

If your husband was asked who his biggest cheerleader is, would it be you?

~Anu

January 5 ~ Job 6-9

"Don't I have a right to complain? Don't wild donkeys bray when they find no grass, and oxen bellow when they have no food?" Job 6:5 (NLT)

Can we just be real?

In the Bible, we read about Job. The faithful servant of God who was caught in the middle of a dialogue between God and Satan. Job's life of integrity towards God ended up turning his life upside down.

As he talks with his friends, Job starts to complain but his friends weren't having it. They insisted that his misfortune was caused by something he did. They applied their misguided understanding of God to Job's situation.

But Job was human so he asks the question, *"Don't I have a right to complain?" (Job 6:5a NLT)*

Yes. I believe he did.

However, in all of Job's complaints he didn't sin. In a very raw and honest way, he let his friends and God know how he really felt.

Most of my life I felt like being "real" with God was irreverent and disrespectful. I thought if I spoke out loud how I truly felt, it would mean that I didn't trust God's plan for my life.

The book of Job actually offers a different perspective. After reading through chapter after chapter of Job's complaints and dialogue between he, his friends and God, we see that God doesn't hold it against him. In fact, when God responds, he tells Job's friends that He is angry with *them* for not speaking accurately about Him, as his servant Job had done.

Can I encourage you to be real with God? What is really bothering you?

Tell your Heavenly Father how you feel. He already knows your deepest thoughts and feelings. He doesn't need you to sugar coat what you're going through. I have personally found a freedom in my relationship with God the more real I get with Him. Regardless of what is bothering me, I know I can pray and tell Him about it.

In response, God gently reminds me that He understands...and that it's going to be okay.

Don't be afraid to be real. Your Heavenly Father can handle it.

~Vijoy

January 6 ~ Job 10-13
*"For the life of every living thing is in his hand, and the
breath of every human being." Job 12:10 (NLT)*

In my neighborhood, we have alleys. On my street, I have a backyard, a small strip of grass, an alley, a brick wall and then 6 lanes of traffic.

As I leave my garage and drive down my alley every morning and every evening, my view consists of a brick wall on one side and the fences of my neighbors on the other side.

One neighbor planted some beautiful flowers on their patch of grass in the alley. There are some stately sunflowers and several lush vines that sprout beautiful orange and pink flowers with yellow pistols. The vines wrap around their fence, dotting the entire patch with these flowers. They are my *'adios'* every morning and my *'welcome home'* every evening.

It seems a bit wasteful. Who plants flowers in an alley? Who's even going to see them back there? The flowers don't know where they are planted. They don't know that they are sandwiched between fence and cement.

They don't complain about the exhaust, noise or even their crummy view. They were planted there by someone, who tends to their needs, and they bloom. Every year.

As Christians, we believe that God has a plan and purpose for each one of us. While we may not enjoy our surroundings, we trust that He is holding us in his hands and has us there for a reason.

You may be there to be the face of Christianity to someone you see on a daily basis, or you could be awaiting your divine appointment.

Maybe you are actively trying to change your surroundings. The crazy thing about these flowers in my alley is that they somehow managed to spread from this fence, across the alley, and wrap themselves around a pole on the other side.

Regardless of where you are now and where you are heading ... bloom. Be fruitful. Bring some color to where you are. Spread some joy.

I see these flowers every day and it's a reminder to me: God has me in his hands. I need to bloom where I am planted.

~Shiney

January 7 ~ Job 14-16
*"But my mouth would encourage you; comfort from
my lips would bring you relief." Job 16:5 (NIV)*

I was in college when two of my classmates died in a boating accident. We were part of an intimate group of friends, and upon hearing of their death, we were utterly devastated.

While I had been to several funerals up until that time, I felt the loss of those young men stung me so much more. Maybe I was at a level where I could understand the meaning of death or I simply realized how young and vibrant they were when they breathed their last breath.

I remember flopping down on my dorm room bed and sobbing while a friend comforted me. We couldn't believe it and couldn't bear it. There were not many words, just sobs and tears in that room. What was there to say? Even though we tried to figure out all the details of their accident, we couldn't grasp the reality that they were gone. The details didn't matter... their silence did. As a group of friends, we recalled the good times that were shared and encouraged each other. There were also a lot of silent moments of pondering.

Isn't it like us when we face an unbelievable situation in life that we try to hash out the details and the reasons and make the story fit into a little box in our minds? We usually end up with more "what-if's" than answers.

How about when we are comforting a friend who is going through a devastating loss or a life event that seems unfair? We want to come up with a reason or play the blame game.

They don't need an explanation; they need a shoulder.

Job's friends failed him when he needed their comfort the most. They blamed him and came up with a list of reasons for his losses. That's not what Job needed. Job responds to their words in Job 16:4 when he says, *"I also could speak like you, if you were in my place"* (NIV). He says if the tables were turned, he, too, could speak. Yet, the difference would be that he would "encourage" his friend to bring him relief (Job 16:5 NIV).

What a lesson in how to handle a difficult conversation when you're with a friend! If you decide to speak, let it be words of encouragement. If you decide *not* to speak, that's okay, too. Your presence alone speaks volumes.

~Elizabeth

January 8 ~ Job 17-20
*"I know that my Redeemer lives, and that in the end,
he will stand upon the earth." Job 19:25 (NIV)*

Has a certain circumstance left you feeling hopeless? No matter how much you pray, it seems as there is no change, no hope. Suddenly, you feel forgotten by God. Even worse, maybe those around you don't seem to have an inkling of how to empathize with you. You just feel alone and misunderstood.

I always knew that I wanted to be a mother. In fact, folks used to call me "Mother Hen" when I was as young as 10 years old. So, you can only imagine how very excited I was when I learned that I was pregnant. I was literally jumping up and down for joy. However, to my dismay, my world appeared to crumble just weeks later as I experienced the sorrow of miscarriage.

How could this have happened? I prayed for this baby. I had already combed through chapters of baby books. I was ready to be a mother. My body writhed in pain and my broken heart was aching. To add insult to injury, hurtful comments were made to me; those bad things happened because I had done something wrong.

After the losses of his children and wealth, Job felt hopeless as well. He felt alienated and abandoned by his wife who told him to curse God. Job felt attacked by his friends' words who were certain that his suffering was the result of something evil that he had done. Job loved God and was a righteous man. But he was filled with grief and he was frustrated.

In the midst of this anguish, Job recognized God's sovereignty and His presence. Job didn't allow his feelings or his circumstances to cloud his knowledge of God. He knew who God was and that He is our Help and our Source whether we are at the mountain top or in the valley. Job said that aloud not only to remind himself but to drown out the voices that were not speaking truth or encouragement.

If you find yourself feeling hopeless today, stand on the truth that God is alive, He is for you, and that He has not left you or forsaken you. God loves you very much and He is your hope. He will lift your head, my Friend.

~Joyce

January 9 ~ Job 21-23
"For he will complete what he appoints for me, and many such things are in his mind." Job 23:14 (ESV)

My husband likes to think he has me all figured out. 19 years of marriage will do that to you. That, however, is reciprocated ... and a recent lunch outing confirmed it.

As busy as the restaurant was, our waitress, who was 7 months pregnant, made every effort to ensure we enjoyed our meal. Once the check was paid, we all started to leave, then my husband said he needed to go back in. And I knew exactly what he was doing.

If you know my husband, you might be thinking something along the lines of ordering dessert but this time, that was not the case.

He went back to give our waitress an additional tip, just a little something extra to express our appreciation.

My husband is generous in every sense of the word so this fits right in line with what I know about him. Knowing him and his character assures me ... I can trust what he's doing even when he doesn't say a word.

It got me thinking about other people whom I know that well and my view of God.

There was a time when I was ready for my life to move forward but God's "inactivity" conveyed that He was just fine leaving me right where I was. I quickly began to wonder if He had really forgotten about me this time.

Sometimes, it feels like God has deserted us and we need to figure out this season on our own. However, that goes against the very essence of who He is.

Job looked everywhere but God was seemingly nowhere to be found. Even though Job struggled with this, he found assurance in what he knew about God.

• *"But he knows where I am going. And when he tests me, I will come out as pure as gold ... So he will do to me whatever he has planned. He controls my destiny." (Job 23:10,14 NLT)*

Our belief in God isn't based on the hope that He will do what we want. It is about having faith in His faithfulness, trusting His heart and knowing His character. Even when it feels like He's walked away and we're left wondering and waiting, we can cling to the promise that He is up to something good.

After all, we know Him pretty well, don't we?

~Anu

January 10 ~ Job 24-28
*"But where can wisdom be found? Where does
understanding dwell?" Job 28:12 (NIV)*

The test scores were in. I breathed a sigh of relief, then told my son I was proud of him and went to bed. The next day, I couldn't resist. I had to tell my boys, *"Don't ever let a test dictate what you can or cannot accomplish."* I was speaking from experience. The experience of a not so great test taker.

I was thankful my son did well, but what if he hadn't? I don't want my children to ever doubt what God can do through them. Tests can make us feel really smart, and believe the sky's the limit, or really defeated and limited. Thankfully, despite our test taking abilities, when it comes to spiritual wisdom, we all have equal access to the same source!

In Job 28:12, Job asks *"But where can wisdom be found? Where does understanding dwell?"* (NIV)

Sapphires may come from rocks, and gold from the dust of it ... but what about wisdom?

Job 28:28b gives the answer. *"The fear of the Lord - that is wisdom. And to shun evil is understanding." (NIV)*

It's not a scary kind of fear. It is a healthy fear of God's divine authority intertwined with an understanding of His greatness. Even in the midst of suffering, Job knew God's power was limitless.

"He (God) wraps up the waters in His clouds, yet the clouds do not burst under their weight." (Job 26:8 NIV)

Job concludes the chapter with the following statement. *"And these are but the outer fringe of His works; how faint the whisper of Him!" (Job 26:14 NIV)*

In other words, *"You ain't seen nothing yet!"*

Tests are important so we should always strive to do our best. But the wisdom that Job is talking about is a wisdom that will take us even farther than the wisdom of this world ever will.

Regardless of where you find yourself today, full of confidence or full of inadequacies, God's wisdom is accessible to all! Don't ever doubt what God can do through you.

"If you need wisdom, ask our generous God, and he will give it to you. He will not rebuke you for asking." (James 1:5 NLT)

~Binu

January 11~ Job 29-31

"So, I looked for good, but evil came instead. I waited for the light, but darkness fell. My heart is troubled and restless ..." Job 30:26-27 (NLT)

Job knew that he was blameless before God. He stood confident in the fact that a just God would not punish someone needlessly. He wanted a chance to advocate to God for himself.

I can empathize with that desire.

In times of struggle, we often think that things would smooth out if the other person could just see our point of view. If they could just understand where you or I are coming from, things would be fine. For example, the meeting with your boss where you think you're going to get a promotion turns into a write up instead. That family celebration that ends in an argument. You think that your life is headed in one direction until it makes a violent turn. *What just happened?* You might have been expecting good, but instead, you watch evil running towards you.

When life doesn't go how you planned... when you can't make lemonade from your lemons ... remember that it doesn't take away from who God is. If we could just see what He sees, we would understand the significance of the detour that we are on.

Stand strong. Stand secure. Our Father sees the bigger picture. He is sovereign through it all. The same God that lead you through the good times is holding your hand through the rough ones. The same God that gave you strength to stand tall in your win is strengthening you to stand tall in your struggle.

God will always take care of his children.

~Shiney

January 12 ~ Job 32-34
*"For God speaks again and again, though people
do not recognize it." Job 33:14 (NLT)*

Have you ever looked for a sign from God to come as a lightning bolt in the sky? I know I have.

What I've found though is that God rarely speaks to me that way. Rather, it is in the ordinary and mundane when I tend to hear and sense God the most.

A few years ago, when our family was going through a difficult time, God spoke to me through dreams He gave to two of my children. Each of them came to me in the middle of the night during that season with very vivid dreams about the current situation and about the future.

I knew immediately that God was speaking through them. Since then, I recognize that God speaks to me through my circumstances, through my loved ones, and even through total strangers.

Elihu, the youngest of Job's friends speaks of this in the book of Job.

"For God speaks again and again, though people do not recognize it. He speaks in dreams, in visions of the night, when deep sleep falls on people as they lie in their beds. He whispers in their ears and terrifies them with warnings. He makes them turn from doing wrong; he keeps them from pride. He protects them from the grave, from crossing over the river of death." (Job 33:14-18 NLT)

I too believe that God is always speaking. But why would God speak to us today in addition to what He has already said to us in the Bible?

I believe it's because He wants us to know that He loves us. He wants us to know that our concerns are not insignificant. He wants us to know that we are not alone.

Do you need direction? Do you need comfort? Do you need reassurance? One word from your heavenly Father can set your heart and mind at ease.

It may take some time and practice to recognize when He speaks to you. But once you do, you will understand that He not only holds the world in His hands, but He holds *your* world in His hands.

~Vijoy

January 13 ~ Job 35-37
*"But You are talking nonsense, Job. You have
spoken like a fool." Job 35:16 (NLT)*

Several years ago, a dear friend of mine was struggling with a health crisis. It affected every role in her life as a daughter, sister, employee, wife, and friend. We watched as it began to limit her sphere of influence to the point that she rarely left her home.

Often times, people would come to her home to visit with her, and the encouragement she received from several of them was the same ... *"Ask God to forgive you for whatever you've done to bring about this illness."* It was crushing for her to hear. What could she have possibly done to deserve this?

Job heard the same messages from his 'friends' during his struggle. They initially came to Job and sat with him in silence as he mourned. However, their silence eventually turned into accusations. They called him prideful, seduced by wealth, and bribed into sin. They repeatedly told him to repent in order to change his circumstances.

Despite the voices around him, Job stood confident in his belief of who he was and who God was. Are we as confident when we walk through difficult circumstances? Do we trust that God is holding us in His hand? What are we speaking over our friends when they walk through difficult times?

God's voice is never accusatory to his children. It is always loving and always seeking the best. Our voice should reflect the same.

~Shiney

January 14 ~ Job 38-39
"Who shut up the sea behind doors when it burst
forth from the womb," Job 38:8 (NIV)

My husband and I were newlyweds when we traveled overseas to the Dominican Republic. The beaches there are beautiful. We rode on horses, took a bike ride through the outskirts of the resort we were staying at, and had dinner on the beach.

We had other memorable moments, like getting seasick on a speedboat and having gas siphoned from our 4-wheeler in the middle of a ride.

Then, there was that near-death experience.

The sun was setting, and my husband and I were enjoying a walk on the beach. The waves felt refreshing against our feet, and before I realized what was happening, I was pulled away from my husband by a massive current. I remember losing my footing and ultimately, control of my body. The force of the water pushed me backward, and I lost all sense of direction.

I came up for air and couldn't hear or see my husband. I was just being pushed back and forth by the massive strength of the water.

Suddenly, I felt an arm grab and pull me. Then, I was back on shore. I felt confused - what had just happened?

My husband later explained that while we were walking together, a large wave pulled us apart, and I was pushed into the ocean. He yelled out for help and out of nowhere, a man heard him, swam, and rescued me.

I could have died that day ... but God saved me.

I could never have appreciated the sheer strength of the water until I was forced into it with no sense of control. In today's passage, God reminds Job that it is He who sets the limits for the sea and decides where the waves should stop.

It is all God. He is ultimately in control.

When I felt helpless and lost in the water, God was in control. He created those waters and He created me. Nothing is a surprise to our sovereign God.

When fear seems to swirl around us and we lose our footing, He pulls us up and leads us to the warmth of the shore. Know that you can trust in a God who holds the waves in the palm of His hand.

~Elizabeth

January 15 ~ Job 40-42
*"The Lord blessed the latter part of Job's life more
than the former part." Job 42:12 (NIV)*

When I was in high school, one of my art projects was to make a clay sculpture. The process was a tedious one. I engaged in this labor of creativity daily. When the vase was too tall to be stored in the usually locked cabinet, it was placed in a cabinet that did not have doors.

Imagine my shock when I walked into class the next day to find that a "lively" teenager thought it would be amusing to punch the vase and ruin its shape. As I tearfully looked at my broken sculpture, all I could think about were the countless hours which now felt like a waste. I was angry and I was disappointed.

Do you ever feel as if you are doing the right thing, only to end up feeling broken by your circumstances? Maybe you're like Job, a righteous person who loves God, a loving spouse, a caring parent, honorable business person and overall, possess a great reputation among those who know you. Then one day, you experience loss, death, illness and ultimately, alienation. You still trust God and refuse to walk away from Him in spite of being told to do so by your own spouse. You feel disheartened as you writhe in physical and emotional pain ... you feel broken.

I'm so glad the book of Job doesn't end there. As one continues to follow his life, he humbles himself in the presence of Almighty God and isn't just restored to the life he once had. The key verse indicates he is blessed twice as much. Wow, what an awesome God we serve!

Though I wanted to give up on my broken vase, my teacher encouraged me that it could be fixed if I would just submit to the process. Not only were we able to repair the vase, it actually looked much better by the time it was all done!

Dear Friend, you may feel broken by your present situation, but just know that you are not beyond repair when you place your life in the hands of God. Acknowledge that you can't do it by yourself, ask Him for help, obey what He instructs, and trust that *"His plans are to prosper you and not to harm you."* (Jeremiah 29:11 NIV) Not only can God fix your circumstances, But He can also make them better!

~Joyce

January 16 ~ Gen 12-15

"So Abram went, as the Lord had told him..." Genesis 12:4 (ESV)

Comfort zone - 2 words that go great together and where I love to be.

I've been at the same job for almost 20 years. I've driven the same car for the past 12 years.

When I go to a particular restaurant, I order the same dish each time I go there. I sit in the same row at church every single week and if someone is in my seat ... well, maybe that's another post for another time.

If you haven't figured it out, I like the comfortable and predictable.

Case in point: we had traveled out of state with my family and once we arrived at our destination, we were ready to eat. By then, we didn't feel like being adventurous. We just wanted a decent meal. So, we ended up having dinner at a chain restaurant that we actually had back home.

Talk about comfort zone. It was safe. It was predictable. We knew what to expect.

We left full.

The next day, my husband consulted a travel guide and we ended up at a local spot. It was different. It was new so we didn't know what to expect. And it was great.

We left full ... and satisfied.

It's a simple thought but maybe it speaks to where you are at right now. What new thing is God asking you to do? Maybe it's time to give it a try.

*"Now the Lord said to Abram, "**Go** from your country and your kindred and your father's house to the land that I will show you. And I will make of you a great nation, **and I will** bless you and make your name great, so that you will be a blessing." (Genesis 12:1-2 ESV)*

Abram's destiny hinged on him leaving the known and going to the unknown. If he would do his part and go, God would do His part too.

"So Abram went, as the Lord had told him..." Genesis 12:4 (ESV)

And the rest is history. Israel's history to be exact.

Stepping out of your comfort zone won't be comfortable but new experiences and fulfilled callings are waiting.

~Anu

V.12.2022

January 17 ~ Genesis 16-18
*"For the generations to come every male among you
who is eight days old must be circumcised..."*
Genesis 17:12a (NIV)

Not sure how I missed it, but I did. The big warning on the side of the taco shell box that states- do not use in toaster oven.

I placed a few taco shells into my new toaster oven, then walked into the other room. As I returned back to the kitchen, I saw flames shooting out of the toaster oven.

There was a reason for the warning on the box. The manufacturer, the creator of the taco shell, was not trying to "control" me. The manufacturer knew that taco shells in a toaster oven equals disaster! But I didn't take time to read *all* the instructions. It was an innocent oversight.

Hosea 4:6 states, *"My people are destroyed for lack of knowledge."* (KJV)

Some may see the Bible as a book of 'Thou shalt Nots.' But the more I read His Word, the more I understand, from Genesis to Revelation, God's love and character is seen. Every word, every *do* and every *don't*, is for our good.

In Genesis 17, God introduces the covenant of circumcision to Abraham. *"For the generations to come every male among you who is eight days old must be circumcised ..." (vs 12a NIV)*

Why was God so specific? Why does the baby have to be eight days old? Why not when it's convenient for the parents? Is God just trying to "control" us?

In the 1900's, medical research discovered Vitamin K coupled with prothrombin causes blood coagulation or clotting. *"On the eighth day, the amount of prothrombin present actually is elevated above one-hundred percent of normal."* (Dr. McMillen/ Apologetics Press)[1] Thus making it an ideal day for a minor procedure, especially before modern day medicine.

In case I lost you at prothrombin or maybe even at taco shells, my point is that our Creator knows us, loves us and truly desires what's best for us. Each and every command or Word of instruction He gives is given out of love.

It is for our good. If we choose to do our own thing, then like me and the tacos, the outcome is on us.

~Binu

January 18 ~ Genesis 19-21
"Then God opened Hagar's eyes, and she saw..." Genesis 21:19a (NLT)

Even though I have been a "Mrs." for 19 years now, my single years still outnumber my married years.

Compared to generations before us, women are staying single longer or are choosing not to get married at all. I love seeing singles who are maximizing this season of their life. They are pursuing higher education or advancing in their careers. They are buying homes and saving towards their future. They are going on mission trips and fulfilling their callings. They are working it!

Unfortunately, I was not one of those singles who was thriving. I was surviving (barely). For me, my season of singleness was a challenging time.

I often felt alone and forgotten by people ... and God.

In the book of Genesis, we come across someone whose life was quite different from previous characters.

Hagar found herself in a position of being a single mom. Rejected by her employer and to an extent by the father of her child, she was sent away and ends up wandering aimlessly in the wilderness.

Once she runs out of water, she seemingly comes to the end of herself, thinking that her life and her son's life are over ... but that's when God reveals Himself to her.

"... Hagar, what's wrong? Do not be afraid! God has heard the boy crying as he lies there. Go to him and comfort him, for I will make a great nation from his descendants. Then God opened Hagar's eyes, and she saw a well full of water. She quickly filled her water container and gave the boy a drink." (Genesis 21:17-19 NLT)

God sees her. He comforts her. He hears her. While He gives her hope for her future, God also assures her of her present. He opens her eyes to see what she thought she was lacking - a well full of water. He opened her eyes to see what was right in front of her.

You may not know God's exact plan or timing for your life but we know this: God sees you. God hears you. He will take care of your present and has a plan for your future.

~Anu

January 19 ~ Genesis 22-24

"Then God said, 'Take your son, your only son, whom you love—Isaac—and go to the region of Moriah. Sacrifice him there as a burnt offering on a mountain I will show you.'" Genesis 22:2 (NIV)

There I was ... in my car ... crying.

"Lord, I can't take any more bad news."

Every difficult situation I had encountered up until that day was dealt with the same way: going from a state of shock and disbelief to becoming numb and finally, feeling angry and asking God, *"Why??"* In my weariness, I found the guts to tell God that I believed I had met my quota of hard times and needed a break.

But God, in His infinite mercy and grace, met me where I was and healed my brokenness. He assured me to trust Him and reminded me of His plans for my life. God gave me strength for each moment.

So that afternoon in the car, I found myself in a different place. Even though I said I couldn't take any more bad news, I didn't stop there. With tears streaming down my face, I continued by saying: *"But no matter what the outcome is Lord, I choose to trust You and I will praise Your name."*

I think about Abraham who had waited for 100 years to become a father. God gave him a promise, but it didn't happen quickly or when he may have expected. Maybe he was tempted to feel some sadness and anger.

And then, he finally was blessed with a son. Can you imagine how excited he must have felt? So that was the happy ending to his story, right? Well, the key verse indicates otherwise, doesn't it? Surely, Abraham must have protested or pleaded with God. But that is not indicated. In fact, all we see is obedience and trust. Abraham went about doing what God instructed to the point where Isaac was laying on the altar to be sacrificed and then, a ram appeared. Abraham didn't know that would be the final outcome, but he trusted God would provide. What an amazing example of trust we see in this chapter of Abraham's life.

His trust in God wasn't conditional. Instead, he believed that God had the best plans for his life.

Even when the outcome was not what I had hoped for, I praised God because I trusted that my life is in His hands. I trusted that He will provide. He has and He always will. Will you trust God regardless of the outcome?

~Joyce

January 20 ~ Genesis 25-26
"'Look, I'm dying of starvation!', said Esau. 'What good is
my birthright to me now?'" Genesis 25:32 (NLT)

Hanger.

I have been accused of displaying this unflattering trait on more than one occasion. I lose my patience, snap at people, or just shut down. My family knows that when I get quiet, something is really wrong. They'd better feed me quickly!

Had I been in Esau's position, I probably would have done the same thing. My moments of hanger expose my vulnerability, and often, my lack of self-discipline. In that moment, my 'birthright' would have seemed so nebulous compared to the very tangible bowl of stew that would be setting off each of my senses. I wouldn't have cared about the larger inheritance, patriarchal respect, or any of the benefits that came with the firstborn birthright. I would have wanted to bury my face in that bowl of stew and sop up the remains with a piece of fresh bread.

A snap decision that affected the trajectory of the lives of two brothers.

We often make decisions based on our senses, not realizing that there is another dimension that we haven't consulted. The faith dimension- where you base your decisions on things that are unseen. What if Esau had stopped for a moment and thought about what he was agreeing to? Let's get super spiritual-what if he had paused for a moment of prayer before gulping down that stew? It could have changed the entire course of the Old Testament.

We all have moments of vulnerability that expose our weaknesses. Whether it be reaching for that second cookie or something more tempting. One is going to put us in the gym longer but the other one could affect more than just our waistline. As Christians, we are called to make decisions based on where our faith would lead us, not just our immediate needs.

The story of Jacob and Esau challenges us to think beyond ourselves. It challenges us to try to see the bigger picture that God has planned for us. Think beyond the immediate circumstance and consider what God's plan is for you. It's better than a bowl of soup - I can promise you that.

~Shiney

January 21 ~ Genesis 27-29
"...This time I will praise the Lord ..." Genesis 29:35 (NIV)

Have you ever felt unloved or rejected? You are not alone.

Leah was all too familiar with that feeling. You see, Leah had a sister named Rachel. The Bible described Rachel as beautiful and having a lovely figure.

And then there was Leah.

Leah is described as having *"weak eyes"*. I'm not sure what that means, but it sure doesn't sound like a compliment.

That was Leah's life. A constant feeling of rejection and striving to be loved and cherished. It eventually came time for Leah to be married. Let's just say, marriage didn't exactly help with her insecurities, it solidified them.

Her father, Laban, actually had to trick her soon to be husband, Jacob, into marrying her.

Laban fools Jacob into believing that he is actually marrying Rachel. But when the truth is revealed, Jacob is furious and Laban agrees to allow Rachel to marry Jacob as well.

Can you imagine Leah's heartbreak as these events unfold?

But God saw Leah's pain, and responded. Rachel struggled with barrenness while Leah had children.

God gave Leah six sons, but even so, we continue to sense her pain with each birth.

With her firstborn Reuben, she says *"It is because the Lord has seen my misery, surely my husband will love me now." (Genesis 29:32 NIV)*

With Simeon, she offers a similar sentiment. *"Because the Lord has heard that I am not loved, he gave me this one too." (Genesis 29:33 NIV)*

When Levi is born, she states *"Now at last my husband will become attached to me, because I have borne him three sons." (Genesis 29:34 NIV)*

Do you get the picture?

But with the birth of her fourth son Judah, something changed. Leah declared *"This time I will praise the Lord." (Genesis 29:35 NIV)*

Even though Leah strived for Jacob's love, at this point she understood that true strength is found in God alone. Rachel eventually bore two sons, Joseph and Benjamin ... but it was through Leah's son, Judah,

that the royal line of David was established. Our Savior, the Lion of the tribe of Judah, came through Leah.

At the time of her death, Jacob finally bestowed on Leah the honor she deserved. While Rachel was buried on the journey to Bethlehem, Jacob buried Leah at the tomb at Machpelah. The tomb of Abraham and Sarah, Isaac and Rebekah, and Jacob and Leah.

Leah's life with Jacob wasn't the happily ever after she probably imagined. But just as God's hand was with Leah, know that God's hand is with you also.

~Vijoy

1/21/2022

January 22 ~ Genesis 30-31
*"Then Rachel said, 'I have had a great struggle with my
sister, and I have won...'" Genesis 30:8a (NIV)*

Has jealousy ever driven you to say and do things that you are not proud of?

When I was a young girl, my best friend and I had a lot in common. We were the same age, we loved to talk, and we had a favorite older friend. This friend was the one we looked up to because she had the prettiest clothes, the trendiest toys, and she always had bubble gum. In other words, she was cool and we wanted to be just like her.

As much as my best friend and I adored each other, you wouldn't know it by the way we treated each other when our cool friend arrived. Suddenly, we were pushing and shoving each other so that we could sit next to our friend, arguing over who sat next to her last time, and ultimately, growing jealous of the one who finally won the fight. Sadly, we were willing to allow this division in our relationship if that meant we could be near our fabulous friend. That's a lot of drama over one friend!

In Genesis chapter 30, we see a similar struggle between sisters Rachel and Leah. Rachel was jealous of Leah because Leah could bear children while Rachel could not. Leah was jealous of Rachel because their husband Jacob loved Rachel more. In Rachel's jealousy, she became dramatic in how she spoke to Jacob and when he succumbed to her demand, Rachel deemed that she had been victorious. When Leah saw that, she made a similar demand of him. But did either of them really win?

In each of these scenarios, the females involved were jealous of each other because one had something that the other wanted. What's a girl to do in such a situation? We need to pray and ask for God's help to overcome this struggle. Then, we need to declare Scripture reminding ourselves that *"A heart at peace gives life to the body, but envy rots the bones." (Proverbs 14:30 NIV)* Remember that love is not jealous. Finally, walk in the fruit of the Spirit.

Those childhood memories made me realize that the envy we each had was destroying relationships which meant a lot. Thank God for His revelation and thank God our friendship survived such a challenge.

Friends, I pray that the words and actions in our relationships are life-giving and reflect God's love.

~Joyce

January 23 ~ Genesis 32-34
"... Esau ran to meet him and embraced him..." Genesis 33:4 (AMP)

The story of Jacob and Esau starts with drama even before they were born. We recall Esau's imprudent decision to trade his birthright for a bowl of stew. Of course, there was also the time when Jacob underhandedly secured the blessing of their father. At that point, Esau vows revenge on his brother.

When it's time for the two to finally see each other again after many years, we expect more drama to unfold. Instead, we see forgiveness.

We don't know Esau's vantage point while this all plays out but we do hear from Jacob. He is rightfully afraid and presents gifts to soften the heart of his brother. In the process of it all, Jacob's heart softened too.

He humbly acknowledges to God that he is "*... not worthy of the least of all the deeds of steadfast love and all the faithfulness that You have shown to your servant, for with only my staff I crossed this Jordan, and now I have become two camps.*" He then goes on to ask for God's help in the situation: "*Please deliver me from the hand of my brother, from the hand of Esau, for I fear him, that he may come and attack me, the mothers with the children. (Genesis 32:10-11 ESV)*

To Jacob's surprise and relief, "*... Esau ran to meet him and embraced him, and hugged his neck and kissed him, and they wept [for joy]." (Genesis 33:4 AMP)*

It looks like Jacob isn't the only one who had a change of heart.

We understand the idea of forgiveness because God has demonstrated it to us. Unfortunately, comprehending something and carrying it out are two different things.

A term used for forgiveness in the Greek is "aphesis" which means "*releasing someone from obligation or debt.*"[1]

It is also important to understand what forgiveness does NOT mean: *excusing unjust behavior, explaining the hurt away, denying the hurt, being a doormat, forgetting, a feeling, conditional or reconciliation.*[2]

As the offender, are we willing to let down our pride and admit our wrong? As the offended, can we extend forgiveness that we have been so freely given? Neither are easy but both are necessary. Jacob and Esau demonstrated the beauty of forgiveness and that just because a story started with drama doesn't mean it has to end that way.

~Anu

January 24 ~ Genesis 35-37
"... he is the Anah who found the hot springs in the wilderness..." Genesis 36:24 (ESV)

It's a typical begats reading.

So and so begat so and so who begat another name that I can't pronounce who begat more names I can't pronounce and they lived to be hundreds of years old.

Until...

"These are the sons of Zibeon: Aiah and Anah; he is the Anah who found the hot springs in the wilderness, as he pastured the donkeys of Zibeon his father." *(Genesis 36:24 ESV)*

Anah isn't a name we typically hear in Sunday School. However, Moses decided to interrupt the genealogy of the children of Israel to give him a special shout out about finding water in the wilderness.

This couldn't have been easy. Remember, these were the days of no technology or engineers telling him where to look. In the middle of a dry, desert land, ANAH found water. Not Joshua. Not Gideon. ANAH found water.

He was just taking care of some donkeys for his dad. Who knows? Maybe he didn't even want to be out there! Then, he stumbles on something that benefits him and probably everyone around him.

Anah's life serves as an example to us. I want to be someone who can find water in the wilderness, the good in the bad, and the light in the dark.

Sometimes, it may seem like those things can't be found no matter how hard we look. So, I guess we're out of luck then...at least we tried!

Um, no. Then it's time for us to step up: to be the good, to shine the light, and to saturate a dry place.

You don't have to look too hard or too long for a wilderness opportunity. It's all around us...the grumpy checker at the grocery store, the complaining co-worker, or the sad friend. The world today is in desperate need of water finders.

The Peace Prayer of St. Francis starts with this: "*Lord, make me an instrument of Thy peace.*"[1] Don't discount what you can do. You are not just a student, just a mom or just a donkey caretaker. You are a cup of cold-water bearer. You are a candle in a dark room. You are a word of peace giver. You are a water in the wilderness finder.

~Anu

January 25 ~ Genesis 38-40
*"When Joseph saw them the next morning, he noticed
that they both looked upset." Genesis 40:6 (NLT)*

Blah days are so...well, blah. When I have those days, I just want to sit there and wallow in my blah-ness.

Joseph probably had every right to consider himself the king of blah days. He couldn't seem to catch a break. First, his brothers hated him so they sold him to slavery. Then, he was falsely accused of assaulting a woman and thrown in prison.

By now, I would be having a major pity party but thankfully Joseph shows us the higher road. You never see him complain. He just continues to make the most of every situation he is in.

Even in prison, he is appointed as the overseer. One day, new prisoners who were former employees of Pharaoh join them. Joseph notices they are having a blah day, so, he asks, *"Why do you look so worried today?"* (Genesis 40:7 NLT)

Here is a guy who has every right to have a permanent woe-is-me look on his face but not Joseph. First of all, he doesn't just look at the other prisoners, he really SEES and NOTICES them. There probably aren't a lot of happy people in prison but Joseph still makes it a point to ask ... *"Why do YOU look worried?"*

Before even asking the question, he could have given them the *"You think you have it bad, wait till you hear my story"* speech but he doesn't do that. His focus is purely on them.

The amazing thing is this one question ended up leading to his own deliverance.

He asked and they answered. They shared their dreams and through God, Joseph was able to interpret them. Long story short, one man is restored to his position and when his boss, Pharaoh, has a dream that needs interpretation, he remembers Joseph. It took some time but it happened. Joseph is released from prison and becomes the #2 man in all of Egypt.

This was all triggered by one question to a couple of people who the world was ready to cast off.

One question.

The next time my blah day decides to come around, I pray that I can make it a point to look around and see who else might be having a blah day. I might find my freedom in that moment too.

~Anu

January 26 ~ Genesis 41-42

"...Can we find anyone else like this man so obviously filled with the spirit of God?" Genesis 41:38 (NLT)

The world has a problem that only you can solve. If you look around you there's always a problem. God has given you gifts and abilities to ultimately achieve His purposes on the earth. And coupled with His spirit, you are uniquely equipped to do what others cannot.

In the Bible, Joseph was a great example of this.

From a young age, Gold told him through his dreams that he would be in a position of power. But at that age, he wasn't ready for it. He told his brothers about his dreams, which only made them jealous of him. Fast forward many years later and so much has transpired. Joseph was thrown into a pit, sold into slavery, wrongly accused, and imprisoned.

Sitting in an Egyptian prison year after year, he might have been wondering where God was in all of this. But the scripture doesn't tell us that Joseph was bitter or angry. Instead, we see that wherever he was placed, he found a way to help. Even in the prison, he used the gifts and the skills he had to do what he could.

Because of the faithfulness he showed during his time in prison, a former prisoner remembered Joseph when Pharaoh had a disturbing dream 2 years later. He was released from prison and brought before Pharaoh. After Joseph heard the dream, he was able to interpret it immediately.

After hearing Joseph interpret the dream and provide wise counsel to Pharaoh regarding what was to come, *"... Pharaoh asked his officials, 'Can we find anyone else like this man so obviously filled with the spirit of God?' Then Pharaoh said to Joseph, 'Since God has revealed the meaning of the dreams to you, clearly no one else is as intelligent or wise as you are ..."* (Genesis 41:38-39 NLT)

And in one moment, Joseph went from prisoner to prince.

Joseph wasn't able to choose what happened to him. He no doubt found himself in harsh and unfair circumstances. *But* he chose to respond in a way that changed his outcome.

Life may have dealt you an unfair hand. But I believe how you choose to respond can ultimately change your outcome. I pray that with God's help your response will be one that will help to serve those around you, and ultimately achieve God's purpose for you on the earth.

~Vijoy

January 27 ~ Genesis 43-45

"...Send the boy with me, and we will be on our way. Otherwise we will all die of starvation - and not only we, but you and our little ones. I personally guarantee his safety ..." Genesis 43:8-9 (NLT)

My daughter is a ball of energy. She talks constantly with one volume: loud. She doesn't walk; she bounces. Since the time that she learned how to walk, she developed this habit of carrying something around the house with her. It was really entertaining when she was just beginning to toddle around. She had this red stool that she would try to carry with her. The thing was bigger than she was and every few steps she would fall down with it. She'd get right back up and do it again. As she got older (and wiser) her items became more manageable. For the last several months, she has taken to roaming around the house with two stuffed animals. They accompany her everywhere.

I don't have a problem with it until it interferes with what she needs to do. Very often, she is slowed down or gets distracted because she won't let go of these little animals. She's extremely independent and wants to do everything by herself, but it's hard to do that when your hands are already occupied.

My words to her are the same each time, *"Put down what you are carrying, and do what I need you to do."* When her hands are full of what she *thinks* she needs, she has no ability to grasp what I want to give her.

In Genesis 43, Judah plans the return to Egypt for food. He has to take Benjamin with him otherwise he might return empty-handed. Simeon is still jailed and no one knows what will be done with Benjamin. The brothers make a huge leap of faith when they return to Egypt. It would have been easier to starve and live in the fear of the unknown than to make that journey. They were willing to sacrifice what they had to possibly receive something greater, and it changed the course of history.

I don't know what you may be carrying around, but I want to encourage you to put it down. God is trying to give you something greater, but he can't if your hands are already full of something that you have deemed is more important. It's impossible to receive when your hands are already full. Put down what you are carrying and receive what God has for you instead. Empty your hands so that He can fill them up.

~Shiney

January 28 ~ Genesis 46-47
"So they brought their livestock to Joseph, and he gave them food in exchange for their horses, their sheep and goats, their cattle and donkeys..." Genesis 47:17a (NIV)

My father always reminded me to use my time and money wisely when I was growing up. He also wanted me to learn the value of the dollar. So, when it came time for me to make my biggest purchase, a brand-new car, he simply watched me sign the papers and hand over the down payment. None of that money came from his pocket. It came from mine. Every single dime.

I joke that he wouldn't even purchase the car mats for me. Dad wanted me to know the feeling of earning and spending. And that I did. The earning was tough - long evenings working in the hospital but the spending was no picnic, either. I remember making those car payments ... just watching a large chunk of my paycheck slip away into an envelope and off to the billing department.

But it was all worth it. By God's grace, I still drive that same car today! I'll give credit to my husband for the maintenance of the vehicle, but there's just something special about working hard for something and reaping the rewards for years to come.

Remember how Joseph was placed in a position of prominence during the famine in Egypt in a way that only God could orchestrate? Pharaoh put Joseph in charge of the entire land of Egypt, and Joseph moved his entire family there to avoid the famine where they were living. At that time, food was available in Egypt but that did not last. Resources were becoming scarce in Egypt, too.

What were the people to do?

Joseph had a plan. Instead of giving the food away, he sold this food in exchange for money.

When their money ran out, he sold the food in exchange for their livestock. When all their livestock was sold, he bought their fields and had the people serve on the land in exchange for food.

Then, he gave them seed to plant in the ground ... for harvest ... for food.

Joseph didn't give the people handouts. They sacrificed, they worked, and finally they reaped the reward.

The Bible reminds us that when you work hard, you will be blessed for it. Looking back, I value my car so much today because of the amount of effort that went into purchasing it. The reward was all worth it, thanks to a life lesson by Dad.

~Elizabeth

January 29 ~ Genesis 48-50
"... this is what their father said to them when he blessed them,
giving each the blessing appropriate to him". Genesis 49:28 (NIV)

Over a year ago, our founding Pastor transitioned out of his position and named his son as the senior Pastor. What was most profound for me about that moment was the blessing he spoke over his son. He declared words of life over his future and then, passed on the mantle with powerful prayer and anointing. What a special moment that was to witness!

The moment must have felt the same as Jacob blessed his grandsons Manasseh and Ephraim. He embraced them and spoke over their future. Then, Jacob blessed his sons. As they gathered around him, he told them what would happen in their days to come.

To speak a blessing over someone means to speak good into their lives and to say what God says about them based on His Word. One of the most powerful things parents can do for their children is to speak such blessing over them.

Following is a simple way to do it:

- Look at your children in the eyes, placing your hands on their heads.
- Tell them that God loves them and they are precious in His sight.
- Thank God for the gifts He has placed in them and how they will be used in the future.
- Declare Scripture over them in a personal way:

You are "fearfully and wonderfully made." (Psalm 139:14 NIV)
You are blessed because you "trust in the LORD" and your "confidence is in Him." (Jeremiah 17:7 NIV)
You "can do all things through Christ who gives you strength." (Philippians 4:13 NIV)
You can confidently say, "The Lord is my helper; I will not fear; what can man do to me?" (Hebrews 13:6 NIV)

Just this past weekend, my husband and son had the privilege of going on a father-son adventure. After engaging in fun "manly" activities together, they concluded the time with each father speaking a blessing over their son. Just hearing about this incredibly special moment brings tears to my eyes. It's been evident that my son felt empowered to walk forward into his future knowing that he has received this blessing from his Dad.

Friend, when we speak a blessing over someone, they receive the confidence to walk into the days to come with hope and excitement. I pray that you are encouraged to speak a blessing over your own children.

~Joyce

January 30 ~ Exodus 1-3
"...When she saw that he was a fine child, she hid
him for three months." Exodus 2:2b (NIV)

Extra! Extra! Read all about it: "Every baby boy that is born must be killed."

Imagine waking up to such a headline. Such was the order given about the Hebrews in Exodus 1:22.

Responses to such news could include:

1) becoming overcome by fear displayed through crying and feelings of panic and ultimately, paralyzed by the fear OR
2) looking to the Source for an answer and being proactive in the solution.

When I think of those circumstances of being a powerless slave in a land where my people were despised, I'm afraid there's a possibility that my response would be the first one. I mean, what could someone in such a helpless position do when hearing that decree?

Exodus 2 reveals the answer. Jochebed, who had just given birth to Moses, hid him for the first three months, then came up with a plan. She made a basket, placed him in it and put it in the Nile River.

I think about the *creativity* and time it must've taken to execute this plan, the heartache involved to separate from her baby, and the *trust* she had in God to provide for this precious baby. The book of Exodus tells us how Moses was rescued by Pharaoh's daughter, nursed by Jochebed, raised in the Pharaoh's palace, and although he fled from Egypt, ultimately, he returned to be the deliverer of the Israelites from bondage and slavery.

Jochebed's response reminds us not to let our emotions control us, but rather display self-control, a fruit of the Spirit. In Greek, *"self-control is egkrateia which means temperance: the virtue of one who masters his desires and passions."*[1] In doing so, Jochebed focused on God to provide her with a plan and resources with clarity and strength.

Whatever circumstances you find yourself in today, at your job, in your marriage or with your children, look to God Who is for you, not against you and Whose plans are to prosper you, not to harm you. Romans 12:21 (NIV) states, *"Do not be overcome by evil, but overcome evil with good."*

You are not powerless or helpless as the enemy would like you to believe. You are more than a conqueror through Christ Jesus! Time to get your game face on and be victorious in the battle!

~Joyce

January 31 ~ Exodus 4-6
*"Now therefore go, and I will be with your mouth and teach
you what you shall speak." Exodus 4:12 (ESV)*

College - it was the best of times; it was the worst of times.

One of those "worst" experiences occurred at the pizza place on campus. I was sitting with a friend and a guy she knew well but whom I had recently met. As we were talking, he told her, *"You talk too much! You include all these details that don't matter!"* I was surprised by his bluntness but even more shocked when he said to me, *"You do the same thing!"*

I had always been a confident person and felt very free to be me. Until that moment.

These words, from this random guy, sent me into a prison of insecurity.

For the next 15 plus years, I would battle his voice in my head. I never wanted to be alone with someone for fear of boring them with my excessive talking. Then, on the flip side, I would try to be funny or say things I thought people wanted to hear. I had lost me.

Eventually, through much prayer and encouragement from the people around me, I started to find myself again.

Now, the irony. What was once my greatest fear and weakness, my words, is now the area God has called me.

When God tells Moses to lead the children of Israel to freedom, Moses repeatedly questions this. Finally, God agrees to send Aaron and makes the point, *"I know he speaks well." (Exodus 4:14b NLT)*

God knew Aaron spoke well but yet He still chose Moses – the tongue-tied, not so eloquent one. It was Moses who shifted his rightful calling to someone else. All because of his insecurity.

God is fully aware others may sing, teach or whatever better than you. It's not about who is more talented, it's about who is called and more importantly, who is obedient.

Insecurity still tries to have its way with me but the difference is now, I give it a good fight. Instead of imprisoning me, it humbles me. When it tries to stop me, I lean on God more. In my weakness, He is strong.

You may feel afraid or unworthy. You may feel insecure. You may have had your own moment like I did in that pizza place. Just like He was with Moses, He is with us. Now, go.

~Anu

February 1 ~ Exodus 7-9

"So the heart of Pharaoh was hardened, and he did not let the people of Israel go, just as the Lord had spoken through Moses." Exodus 9:35 (ESV)

What phrases have people used to describe you?

- Never met a stranger
- They would give you the shirt off their back.
- Beautiful on the inside and out

There are people in scripture who were known by a certain phrase.

- A man after God's own heart - David
- A friend of God - Abraham
- For such a time as this - Esther

I'd take any of the above for the distinguishing marker on my life but there are other phrases I don't want. Like the one used to describe Pharaoh...

A hardened heart.

I may not want it but unfortunately, it sometimes applies.

Repeatedly, the Bible says that Pharaoh hardened his heart. Each time, Pharaoh thought he was in control and asserting his power. He was wrong.

God, in His sovereignty, used Pharaoh's hardened heart for His own purposes.

"For by now I could have put out my hand and struck you and your people with pestilence, and you would have been cut off from the earth. But for this purpose I have raised you up, to show you my power, so that my name may be proclaimed in all the earth." (Exodus 9:15-16 ESV)

We look at the life of Pharaoh and quickly judge his obvious and blatant disregard for God's instructions. But again, haven't we found ourselves in that place too?

That time He told us to go pray for someone who needed healing. Or when we knew we were supposed to be merciful but we extended judgment instead. Maybe when we allowed other things to take priority in our lives above God.

We can harden our hearts because of past hurts, present circumstances, or like Pharaoh ... pride.

What happens when clay gets hard? It becomes almost impossible to be molded into what the potter intended. The same is true with our hearts. God wants more for us.

"But we have this precious treasure [the good news about salvation] in [unworthy] earthen vessels [of human frailty], so that the grandeur and surpassing greatness of the power will be [shown to be] from God [His sufficiency] and not from ourselves." (2 Corinthians 4:7 AMP)

That's a description I wouldn't mind having.

~Anu

"... Go, but bless me as you leave." Exodus 12:32 (NLT)

Have you ever had the very people who give you trouble ask for your help in their time of need?

I've seen this at work in my own life. Throughout my career, I've had to deal with difficult people who seemed to dislike me without even giving me a chance. For whatever reason, I could not do right by them no matter how hard I tried. But I saw those same people drawn to me, asking for my help and even my advice in their own personal lives. Perhaps this happened because they saw something different in me.

We see a similar situation in the book of Exodus in the Bible.

The people of Israel found themselves enslaved in Egypt for over 400 years. God heard their cries and sent Moses to help lead them out of Egypt.

But God wanted to put his glory on display so that both Israel and Egypt would know that it was only God that delivered them.

He chose Moses, an unlikely Hebrew with a speech impediment, to stand before Pharaoh and boldly ask to let his people go. Although Moses initially resisted, he reluctantly agreed to go.

As we know the story, Moses tells Pharaoh if you don't let us go, God will bring plagues upon the land of Egypt. But Pharaoh was unyielding, and one by one, God sent devastating plagues over Egypt.

Eventually after the final most terrifying plague, death to all the firstborn sons in Egypt, Pharaoh agreed to let them go.

But then something interesting happens.

Pharaoh says to them *"Take your flocks and herds, as you said, and be gone. Go, but bless me as you leave"* (Exodus 12:32 NLT)

Pharaoh understood something at that moment. He saw that these people had the favor of God over them. Through the plagues, he saw God's power and might on display and he recognized that God was with the children of Israel. Even though Pharaoh didn't worship or serve the God of Israel, *he wanted what they had.*

Our lives are no different. Can we be the same reflection of God's glory to a hurting and broken world today?

My prayer is that I am willing to let the world see God at work in me, and in turn those who don't know Him will come to know Him in a real and personal way.

~Vijoy

February 3 ~ Exodus 13-15

"... Why are you crying out to me? Tell the people to get moving! Pick up your staff and raise your hand over the sea ..." Exodus 14:15-16 (NLT)

Most of us who grew up in church have heard it said *"Stand still and see the salvation of the Lord!" (Exodus 14:13 NKJV)* as quoted from Moses to the people of Israel soon after they left Egypt and were faced with the Red Sea in front of them, and Pharaoh and his army behind them.

But when I was reading this passage recently, I noticed something I had not noticed before. *Moses* is telling the people to stand still and watch the Lord rescue them. But *God* is telling Moses, *"Why are you crying out to me? Tell the people to get moving! Pick up your staff and raise your hand over the sea ..."* *(Exodus 14:13,15-16 NLT)*

It seems the answer may not always be to stand still, but to get moving. What do you do when you don't know what to do? According to many recovery programs, you don't have to have it all figured out. You just have to do the *next right thing*...followed by, the next right thing, and then the next right thing.

Life can seem overwhelmingly complicated at times. As humans, I think it's in our nature to take on the weight of something that we were never meant to take on.

God only gives us light for the step that is in front of us, not the entire road ahead.

"Your word is a lamp to guide my feet and a light for my path" (Psalms 119:105 NLT).

So, when we get overwhelmed because we don't know how it's all going to work out, we should remember that God never asked that of us. He asks us to take a step, and trust him.

My friend, for the circumstance you find yourself in today, what is the next right thing you can do?

Is it making a phone call or sending a text to someone you have a strained relationship which may eventually lead to restored relationship? Is it getting up from your chair and taking a 10-minute walk to start the process of a healthy lifestyle?

Is it going next door to your neighbor's house and getting to know them, so that they may be more open to hearing the gospel of Jesus because it's coming from someone they know?

Whatever it is, don't let whatever end you have in mind overwhelm you and keep you from doing the right thing you can do now. There's a good chance it will eventually bring you to the place you desire to be.

~Vijoy

February 4 ~ Exodus 16-18

"If you do this and God so commands, you will be able to stand the strain, and all these people will go home satisfied." Exodus 18:23 (NIV)

A few days ago, as I passed by my kids' playroom, I was amazed at how chaotic and disorganized it appeared. Puzzle pieces, cars, balls, and paper littered the floor. It was past time for a major clean-up. Every toy needed to be in its proper home, and I could have easily had that room tidied up in ten minutes.

Instead, I decided it was time to teach my 4-year-old to take responsibility. I tasked him with this duty ... and surprisingly, he mastered the job. About thirty minutes later, I came back to an organized room with a visible floor.

Recently, roles at my workplace have been in transition, which means that certain responsibilities I had a few weeks ago have been transferred to my colleagues.

The job of the audit, which I had been doing, has now been handed over to an employee who is not familiar with the process, but otherwise qualified to handle it. I've had to let it go and move on with the new responsibilities on my plate.

In both these situations, a project that I could have done easily was given to another capable person. In other words, I had to delegate to someone I could trust. While delegating can be painful, especially for perfectionists, it helps to lighten the load.

Are you one of those people that just can't let go? You just know how to do it SO MUCH BETTER? You can't trust anyone else because of fear that they will mess up? It's time to give up control.

Moses was taught this lesson by his father-in-law when he was serving as a judge for the Israelites. From morning until evening, Moses took on the role of resolving disputes and teaching the people God's laws. Anyone with a 9 to 5 job can attest that this sounds exhausting!

Jethro, Moses' father-in-law, suggested that he delegate the simple cases to trustworthy men, and that Moses take on the more difficult ones. Three benefits would take place if Moses were to follow this plan:

1.   The load would be lighter
2.   He would stand the strain (less stress!)
3.   The people would be satisfied

Like any good son-in-law, Moses listened to Jethro ... and so should we.

Release stress and responsibility. Trust the qualified people around you. You will be happier and will even be able to empower others.

~Elizabeth

February 5 ~ Exodus 19-21

"You shall not covet your neighbor's house. You shall not covet your neighbor's wife, or his male or female servant, his ox or donkey, or anything that belongs to your neighbor." Exodus 20:17 (NIV)

Have you ever watched young children play together? Each one can be happily playing with their toy until they notice the toy that their peer is playing with. Suddenly, you hear "I want that!" and see a hand rushing to grab what appears to be better.

I was raised with the best of everything. However, when I was a teenager, I noticed classmates who owned designer purses and clothes. Suddenly, what I had did not seem to be enough and I felt unhappy. I desired to have what they possessed.

But this must be struggles limited to our younger years when we lack maturity and understanding, right? Well, unfortunately, this desire can rear its ugly head at any stage in life. Maybe you have found yourself riding in your air-conditioned car listening to music until you arrive at your friend's house and see their new car. It looks so luxurious that now, your car seems like a jalopy and all you want to do is purchase what your friend owns.

According to the Merriam-Webster Dictionary, to covet is defined as to *"desire wrongfully what belongs to another."[1]*

Among the Ten Commandments that God gave to Moses, He addresses this issue in the tenth commandment. This law was put in place to teach us right from wrong in our relationships with others. What we may dismiss as harmless desires actually are sinful.

In addition, when our hearts are in this place of wrongful desire, we are communicating to God that we are not content with what we do have. Whether we are unhappy with the material possessions we own or the relationships we are in, our lack of satisfaction conveys that we are not grateful for our blessings. Boy am I sorry for not giving thanks to God for all that I did have as a teenager!

The Bible reminds us that "*... those who seek the Lord lack no good thing."* *(Psalm 34:10b NIV)* The Apostle Paul said, "*I have learned to be content whatever the circumstances." (Philippians 4:11b NIV)*

Lord, please forgive us for coveting. May our hearts be content and grateful at all times because we know that You are good and greatly to be praised. Amen.

~Joyce

February 6 ~ Exodus 22-24

"I will drive them out before you little by little, until you become fruitful and take possession of the land." Exodus 23:30 (NASB)

When my car needed an alignment, my husband wanted to come with me to get it done. I really wasn't sure why because I had done this on my own before. It seemed simple enough - just tell the guy at the counter, *"I need an alignment."*

Apparently, there was a little more to it than that.

Once we got there, my husband started talking in car language that sounded like "blah, blah, blah" to me but it made sense to the guy. He then asked them to *"toe it in by 1/10 of an inch"*.

See? Blah, blah, blah.

The "toe it in" part was new to me but I did understand the "1/10 of an inch" part. That wasn't very much so I asked my husband about it. He said with my particular car, that minor adjustment actually helps prevent some of the wear and tear on the tires and gives them longer life.

1/10 of an inch does that.

In life, we often feel like in order for big things to happen, big changes need to be made.

What about considering smaller adjustments?

"I will not drive them out before you in a single year, that the land may not become desolate and the beasts of the field become too numerous for you. I will drive them out before you little by little, until you become fruitful and take possession of the land." (Exodus 23:29-30 NASB)

We all know God can do big things. We've already seen His power demonstrated in creation and the parting of the Red Sea. This time around, He uses a different approach. He knows if He does it all at once, it will be too much for the Israelites. On the other hand, if He does it little by little, they would get strengthened along the way.

I think the same applies to us. Maybe we could spend a little less time on social media rather than completely eliminating it. Only eating salads sounds like a good idea but we could start by just adding one more vegetable to our meals. If jumping from one verse to a whole chapter seems intimidating, try reading a few more verses instead.

On the journey to accomplishing our goals and entering our promised land, small changes can have a big impact.

Inch by inch. Little by little, we're getting there.

~Anu

February 7 ~ Exodus 25-27

"Tell the Israelites to bring me an offering. You are to receive the offering for me from everyone whose heart prompts them to give." Exodus 25:2 (NIV)

Some people are natural givers. I'm not one of those people. I am a natural saver. My husband, on the other hand is one of those people.

So, as one might expect, our first few years of marriage were interesting. It was a constant tug of war. But after a few years, with the help of our financial advisor, I thought we were doing good. We tithed, gave to missions, and even saved a little. What more could God want?

One day, my husband and I received a small but unexpected check from someone who had owed us money, money we both had forgotten about. I was excited, unexpected money is always nice. I couldn't wait to put it in savings. My husband was happy too, but he had something else in mind.

My husband: *"Hey, would you be okay if we gave that money to——ministry."*
Me: *"Really?"*
My husband: *"Oh, okay...no problem. We don't have to."*

I thought I won that game of tug of war, but I didn't. Within one week, lightning literally struck our home. Thankfully, no one was hurt and the damage wasn't too bad...but that unexpected check now went towards unexpected home repairs. Some may call it a coincidence, but I knew better.

God used lightning to transform my heart.

In Exodus 25:2, God delivers a message through Moses. *"Tell the Israelites to bring me an offering. You are to receive the offering for me from everyone whose heart prompts them to give." (NIV)*

God had just brought these people out of slavery, parted the Red Sea, given them food to eat and water to drink. It was time for a heart check.

God wanted the same from me.

He had delivered me from who knows what and provided an endless supply of everything to meet my every need. It was time for a heart check.

I believe God wants us to be wise stewards of every penny He has given us. He wants us to save, but He also wants us to give. Give generously and give extravagantly. Give, not out of compulsion, but out of an overflowing heart filled with gratitude. God doesn't long for my money, He longs for my heart.

So, what more did God want? He wanted to transform my heart.

~Binu

February 8 ~ Exodus 28-29

"There are to be twelve stones, one for each of the names of the sons of Israel, each engraved like a seal with the name of one of the twelve tribes." Exodus 28:21 (NIV)

Several years ago, my husband lost his job. We were all on my husband's insurance, and he was the primary breadwinner for our family. My son was 18 months old, and I was working part-time at two different jobs. Thanksgiving, Christmas and New Years were only a few weeks away.

I have to admit that I panicked. We tithed and gave consistently - why would God allow this to happen?

My husband received a severance package. We had a team of prayer warriors interceding for him to find the right job. We sought advice from our financial counselor. We purchased a health insurance plan. When I informed my manager at my second job, his response was *"Work as much as you want, whenever you want. The schedule is yours. I will accommodate whatever you need."*

My husband was out of work for only 4 months. During this time, we didn't miss a payment. We didn't get sick. When he started work again, we canceled our health insurance, and they sent us a refund check pro-rating the month that we didn't use. Since he returned to his previous company, he was told that he would have to repay his severance (the pre-tax amount). He worked out a repayment plan, but the HR representative in charge of his case quit and never filed the paperwork. He was hired into a new department with a better income and opportunity for growth. Only God could have orchestrated it like this. When the four months were over, we were better off than before. He is now the manager of this department.

God is in the details. He LOVES details. These chapters demonstrate God's passion for details. After outlining the clothing for the priests and the design of the ephod, there is a beautiful detail that God desires. On the chest piece for the priest, there are to be 12 stones, each one inscribed with one of the 12 tribes. The stones are to be set in gold and positioned over the priest's heart. Every time the priest enters the presence of God, he is not just there representing himself. He is carrying the tribes with him.

The details in your life are not by coincidence, but rather a nod from God. The details demonstrate His glory.

~Shiney

February 9 ~ Exodus 30-32

"And I have filled him with the Spirit of God, with wisdom, with understanding, with knowledge and with all kinds of skills." Exodus 31:3 (NIV)

When I was young, I was convinced because I couldn't sing or preach, I was not called to do God's work. Thankfully, the lives of Bezalel, Oholiab and even my brother-in-law have taught me otherwise.

Exodus 31:1-3 makes it clear that God doesn't just place His Spirit upon pastors, preachers or musicians. He fills even craftsmen *"with the Spirit of God"* to accomplish His purpose. *"See, I have chosen Bezalel and I have filled him with the Spirit of God, with wisdom, with understanding, with knowledge and with all kinds of skills- to make artistic designs....and to engage in all kinds of crafts. Moreover, I have appointed Oholiab to help him." (NIV)*

Bezalel and Oholiab were instrumental in the building of the tabernacle.

I love to see the uniqueness of God's gifts across the body of Christ. They are as varied as the people who possess them. In his book, Glory Days, Max Lucado writes, *"Ability reveals destiny. What is your ability? What do you do well? What do people ask you to do again? What task comes easily? What topic keeps your attention? Your skill set is your road map. It leads you to your territory. Take note of your strengths."[1]*

I have a friend with a real knack for interior design. It's not her career, but it is her gift. When I moved into my new home, I was intimidated as I stared at my high ceilings and empty walls. She, on the other hand, looked with excitement at the same bare walls and willingly offered to help. My brother-in-law has an unusually high aptitude and passion for cars. A few years ago, he organized an outdoor car show at a local children's hospital. What a blessing it was to so many children and their parents.

In the movie, *Chariots of Fire*, Eric Liddell, the Scottish Olympian and missionary, says it best, *"I believe God made me for a purpose, but He also made me fast. And when I run, I feel His pleasure."[2]*

What causes you to feel God's pleasure?

It may not sound super spiritual. Whatever it is, embrace it! You never know, maybe it will bless your neighbor. Maybe it will bless the nations!

~Binu

February 10 ~ Exodus 33-35
"... For he is a God who is passionate about his relationship with you" Exodus 34:14 (NLT)

Moses had an incredible relationship with God. God and Moses spoke *"face to face, as one speaks to his friend." (Exodus 33:11 NLT)* God calls Moses his friend and reveals His glory to him. He makes a promise to go with Moses and give him rest. His intention in the book of Exodus was to dwell among his people.

There's a game changer buried in this reading. If you blink, you might have missed it. It sets the perspective for the rest of the Bible.

Buried in the Lord's instructions is this one line that will change your life.

He is passionate about YOU.

My eyes swell with tears every time I read it.

Our God doesn't want you to just serve him blindly, perform some rituals, give him your money and be in bondage to him for life. He wants to be in relationship with you. He cares about YOUR life. Your ups and downs. Your wins and losses. Your smiles. Your tears. He thrives on every detail.

Passion is a word often reserved for dating or marital relationships. Passionate people can't wait to talk to each other, spend time with each other, just be near each other. They stay on the phone for hours.... *"No, you hang up first!"* They want to hold hands, memorize each line on their beloved's face, smell their loved one's scent.

If you don't have that here on earth, let me encourage you that you have it in your Heavenly Father. He longs for time with you. He longs to talk to you, touch you in your moment of need, gaze at your face. He is passionate about you.

It's humbling to know how much God loves us. It's even more humbling to think of my response to this passion.

You can never out love God. You can only accept it and relish it.

~Shiney

February 11 ~ Exodus 36-38
"... The people are bringing more than enough for doing the work the Lord commanded to be done." Exodus 36:5 (NIV)

I got my first paycheck when I turned twenty-one. Since my parents would not allow me to work before I finished college, it was after years of sweat and tears that I finally got to feel that check in my hands. It was a great feeling.

All of my young adult life, my father had taught me the importance of tithing, so when I received that first paycheck, I knew it didn't all belong to me. In fact, from what I recall, I gave away all the money from that check. And it wasn't painful.

I knew that it was only by God's grace and my parents' support that I had achieved a job, so while yes, I earned the money, I owed it back to the ones who got me there.

Remember when Moses was invited to the top of the mountain, covered with a cloud, to meet with God? One assignment the Lord gave Moses during those 40 days and nights was to have the people build a sanctuary for Him so that He could dwell among them.

The Lord gave Moses specific requirements on this build, and He asks that the Israelites bring an offering to him from *"each man whose heart prompts him to give."*

The people responded well.

They brought *"more than enough"* for the work that the Lord commanded to be done. So much so that Moses had to send an order for the giving to stop.

Imagine that today. What if God's people gave so much that leaders would have to refuse their generosity? Unfortunately, many people do not realize the blessing they would receive when they sow into God's kingdom. They miss the opportunity to thrive and instead choose to live "just barely making it".

From that first paycheck to the very last one I received, I have given God what belongs to him, and hope to give more. I realize that He is not concerned about the amount, but the condition of my heart.

Can we give so that there is "more than enough" for God's work to be done? May we trust that He will provide exceedingly beyond our needs when we take that leap of faith.

"Each of you should give what you have decided in your heart to give, not reluctantly or under compulsion, for God loves a cheerful giver." (2 Corinthians 9:7 NIV)

~Elizabeth

February 12 ~ Exodus 39-40

"Moses inspected the work and saw that they had done it just as the Lord had commanded. So Moses blessed them." Exodus 39:43 (NIV)

"Enough about me ... what do you think about me."

We laugh, but isn't it true? I may not say it, but there are times, I think it.

Sociologist have said, we are, by far, the most narcissistic culture. Think about it. We build pages around ourselves so others can express how much they "like" us and then wonder why we are more depressed than ever before.

We are not alone. If you know anything about the children of Israel, you know they were also the classic example of me-centric people. Once they were out of Egypt, they celebrated for about a day or two, but then the complaining began.

Chapter after chapter, we hear the same repeated phrase said in many different ways ... 'Moses, what can you do for me?'

But then something changes. They are given a task to work on.

Moses has heard from God. He gives the people very specific instructions concerning the construction of the tabernacle and all that goes into it - the Ark of the Covenant, the table of showbread, the lampstands, the priestly garments, etc.

The Israelites were now on a mission. God's mission.

And as the Israelites begin to follow God's instructions given through Moses, something strange happens. *For the next few chapters, their complaining stops.* From creating curtains made from goat hair to constructing frames made from acacia wood, the children of Israel are busy doing God's work.

After an overwhelming amount of detail, Exodus 39 ends with these final verses. *"The Israelites have done all the work just as the Lord had commanded Moses. Moses inspected the work and saw that they had done it just as the Lord had commanded. So, Moses blessed them." (vs 42,43 NIV)*

Finally, the children of Israel did something right....and God acknowledged their work and blessed them.

The same principles apply today. When we focus on what others are *not* doing to meet our needs, things inevitably go south. But when we focus on God and pour ourselves into His will and mission for our lives, His blessing will be upon us. The by-products of peace and unity are sure to follow.

Are you in a me-centric slump? Look around you. There are so many people who could use your help.

"So really, enough about me ..."

~Binu

February 13 ~ Leviticus 1-4

"He shall lay his hand on the head of the burnt offering [transferring symbolically his guilt to the sacrifice], that it may be accepted for him to make atonement on his behalf." Leviticus 1:4 (AMP)

Oooohhh Leviticus.

It's the usual ending point of anyone on a "Read Through the Bible" plan.

Admittedly, Leviticus is not the easiest of reads. There are a lot of details that may have you blushing and asking ... *was that really necessary to include?* Since we know and believe that ALL SCRIPTURE is God-breathed, the answer to that is a resounding yes.

Leviticus is a book that on its own may seem like it just pertained to the Israelites of that day. But as you continue to read it, you will catch glimpses of what we know is to come ... the sacrifice of Jesus for our sins, once and for all.

"He shall lay his hand on the head of the burnt offering [transferring symbolically his guilt to the sacrifice], that it may be accepted for him to make atonement on his behalf." (Leviticus 1:4 AMP)

As we start the book of Leviticus, here is something else to keep in mind. The children of Israel are now on their own as a nation. If you live in the United States, you may recall our history as a new nation. Our founders created the constitution along with federal laws.

Much like that, the Levitical laws were necessary for the people of Israel to be governed and their well-being. In your role as a mom, you know much more than your children do so you instruct them accordingly. That's what God is doing for His children.

The laws also provided a way for God's people to enter into His presence. Of course, He wants holiness from them but you know what else He wanted (and still does)? Relationship. That's why we were created and through all of the sacrifices and laws, it happens. Spoiler: The book of Numbers begins with Moses speaking to God IN the tent, instead of FROM the tent.

The Bible Project[1] provides this wonderful overview of Leviticus:

- Chapters 1-7: Ritual sacrifices
- Chapters 8-10: Ordination of the priests
- Chapters 11-15: Ritual purity
- Chapters 16-17: Day of Atonement
- Chapters 18-20: Moral purity
- Chapters 21-22: Qualifications and standards for the priests
- Chapters 23-25: Annual feasts
- Chapters 26-27: The call to faithfulness

Leviticus is a part of the children of Israel's story ... and ours.

~Anu

February 14 ~ Leviticus 5-7
"The Fire on the altar must be kept burning; it must not go out..." Leviticus 6:12a (NIV)

And you thought your church collected too many offerings. Try living in Old Testament Times.

Burnt offerings, sin offerings, grain offerings, fellowship offerings, there was even a wave offering.

Commit an *unintentional* sin, time for a sin offering. Commit a sin *unintentionally regarding any of the Lord's Holy things,* time for a guilt offering. Want to express gratitude? Time for a grain offering. What was the significance of the burnt offering? It honored God's holiness and invited His presence.

These offerings required much more than putting a few dollars in the offering plate.

The burnt offering involved the slaying of an animal, the draining of its blood and the priest putting on special linen clothes, including linen undergarments. (TMI, I know but it's in the Bible...I promise.)

God provided the flame for the burnt offering, but the people were required to bring the sacrifice and *maintain* the fire.

"The Fire on the altar must be kept burning; it must not go out. Every morning the priest is to add firewood and arrange the burnt offering on the fire ..." (Leviticus 6:12a NIV)

The fire was a reminder of God's presence and it was to "not go out."

We live in good times, y'all.

Because of Jesus Christ, all we have to do now to experience God is this ... *"Draw near to God, and He will draw near to you." (James 4:8 ESV)*

There is no need to gather firewood and no need to put on linen garments. But one thing remains the same ... *we must be intentional.* We cannot let the fire go out. Sounds easy, but with so many things competing for our attention, this may be easier said than done.

What does 'keeping the fire burning on the altar' mean for you?

For me, it means *intentionally* spending more time each day in worship, in my Bible and in prayer and less time scrolling mindlessly on my phone. It means being *intentional* about getting together with fellow believers when I'd rather be at home. It means saying 'no' to certain things, so I can say 'yes' to God.

What does it mean for you?

~Binu

February 15 ~ Leviticus 8-10
"And Moses said to the congregation, 'This is the thing that the Lord has commanded to be done.'" Leviticus 8:5 (ESV)

I was one of those weird kids at school. I liked to be at the front of the class.

That meant you were "in charge" ... of your row.

But the front row seats weren't on a first-come, first-served basis. They were assigned by the teacher.

For non-weird kids, they didn't really care where they sat.

I wasn't one of those kids.

I was upset when others were chosen for the front row and I wasn't. One time, I even begged my mom to call the teacher and ask her to move me to the front.

Bottom line - it's hard when someone else is chosen for a position that you wanted - in the classroom, boardroom or even Sunday School room.

As a kid, my mom just had to make a phone call. As an adult, it's not that easy.

In Leviticus 8, we read about the ordination of Aaron and his sons into the priesthood. They were the chosen ones for this highly respected position and served as the liaison between God and His people.

I wonder if there were others who thought the same as I did in my third-grade class. *Why wasn't I chosen for that position? I wanted to do that! I would be really good at it too!*

The answer is simple. *"And Moses said to the congregation, 'This is the thing that the Lord has commanded to be done.'" (Leviticus 8:5 ESV)*

Just like the teacher determined our classroom seating arrangement, the Lord established that Aaron and his sons would serve as priests.

Why were they chosen and not someone else? We know that the descendants of Levi were the priestly tribe but why not any of the other tribes? Why the Levites and why Aaron?

Because God commanded it.

I may not be in school anymore but I still struggle with understanding why God has chosen certain people for certain assignments. Assignments that I want. Assignments that I feel like I would be good at.

Over the years, there is one thing that has brought me assurance: The Lord commanded it. For whatever reason, He chose them and not me. I may never know why but I know His heart toward me is good and that His ultimate purpose for my life will prevail ... whatever position I find myself - in the front row or not.

~Anu

February 16 ~ Leviticus 11-13
"For I, the Lord, am the one who brought you up from the
land of Egypt, that I might be your God. Therefore, you must
be holy because I am holy." Leviticus 11:45 (NLT)

God is in the details.

Leviticus very specifically lists the food that the people of Israel could and could not eat.

But why did it matter what they ate?

You see, this generation of Israelites were born into slavery. As slaves, they didn't get a choice on how to conduct their lives. They did what they were told and weren't allowed to question it.

So now with their newly found freedom, they needed some instruction on how to practically live their lives.

God tells Moses very specifically what his people should and should not eat. Leviticus 11 is so specific that it can seem downright petty. *Why can't I just eat what I want? What's the big deal?*

This was a time before the world knew anything about nutrition and what we need to eat to be in optimal health. But God knew. He is the one who uncovered these mysteries to man today.

Back then, God knew He needed to give His people specific instructions. If we look at the instructions He gave, especially regarding food, we can see that in doing so, He was using these laws to preserve their health and wellness.

There were also skin diseases that kept people isolated from the rest of the people. The specifics He gave to His people were to protect them. His laws helped stop the spread of infectious diseases among the people of Israel.

To many it seems like lists of strict rules from a God who just wants to control us. But I understand now that His laws were given because He loves us. When good parents give their child boundaries, it's because they love them.

Our Heavenly Father knows what happens outside of the boundary He has given us.... sin and ultimately death. At a time before science had understood what we know today, God lovingly gave laws to protect and preserve his children.

I am so grateful to serve a God that is in the details. Not only in the giving of his laws, but in every detail of my life. He doesn't miss a thing. He knows when one strand of hair falls from my head.

Knowing God is in the details, I can trust Him with the details of my life and my future.

~Vijoy

February 17 ~ Leviticus 14-15

"... they must remain outside their tents for seven days. On the seventh day they must again shave all the hair from their heads, including the hair of the beard and eyebrows..." Leviticus 14:8-9 (NLT)

Several years ago, a television show did a vignette where it showed a doctor sneezing into his hand. For viewing purposes, the sneeze turned his hand green. He didn't wash his hand and went on to touch a doorknob, which turned green as well. Someone else came up and touched the same doorknob and the germs were then transferred to them, turning their hand green. The germs were passed on and on until they ended up infecting an elderly woman, and she eventually succumbed to a disease that started off as an innocent sneeze. It was a great illustration of how the simple act of washing hands could stop the spread of infection.

God's instructions here are attempting to stop an infection before it even starts. He is preparing to dwell among His chosen people. His instructions have been pared down from procedural offerings now to specific personal issues. He is preparing for His tabernacle to be built in the midst of this massive nation.

Imagine for a moment what that would have looked like. All the noise. People coming and going from their daily routines into and out of the building where the presence of the Lord dwells. Imagine the smells and chaos as people brought their animals to be presented as sacrifices. Can you see the mess of the grains, oils, and wines? From the field to the home, into a basket, into the tabernacle. It was critical that His people did not defile themselves in any way before entering in the tabernacle or when touching anything that would enter the Lord's presence.

Thank God that we don't live in those times, right?

Well, maybe... God dwells with us and within us, right?

In your home, your car, your cubicle. He is there. Everything that we say, touch, and see can have an impact on our relationship with our very present God. You and I have direct access. Our personal holiness is just as important now as it was back then. It's a matter of just asking God, "Forgive me. Cleanse me from my sin."

We strive to be holy because He is holy.

~Shiney

February 18 ~ Leviticus 16-18

"For the life of a creature is in the blood, and I have given it to you to make atonement for yourselves on the altar; it is the blood that makes atonement for one's life." Leviticus 17:11 (NIV)

Last week, I had one of those days. I was easily irritated and touchy, and my husband could sense it in the way I was interacting with the family. I knew he noticed my mood, although he chose not to say anything in that moment.

Looking back, I felt ashamed at my behavior, and even though I could have come up with a few excuses, it wasn't enough. I was still responsible for my words. That night, I sat next to my kids as I put them into bed and asked them for forgiveness.

I confessed it to my Father in heaven, too. He had witnessed me. I prayed, and I knew I was forgiven.

What a burden off my shoulders to know that while I had made a mistake, I was forgiven. I didn't have to feel ashamed for a minute longer after confessing my sin to my Father God that night.

A few days later, my husband and I talked about how I had reacted, and it was comforting to acknowledge that although I could have handled things differently, I did not need to feel condemned.

Jesus' death on the cross made a way for every man and woman to be forgiven. He paid the price for every sin and shameful thing we have done. His *blood*, which has life, allowed for "atonement", the reconciliation of God to us.

The Bible says, *"For the life of a creature is in the blood ... it is the blood that makes atonement for one's life." (Leviticus 17:11 NIV).* Prior to the death of Christ on the cross, the blood of bulls and goats would make atonement for the people ONCE A YEAR! Can you imagine the shame and condemnation that would build over time? I was feeling guilty in a matter of minutes after my sin!

What is causing you to constantly feel guilty and apologetic? Confess your sins and know that you are already forgiven! While we play a part in asking for forgiveness, the price was paid through the blood of Jesus.

"Jesus paid it all, all to Him I owe; Sin had left a crimson stain, He washed it white as snow."[1] (Lyrics by Elvina M. Hall)

~Elizabeth

February 19 ~ Leviticus 19-21
"The Lord said to Moses, 'Speak to the entire assembly
of Israel ...'" Leviticus 19:1,2a (NIV)

I had my Bible open to the book of Leviticus when my sixteen-year-old son decided to plop right next to me. Peering over my shoulder, a few verses caught his eye. "*What in the world? 'Do not cut the hair at the sides of your head or clip off the edges of your beard.' Is God talking about fades?"* He kept reading.

Leviticus is a difficult book for readers of any age or spiritual maturity. In fact, it's usually the book that makes good intentioned '*I'm going to read the Bible in a year'* Christians stop their Bible reading plan.

Leviticus literally means '*to the Levites'*, but this law was spoken by God to Moses *to the entire assembly* of Israel.

Unlike the book of Psalms, Proverbs and much of the New Testament which reads like a devotional book, Leviticus does not. This book reads more like a health or safety manual....and we all know how exciting those books can be.

Leviticus discusses everything from offerings, uncleanliness, feasts, vows, land ownership, the Day of Atonement and so much more. Some chapters are very difficult to read through, but please don't give up! Keep reading! By the end, this book will give you a greater understanding of the culture and help you see God's big picture and plan more clearly.

That evening, as my son continued to read on, I cringed. I knew what was coming up. It was laws regarding "inappropriate relations" with animals and close family members. I wanted so badly to close my Bible. But I didn't. I reminded myself, my son is sixteen, not six ... he can handle this ... and so can I. The more I read through the Levitical laws, the more I am convinced that only one person could satisfy all of this: Jesus Christ. I am thankful He came, not to abolish the law but to fulfill the law.

Thank You Jesus for the finished work of the cross!

~Binu

February 20 ~ Leviticus 22-23
"You shall not offer anything that has a blemish,
for it will not be acceptable for you."
Leviticus 22:20 (ESV)

A lot has changed since the days of the Old Testament. There are terms and guidelines for worship that we no longer use in the modern church today.

Various offerings like burnt offerings and peace offerings were acceptable as long as they met certain criteria. God also appointed specific feasts, a "holy convocation", when the people were to gather together. This included the Feast of First Fruits and the Feast of Trumpets which were to be handled in a particular manner.

The change is a result of God's ultimate plan to reconcile people to Himself through His son, Jesus Christ. While we may not have to follow the specific laws and regulations of Leviticus when it comes to our worship, there are still principles that we can apply.

Unfortunately, it seems that we may have run so far from the letter of the law to the point of neglecting the heart of it.

God still deserves our best.

One person's idea of worship "without blemish" is going to be different from someone else's. To some, that means dressing up on Sunday and singing hymns. Others may picture exuberant worship with lifted hands.

The method may be different but there are two things that are essential: worship in Spirit, worship in truth.

"... true worshipers will worship the Father in spirit and truth, for the Father is seeking such people to worship him." (John 4:23 ESV)

There is obviously still some significance to what we do on the outside but Jesus' primary requirement for worship focused on what was happening on the inside.

Where are my mind and heart when I step into service on a Sunday? There have been times when I was clapping my hands to a song and thinking about what we were going to have for lunch instead of the words I was singing. What about my quiet time during the week? If it's become an item on a checklist, then is that really worshipping in Spirit and truth?

We're not going to always get this right and thankfully, He doesn't expect perfection from us. But I still want to give Him my all when I worship ... and my best.

~Anu

February 21 ~ Leviticus 24-25
"... When you enter the land I am going to give you,
the land itself must observe a sabbath ..."
Leviticus 25:2 (NIV)

How are you? *Busy.* It's a common response to a common question.

Busyness isn't always bad. Certain seasons of our lives are inevitably busy. And sometimes busyness can simply mean our lives are full. Remember the Proverbs 31 woman? She got up early, spun wool, inspected fields, helped the poor, and stayed up late. But when does busy become too busy?

Maybe when it begins to affect our mental, physical or spiritual health. When we are so busy, we have no time or energy left for God- the one true source of energy and strength.

In Joanna Weaver's book, "Having a Mary heart in a Martha World," Joanna writes, *"I can get to running so fast that I leave everything behind. Not just God. Not just people. I can lose my own soul as well."* [1]

So, what is the practical solution? It's the same as it has always been. *The fourth commandment.*

God, in His infinite wisdom, knew the negative effects of a continuous nonstop busy lifestyle, so He not only gave us permission to rest, He commanded us to rest. Once a week, we are instructed to cease from our busyness and observe a regular period of extended rest. God gave us a Sabbath. In Hebrew, the word Sabbath literally in means a 'ceasing of labor.'

In Leviticus 25:2, the Lord instructs the Israelites that even the land must observe a Sabbath. *"When you enter the land I am going to give you, the land itself must observe a sabbath ..." (NIV)* He told them to sow, prune and gather for six years. *"But in the seventh year, the land is to have a sabbath of rest." (vs 4 NIV)*

In other words, work hard, but when I say rest, rest. Don't worry, during this time of rest, God will take care of you and your fields.

Maybe you feel as if you can't afford to 'cease' for a full day. I understand. Try setting aside one morning, one afternoon or one evening a week. Whatever the time period, let's be intentional and schedule ... nothing. Spend time with God and spend time with those who matter most to you.

If we take the time to *"cease from our labor,"* God *will* refresh our souls.

~Binu

February 22 ~ Leviticus 26-27

"If you follow my decrees and are careful to obey my commands, I will send you the seasonal rains. The land will then yield its crops, and the trees of the field will produce their fruit." Leviticus 26:3-4 (NLT)

In Leviticus 26, we see an outline of the blessings that the Israelites would receive if they followed God's commands and the curses that would follow if they disobey. Beginning in verse 3, God is promising incredible blessings to the same people who seem to have a selective memory and remembered Egypt to be so much better than it actually was. The same people who moaned about missing the food in Egypt without recalling the slavery that accompanied it.

I can just hear their responses now...

"I will send the seasonal rains" = Rain is going to wash out my outdoor plans this weekend. Hope that it doesn't make my tent leak.

"Your land will be fruitful with extended harvest times" = Extended harvest times means more work for me!

"You will have peace and protection from your enemies" = Enemies? You mean that there are people out there that don't like me? How is this possible?

Favor. Fulfillment. Surplus. = WHERE is all of this surplus going to go? Am I going to have to get rid of some of my old stuff to make room for my new stuff? Groan - do you know how long that's going to take??? And I really like some of my old stuff!

These seem like petty complaints to moan about in the midst of receiving God's blessing, but we do it all the time. We get mad when our day doesn't go the way the planned. Mad when we don't get that job. Mad when our car breaks down.

God has promised to live and walk among us. That means that He might interrupt and mess up your day a little bit. There is blessing in all of these little hiccups of life - a chance for the Holy Spirit to come and wreck your day. It gives us a chance to veer out of our lane and move into the better picture that God has planned for us.

Can you accept the good with a little not so good? Can you deal with a little rain to accept His provision for your life? You can work a little harder for the tradeoff of satisfaction and security that comes from our Heavenly Father, right? You may still have enemies that you have to chase off, but you will have supernatural strength to do it.

As long as God is in it with you, you can handle it.

~Shiney

February 23 ~ Numbers 1-2
"So the Israelites did everything just as the Lord had commanded Moses." Numbers 1:54 (NLT)

A couple of years ago I was praying about the direction God wanted me to go for that year.

What I strongly felt was that God wanted me to clear up the clutter and organize my home. It seemed like a strange request to hear from God. But the more I prayed the stronger I felt it.

You see, clutter was a big part of my life. I'm not sure why, but I felt like it was easier to stack piles of mail and deal with it later, than to put things away as they came through my door. But what I didn't realize until later was that the disorganization of my home added a layer of anxiety and chaos to my heart and mind.

So, in that year, I finally decided to do something about it. I did my best to do what I could on my own, and when I couldn't do anymore, I enlisted the help and encouragement of those around me.

In the first and second book of Numbers, God asks something similar of Moses and Aaron. He asks them to take a census in order to organize and mobilize the people of Israel. At this point, it had been one year since they left Egypt. And yet they were still wandering in the desert without a real sense of purpose or direction. But God needed his people to be organized and ready to be able to take on the promised land. Per God's direction, each tribe was methodically counted and aligned in a very specific formation around the tabernacle of God.

Now, with an army of more than 600,000 strong, the tribes of Israel were now mobilized and ready to fight.

What is God asking of you in preparation for what He wants to do in your life?

You might be surprised that what He is asking of you is way more practical than spiritual. And it might be the very thing you need to be able to receive what He wants to give you. I want to encourage you today to take an inventory of your life.

Listen and act on what God is asking you to do, because He might just be preparing you for what is about to come.

~Vijoy

February 24 ~ Numbers 3-4
"Call forward the tribe of Levi, and present them to
Aaron the priest to serve as his assistants."
Numbers 3:6 (NLT)

There is a fantastic kids' book called "The Day the Crayons Quit" by Drew Daywalt[1]. It's the story of a little boy named Duncan who goes to take out his crayons in class to color an assignment. Instead of crayons, he finds a stack of letters, addressed to him, in his crayon box. Each crayon has written a letter to Duncan.

Red goes first. He complains about how he has to work all year long, even on holidays, coloring everything from fire engines and apples to Santa Claus on Christmas. Next is purple who complains that his color ends up outside the lines.

Beige complains about his general lack of work and that he's called light brown or tan instead of his actual name. Gray complains about his heavy workload of coloring large things such as elephants, rhinos, hippos, and whales. He requests to color tiny rocks and pebbles instead for a break.

White complains about how he can't be seen without the outline of another color or can't make an image without the help of another crayon. The green crayon is happy with its workload, but he writes to notify Duncan of the rift between the yellow crayon and the orange crayon. Apparently, they had an argument over which one was the actual color of the sun and now are no longer speaking to each other. It's a fun read and with beautiful ending.

The crayons' complaints sound similar to the complaints we often have about our own roles in ministry. In this reading, we see that God was very particular to assign specific responsibilities to the Levites, knowing that each of these details was critical.

In the body of Christ, we each have our responsibilities and duties. We are the hands and feet of Christ. We cannot work independently of each other. We must work together.

Each of us are gifted with different skills that are suited to our task. Not one of us is more important than the other. We are all needed in the kingdom to pursue the same, singular purpose.

We cannot adequately color our world with God's love without leaning on each other. We are all in God's box with different strengths and must come together to fulfill His plan on the earth.

~Shiney

February 25 ~ Numbers 5-6
"... They must fulfill the vows they have made, according to the law of the Nazirite." Numbers 6:21 (NIV)

My father was the pastor of my church when I was growing up, and I was the eldest child.

Given this position, I would constantly be reminded to set an example for the other women in our church in my attire and attitude. It was a tall order. Most first-born children understand this pressure.

People were watching me, and I knew that any slip-up could convey a negative impression on my father, so I was careful.

At the time, I didn't fully understand my parents' requirements on dressing modestly or refusing certain social events, but I obeyed their rules. With time, I began to realize that the innate nature of my role as the daughter of a leader would lead people to view me as a leader, as well.

Looking back, I realize their intentions. My parents wanted me to be set apart.

The Israelites were given certain requirements to those who desired to make a special vow- a vow of separation to the Lord as a Nazirite. Specific obligations, such as abstaining from drinking wine or grape juice, keeping hair long, and avoiding dead bodies, were prohibitions given to any man or woman seeking this act of devotion to the Lord. The outward signs were an expression of an internal devotion to God.

As an adult, I have come to realize that an inward devotion to the Lord should automatically bleed out into how we speak and act and even in the way we physically present ourselves.

As Christ-followers, we have freedom in how we dress or socialize, yet we realize that as a child of God we should carry ourselves in a way that is unique and set apart. Our choices can positively impact others that may not know Him.

God's desires your devotion. While it may not necessarily be a Nazarite vow you are taking, it could mean making appropriate choices in appearance, diet, or who you are associating with.

Know that it is your heart that God is after, and that you are His daughter. May others realize through your words and actions that the Lord's face is shining on you and that He has written His name on your heart.

~Elizabeth

"And when Moses went into the tent of meeting to speak with the Lord, he heard the voice speaking to him..." Numbers 7:89 (ESV)

I was surprised when I looked at my calendar one particular day: *"Text mom/ dad you're proud of them!"* I quickly realized it was my husband who added the event to our calendar.

The reason for the text? My in-laws were leaving to do medical missions work in the Philippines.

The reason for adding it to our calendar? He was being intentional.

The word "intentional" has gotten a lot of buzz over the past few years. The definition simply says, *"done on PURPOSE, deliberate."*[1]

My husband, Lance, knew as the day progressed, he would likely forget to text them. He also knew this was something he wanted to do so he did something about it.

Even for me, when I've seen his personal calendar, he has a weekly reminder about reading my blog post because he knows that I write on a particular day.

I can hear it already. Some may say he should just remember that on his own. That is one way of looking at it but I know with all we have going on sometimes, we both struggle with remembering things. So, the fact that he would go out of his way to remind himself to read my posts actually meant a lot to me.

There are plenty of things we know we should do and things we just want to do, like texting our parents or reading a post...but if we aren't intentional about doing them, they may not happen.

Maybe for you it's something like exercise or following up with a friend who is going through something. It could even be your time with God.

Good things are more likely to happen when we are intentional about good things.

"And when Moses went into the tent of meeting to speak with the Lord, he heard the voice speaking to him..." (Numbers 7:89 ESV)

When you put yourself in a position to have a conversation with God – when you are intentional about your time with Him, God will speak.

Determine what those things are that you keep saying "I need to do that..." or "I really should...". Then, set yourself up to win by doing what you can to make it happen...get an accountability partner, write yourself a note or maybe add it to your calendar. I've heard that works pretty well.

~Anu

*"And Moses said to them, 'Wait, that I may hear what
the LORD will command concerning you.'"*
Numbers 9:8 (ESV)

I'm a Texas girl. Born and raised. I've lived in the Dallas area since I was 2 years old. I love my city. I know my city ... well, at least I thought I did.

Recently, I've ventured out to some parts of town where I haven't been before. Each time I got in my car, I had this conversation with myself: *"Who needs a GPS? I survived a lot of years without a map app or a smart phone. My friends even tell me I am good with directions. I GOT THIS!"*

Well, it turns out, I didn't have it. In each situation, I found myself "exploring" these new parts of town and eventually asked my smart phone for some help. Once I did, I was on my way again ... this time in the right direction.

"And Moses said to them, 'Wait, that I may hear what the LORD will command concerning you.'" (Numbers 9:8 ESV)

This is Moses we are talking about. The same guy who was used to bring on the plagues in Egypt and part the Red Sea. The one who talked to and heard from God on a regular basis. The only person God wanted to keep around but relented when Moses interceded.

This same guy, Moses, encountered a situation he was unsure about.

Sometimes, I feel like I should be at a place where I immediately know what I should do. That is definitely not the case for me. However, the life of Moses reassures me that it may never be the case which may be a good thing.

If I always have things figured out, I may give myself too much credit and start thinking "I GOT THIS!". The uncertainty reminds me (almost daily) that no matter how far I am in my walk with God, I am still utterly and completely dependent on Him.

Even when I think I know, I will never go wrong stopping to ask Him for directions. I can't do anything in my own power. I need Him.

And I guess I need my GPS too.

~Anu

February 28 ~ Numbers 11-13
"... We should go up and take possession of the land, for we can certainly do it."
Numbers 13:30 (NIV)

Joshua and Caleb.

My two favorite Bible characters. I even named my children after them... Joshua's leadership, Caleb's feisty spirit. Put them together, they define courage. Their story is found in Numbers 13 and 14.

A little after the Red Sea parted, Moses sent twelve spies to explore the land of Canaan, the land God promised the Israelites.

Ten of the spies reported, *"We can't go up against them! They are stronger than we are ... the land will devour anyone who goes to live there...We even saw the giants, the descendants of Anak. We felt like grasshoppers." (my paraphrase)*

Joshua and Caleb walked the same streets, saw the same land and the same giants.

But they had a different report.

"The land we traveled through is a wonderful land. If the Lord is pleased with us, He will bring us safely through...." (my paraphrase again)

Unfortunately, all of Joshua and Caleb's faith and optimism did not change the mindset of the community. The Israelites believed the land was unattainable and wanted to stone anyone who disagreed with them.

Fast forward about forty years.

Joshua and Caleb are the only two people of the approximately one million Israelites who actually made it to their intended destination, the Promise Land. What made them different?

Joshua and Caleb didn't deny the problem. They compared the problem to their God. The other ten compared the problem to themselves.

So, where is your Canaan? What is your Promise Land?

Maybe it's when that dream of yours is finally fulfilled or maybe it's when, as Max Lucado puts it in his book "Glory Days"[1] - *"You stand at the intersection of your skill and God's call."* He goes on to say... *"Canaan is a life in which we win more often than we lose, forgive as quickly as we are offended, and give as abundantly as we receive. We serve out of our giftedness and delight in our assignments."*

So, whatever that Promise Land is to you, expect naysayers, but don't let their negative words stop you from starting. *"People have a right to say what they want. And you have a right to ignore them." (Lucado)[1]*

Joshua and Caleb stood their ground and God took note of it. They were two in a million.

Stand your ground and enter in.

~Binu

March 1 ~ Numbers 14-15, Psalm 90
"Teach us to realize the brevity of life, so that we may grow in wisdom." Psalm 90:12 (NLT)

Despite my heritage, my ability to cook Indian food is very (very) limited. Thankfully, my parents and in-laws have no problem sending food for us ... their grown children.

Recently, it hit me that one day, I wouldn't have that. Sure, I could go to an Indian restaurant but I wouldn't have my mom's cooking. My grandmother lived to be 92 so God willing, my mom has a long way to go. But it doesn't change the fact that at this stage in life, the time I have left with my parents may be less than what I already had.

It's a sobering but potentially impactful thought that can affect every aspect of our relationship with our parents – how we talk to them, how we listen, how we treat them, the time we spend with them and so much more.

Scripture puts it like this, *"Teach us to realize the brevity of life, so that we may grow in wisdom." (Psalm 90:12 NLT)* Something happens to our thinking when we understand how limited our time is.

In his message, "Don't Waste Your Family"[1], Pastor Ben Stuart offers this suggestion regarding our parents: *"Stay connected to them. Speak graciously to them. Speak gratefully to them. Thank them for what they have done in your life – for bringing you into existence if nothing else. And for dropping $250,000 to raise you."*

He goes on to say, *"Even if your family doesn't deserve it, you aren't doing it for them, you do it for the Lord. If Jesus, while He was dying for the sins of the world...could look down and make sure His mother is taken care of by one of His disciples, you can call your mom."*

We no longer have to clean our room or make our bed at their command but they are still our parents. They may not have always gotten it right but neither have we. Trust that they did the best they could to raise us and now let's do the best we can to honor them. Make the most of the time we have with them ... it is worth savoring.

~Anu

March 2 ~ Numbers 16-17

*"Then he said to Korah and his followers, 'Tomorrow morning the
Lord will show us who belongs to him and who is holy. The Lord will
allow only those whom he selects to enter his own presence.'"*
Numbers 16:5 (NLT)

Do you feel like your background dictates your future? Were your parents divorced, or maybe alcoholics, or filled with bitterness and anger? It's hard to believe that your life will end up any different from theirs.

But it doesn't have to.

In the scripture we read about a man named Korah who lead a rebellion against Moses and Aaron. Korah planted seeds of doubts in the people's minds which questioned Moses and Aaron's leadership. But Korah had already been given a special responsibility in ministry.

You see, Korah was also a descendant from the tribe of Levi, just like Moses and Aaron. And as a Levite, he and his family were already set apart to serve God and his people.

But that wasn't enough for Korah. He wanted more.

As a result of Korah's rebellion, Moses called upon God to prove to the people that he was indeed chosen by God to lead Israel.

God's answer was swift and undeniable.

The earth opened up and literally swallowed up Korah, his followers, and their families right before their eyes. But several chapter later, the scripture mentions something significant.

"But the earth opened up its mouth and swallowed them with Korah, and fire devoured 250 of their followers ... However, the sons of Korah did not die that day." (Numbers 26:10-11 NLT)

Did you catch that? While most of the other followers of Korah and their families died that day, Korah's sons did not die with him. So, what ever happened to the sons of Korah?

When we read the book of Psalms, the writers credit some of the most beautiful Psalms to the sons of Korah. One of the most notable reads *"As the deer longs for streams of water, so my soul longs for you O God". (Psalm 42:1 NLT)*

Coming from their particular background, you would expect them to do what their father did.

But they did not. Rather, they chose to serve God as they were intended and the Psalms they wrote reveal their lives took a beautiful turn for good.

I hope you know that your life can be different too. Despite your family pedigree or your past, God can turn your story into something more beautiful than you ever imagined.

~Vijoy

March 3 ~ Numbers 18-20

"You and Aaron must take the staff and assemble the entire community. As the people watch, speak to the rock over there, and it will pour out its water..." Numbers 20:8 (NLT)

Several years ago, when I was going through a difficult time, a friend reached out to me. At the time, we were good friends, but not the kind that would talk every week. However, she knew that I was in a rough spot, and she and her husband felt an urging to come and pray with my family. I did not call her; she reached out to me. She had never experienced what I was going through, but as we visited, it was clear that God gave them a word for us that was a healing balm and pushed us in our faith.

Whenever I sit back and reflect on that time, I can honestly say that I don't know how I would have made it through that time without her visit. Years later, I still thank God that my friend listened to His instructions and met with us.

Following God's instructions seems easy. You feel His nudging, but you may or may not chose to answer it. How many times do we hear what God is telling us to do but casually ignore his instruction?

Moses was instructed to bring the staff and command the rock to pour out water. Instead, Moses only partly obeys, striking the rock to produce water. Throughout their journey, God had been proving himself to the Israelites by various signs and miracles, using these works to build their faith. In this moment, Moses robbed God of a miracle.

Are you someone's miracle? Are you withholding a word for someone that could be the momentum they need to conquer their hill? Listen to the nudging that God places in your heart. Make that phone call. Visit with that person. Speak what God has told you to say.

I am grateful for my friend that listened and obeyed. It challenged my faith in a way that changed my walk. A few years later, when my family was facing a different struggle, my husband called up these same friends and asked them to stand with us in prayer. They responded with immediate prayer and stood in faith for us when we were running low.

Follow His instruction so that His work may be completed through you. You never know what miracles you may be holding.

~Shiney

March 4 ~ Numbers 21-22
"Balaam's donkey saw the angel of the Lord standing in the road
with a drawn sword in his hand." Numbers 22: 23 (NLT)

I have been called many names in my lifetime. Some good: sister, wife, mother, friend. Some not so good: brat (I have an older brother), antagonizer (by my brother), instigator (my brother again- we really do love each other). I have probably even been called a donkey, just in a different form.

In Numbers 22, when Balaam gets on his donkey to go to where the Israelites are camped, God sends an angel to stop him. Balaam does not see the Angel, but the donkey sees it as it approaches three different times and even tries to yield to the Angel. Each time, the donkey is beat by its master, because it sees what the master does not. Finally, the donkey turns to Balaam and has a conversation with him. (I always thought that it was interesting that Balaam does not seem fazed by his talking donkey...)

The donkey saw what the human couldn't. I have a dog, and I know that he senses things that I cannot. One time, we went for a walk, and when we got to the end of the street, he just sat down. He would not go forward. I pulled him, but he would not budge. Finally, when I turned around to go back home, he jumped up and happily trotted home. We got home, I closed the door, and it started pouring. Had we continued our walk, we would have been drenched. He sensed something that I didn't.

Sometimes I think that my eyes are so fixed on what is in front of me or on whatever mission I happen to be on that day, that I do not see anything else. I don't see that the traffic is heavy to force me to stay in the car and worship just a minute longer. I over analyze situations in my life, forgetting that God is working things in the background that I cannot see. I get so easily overwhelmed that I forget to ask God to order my steps in a productive way.

I wish that I could be like that donkey and be so in tune with God that I see the angels all around me. I wish that I had the confidence of that donkey to speak to the Balaams in my life and call them to the carpet.

Be a donkey.

~Shiney

March 5 ~ Numbers 23-25
"... Must I not speak what the Lord puts in my mouth?" Numbers 23:12 (NIV)

Have you ever been in a position where there were expectations of you except you did not meet them? You just felt the Holy Spirit tug at your heart and you knew that you do had to do differently than what was expected from those around you.

I remember being in a position where the standard that was set lacked integrity. However, the expectation was that I would go along with it because that's what everyone else did. I knew my position was on the line, but I also knew what was right and what was wrong in God's sight. I decided not to meet those expectations because I wanted to obey God.

As you can only imagine, I was not met with a positive response. In fact, the next several months were the worst of my life. But God was with me and He kept me. I have no regrets because I knew I did what was right by obeying Him.

King Balak's expectation of Balaam was to curse Israel. To Balak's dismay, every time Balaam gave a prophecy, he blessed Israel. He was angry because Balaam was not doing what he was paid to do. Balaam's response is found in the key verse.

You and I may face similar circumstances whether the expectations in question stem from our work environment or our cultural background. We are asked to speak a certain way or behave a certain way. The question we have to ask ourselves is will we respond as God is prompting us to or will we ignore Him because our fear of man is greater?

"The fear of the Lord is the beginning of wisdom; all those who practice it have a good understanding." (Psalm 111:10 NIV)

When we have a revelation of who God is, with our eyes and ears being opened to see and hear what He is revealing to us, then our hearts are inclined to obey Him at all costs. Those around us may not be happy with us. They may be disappointed and even infuriated. But I pray that we would have the courage and the strength to obey what God is telling us to do.

Dear Lord, may our hearts be obedient to speak what you tell us to say without fear or hesitation. Amen.

~Joyce

March 6 ~ Numbers 26-27
"The daughters of Zelophehad are right. You shall give them possession of an inheritance..."
Numbers 27:7 (ESV)

Fighting like a girl is a good thing.

That was the case especially with the daughters of Zelophehad: Mahlah, Noah, Hoglah, Milcah, and Tirzah. At this point, only sons were given an inheritance but there were only daughters in this family. So, it says that these women "*... stood before Moses and before Eleazar the priest and before the chiefs and all the congregation ...*" *(Numbers 27:2 ESV)* and petitioned for their father's inheritance.

Can you imagine what they must have been feeling as they walked forward? Maybe they started questioning themselves. Maybe one sister changed her mind but the others talked her back into it. What if Moses said no? They could be completely humiliated.

If they felt any of that, they didn't let it stop them. Good thing they didn't because (spoiler) the outcome is a good one.

"Moses brought their case before the Lord. And the Lord said to Moses, 'The daughters of Zelophehad are right. You shall give them possession of an inheritance among their father's brothers and transfer the inheritance of their father to them.'" (Numbers 27:5-7 ESV)

Moses took their request seriously. And so did God.

I don't know if guys get the same feeling when they read this story as I did ... but my heart smiled. I love their boldness. In a time and culture where women aren't usually involved in these types of matters, they stepped up, completely going against the norm and received what they asked for.

There are certain situations when we should just "be still" and let the Lord fight our battles. However, this story has reminded me that sometimes in order to get the promise, you may have a part in the fight. Jacob wrestled an angel to get a blessing. The Israelites fought (repeatedly) to claim their territory. These brave women, the daughters of Zelophehad, petitioned to receive their inheritance.

In scripture, there are plenty of examples of women who fought messy by taking shortcuts and trying to do things their own way. Not these girls. Mahlah, Noah, Hoglah, Milcah, and Tirzah were respectful to those in authority and submitted themselves to the process.

Whatever your calling, whatever your promise, whatever your inheritance ... don't shrink back. Fight like a girl and go for it.

~Anu

March 7 ~ Numbers 28-30
"On the first day of the seventh month hold a sacred assembly and do no regular work..."
Numbers 29:1 (NIV)

I am a big multi-tasker. Cooking, cleaning, catching up with an old friend. All three can be done simultaneously in my house. Throw a load of laundry in the washer, begin to prep for a meal, talk on the phone...why not do it all at the same time? Even at my workplace, I'm somewhat of a 'Time Dictator'. Ask my co-workers. I can't tell you how many times they have heard me say, *"If you are unable to work and talk at the same time, let's save the talking for later."*

But when I get into God's presence, I am forced to switch gears. You see, God desires something different of me. He wants 100% of my attention. He asks that I step away from multi-tasking and from all of the distractions. God asks that my time with Him be time with *Him.*

In Numbers chapters 28 and 29, God gave the people strict orders regarding His Sacred Assemblies. The Passover, the Feast of Weeks, the Feast of Trumpets, the Day of Atonement, the Feast of Tabernacles. All required setting aside one's daily (or even weekly) routine, coming together, and offering something of value to God. Keep in mind, this was in addition to the once a week God- honoring Sabbath days.

Regardless of the festival, feast or assembly, God repeated one key phrase throughout these chapters, *"Do no regular work." (NIV)*

God wanted His people to deny themselves and their schedules and focus on Him.

He knows if we choose to step away from our phones, our calendars, and our agenda ... we have the opportunity to experience more of Him.

~Binu

March 8 ~ Numbers 31-32
"Moses sent them, a thousand from each tribe, to the war, and Phinehas
the son of Eleazer the priest to war with them, and the sacred vessels
[of the sanctuary] and the trumpets to blow the alarm in his hand."
Numbers 31:6 (AMP)

Cancer. Chronic illness. Alcoholism. Depression.

Long term battles. Emotional struggles. Day to day warring. Life becomes exhausting. Some of us know the nature of these battles too closely.

When the Israelites were called to war, they had an interesting battle formation we see repeated several times throughout the Bible. They were led by the priests, the sacred objects from the sanctuary, and trumpeters or musicians. My intellect says that this would be placing your weakest, least prepared men at the front line, meeting battle face to face. These men are not trained to fight.

This formation seems like it would result in a slaughter of your most sacred people.

I don't know much about war strategy, but let me compare this to something that I do know about- football. Occasionally during football games, the crowd will break into a team chant or team song. The Minnesota Vikings have the "Skol chant", and the Washington Redskins have a popular team song as well. It's usually heard during a particularly critical time in the game, often when the team needs to score or when they need to stop a score from happening. We've all heard those chants...one fan starts it, and it spreads like wildfire until it becomes a deafening roar to the opposing team. It unifies the crowd and the team and hopefully spurs them onto victory.

Now, it doesn't seem so crazy.

God's battle plan puts the singers, musicians and encouragers at the frontline to set the tone for the battle. They are establishing unity among the warriors and inviting God to intervene on their behalf. What better way to lead men into a war than with God's presence at the front, facing the enemy head on?

In the powerful song "No Longer Slaves" by Bethel[1], it says *"We've been liberated from our bondage. We're the sons and the daughters. Let us sing our freedom!"* As we face our struggles today, let us not forget to let God's presence lead the way for us. Let us allow Him to meet our enemy head on, face to face. Lead with God's word and worship. Meet Him daily, at your altar or sacred space that you have created for Him. Let His presence wrap around you as you go through your day.

~Shiney

March 9 ~ Numbers 33-34

"Speak to the Israelites and say to them: 'When you cross the Jordan into Canaan, drive out all the inhabitants of the land before you. Destroy all their carved images and their cast idols, and demolish all their high places.'"
Numbers 33:51,52 (NIV)

I have goals, you most likely have goals, and the Israelites had a goal. We all long to reach a Promised Land.

In Numbers 33:51-53, God gives strict orders to the Israelites concerning their goal.

'When you cross the Jordan into Canaan, SET UP A HAMMOCK, AND RELAX IN THE SUN, for you have finally arrived.'

Actually, it doesn't say that. *I just wanted to see if you were paying attention.*

It says... *"When you cross the Jordan into Canaan, DRIVE out all the inhabitants of the land before you. DESTROY all their carved images and their cast idols, and DEMOLISH all their high places. TAKE POSSESSION of the land and settle in it, for I have given you the land to possess."* (NIV)

In other words, 'Children, there is still much work to be done...even once you arrive.' Sure, they were promised a land flowing with milk and honey. But as my pastor once said, *'In the Promised Land, milk and honey weren't found on shelves in jars and jugs at the grocery store ready for their consumption. They had to continue to work for it.'*

So, whatever your Promise Land may be...better health, better relationships, or a better grip on your finances...if your feet are moving in the right direction, you might already be there. Don't get discouraged by all the work still to be done around you.

Because the truth is ... do we ever fully "arrive" anywhere? Once we reach one level of God ordained success, God usually has another level He wants to take us to.

The journey and the work involved are all a part of the destination. It was a part of the Israelites' Promised Land and it is most likely a part of ours.

~Binu

"Six of the towns you give the Levites will be cities of refuge, where a person who has accidentally killed someone can flee..." Numbers 35:6 (NLT)

Flashback to your childhood. Remember the game 'tag'? You get to be 'it' and the rest of your friends run away from you to avoid being tagged by you. Once you finally catch up to one of your friends (most definitely the slowest one), you tag them, and then you take off running!

Usually, at some point in the game, you establish a 'base'. That's your safe haven. Your only break during the game comes when you finally reach 'base'. It becomes your place of refuge in this relentless, reckless game. You can rest, catch your breath, and figure out your next move.

Even before the New Testament, God had grace for his people and their mistakes. Long before the birth of Jesus, God had a plan to redeem his people. He knew that they would need shelter from the craziness of life.

As Israel was establishing its territories, God was specific to include cities of refuge for his people. God wanted a place of grace for those who had found themselves in troubled situations. He wanted to give them a place for a second chance. A base for His very own people.

God knows that accidents happen. God knows that we make mistakes. He has compassion for us. He has grace for your mistakes, too.

Let him be your refuge that you run to. Let him be your home base.

~Shiney

March 11 ~ Deuteronomy 1-2

"... These forty years the Lord your God has been with you, and you have not lacked anything." Deuteronomy 2:7 (NIV)

"They are letting people go." Words you never want to hear at work. Hearing this pierced the hearts of our work family. Uncertainty hung in the air ... who were they keeping and who would leave? We were suddenly thrust into a whirlwind of uncertainty.

I remember being in this season of doubt eight years ago when I was looking for my first job. I was a new graduate and needed a place to work, and so I tidied up my resume, mailed it out to the masses, and waited.

My husband and I prayed for the place God wanted us to be, and He opened the door to an amazing company. Truly, it was a dream come true and it was also a relief to finally end the process of updating resumes, interviewing, and searching.

There is something about reaching the end of a process that is satisfying. But, even more so when you know that God is in it.

In the book of Deuteronomy, Moses reminds God's people that the Lord has been with them all along their 40-year journey through the desert as they fought battles to take possession of the land that God promised them. There were even countries God told them to avoid possessing.

One such king they had to defeat was Sihon, an Amorite. God told the Israelites that Sihon would be defeated...and this promise came even before the battle even happened.

How? God put the terror and fear of the Israelites on all the nations under heaven. The nations would tremble and be in anguish of them. So, ultimately, the battle was won even before any bloodshed because God was in it. He was "preparing" the Israelites for victory.

That's what gives me peace when I am thrust into that stomach-dropping, breath-stopping place of uncertainty. God is in this, and He is preparing the way for my victory.

I am in a season of unpredictability right now. How about you?

How should we handle it? The only way we know we will have victory is by walking out our faith. This is where our faith gets tested. And how do we pass this test?

We trust in a Father that has brought us through hot, sticky deserts in the past, and we thank Him in advance for our triumph. It's coming ... because God is in this.

~Elizabeth

March 12 ~ Deuteronomy 3-4
"But commission Joshua, and encourage and strengthen him,
for he will lead this people..." Deuteronomy 3:28 (NIV)

A few weeks ago, my husband and I were commissioned as Elders at our church. We were filled with emotion as our Pastor and the congregation prayed over us. It was just an incredibly humbling moment for us. What an honor to be installed into this position.

When we married, we knew that we wanted to serve in the ministry, but never had we imagined that it would be helping married couples. It's not something we were familiar with. We felt as if our own marriage had been through many trials, braving through each storm with God's help. We decided to share our experiences within the small group setting.

Then, a few years ago, we were asked to coach couples and we agreed. We learned a great deal from our mentors. We worked hard to learn the ropes of a new program that had been launched on our campus but we struggled with feeling qualified to do the job. I am so thankful for the faithful leaders who encouraged us and prayed for us, which really caused a shift from feeling inadequate to feeling confident. Now, here we were moving into a new season. God is just amazing, isn't He?

God instructed Moses to commission Joshua as the one who would lead the Israelites into the Promised Land. He was told how to empower Joshua. Leading the people would not be an easy endeavor and God knew exactly what was needed to fully equip Joshua.

Perhaps you are in a position where you recognize there is someone in particular who is ready to be elevated to leadership. There is wisdom in using this model laid out in the Bible by:

1. Officially charging them with the function they are to complete
2. Giving them support and advice so that they will do well in this new position
3. Reinforcing that they have what it takes to fulfill this new role

1 Thessalonians 5:11 (NIV) reminds us to "*... encourage one another and build each other up.*" Empowering others to lead gives them the confidence they need to take on a role which can seem overwhelming and one that they do not feel qualified to do.

Lord, help us to empower those who are called to lead and to equip them to do the job with excellence. Amen.

~Joyce

March 13 ~ Deuteronomy 5-7

*"These commandments that I give you today are to be on your hearts.
Impress them on your children. Talk about them when you sit at home
and when you walk along the road ..." Deuteronomy 6:6,7a (NIV)*

My firstborn son received his drivers' permit earlier this year. So, there we were, in a parking lot, ready to practice. I asked my younger son to buckle up as his big brother was about to take over the wheel. When I turned around, I couldn't help but laugh. He had every seat belt in the backseat somehow strapped on him. What a perfect image of what I was feeling at that exact moment.

Every stage of raising these little ones is exciting but scary.

I'm no parenting expert, as I'm still in the thick of it, and I'm learning new things every day. But thankfully, over the years, I have received some great advice from those who are both decades and even just a few years ahead of me. Either way, their wisdom is priceless and I'll take it.

1. *Pray.* Don't ever underestimate the power of prayer. It really is the most powerful tool we have. Pray for the present and for the future. It's never too early or too late to start praying for our children's schools, colleges, friendships, spouses, careers, and ministries. If possible, set aside one day a week (or even a meal a week) to fast and pray specifically for their future.
2. *Protect them.* Not just from obvious predators but from themselves. Even the best of kids left to themselves and to their own curiosity may do things they normally wouldn't do. Be present. Innocence can be stolen in seconds. We shouldn't be paranoid, but we should be vigilant and wise.
3. *We are raising children to become adults.* Not children to become bigger children. Give them age appropriate responsibilities. You may be able to hire a house cleaner now, but most likely, you were on your own when you went off to college or in the early days of your career. Let's not raise slobs.
4. *Don't rely on Sunday School alone.* Two hours a week isn't much time to teach our children everything they need to know about our faith. Teach them the Word of God practically through everyday life experiences. Be intentional and be engaged. Take advantage of every minute.
5. *It takes a village.* Surround yourselves with good friends and family who are willing to pour into and be positive mentors to your kids.

Sit back and enjoy the ride. It'll be over before we know it.

~Binu

March 14 ~ Deuteronomy 8-10

"He led you through the vast and dreadful desert, that thirsty and waterless land, with its venomous snakes and scorpions. He brought you water out of a hard place." Deuteronomy 8:15 (NIV)

Do you ever wish deserts had warning signs as you enter in?

Maybe a flashing yellow light to warn you that a dry and weary land is up ahead. Unfortunately, no such signals usually exist. Emergencies are just that. Sudden and immediate with no time to mentally prepare yourself.

One minute you're making plans to pack for spring break, the next minute you're packing for a hospital stay.

Just. Like. That. My family entered the desert.

In Deuteronomy 8:15, we read *"He led you through the vast and dreadful desert, that thirsty and waterless land, with its venomous snakes and scorpions..."* (NIV)

After such an extravagant exodus out of Egypt, why would God lead those very same people through a dreadful desert? God gave them a nice, safe pathway through the Red Sea. He could have done the same for them in the desert but He didn't.

Earlier in the same chapter, Moses explains why. *"The Lord your God led you all the way in the wilderness these forty years, to humble you and to test you in order to know what was in your heart..." (vs 2 NIV)*

It's one thing to sing, teach, preach, pray, and write nice little blogs while we are up on the mountaintop, but it's a whole other story to do those things when we are in the valley. The more I read, the more I realize ... desert routes may not be *my* preferred route of choice, but it seems to be *God's* preferred route. For it's often in the desert, He is able to perform the miraculous ... in us, through us and all around us.

Sure, there were scorpions in the desert but there were also miracles in the desert: manna on the ground, drinking water from a rock, quail from the sky, shoes and clothes with a lifetime warranty. All were amazing miracles God performed as the Israelites wandered *in the desert.*

Deuteronomy 8:15 begins with a description of the dreadful desert and venomous snakes but the verse ends with a miracle displaying God's power and provision,

"He led you through the vast and dreadful wilderness, that thirsty and waterless land, with its venomous snakes and scorpions. He brought you water out of a hard rock." (NIV)

Whatever it is you are going through today, be encouraged. God often performs the miraculous, in the desert.

~Binu

March 15 ~ Deuteronomy 11-13
"then the Lord will drive out all these nations before you, and you will dispossess nations larger and stronger than you." Deuteronomy 11:23 (NIV)

At a recent meeting, the leader of our Bible Study asked us about big dreams we may have. It made me think about my future ... *and my past.*

Can I share an entry from my prayer journal 16 years ago? I had a dream that seemed unattainable:

"Lord, sometimes {I am} fearful of my passion and desire to be a doctor. Is it taking over my love for You? Lord, it's like I want it so bad, but I'm scared of it too. Please Lord, show me the way. If it is not your will Lord, please show me. I don't want to do it for myself, but for you Lord, because I love you."

I was desperate for this dream to come true but it just seemed so out of reach. It took many prayers, missed social events, applications, interviews, and *years* before my dream materialized.

I could not believe it when I was finally accepted into a medical school. All I can say, *even today*, is that God's grace was on me.

Throughout it all, writing in my prayer journal helped me see where God had brought me. My dream seemed too big, but God made my dream come true. Even now, I have other "big" dreams which I want to record. That way, I can again look back and say that God's grace made it happen.

There is a quote that I love, *"Don't tell God how big your storm is, tell your storm how big your God is."*[1]

When the Israelites were being led to the promised land, the Lord assured them He would *"drive out the nations that were there before them"*, and the Israelites would dispossess nations larger and stronger than them (Deuteronomy 11:23 NIV).

Only God can equip you to take on something that seems impossible.

What is your *impossible* dream? Tell your dream how big your God is, and be prepared to praise Him when those dreams come to pass.

~Elizabeth

"... For seven days eat unleavened bread, the bread of affliction ... so that all the days of your life you may remember the time of your departure from Egypt." Deuteronomy 16:3 (NIV)

I bought my first journal at a fifth-grade book fair. My life was pretty simple back then. My daily entries usually consisted of the weather or what I ate for dinner. Nothing too deep, just the facts.

As the years progressed, so did my journal entries. Some pages were still fun and light hearted, but some pages were filled with pain, heartache and confusion. Looking back, I cringe at my mistakes, I thank God social media wasn't around just yet and I rejoice in God's unconditional love and mercy.

In Deuteronomy 16, Moses instructs the people to NOT forget what God has done.

"Observe the month of Aviv and celebrate the Passover ... because in the month of Aviv He brought you out of Egypt by night ... for seven days eat unleavened bread, the bread of affliction, because you left Egypt in haste- so that all the days of your life you may remember the time of your departure from Egypt." (1,3b NIV)

What an interesting request. For seven days, God asks the children of Israel to eat what they ate the night they departed from Egypt. God desired that His children taste the unleavened bread again, the bread of affliction.

I don't know about you, but I can get so far removed from a past hurt, I find it difficult to even relate with those going through similar circumstances. But in order for us to truly minister to the hurting, *we can't forget*. God doesn't want us to sulk about our past mistakes, He wants us to learn from them, never forget how far He has brought us and be a source of hope to those around us.

If you don't already do so, I'd like to encourage you to start journaling. It's easy. Simply write down your thoughts. Then, as you look back on past entries, I believe you will be encouraged and you will be able to encourage others. For the God who delivered you from past struggles, is still with you today.

"With all my heart I praise the LORD! I will never forget how kind he has been." (Psalm 103:2 CEV)

~Binu

March 17 ~ Deuteronomy 17-20
*"Then the officers of the army must address the troops and say,
'Has anyone here just built a new house but not yet dedicated
it? If so, you may go home!'..." Deuteronomy 20:8 (NLT)*

Several years ago, before my children were born, I was in the choir at church. Our practices were during the week, so I would rush home from work, attempt to cook and eat something for dinner, and then head back out into the rush of traffic to get to rehearsal on time. On Sundays, we were to be there an hour before the service started for sound check and one final rehearsal.

The choir would also sing at other special events - our worship conference, women's conference and anniversary conference. Each of these events included additional rehearsal time during the week and weekend, but it didn't seem like a chore to me because I really enjoyed it.

Once I had kids, my time in the choir came to an end. I was sad, but I knew that juggling my work life and home life wouldn't leave me with much spare time. Our church strongly encourages volunteerism, so I felt guilty just sitting during this season of my life. I wrestled with that idea for a while, trying to find a place where I could fit in. Nothing seemed like a good match for my time constraints and for where I wanted to serve.

I began attending a Bible study (now known as Whispers and Fringes). I attended consistently for a year or two, and then I was asked to come on as a leader. God knew that I needed time to care for my family, and He opened a door for me at the right time, with the right ministry.

In Deuteronomy 20:8, there are specific instructions for men as they go off into battle. Haven't dedicated your house yet? Go home and do it. Haven't enjoyed the grapes from your vineyard? Go have some wine. Haven't married your woman? Go put a ring on it. The message seems clear to me: take care of your home and then join the battle.

Some of you might be in the same season that I was in...struggling to serve and manage your family. God knows your heart. Take care of your home and He will open the right doors for you in the right time.

~Shiney

March 18 ~ Deuteronomy 21-23
"... You must not desecrate the land the Lord your
God is giving you as an inheritance."
Deuteronomy 21:23 (NIV)

I put my 4-year-old behind the wheel. He wasn't tall enough to hit the pedals, but that was okay because I was. Being a car guy at such a young age, this was a dream come true. He revved, revved, revved the engine, and we were off!

No, he hasn't gotten his license yet ... nor are we doing anything illegal. We were in the safety of bumper car at a theme park.

Soon, my son realized that no matter how hard Mommy pushed the pedal, there was a limit to his speed. He was swerving to the right and to the left, but the bumpers limited him from going too far off course. He even realized at one point that his own steering wasn't keeping the car on track!

All the safety measures were put in by the bumper car company to ensure children could enjoy being behind the wheel without the consequences of irresponsible driving. Don't you wish we had bumpers and boundaries to keep us on course? We do!

The passage today lists a few guidelines that the Lord gave the Israelites to set them apart from the rest of the nations. Again, and again, he asked His people to these laws to "purge evil" from their midst. There were rules on unsolved murders, inappropriate relationships and clothing (even referencing cross-dressing!), and rebellious sons. God had a special purpose for them and wanted to make sure His people would reflect His own character.

While we live in the age of grace, we understand that the law was actually given as a gift to humanity- to be set apart. We have a charge from our master, our Lord. Jesus said in Matthew 10:16, *"Look, I am sending you out as sheep among wolves. So be shrewd as snakes and harmless as doves..." (NLT).*

We were not asked to live in a bubble or be part of the Christian Country Club. We are sent out to a world that needs to hear and see the grace of Christ being lived out, and we do that by living a way that reflects Him.

Jesus is putting us behind the wheel, but ultimately, when we believe in Him as our Lord, He takes control of it. May we know our boundaries and be mindful of Whose character we should display.

~Elizabeth

March 19 ~ Deuteronomy 24-27

"... you are his people, his treasured possession as he promised, and that you are to keep all his commands. He has declared that He will set you in praise, fame and honor high above all the nations he has made and that you will be a people holy to the Lord your God, as he promised."
Deuteronomy 26:18-19 (NIV)

Maybe you have heard of The Five Love Languages.[1] It is a book written by Gary Chapman for couples to understand how a spouse feels loved. Reading this book was an eye opener for our marriage as it confirmed how each of us feels loved in very different ways.

You see, for years my husband was buying me expensive gifts. While I appreciated them (and was astounded by their cost!), I just wasn't feeling "the love". We realized it is because I actually feel loved when I receive words of affirmation. In other words, when I am told that I am loved and appreciated, it makes me feel as if I'm on top of the world! It could literally be handwritten on a napkin and it would seem like I just received a million dollars.

I imagine that is how the people of God felt when the declaration from the key verses was made over them after they said they would observe His laws.

Wow! How deep, how wide the Father's love is for His children! I know that as His children we are recipients of material blessings, miracles, and so much more. However, it is quite powerful to receive God's affirmation, His support, and encouragement, His promises. We read in the Bible how *"The tongue has the power of life" (Proverbs 18:21 NIV)* and that's what His spoken word does for each of us!

May this encourage each of us today to use our words to express our support for those around us. May our words build others up and remind them of how much they are loved by God.

~Joyce

March 20 ~ Deuteronomy 28-29
"And all these blessings shall come upon you and overtake you,
if you obey the voice of the Lord your God." Deuteronomy 28:2 (ESV)

Who doesn't love a plan with guaranteed results?

Eat this every day and lose 10 pounds. Get this degree and you get that particular job. Do these 5 things for better communication with your spouse.

That's what the children of Israel had going for them. While there were many laws, the results were always guaranteed.

With obedience came blessings. *"And if you faithfully obey the voice of the Lord your God, being careful to do all his commandments that I command you today, the Lord your God will set you high above all the nations of the earth. And all these blessings shall come upon you and overtake you, if you obey the voice of the Lord your God." (Deuteronomy 28:1-2 ESV)*

But on the other hand, disobedience resulted in curses. *"But if you will not obey the voice of the Lord your God or be careful to do all his commandments and his statutes that I command you today, then all these curses shall come upon you and overtake you." (Deuteronomy 28:15 ESV)*

It's the simple notion of good things will happen to good people and bad things will happen to bad people. But if we're being honest, this isn't how it necessarily works anymore, is it? We've all seen and even experienced the opposite. Good things happen to bad people while bad things happen to good people.

Does this mean the Old Testament promises are null and void? Not so ... according to John Piper. He provides this explanation: *"... we are heirs of all the promises, we have to take into account that those promises may be fulfilled differently today because of the changes that have come into history through the words and the work of Jesus."*[1]

As we've entered the new covenant, the beauty of our lives with Christ is not the predictability. It is the assurance we have of God's faithfulness ... that all things work together for good.

So, we may not get that job that we rightfully earned and those 5 pounds may not shed that easily even when we've eaten cucumbers all day, every day. In spite of *those* results, through it all, He is doing something better in us. For our good. For His glory.

~Anu

March 21 ~ Deuteronomy 30-31
"... Love the LORD your God ... keep his commands, decrees and laws ... and the LORD your God will bless you in the land you are entering to possess." Deuteronomy 30:16 (NIV)

It all happened so fast. I blinked and somehow, I went from carrying a very heavy car seat to staring at a stack of college introductory letters.

My husband said it best, *"When I saw those letters on the table, it hit me. One day our boys will be gone."*

Moses was just a baby when his mother, Jochebed, had to let him go. But what if Jochebed held on to Moses? Who would have blamed her? There was a crazy madman out there desiring to kill every Hebrew baby boy. What if her waterproof basket plan failed?

Despite all the what ifs, Hebrews 11:23 (NIV) tells us, Jochebed recognized Moses was *"no ordinary child."* She knew he had a unique destiny. So, she released her sweet baby boy into the Nile River ... not because she wanted to, but because she knew she had to.

God has called us to do the same.

We live in a scary world. As in the days surrounding the birth of Moses, we also have an enemy out there who desires to destroy our children. A quick trip to the mall last week was enough to remind me of this. Have you seen the explicit wall advertisements these days? One glance and my heart sank.

Like Moses, our children are not *"ordinary children."* God has placed a unique calling within them.

Jochebed released her son in order to save his life. In turn, eighty years later, God used Moses to save and rescue the lives of one million Israelites from slavery.

Now it's Moses turn. He is 120 years old. He knows his end is near. What does he say to the children of Israel just before he releases them? He repeats the same message he has said to them for the past forty years.

"Love the LORD your God ... walk in obedience to him ... keep his commands, decrees and laws...and the LORD your God will bless you in the land you are entering to possess." (Deuteronomy 30:16 NIV)

Like a broken record, I believe God wants us to send our children out with that same command. And when we do, remember, we are not releasing our children into the hands of crazy mad men. We are releasing them into the hands of our loving Heavenly Father and into their God appointed destiny.

~Binu

"... Let the beloved of the Lord rest secure in him, for he shields him all day long, and the one the Lord love rests between his shoulders." Deuteronomy 33:12 (NIV)

My children love to be carried. They often beg my husband to lift them up and carry them upside down or to give them a piggy back ride. Their faces light up with this nervous excitement as they crawl onto my husband's shoulders. As he trots around the house with each one on his back, you hear laughter and shrieks of delight.

I know that we will eventually reach the stage where these kinds of things will no longer happen. At some point, our kids will either no longer ask for piggy back rides or they'll be too big for us to carry around. Just another rite of passage as our children grow.

Imagine if you could enjoy it again. Imagine if you could crawl up into your heavenly Father's shoulders and let him whirl you around the room. Imagine that you could go running through your backyard or the halls of your house on someone's shoulders (without fear!). How exhilarating would that be? When was the last time that you felt that carefree, sheer joy that you did as a child?

As Moses' time draws to a close, his blessing to the tribe of Benjamin speaks to all of us. You are the beloved of the Lord. He shields you all day long. He wants to lift you up and carry you. He wants to give you rest and joy.

Maybe you didn't have a healthy relationship with your earthly father. Your heavenly father is ready, arms open, to raise you up and remedy that.

~Shiney

March 23 ~ Joshua 1-4

"... These stones are to be a memorial to the people of Israel forever." Joshua 4:7b (NIV)

We read about miracles in the Bible including what the Israelites experienced on their way to the Promised Land. As soon as the priests set foot in the flood-level waters of the Jordan River, the water *stopped* flowing. The *whole* nation has crossed on *dry* ground.

Miracles, however, aren't limited to the Bible. I experienced one that saved my life as a new mom. One morning, my baby wasn't feeling well, so I hastily took her to the pediatrician and then, went to work. As I entered the parking lot, I felt a painful sensation on the right side of my head but ignored it as I dashed up to the office.

As I talked to co-workers and sent emails, it was evident that my words were not making sense and I was rushed to the ER. Unfortunately, they were unable to figure out what had happened.

Then a friend referred me to a neurologist who sent me to have a picture of my heart taken. We discovered that I had a hole in my heart which normally closes up at birth. A blood clot had passed through that hole and caused me to have a mini-stroke. Immediately, I was sent to a surgeon and the hole had been closed off.

I was told that it was a miracle I was able to deliver my baby without any complications from the unsealed hole.

Being that this happened over a decade ago, it is easy to forget about as life goes on. That's when I am reminded of memorials. Joshua instructed a man from each of the twelve tribes to take a stone from the Jordan River which they just crossed. When asked why he explained that they would serve as a sign that they were able to cross the Jordan River on dry land.

I have a framed picture of my newborn and me on my nightstand, which is my memorial of God's miraculous, wonder-working power.

As you reflect on your life, think about the miracles you have experienced. It's easy to lose sight of their value without a memorial. Make sure you have one so "In the future, when your children ask you, *'What do these ... mean?'"* *(Joshua 4:6 NIV)*, you can tell them what the Lord has done.

~Joyce

March 24 ~ Joshua 5-8

"Now when Joshua was near Jericho, he looked up and saw a man standing in front of him with a drawn sword in his hand. Joshua went up to him and asked, "Are you for us or for our enemies?"
Joshua 5:13 (NIV)

I love to watch my boys play basketball, but this particular game was a little different. They were facing each other. So, I did as any good parent would do, I cheered for both of them.

They are both my children. It didn't matter to me who won. I wanted them to learn (and have some fun) from this experience.

In the book of Joshua chapter 5, Joshua is getting ready to conquer the land of Jericho. Verse 13 states, *"Now when Joshua was near Jericho, he looked up and saw a man standing in front of him with a drawn sword in his hand. Joshua went up to him and asked, "Are you for us or for our enemies?"* (NIV)

God's Response: *"Neither, but as commander of the army of the Lord I have now come." (vs 14a NIV)*

I don't know about you, but when I face a dispute or a heated argument, I want to make sure all involved *and maybe even those not involved* are aware of my side of the story. I also tend to offer up suggestions in prayer as to how God can "fix" my situation and my opposer.

But God loves all of his children. Max Lucado writes, *"God doesn't take sides. He is never against his children. Even the evil Canaanites, who had long ago turned to worshiping idols, were candidates for His mercy. Had Jericho turned and repented, God would have received them as He received Rahab. He is for His children. And He is for you." [1]*

So, what did Joshua do in response to the Lord's reply?

Joshua fell facedown to the ground in reverence and asked Him, *"What message does my Lord have for His servant." (vs 14b NIV)*

In other words, 'What message does the Lord have for ME?'

Are you up against your own Jericho today? Opposition can be found anywhere. At home with your family, at work or even at church amongst friends and fellow believers. Whatever or whoever your opposition may be, can I encourage you to do as Joshua did?

Rather than asking God to *fix* your opposer, ask the Lord if He has a message for YOU. God loves you and wants to cheer you on. But He loves all His Children and He wants us to learn, mature, and have some fun from life's experiences.

~Binu

March 25 ~ Joshua 9-11

"Then Joshua summoned the Gibeonites and said, 'Why did you deceive us by saying, 'We live a long way from you,' while actually you live near us?'" Joshua 9:22 (NIV)

I had just graduated from my training and was seeking a stable job. We all know the challenges of looking for a job - cleaning up our resume, sitting in front of a computer searching and searching, calling potential employers, and finally interviewing for the position....it all takes a bit of work.

Yes, we do it because that's what it takes.

I had just been married for about 2 years when my husband and I were on this search. We were hoping to move and needed to choose between two major cities. So, we put my resume out there and even mailed it to places that weren't even hiring, hoping for a break.

But you know what we did before we actually put them in the mailbox?

We prayed over the manila envelopes that were stamped and ready to be sent off. We inquired of God where He would want us because this not only meant a major career decision, it was also where we would likely start our family. Asking God for wisdom was more powerful than any of the background work that went into mailing those resumes.

In our reading today, we see Joshua, the leader of the Israelites, asking God for wisdom in how to destroy his enemies ... except for one important time. In the middle of his conquests, a group of people deceive Joshua and the other Israelite leaders by stating that they are servants coming to live among them. In reality, they were residents of a neighboring country that was to be destroyed.

In an effort to save themselves from the wrath of Joshua and the Israelites, these strangers clothe themselves as destitute servants and ultimately deceived God's servants. How did this happen? Because God's people did not inquire of the Lord.

When we make major decisions without seeking God's direction and favor, we may miss a blessing or possibly suffer consequences.

I finally made a decision to join an organization that proved to be one of my greatest blessings. I saw the favor of God on me as I served in this group for many years, and my leadership skills were strengthened with the colleagues He put in my path.

What major decision do you have to make? Ask God for wisdom, and He will open up doors you never imagined you could walk through.

~Elizabeth

"... I ... followed the Lord my God wholeheartedly." Joshua 14:8b (NIV)

I have difficulty talking to others about my accomplishments. I struggle with the idea of sounding prideful. But the truth is that when I feel led to share about something I've done, my motive isn't to brag. Instead, it is to tell others about how God helped me achieve something that I didn't think was possible.

So, I am going to take a leap out of my comfort zone and share the following with you. Once upon a time, I enjoyed writing and speaking in public. In fact, I was able to submit a few writings and speak at some wonderful events. Then, my life changed dramatically and I decided to give my best to the new things on my plate.

Years passed and to my great surprise, being able to write and speak in public have actually resurfaced with being involved in Whispers & Fringes. I am so grateful to share what God puts on my heart for His children and I am humbled that He would use me in this ministry.

The purpose of me sharing this is to give hope that with God all things are possible. I am bragging on God and how He keeps His promises. But I had to work up the bravery to move past the misperception that this sounds boastful and pray that it solely points to God.

I imagine a great deal of courage was required for Caleb to approach Joshua. He reminded Joshua of what he was able to accomplish forty-five years earlier to bring back a report based on convictions rather than fear. He also reminded Joshua of the promise yet to be kept to him of giving him land as an inheritance. What Caleb said could have been perceived as prideful and demanding but it was understood that God empowered him to be a faithful follower and vigorous warrior. As a result, Joshua blessed Caleb and gave him the land of Hebron as his inheritance.

Before sharing your accomplishments, ask yourself if the purpose of doing so is to point others to God and His power. If your answer is yes, then the struggle with being proud or arrogant can be dismissed. Prayerfully share what God has helped you achieve and may He be glorified.

~Joyce

"So Joshua said to the people of Israel, 'How long will you put off going in to take possession of the land, which the Lord, the God of your fathers, has given you?'" Joshua 18:3 (ESV)

My nephews have always been pretty easy to please. Give them a basketball and a hoop and they are good to go.

One afternoon, I took them to our neighborhood amenity center to play. We hadn't been there very long when a group of guys started walking toward the court, with a basketball in hand. Before the guys even said a word to us, I told my nephews, *"Let's go"* and we left the court.

I immediately regretted doing that. We were there first and had no reason to end our game early just because they showed up. What example did I set for my nephews that day?

I think as Christians that we can do this too. When a challenge presents itself, we assume that because things got hard, it must not be God's will...and we take our basketball and go home.

In the book of Joshua, we read about the land allotted to the children of Israel. Even though the land was theirs, they still had to claim it. It seems simple enough...but apparently wasn't. Some tribes neglected to take what belonged to them.

"So Joshua said to the people of Israel, 'How long will you put off going in to take possession of the land, which the Lord, the God of your fathers, has given you?'" (Joshua 18:3 ESV)

I don't know what stopped those tribes from claiming what was theirs but I know what has stopped me in the past.

Intimidation. Insecurity. Opposition. Fear.

God's will doesn't mean things will always be easy. Just ask David who had to fight a giant or Esther who put her life on the line for the sake of her people. What is rightfully yours may not be handed to you on a silver platter. Are you willing to stand your ground and make the claim?

I don't own the basketball court in our neighborhood but for that afternoon, it was ours. I let fear stop me (and the children with me) from possessing it. I won't make that mistake again when we go back to the court but will I remember it in other areas of my life? I pray I do...and I hope and pray the same for you too.

A challenge doesn't mean game over. It means we may just have to step up our game.

"... be strong and courageous..." (Joshua 1:9 ESV)

~Anu

"... And he built up the town and settled there." Joshua 19:50 (NIV)

As I exited the highway, I noticed a sign in an empty grass lot across from my subdivision. It read, "Upscale Grocery Store, Coming Soon." My heart literally skipped a beat.

Maybe I should explain.

I had been praying for a job closer to home. When I saw the sign, my mind began to race. Could this be it? Will the store have a pharmacy inside of it? And if it does, will they even hire me? At that moment, I felt God say, *"That's Yours."*

In the book of Joshua chapters 19 and 20, God is assigning portions of the Promised Land to the tribes of Israel. Tribe by tribe, clan by clan, God says to each man in so many words, *"That's yours."*

The Simeonites received territory within Judah, the tribe of Zebulun had its boundary as far as Sarid. Issachar's allotment included Jezreel. Every allotment was strategically assigned by God.

In Joshua 19 we are told the final allotment of land was given. It went to Joshua.

"When they had finished dividing the land into its allotted portions, the Israelites gave Joshua son of Nun an inheritance among them, as the Lord had commanded. They gave him the town he asked for- Timnath Serah ..." (vs 49,50a NIV) Scholars say the land wasn't anything fancy ... but to Joshua, it was his territory of inheritance. Joshua had been ready and waiting for this for forty years.

In Hebrew, the name Timnath Serah signifies a *'portion of abundance,'* or God's abundant provision.

The verse goes on to say, *"And he built the town and settled there." (vs 50 NIV)*

God has given each of us an allotment. The schools and churches we attend, the jobs we go to, our homes, our neighborhoods, our cities ... it may not look like much at first, but remember, God has strategically placed you there. He is saying, *"That's yours. That's your allotment, your sphere of influence, your Timnath Serah."*

By the way, about a year after seeing that sign, the empty grass lot was transformed into a beautiful grocery store ... and God was right, it was mine. For the past ten years, it's been my Timnath Serah. A place of God's abundant provision.

Wherever God places us, He entrusts us. However long or short the season, let us be faithful.

~Binu

March 29 ~ Joshua 22-24
"... But as for me and my house, we will serve the LORD." Joshua 24:15b ESV

Are you praying together with your husband?

I grew up in a home where we read the Bible and prayed together, every single night. I'm not saying that my sister and I always stayed awake but we were present and accounted for.

When I got married, I envisioned doing the same thing with my husband... minus the falling asleep part. But for some reason, that didn't happen.

Don't get me wrong. My husband and I do pray together but making it into a daily routine never stuck. Blame my weird work hours or our very different sleep schedules. Whatever the case, it wasn't happening the way I pictured it would.

I used to get frustrated and, in my mind, blame him. After all, isn't he our spiritual leader? Why doesn't he take charge and make it happen?

What I've come to realize is that my husband may be the spiritual leader of our home but that doesn't mean he is the only one responsible for our prayer life together.

I may be the primary chef (and I use that term loosely) but my husband can still cook a meal for us. And he does. Yesterday, in fact. He knows way more about cars than I do but that doesn't mean I can't get the oil changed. And I did. Last week.

Don't let the enemy tell you that it has to be your husband who initiates prayer. If you end up asking your husband to pray with you, that doesn't usurp his role as the leader. It allows us as wives to fulfill our role as his helper. Plus, if we let pride step in and just wait for our husbands to always initiate our prayer time, the only one who wins that game is the enemy because we miss out on that Spirit-prompted opportunity to pray.

I'm thankful for the godly husband I have who absolutely serves as the head of our home and my spiritual leader and covering. But just like I step in to help where I can with the car and other non- "typical wife" things, I can serve him by offering myself as a willing prayer partner with him. That is a win-win for both of us.

"... But as for me and my house, we will serve the LORD." (Joshua 24:15b ESV)

~Anu

March 30 ~ Judges 1-2

"... And there arose another generation after them who did not know the Lord or the work that he had done for Israel." Judges 2:10 (ESV)

As I watch my kids grow in the various stages of their life, I find myself thinking back to my own childhood and compare my children to myself at their age. In comparison, my children's relationship with God is very different from my relationship with God at their age.

As a parent, in order to shield them from some of the harsh realities of life, I've found myself on many occasions doing my best to step into their world to make it as ideal as possible.

You see, my childhood was full of trials and hardship - far more than my children have had to endure. But because of that, I found myself leaning into the Lord and developing a personal relationship with the Lord at a very young age. I found the Word of God to be full of hope and encouragement during those difficult times.

In the book of Judges, we read that the people served God during the lifetime of Joshua. They had witnessed firsthand what God had done for Israel. Once that generation died, the next generation worshipped idols and turned away from the God of their ancestors.

These scriptures disheartened me so much. Why?

After being led by Joshua and winning hard fought battles, God gave them victory over their enemies. The people of Israel were finally living out the fulfillment of what was promised to Abraham, Isaac, and Jacob so many years before.

But the faithfulness and the goodness of God was not carried forward to the generations that came after Joshua. The scripture says *"... And there arose another generation after them who did not know the Lord or the work that he had done for Israel." (Judges 2:10 ESV)*

Reading this passage made me realize that my job as a parent is to help my children develop a faith in God that is their own, apart from me.

At times, I have to let them experience disappointment and pain so that they can develop their own relationship with God and experience His faithfulness first hand. My prayer is that as they experience disappointments and challenges, they would lean into the Lord and find, He is not only my God, but He is also *their* God who loves them and has a good plan for their life.

~Vijoy

March 31 ~ Judges 3-5
"Now Deborah, a prophetess ... was judging
Israel at that time." Judges 4:4 (ESV)

Deborah was a judge who found herself also accompanying the Israelite army to war. The entire army was defeated except the commander, Sisera, who managed to escape ... temporarily. Until he ends up in Jael's tent then it is good-bye Sisera.

What's not to love in this story? The bad guys lose. The good girls win.

Once the battle is over, Deborah puts her musical skills to work and composes a song of praise to God for their victory. She thanks God for the part she was able to play but also thanks Him for Jael.

"Most blessed among women is Jael, the wife of Heber the Kenite. May she be blessed above all women who live in tents." (Judges 5:24 NLT)

How refreshing is that?

Many of the female relationships we had seen in scripture prior to this weren't exactly BFFs. Do you remember the drama between Sarah and Hagar? And the sisters, Leah and Rachel?

What makes Deborah different from these women? She didn't give in to the comparison game. She was confident in who God made her to be and the unique role He had for her life. When Jael steps on the scene, Deborah could have felt threatened. Instead, she celebrates Jael's role as the one who killed the enemy.

Unfortunately, the story of Deborah and Jael was the exception rather than the rule in scripture and even today. We still see women struggle in their relationships. But it doesn't have to be that way.

Instead of comparing, let's run our race, *in our lane,* doing what God called us to do. Rather than being insecure because someone else seems better at something, let us celebrate their victory and *"rejoice with those who rejoice".* When jealousy wants us to tear someone down, we should build them up instead.

You don't even have to write a song like Deborah did. A call, a text, a little shout out on social media ... it's as easy as that. It doesn't even have to be about something big like winning a battle or creatively using a tent peg.

Tell your neighbor her garden is beautiful. Let the girl on the worship team know that she nailed that solo. Is your friend an awesome cook? Don't just think it - say it!

Do your thing and encourage others to do their thing. Together, we can win some battles.

~Anu

April 1 ~ Judges 6-7
"The Lord turned to him and said, 'Go in the strength you have and save Israel out of Midian's hand. Am I not sending you?'" Judges 6:14 (NIV)

I didn't feel qualified for a leadership position at work and was not sure if I wanted to take on more responsibility.

My husband, being my biggest cheerleader, encouraged me to apply. He knew the potential in me that I couldn't see. By God's grace, I interviewed and got the position. The training that my company offered helped me with the challenges that come with any leadership position.

Nevertheless, I knew it was God who put me there.

Gideon was a man asked by God to lead the fight against one of Israel's enemies, the Midianites. Gideon's response to *this* leadership position?

A little like mine.

He told the Lord that he was from the *weakest* clan ... and on top of that, he was the *least* in his family.

Have you ever felt that way? Weak, the "least", and underqualified?

Two days ago, I went to a leadership meeting along with other leaders in the organization. As I walked through the building, I couldn't believe I was there. I had an opportunity that many people would love to have ... and you know the best thing about it all? I didn't do it on my own!

God brought me there. I *know* it. How? Because despite my past failures, God gave me favor.

There are others that are better qualified, but God has positioned me there.

Why would God ask a weak man from a weak family to lead an army? Why didn't God choose the strongest man in the most qualified family to lead? Because Gideon had no other choice but to rely on God's strength to do the job. As soon as Gideon told the Lord that he was not qualified, the Lord said, *"I will be with you ..." (Judges 6:16 NIV)*

Why would God ask a weak person like me to lead at the workplace? Because I have no other choice but to rely on God's grace and strength. Many times, I have talked to God and let him know that. *"God, I don't know what to do. Please give me direction."*

That's all I need ... and that's all you need too.

What has God called you to that you feel unqualified to do? Just as God told Gideon, go in the strength you have. He is sending you.

~Elizabeth

April 2 ~ Judges 8-9
*"And the land had peace and rest for forty years in
the days of Gideon." Judges 8:28b (AMPC)*

I am a history buff. I love reading about the successes and failures of the past to learn from it. I am particularly intrigued by courageous leaders who left an imprint in history to make our world a better place to live.

Combatting injustices and fighting for freedom especially captivates my heart. The sacrifices such leaders made, the love they had for humanity, and the humility which they walked in leaves me feeling grateful for their contributions. But it also inspires me to lead with such passion.

There are many leaders who come to mind that fit this description. One, in particular, is Rev. Martin Luther King Jr. He was a pastor and well-known for being a civil rights activist. What distinguished his approach was he did so through nonviolence and peaceful marches.

It was one thing for me to learn about him when I was in school. But it was quite another thing for me to sit in the pew of Ebenezer Baptist Church in Atlanta, Georgia where he ministered and listen to recordings of his sermons. There was determination, loyalty, and passion all exhibited by a servant of God. Although what he believed in cost him his life, segregation in the United States ended. The church I attend is as diverse as Rev. King had dreamed and I am eternally thankful.

Leadership is not an easy or glamorous task. But we can learn a great deal from the ones who embraced it and were successful at it.

An example of such a leader found in the Bible is Gideon. We read how he did so through a myriad of challenges: Gideon was able to pacify the Ephraimites who were offended. He was victorious in battle against the Midianites. Gideon corrected the men of Succoth and Penuel ... to name a few.

When the people recognized his valuable contribution, they requested him to rule their government, but he declined and said the Lord would rule over them. As a result of his leadership, the country was at peace for forty years.

Being a leader requires vision, being able to guide and motivate, and make tough decisions. These examples of successful leaders demonstrate that with God's help, it can be done and impact countless in life-changing ways for His glory.

~Joyce

"And Jephthah made a vow to the Lord and said, 'If you will give the Ammonites into my hand, then whatever comes out from the doors of my house to meet me ... shall be the Lord's, and I will offer it up for a burnt offering.'" Judges 11:30-31 (ESV)

Do you ever say things you don't mean just because they sound good?

"I'd be happy to help you move."

"We should get together sometime."

"You can have the last bite!"

Even as a kid, when I was asked why I liked Sunday School, I responded with *"Because I like to learn about Jesus!"* At that moment, all the parents started smiling and nodding their heads in approval. I was glad I hadn't gone with my first choice (the candy and snacks) but instead went with what I knew they wanted to hear.

Those examples are trivial but what we say matters.

We don't know what was running through Jephthah's mind one fateful day but what came out of his mouth changed his life forever. Scripture doesn't paint him as someone whose heart was in the wrong place but we do see that he was ready to be the leader over his brothers...the same people who had driven him away years ago.

"And Jephthah made a vow to the Lord and said, 'If you will give the Ammonites into my hand, then whatever comes out from the doors of my house to meet me when I return in peace from the Ammonites shall be the Lord's, and I will offer it up for a burnt offering.'" (Judges 11:30-31 ESV)

That "whatever" turned out to be his daughter.

Why would he make such a vow? Is it possible he thought it was what God and the people wanted to hear? Sometimes we say and do things for the sake of how they appear, not because God really requires it of us.

Our words impact our lives. James 3:6 (NASB) says the tongue *"... defiles the entire body, and sets on fire the course of our life ..."* The book of Proverbs provides the warning and encouragement that *"Death and life are in the power of the tongue ..." (Proverbs 18:21 ESV).* Jephthah experienced that in the most literal way possible.

As the saying goes - say what you mean and mean what you say. There is a freedom in knowing we can be real with God because He wants *"truth in the inward being" (Psalm 51:6 ESV)* ... and that is what we always want to offer Him.

~Anu

April 4 ~ Judges 13-15
"... He will begin to rescue Israel from the Philistines." Judges 13:5 (NLT)

Samson was Israel's judge for 20 years. He began his life as a man set apart by God, born with the purpose of beginning the rescue of Israel from the Philistines. That's a heavy plan for a young man with a temper and an affinity towards bad chicks.

Samson's life was definitely colored by struggle and conflict.

In Judges 14, we read the story of his first marriage. His parents don't approve, and verse 4 tells us that his mother and father didn't realize that *"the Lord was at work in this, creating an opportunity to confront the Philistines, who ruled over Israel at that time." (NIV)* Samson kills 30 Philistines and loses his wife to his best man. When he discovers that she's with another man, he kills another thousand Philistines.

He falls in love again, with another bad girl, who repeatedly shows him her true nature. Blinded by love, he ignores the warning signs and falls into her trap, eventually leading to his ultimate downfall.

In his final act, a blinded, publicly humiliated Samson takes out more Philistines, and all of their leaders than he had done during his *entire* lifetime (Judges 16:30). He left the Philistines weakened in number and without a leader to guide them.

He wasn't perfect. He had his issues. It sounds to me like he still fulfilled his purpose.

As Christians, we know that we have a purpose on our lives, but often we get bogged down in conflict, struggle, and maybe even death - physical or emotional. It may feel like we're not walking it out. Samson wasn't perfect, but we know by his final prayer that he retained his faith in God. He walked out his faith and lived out his purpose, although it seemed as though he took a winding path to get there.

Don't let your faith be wounded by the struggles you face. Don't let your own imperfections push you away from God or his purpose on your life. Talk to God. Lay it all out for Him and don't leave out the ugly parts. Give it to Him and let Him complete His purpose in you.

~Shiney

April 5 ~ Judges 16-18
"Then she called, 'Samson, the Philistines are upon you!' He awoke
from his sleep and thought, 'I'll go out as before and shake myself free.'
But he did not know that the Lord had left him." Judges 16:20 (NIV)

I was 18 years old when I made the choice of my college major, and later my career.

My mom was enjoying her occupation as a pediatric nurse, so she encouraged me to pursue it as well. I remember lying on my parents' bed with her and with the college course catalog (remember those??), choosing a major, looking at credit hours, and calculating how long it would take me to graduate.

I remember feeling a little uneasy at first about the decision, but after a lot of thought and prayer, and *really* because I could trust my mother's discernment, I moved forward.

And I'm glad I did.

That decision shaped a lot of my character and had a lot of bearing on how I treat my patients today.

Our parents didn't have all the answers back then, but they trusted in a sovereign God, so they guided us in the best way they knew.

We have been reading the story of Samson as a family. Although set apart by a Nazirite vow, Samson had several choices he had to make. When it came to decision making, he made several decisions that showed poor discernment.

Take, for example, the time he took honey from the carcass of a lion he had killed. As a Nazirite, he was not allowed to touch a dead animal, yet he *still* chose to do so.

We also can't forget the decision he made to give away the secret of his strength to a woman he loved, but a woman who didn't believe in the true God. He made a choice ... a *poor* one. Prior to Samson meeting this woman, his parents had disagreed with his decision to find a wife among ungodly people.

Samson later died with this group of people after God had strengthened him once more and allowed him to kill *"many more when he died than while he lived." (Judges 16:30 NIV)*

God has given us many opportunities to make choices. We need to make sure that we are relying on the guidance of trustworthy, godly people. As we see from Samson's story, there are consequences for poor decisions. We've all suffered from those.

There are also rewards to the good ones we make. Get away from the noise and open your Bible. God will guide you to the right verses, the right people, and ultimately, the right decisions.

~Elizabeth

April 6 ~ Judges 19-21
*"In those days Israel had no king; all the people did
whatever seemed right in their own eyes."*
Judges 21:25 (NLT)

Reading through the last few chapters in the book of Judges, I feel like I'm watching a soap opera and horror movie all at the same time. The latter part of the book delves into the depravity evident in Israel when *"... the people did whatever seemed right in their own eyes." (Judges 21:25 NLT)*

One story chronicled here is about a Levite man who marries a concubine. She gets upset with him and goes back to her father's house. After a few months, he goes to her father's house to bring her home. When he tries to take his wife and leave, her father insist that he stay for one more night, which ends up being several nights.

After five nights, he finally decides he has to leave, even though it is late in the day when they begin their journey. So, they end up staying overnight in Gibeah, a town of the tribe of Benjamin.

That night in Gibeah, they encountered lawless, vile people who want to violate him. After a back and forth conversation with them, the Levite throws his wife out to the townspeople, who take turns violating her all night long. She returns to her husband in the morning, collapses and dies at his doorstep.

Her husband takes her lifeless body home with him. Once home, he cuts her corpse into 12 pieces and sends a piece to each of the tribes of Israel to show them what the tribe of Benjamin has done. The tribes of Israel unite against tribe of Benjamin and proceed to kill the majority of them.

This horrific story shows us how far sin can take us. The people of Israel turned their backs on God's laws and gave into whatever felt right for them.

What resulted was one of the darkest times in Israel's history. They were consumed by their desires and their sin took them to places they probably never imagined they would ever go.

But there was still hope. No matter how far Israel fell, when they turned to God, He always provided a plan of redemption for them.

My friend, has your sin taken you farther and deeper than you ever thought you would go?

Know that you are not too far gone. Just like He brought Israel back from their darkest days, He can do the same for you.

~Vijoy

April 7 ~ Ruth 1-4

"'Where you die I will die, and there I will be buried. May the Lord deal with me, be it ever so severely, if even death separates you and me.'" Ruth 1:17 (NIV)

I was in the early training stages of my career, and my first clinical rotation took place in a nursing home. My assignment was to get the medical history from a frail, elderly woman who could not see very well.

After getting a thorough history, I got up from the chair with my clipboard and started walking toward the door. She continued to chat, telling me a bit about her family. It had nothing to do with her medical history.

I could tell she didn't want me to leave. She was hungry for someone to listen.

New to patient care, I didn't know how to exit without appearing rude, so I stayed. As a student, I was given limited time in each room, so I felt a bit of anxiety, but I just didn't know how to peel away. About twenty minutes later, my instructor snuck her head in the door and commented that we should be heading out.

Once in the hall, my teacher explained the importance of knowing how to bring a conversation to a close when the patient trails off. I felt embarrassed, but it was a lesson learned.

Admittedly, over the years, I have come across many instances when I have had to redirect the conversation because of tangential ideas or thoughts from the patient.

But you know what I have also learned? Those who are elderly and have walked the same roads we are currently treading have SO MUCH WISDOM!

It is easy to forget the generations that have gone ahead of us. We get caught up in technology or the latest fads, and we forget that sometimes, the basic principles of life transcend time.

Ruth was a young woman who followed the advice of someone older and wiser, and she was blessed for it. I love to see how she respected her mother-in-law and because of her obedience, was blessed with a child who would be in the ancestral line of Jesus Christ!

The next time you see an elderly man or woman, invest some time to hear their story. You may be surprised at what life experiences they will share and how their wisdom can change the course of your life.

Lord, may we honor those who have gone before us and give us the wisdom to share our story with those who will come after us.

~Elizabeth

April 8 ~ 1 Samuel 1-3
*"Samuel did not yet know the Lord because he had
never had a message from the Lord before."*
1 Samuel 3:7 (NLT)

Sometimes I feel like I live my life in cycles. The work/school week cycle. The cooking/grocery cycle. The laundry cycle. You're familiar with these cycles, right? It's how I mark my days that turn into weeks, that turn into months, and before I know it another year has gone by and I feel like all that I have done is worked, cooked and washed clothes.

In times of monotony, I crave something to break up the cycles. I would really love to hear some direction from God. Anything - *"Yes, my daughter, you have prepared that dinner so well that I will bless you and your family 100-fold."* So, probably not that, but something to let me know that I haven't slipped out of His thoughts.

In chapter 3, we read about Samuel's early stages of serving the Lord. He is living with Eli, the priest, and he is called out of bed in the middle of the night. Samuel thinks that Eli is calling him and he runs to Eli to answer.

The Message version, verse 7 says *"This happened before Samuel knew God for himself."* I read this and was like *"God, you spoke to him and he didn't even really know you yet! I know you and I am not hearing anything!"*

Here's what I realized about Samuel:

1. He was *submitted*. His mother had promised him back to God's service. He was living with Eli and learning the ministry from him. What am I submitted to that will help me hear from God?
2. He was *responsive*. The Bible says that when he heard God's voice, he jumped up. He didn't sit and wonder who it was that was speaking to him or if he had really even heard a voice at all. Am I responsive when I sense the nudging of the Spirit?
3. He was in *silence*. It was deep in the night when Samuel heard God's voice. Quiet darkness. No visual stimulation. No auditory stimulation. Am I creating silence for the Lord to speak?

Samuel grew into one of the most prolific prophets in the Bible. He was willing and obedient, a recurring theme among those who were used by God. Before God can use me to bring change around me, I know I have to start by changing myself first.

~Shiney

April 9 ~ 1 Samuel 4-8

"... it is not you they have rejected but they have rejected me as their king. As they have done from the day I brought them up out of Egypt until this day, forsaking me and serving other gods, so they are doing to you." 1 Samuel 8:7-8 (NIV)

Rejection. It's painful to experience. It's uncomfortable to talk about. Yet, it's real and it happens.

I have been in relationships where everything appeared to be going well from my perspective. Then one day, an invitation was declined. I heard hurtful words. Ties in the relationship were severed because expectations were not met.

And the pain seemed unbearable. What did I do wrong? How could I have done things differently? I must be a bad person. Such negative thoughts overtook my mind. Joy was stolen and peace was robbed.

It seems that Samuel could relate to what I felt when the elders of Israel requested that he appoint a king to lead them ... after all that he had done for them. He had been interceding for the Israelites which caused the hand of the Lord to be against the Philistines. He had been serving as judge over Israel all the days of his life. And this is how they thanked him ... how hurtful.

What breaks my heart even more is God's response to Samuel's displeasure in the key verse. These words sting so deeply and overwhelm me with sorrow.

While I have been sobbing over the rejection I experienced, I can't even begin to imagine how many times we as God's children have hurt His heart when we have rejected Him. You know those times when we decide that our plans are better or we look to something or someone to be our source and turn away from God.

Basically, we're saying "Thanks, but no thanks" and walk away from our First Love.

My prayer is that we would have a revelation when we are tempted to go down this slippery slope and not fall into the trap of rejecting the King of kings and Lord of lords. May we always be careful to give Him all the glory, honor and praise He is worthy of. May we remain in relationship with the God of miracles, the Maker of heaven and earth, our Provider, our Source, our Redeemer.

~Joyce

April 10 ~ 1 Samuel 9-12

"And Samuel said to all the people, 'Do you see him whom the Lord has chosen? There is none like him among all the people.' And all the people shouted, 'Long live the king!'" 1 Samuel 10:24 (ESV)

If you know the story of Saul, it's hard to read about the beginning of his reign without thinking about how it ends.

He didn't go looking to become king. God sent Samuel, the prophet, to look for him. When Samuel even starts the conversation with him, Saul is at a loss as to why.

Was Saul being humble? Possibly. But as we continue reading, it seems that his response was based on his insecurity. There is a difference.

We often confuse the two because both can look like someone is "shying away" from the spotlight, stage or whatever the situation is. It's the heart behind it that is the factor.

Humility does it for the sake of others. Insecurity does it for the sake of ourselves. We're afraid of what people will think or that we're going to embarrass ourselves so we step away.

Rick Warren said, *"True humility is not thinking less of yourself; it is thinking of yourself less."[1]* It seems the opposite is true about insecurity: Insecurity IS thinking less of yourself (a decreased self-value) but thinking of yourself more (frequently).

In spite of Saul's initial resistance to his new assignment, he starts out strong. The gift of prophecy, the promise that God is with him, a new heart ... God was equipping the man he had called. And Saul operated in that. When people spoke against him, he kept his peace rather than retaliating. He acknowledged God as the one who brought them the victory in battle.

Saul's insecurity almost stopped him from stepping up. When he submitted to God, he was used powerfully. Unfortunately, it was also his insecurity that would ultimately result in his downfall as king. When Saul yielded to his own feelings, God rejected him as king and chose someone else to take his place.

We can mask our insecurity temporarily but if we don't surrender that part of our lives to God, it will seep out when we are pressed.

"... God opposes the proud but favors the humble." (James 4:6 NLT) Pray for humility. Pray that God would heal our insecurities. The end of our stories depends on it.

~Anu

April 11 ~ 1 Samuel 13-14
"There were no blacksmiths in the land of Israel in those days. The Philistines wouldn't allow them for fear they would make swords and spears..." 1 Samuel 13:19 (NLT)

I wasn't a very competitive kid, but come "sword drill" time (aka Bible Reference Competition), I was all in.

In case you are unfamiliar, a sword drill is a competition in which one person would stand in front of the church and call out a scripture reference. The congregation would then frantically flip through their Bibles in search for the verse. Whoever found it first, read it out loud and received a point. At the end of the competition, the person with the most points, won. Its purpose is to entice the younger generation to know their Bibles.

In my Bible reading, I came across a passage which took me back to those sword drill days.

1 Samuel 13:19 states, *"There were no blacksmiths in the land of Israel in those days. The Philistines wouldn't allow them for fear they would make swords and spears." (NLT)*

The Philistines saw to it that the Israelites had no blacksmiths. No blacksmiths meant no weaponry. No weaponry meant no proper way to defend themselves. For decades, this put the Israelites at a great disadvantage. They were constantly subject to neighboring bullies.

Fast forward to today. The enemy's tactic has not changed.

The Bible is our sword (Hebrews 4:12). The enemy will do everything He can to unequip us ... so he distracts us.

Satan isn't intimidated by the number of Bibles in my home. He doesn't even care that I've downloaded it on my phone and read an occasional verse of the day.

He doesn't care that I have a sword...if I never really use it.

We live in a day in which a million things fight for our attention. If we allow the distractions to win, then we will fall like Adam and Eve in the garden... hearing only the voice of the serpent and questioning what God really said (Genesis 3:1).

Sword drills were great, but even that didn't intimidate the enemy. It's when we open up our Bibles, or our Bible app, and know how to use our swords. It's when we allow God's Word to penetrate and pierce our souls. Then, we will see true victory over any and every situation we may be facing.

The enemy took away the Israelites swords. Don't let him take away yours.

~Binu

April 12 ~ 1 Samuel 15-17

"When the Philistine arose and came and drew near to meet David, David ran quickly toward the battle line to meet the Philistine." 1 Samuel 17:48 (ESV)

The first year of my marriage, I had one primary prayer:

"God, please change my husband. Amen."

That was the prayer of a girl who was convinced that all I needed to do to make my marriage better was to say a prayer, prop my feet up and watch God do His thing...with my husband.

Wrong assumption.

"Then David said to the Philistine, 'You come to me with a sword and with a spear and with a javelin, but I come to you in the name of the Lord of hosts ... the battle is the Lord's, and he will give you into our hand.' When the Philistine arose and came and drew near to meet David, David ran quickly toward the battle line to meet the Philistine." 1 Samuel 17:45, 47-48 (ESV)

The phrase, *"The battle is the Lord's"*, is something we hear often in Christian circles and it is unquestionably true. However, someone still had to strike the giant down.

Could God have done it on His own? Absolutely – we've seen that happen too. More often than not though, He uses people...from a shepherd boy like David to a woman with a tent peg (Jael in Judges) to a committed daughter-in-law (Ruth) and even a boy with a sack lunch...to accomplish His will on the Earth.

David was able to act in confidence because he knew the battle was the Lord's BUT he recognized that Goliath had been delivered into HIS hand...so now it was David's move.

What giant are you facing? What move do you need to make?

Looking for a new job? Send out your resume. Want to make amends with a friend? You make the call first instead of waiting on her. Having financial struggles? Say no to Amazon Prime and yes to saving more.

Striking down the giant in our marriage meant changing the focus of my prayer to God fixing ME. It required that I stop expecting perfection. It involved preferring each other when I really preferred to have my own way. It meant apologizing sooner and forgiving even when I didn't forget.

My fellow giant slayers – we can trust our God in every battle knowing He will do His part...just don't forget to do your part too.

~Anu

April 13 ~ I Samuel 18-20, Psalms 11,59
"Saul was then afraid of David, for the Lord was with
David and had turned away from Saul."
1 Samuel 18:12 (NLT)

Have you ever been persecuted without just cause? You were simply doing what you knew was right and someone just didn't like you?

I've had some experience with that. From a teacher or boss who it seemed had it out for me, to friends or family who seemed to think that I was out to get them.

Human nature, including mine, apart from God, tends to be self-serving, jealous, and self-centered. Bible personalities were no different.

In the book of 1 Samuel, we are introduced to David, a young shepherd boy who valiantly killed Goliath, the Philistine giant who had been taunting the people of Israel for some time.

King Saul eventually appoints David as commander in his army. David was so successful that Saul took notice. But instead of celebrating David's victories, Saul became jealous and afraid of David.

"Saul was then afraid of David, for the Lord was with David and had turned away from Saul." (1 Samuel 18:12 NLT)

Scripture after scripture, we see the more Saul recognized that the Lord was with David, the more Saul became afraid and threatened by David.

I am reminded of how our enemy, Satan, must feel about us every time he sees that God is with us. Just like Saul who was once in a good relationship with God, Satan too was once in good relationship with God.

Once Satan fell, he has made it his mission to bring us out of relationship with God. The scripture says *"... He prowls around like a roaring lion, looking for someone to devour." (1 Peter 5:8 NLT)*

Satan's only goal is to steal, kill, and destroy. Why? So that ultimately, we will turn our back on God. Does the enemy see your relationship with God and become jealous and afraid? I believe so but we can't give into his schemes. Like David, we must keep fighting the fight honorably and know that God's purpose for us will prevail if we do not give up.

If your enemies are jealous and afraid of you, know that you just might be doing something right.

~Vijoy

April 14 ~ 1 Samuel 21-24
*"David asked Ahimelech, 'Do you have a spear or
sword of any kind around here?'..."*
1 Samuel 21:8 (MSG)

I have been told (many times) over the course of my life that I have a big mouth. I am sarcastic by nature and sometimes too quick witted.

When I was in college, I was invited, by my cousin, to a game night with her co-workers. It was a crowd of people that I had never met before. We were playing a game where the team has to guess a word that their teammate is describing. The describer has a list of words that they are not allowed to use while trying to get their teammates to guess the correct word.

During one turn, a younger guy was up, and he was struggling to describe his given word. Exasperated, he said *"Me... What am I? How would you describe me?"* Without thinking, I yelled out *"A nerd!"* I knew nothing about him and just blurted that out based on his physical attributes. I have no recollection of the rest of the evening. I know that I embarrassed him and embarrassed myself. I wish to this day that I could take that back.

Words are powerful. Fast forward 20 years, and here I sit, still trying to hone my wit and words and turn them into something useful and powerful.

David is on the run from Saul, and when he arrives at Nob, he casually asks the priest for food and a sword. Why on earth would the priests have weapons? Not only do they have a sword, but it is the sword of Goliath.

When David originally got the sword, he was too small to fit into Saul's armor, much less wield the sword of Goliath the giant. Now David has returned to it, and we can surmise that his life experiences and physical growth have prepared him to better manage this weapon - HIS weapon.

What is your secret weapon? What's that gift that the devil is trying to trick you into thinking is a curse? It is not a curse. Give it to God. Give yourself some room to grow and see how God refines you and your ability to use your secret weapon!

~Shiney

April 15 ~ Psalms 7,27,31,34,52
"O taste and see that the Lord is good; Blessed is the man that trusteth in Him." Psalm 34:8 (KJV)

I passed by my bedroom a few weeks ago and saw my twelve-year-old son, Caleb, sitting on the bed. He held a small vial of anointing oil in his hand. When I inquired as to what he was doing, his reply was short and to the point. *"Just praying for my skin to heal."* I watched him continue to dab the oil on his eczema patches.

Although my heart sank when I heard him say those words, my heart also leapt.

I was reminded, God never wastes a hurt.

Caleb has dealt with eczema since he was very young. We have prayed, seen dermatologist, applied prescription creams, natural oils, changed detergents and his diet ... but he still struggles.

As we wait on the Lord for healing, if eczema draws my son nearer to God, then I must give God praise. For He is still faithful to His Word and causes all things (even eczema) to work together for the good of those who love Him.

Trust me, I would love to shield my children from all trials. But perhaps it's good that I cannot. For it's through life's struggles that they will experience God for themselves ... His power, His peace, His presence.

Psalm 34:8 states, *"O taste and see that the Lord is good; Blessed is the man that trusteth in Him." (KJV)*

Think about it, even the best description using the most detailed adjectives can't do justice to a piece of chocolate cake. You just have to taste it for yourself!

Sermons and teachings may offer us an understanding of who God is, but nothing can take the place of experiencing God for ourselves.

My son is young and his journey has just begun. Eczema isn't his first trial and it won't be his last. But through each difficult situation, my prayer is that his personal relationship with Christ will only grow deeper. He will learn, the God of Abraham, Isaac and Jacob is also the God of Caleb.

Whatever you are facing today, please know, He is also the God of (insert your name).

~Binu

April 16 ~ Psalms 56,120,140-142
"... I call on the Lord in my distress, and he answers me." Psalm 120:1 (NIV)

When I invited Jesus to live in my heart, I knew my life wasn't going to be easy but I didn't think it would be this hard. It certainly has difficult people and difficult circumstances to deal with.

I encountered some of the most challenging people in my life in my early twenties. They were rude and they spoke poorly of me. I felt like an outcast and all alone. I cried incessantly and I was stressed beyond belief. I didn't know what to do.

It seems that David felt the same about Saul's wrath and anger toward him. These Psalms illustrate how he communicated with God through such unbearable circumstances. David expressed his honest thoughts and feelings. He did not hold back from complaining about his enemies and the indifference of his friends. David was hurt and didn't attempt to sugarcoat his pain and disappointment.

That was eye-opening for me to read and comprehend. I did not feel as if I could verbalize my complaints about people to God. I did not want God to think that I was ungrateful but just because I wasn't saying it aloud doesn't mean I wasn't thinking it. God knew what was running through my mind and these Psalms show that we have the freedom to be transparent with God.

But David didn't stop there. He knew that God would comfort him. David sought the Lord because he knew God was his Refuge. He asked God for protection. David encouraged himself in God and he trusted that his troubles would end in due time. David emphasized that when feeling distressed, prayer is the answer. He asked God for His favor and help and for His mercy and grace. David expected that God heard him and would deliver him.

During my own trying situations and many tears, I also learned to find such comfort in God's presence. As I shared my heart with Him, I waited in expectation for the answer and it came in His perfect time. What a gracious God we serve!

Whatever it is that you are walking through today, communicate with God. He can handle your complaints, but also trust that He will comfort you. Keep your eyes on God from where our help comes from.

~Joyce

April 17 ~ 1 Samuel 25-27
"This man's name was Nabal, and his wife, Abigail,
was a sensible and beautiful woman..."
1 Samuel 25:3a (NLT)

How do you handle moody, angry or just plain foolish people?

Anyone who knows me knows that I have no tolerance for nonsense. If I can, I walk away from those people ... and I stay away.

But what if we can't walk away? What if it's people we work with or live with, what if it's family or someone we are forced to encounter often? Then, what?

There is a story in the Bible of a woman who faced foolishness every day. She was married to Nabal, a man whose name literally means fool.

Her name is Abigail and her story is found in 1 Samuel 25.

David and his men are on the run from King Saul. David is hungry and requests food from the wealthy but foolish sheep shearer, Nabal. David and his men had been providing protection to Nabal's shepherds so this seemed like a deserved payback.

But Nabal brashly rejected David's request for food. Now, David is both hungry and angry. He swears to kill the men of Nabal's household.

Abigail is told about David's plan to kill her family. She quickly gathers food, meets David on the road, and pleas for his mercy.

She carefully crafts into her 'plea' a little mention of David's slingshot, nothing like food and a mention of a past accomplishment to boost a man's ego. She speaks into his future and urges him to not waste his time on needless bloodshed. David listens and relents.

Soon after these events, Nabal dies and David asks Abigail to be his wife. Abigail is no longer the wife of Nabal, *the fool*. She is now the wife of David, *the future king of Israel*.

The message of this story is simple - Abigail understood her position of influence and her ability to change her surroundings, rather than her surroundings changing her.

Abigail stayed consistent.

She didn't sulk about her lot in life. Being married to Nabal couldn't have been easy. The Bible describes Abigail as beautiful and intelligent, and that she was. She never missing a beat and saved the lives of many.

Whatever or whoever you are facing today, I pray you understand *your* position of influence. Like Abigail, God can use *YOU* to change and even save the lives of those around you.

~Binu

April 18 ~ Psalms 17,35,54,63
*"... You probe my heart...You examine me at night
and test me..." Psalm 17:3 (NIV)*

I was determined. It wasn't going to happen again.

The last time I went through airport security, I mistakenly left a bottle of water in my purse. The security scanners caught it and I was asked to step to the side. I then went *behind the curtain* for a more *thorough* search. So, I was determined. *That* wasn't going to happen again.

Fast forward one year.

I was getting ready to board a flight back home. I double checked my bags. No bottled water, no perfume, no lotion, and no liquids over 3.4 ounces. With my head held high, I confidently walked through the airport security scanner.

The agent looked shocked. *"Oh my! Could you please step to the side?"* She showed me her monitor. The gray striped shirt I was wearing lit up her screen.

The Bible tells us over and over again, God does in the spiritual what the airport scanner did in the natural. He examines us.

"You probe my heart ... you examine me at night and test me." (Psalm 17:3 NIV)

"I the LORD search the heart and examine the mind..." (Jeremiah 17:10 NIV)

"For the LORD searches all hearts, and understands every intent of the thoughts..." (1 Chronicles 28:9b NASB)

After I landed, I checked my shirt. Sure enough, 78% cotton, 15% polyester, and 7% metallic. I had no idea. Is metallic even a fabric?

And maybe I have no idea what all God sees as He examines me.

Unforgiveness from years ago, jealousy from today's search on social media, a little bit of innocent gossip, hints of racism, gluttony and even some greed. I may be able to fool others, and even myself, but *nothing* gets past God. He sincerely desires that we be free from *anything* which could detain us or hold us back. (Hebrews 12:1)

I learned two lessons from my airport experience. Metallic can be used in fabric ... who knew? And ... it doesn't take much, in the natural or in the supernatural to slow us down and keep us from where we need to go.

"Search me O God and know my heart; test me and know my anxious thoughts. Point out anything in me that offends you, and lead me along the path of everlasting life." (Psalm 139:23-24 NLT)

~Binu

April 19 ~ 1 Samuel 28-31, Psalm 18
"... As surely as the Lord lives, you have been reliable ...
but the rulers don't approve of you."
1 Samuel 29:6 (NIV)

Have you had a door close in your life? Or maybe even slam shut? Don't take it personally.

On second thought...if you are a believer, asking God for His will to be done in your life, maybe you should take it personally.

In 1 Samuel 29, David is on the run from King Saul. He is tired and worn out and finds a safe haven in an unlikely place, amidst the ungodly Philistines.

David became so chummy with his new found friends, he offered to join their army. King Achish was ready and willing accept David's offer, but the other Philistine rulers resisted. They had heard about David's great reputation as a leader in the Israelite army. *"Isn't this the same David about whom the women of Israel sing in their dances ... He can't go to battle with us. What if he turns against us in battle and becomes our adversary?" (My paraphrase vs 4,5)*

David might have forgotten his calling, but God didn't.

A couple of chapters later, Saul dies and David is appointed king.

Imagine if God hadn't closed that door? What would have become of David? Would we still have our Psalms? The great King of Israel might have become the not so great king of the Philistines.

Isn't God good?

We all have a story like David. I know I have tried to open certain doors, doors which would have led me down some pretty crazy paths. Thankfully, God in His mercy, closed those doors. What seemed like rejection proved to be God's hand of intervention and grace.

I bet He has kindly closed doors for you too.

So, take heart and don't be discouraged when more doors appear to be closing rather than opening. Give it time. I believe you will one day look back and see, it was the hand of God closing those doors.

For the same God who cared enough about the destiny of David, cares about your destiny too.

~Binu

April 20 ~ Psalms 121,123-125,128-130
"Those who trust in the Lord are like Mount Zion,
which cannot be moved, but abides forever."
Psalm 125:1 (ESV)

Do you find yourself in a dry season with God? Do you find it difficult to connect with Him? I do. And it's more often than I want to admit.

Growing up in the faith, I feel I was implicitly taught that if you do "A" and "B" then you can expect a result of "C". But what happens when A+ B doesn't equal C?

I go back to the basics. I turn to the scripture and go back to what I know to be truth.

In the Bible, David was no stranger to this feeling.

David's relationship with God looked more like a roller coaster than a steady line. He went from the high of seeing God deliver a giant into his hands and bringing him into the favor of King Saul, to running for his life from that same king.

And through it all David chronicles his emotions in the many Psalms that he wrote. David's emotions were raw and real. He boldly questions God's fairness and tells God directly that He has abandoned him and has allowed his enemies to get away with evil. We watch him go from the highest of mountains to the deepest darkest valleys.

But David always comes back to the place of realizing that God is who He says He is. David's writings shift from hopelessness to declaring the love and faithfulness of God.

David beautifully writes that we are safe in God's protection because "... *he who watches over Israel never slumbers or sleep." (Genesis 121:4 NLT)*

He boldly declares, *"Those who trust in the Lord are like Mount Zion, which cannot be moved, but abides forever." (Psalm 125:1 ESV)*

He also writes that those who obey the Lord will enjoy the blessing of family and see God's faithfulness into the next generation. *(Psalms 128)*

Yet, with all David's ups and downs, God still declares that David is "... *a man after his own heart." (1 Samuel 13:14 NLT)*

I am encouraged today that God can handle my ups and downs too. I am encouraged that even in my dry season, God is still who He says He is. As I get back to the truth that I know, I always find that God meets me there and brings me through.

~Vijoy

"Then they all came and urged David to eat something while it was still day; but David took an oath saying, 'May God deal with me... If I taste bread or anything else before the sun sets!'"
2 Samuel 3:35 (NIV)

We've all found ourselves in the position of being offended. A friend says something or does something that gets you prickly, and *bam* - you are offended.

Often times, this position sends me onto a slippery slope. A few offensive comments will start a running tally of all of the possibly offensive things that this person has said or done. This plays in my head like a highlight reel (or low light reel), reminding me of all the things about this person that rub me the wrong way.

It's easy to stay in the position of offense. It's easy to stay angry, ignoring phone calls or texts, or avoiding social engagements to ensure that your paths don't cross until you're good and ready for them to cross. It takes an effort to mentally propel yourself above these issues.

David deeply mourns Saul death, to the point of having Saul's murderer killed. Remember, it was just a few chapters ago when Saul was hurling his spear at David and hunting him down, attempting to kill him. David's stance consistently is that Saul is anointed by God, and this makes him untouchable.

Abner was Saul's commander in chief. After David kills Goliath, Saul inquired about David, and Abner was the one who brings David, with Goliath's head still in his hands, to Saul. Abner also helps Saul's son take over as king after Saul's death, but eventually switches sides and tells David that he will help him take rule of all of Israel. David also mourns Abner's death in a very public way (mostly to show that he didn't kill him) instead of celebrating a good riddance.

When we get offended, it's hard to step back and separate the person from the action. No one would have blamed David for being relieved or even happy at the death of Saul. After all, it opened the door for him to take over. Abner created his share of conflict for David as well, and it would have been a relief for David to have him gone. David chose to rise above the offense and remember the person, their life, and their value in God's eyes. Each of us is valuable. We each have our good and bad qualities. We need to strive to rise above the offense.

~Shiney

April 22 ~ Psalms 6,8-10,14,16,19,21
*"What is man that you are mindful of him, the son of
man, that you care for him?" Psalm 8:4 (ESV)*

Ever since my youngest son was born, he was always watched by myself or his grandparents.

As he neared the age of 3, I knew it was time to transition him to preschool for a couple of days a week.

When he got to class on the first day, he was so excited. He put his things down and started to play. His excitement quickly turned to anxiety and tears when he realized I wasn't going to stay with him.

I said goodbye and quickly left, but stayed around the corner to make sure he was okay. I could hear him wailing loudly, as his teacher tried to comfort him. I left upset and feeling guilty, wondering if I had made a mistake.

For weeks leading up to this day I had been praying for him to be okay. I even put it out as a prayer request to everyone I knew who would pray for him. As I left him at school that morning, my heart wanted to just take him home and let him try again next year.

When I came to pick him up the first day, his teacher said he was teary eyed on and off, but eventually he was happy to paint and play outside. She even said that when nap time came, my son was trying to comfort an anxious child in his classroom by patting her back and saying *"It's okay, your Mama's coming soon".*

When day 2 rolled around, he cried again when he was dropped off, but the tears lasted only a few minutes. Eventually his teacher posted a picture online showing my son playing and participating with the class. My heart was overjoyed and filled with gratitude.

God reminded me that the things that matter to me also matter to Him. As busy as God is with running the universe, He still takes the time to hear the cries of my heart.

In scripture, King David asks *"What is man that you are mindful of him, the son of man, that you care for him?" (Psalm 8:4 ESV)*

My friend, know that God's heart is stirred by the things that concern you. He hears your cries, and He wants you to know that He cares about you.

~Vijoy

April 23 ~ 1 Chronicles 1-2
"These are the earliest generations of mankind ..." 1 Chronicles 1:1 (TLB)

Since I was a child, one of my favorite pastimes is to look at photographs. My parents had kept their pictures in photo albums. I could spend hours just perusing through each one, studying the faces and learning the stories behind each picture. I was able to see where my parents grew up, to see them grow through the years, and to understand how much God's favor has been upon them.

Those photographs allowed me to connect to the history that I wasn't present for but now felt a part of because the moments had been preserved. Between special occasions and family vacations, memories of relationships were there for me to see and appreciate.

As I grew older, the passion for capturing such moments developed and I can often be found behind a camera. It has just always been important to me to document my history, especially for my children and their children to look back upon and know their roots.

These two chapters may seem like just a list of names that we can easily glance over. I mean what's the big deal with all these names? Why is it even included in the Bible?

Like the photographs reflecting my history, this list of names became a historical record for the Israelites. We find that they were just returning to Israel after living in captivity in Babylon. Having this list of names recorded not only reminds them of their genealogy, of the family and tribe they came from, but also that they are still God's chosen people.

Beginning with Adam, we see the line continues to Abraham and eventually, to the twelve sons of Israel. After being displaced and lacking freedom, it is refreshing to be reminded of where one came from, how God has blessed generation after generation, and that He has still much more in store for their future.

History isn't always pretty and neither are family relationships. But it's a part of who we are and ultimately, demonstrates how God's hand has always been upon us.

Take a moment to thank God for where you've come from, where you are today, and where you are headed with His grace. Then, document your history for your future generations to see and express gratitude for.

~Joyce

*"In God we have boasted continually, and we will give
thanks to your name forever." Psalm 44:8 (ESV)*

It's one thing to have confidence. It's another to have *"foolish confidence"*, as mentioned in Psalm 49:13 (ESV). What's the difference?

Your first thought may be the people who make the blooper reel of the talent shows we watch on television. There is some truth to that but it can go much deeper than our ability to carry a tune.

If we look ahead to the words of Jesus, He talks about the wise vs the foolish man. The wise man built his house on the rock; the foolish man built his house on the sand.

Maybe you know how the rest of the story (or song) goes: the rain, flood and wind came. In spite of the storm, all was well for the man whose house was founded on the rock. Unfortunately, that was not the case for the man who built his house on the sand.

"... it fell, and great was the fall of it." (Matthew 7:27b ESV)

It's easy to look at a man choosing sand as a foundation and judge his poor choice. But if we're honest, we've all been there in one way or another.

We place our confidence in things that are as shifting as the sand and build our lives on them.

Our looks, jobs, friends, titles, and skills may temporarily provide some footing for us to stand. However, all it takes is time, one wrong decision, or a diagnosis outside of our control ... and our source of confidence is gone.

As many victories as David had, his confidence was never in himself. He recognized that his help came from the Lord, the maker of Heaven and earth.

"For not in my bow do I trust, nor can my sword save me. But you have saved us from our foes and have put to shame those who hate us. In God we have boasted continually, and we will give thanks to your name forever." (Psalm 44:6-8 ESV)

When we make our boast in Christ alone, we build our lives on the rock that is unchanging. Even when the rains come down and the floods go up, our lives will stand firm.

~Anu

"... God granted what he asked." 1 Chronicles 4:10b (ESV)

I love being an aunt. If my nephews and nieces want something from me, a presentation with a PowerPoint would be cute but not necessary.

All they would need to do is come ask.

Unfortunately, we've seen prayer approached with that same type of formality. We feel we have to say things just right or else our prayers won't be answered.

Nestled in a genealogy chapter is a simple prayer by a man named Jabez.

"... 'Oh that you would bless me and enlarge my border, and that your hand might be with me, and that you would keep me from harm so that it might not bring me pain!' And God granted what he asked." 1 Chronicles 4:10 (ESV)

When Jesus teaches His disciples how to pray in Luke 11:2 (ESV), He begins with, *"When you pray, say..."*. In this context, the word "say" in Greek essentially means, *"bringing a message to a closure...laying it to rest."*[1] So, it isn't really what we are saying as much as how. The focus is the posture of our heart in giving the request to God and leaving it there.

When you look back at other stories in the Bible, there wasn't a specific type of prayer mandated. It has always been demonstrated as a dialogue with God.

Think of Abraham interceding for his nephew, Lot. Moses asking God to spare the children of Israel. The Psalms of David. Hannah weeping bitterly, praying in her heart while moving her lips but not saying a word.

When Jesus was on the cross, He uttered short phrases to His Father, expressing His pain at feeling forsaken and His request for forgiveness of those who had done this to Him.

Genuine, honest conversations with God. That's all it takes.

The prayers of Jabez and Jesus provide beautiful examples of how we can pray. We even have the ability to use those exact words along with other scripture. However, we can rest assured that God isn't looking for our words to line up like the numbers on a combination lock so He can finally answer our prayers. He is a good Father who just wants to hear from us, His children. We can trust Him to listen not as a result of what we said, but because of who He is.

~Anu

April 26 ~ Psalms 73,77-78
*"Whom have I in heaven but you? And earth has nothing
I desire besides you." Psalm 73:25 (NIV)*

My three-year-old son just recently got into the habit of saying, *"It's not fair!"* His big sister had gotten a special treat one day, and he wanted one, too. He had forgotten all about the candy he had received just a few hours before.

Earlier in the week, my daughter told me it wasn't fair that I wouldn't allow her to do something her friends got to do. In her mind, it just wasn't fair.

Typical for young kids, right? Some things just don't seem to add up in their naive minds. Therefore, it isn't fair.

What about us, adults? We have a few years under our belt but don't we *still* think the *same* sometimes? Life isn't fair.

Like the gorgeous celebrity who is making decisions that are compromising her integrity, yet has fame, perfect Facebook photos, money, and a keen fashion sense. No fair!

King David noticed this trend, too. He says, *"For I envied the arrogant when I saw the prosperity of the wicked. They have no struggles; their bodies are healthy and strong." (Psalm 73:3-4 NIV)*

He says, *"Was it for nothing that I kept my heart pure...?"*

Don't you wonder the same thing when you see people who aren't walking with the Lord prosper? It's not fair!

David has a light-bulb moment when he entered the sanctuary of God. He realized that *"they are like a dream when one awakes" (Psalm 73:20 NIV)*. He even admits to feeling *"grieved"* and *"embittered"* and realized that he was so foolish and ignorant for envying the wicked. (Psalm 73:22 NIV)

Sometimes, desiring what others have can lead us to the point of bitterness, just like David experienced. That is *not* how God called us to live.

What a beautiful way David ended this chapter, *"Whom have I in heaven but you? And earth has nothing I desire besides you." (Psalm 73:25 NIV)*

Nothing in this world can satisfy the longings of your heart than Jesus. Absolutely nothing.

Life isn't fair but neither is God's grace. He made the ultimate sacrifice for you when you were still a sinner and made you clean. Nothing fair about that ... but He did it anyway because He loves you so much.

~Elizabeth

"... They carried out their work, following all the
regulations handed down to them."
1 Chronicles 6:32 (NLT)

Do you ever ask yourself what is your place in this world? Maybe you feel as if you are not gifted to write books, sing songs, or speak on a stage in front of the masses.

I have good news for you. Neither am I. But that doesn't mean what I do is any less important than the ones out front and center.

In the Bible, we see a similar scenario.

You see, from the tribe of Levi, only Aaron and his descendants were allowed to carry out the role of high priest in the tabernacle and temple of God. The high priest had the important job of going into the Holy of Holies to stand in the presence of God and sprinkle blood on the mercy seat in order to atone for his sins and the sins of the people.

This role, I imagine, was seen as the most glamorous of all the temple duties.

But there were so much more than just the duties of the high priest.

The scripture lays out specific tasks assigned to the rest of those who descended from the tribe of Levi. Those roles included gatekeepers, musicians, singers, assistants to the priest, and so on. Each of those roles was specifically assigned to each family descending from the tribe of Levi.

The temple could not run if the only job that was fulfilled was that of the high priest. Every role was important and necessary.

And as they worked together, the scriptures say *"... They carried out their work, following all the regulations handed down to them."* (1 Chronicles 6:32 NLT) In other words, they faithfully served the Lord in the roles they were given.

What is your role in faithfully serving the Lord?

For me, I find that I thrive out of the spotlight and behind the scenes. For those I work with and for those I serve in ministry with, I am grateful for the abilities God has given me to support them and to help contribute to the overall success of the organization.

For you my friend, whether you find yourself out front or behind the scenes, I pray you would know...your role is important and necessary to accomplish what God is doing in the earth.

~Vijoy

April 28 ~ Psalms 81,88,92-93
"Do you show your wonders to the dead? Do their spirits rise up and praise you?" Psalm 88:10 (NIV)

It was a Sunday morning. My family had left for church, and I was still at home getting ready to leave for work instead. My phone rang. It was my dad. He has a knack for calling on Sunday morning as we're rushing out the door. Usually, it's an invitation for lunch or an inquiry to see if we plan on watching the football game later. So, I didn't answer. Instead, I let it roll to voicemail.

He didn't leave a voicemail but immediately called back again. (This is the way he works. He just keeps calling until you answer or he gets fed up.) I still didn't answer. When he called back the third time, he left the voicemail that no one wants to hear: "*I am taking your mom to the hospital. I think that she's had a stroke.*"

My blood froze. I could barely push the screen to call him back. My hands were shaking and my voice trembled. He answered and told me that my mom had woken up with a massive headache, slurred speech and wasn't able to walk without support. I made arrangements for someone to cover me at work and drove down to meet them at the hospital.

Thankfully, her workup was negative for a stroke and her symptoms resolved without any lingering effects. They kept her overnight at the hospital and I had the opportunity to stay with her. When she relayed the details to some family members later in the day, she said "*I was laying there, I was telling God 'If I can't lift my arm up, how will I praise you Lord? If I cannot speak, how will I worship you?'*" She had faith that God would heal her to continue to reflect His glory.

In Psalm 88, David poses some similar questions to God. Can the grave, destruction, or darkness reflect who God truly is? Not the way that His own children can. We have a duty to reflect the attributes of God in our daily lives, and He has equipped us with the ability to do it. Sometimes we take for granted that we have health and the ability to do so. Take the time today to spend some time with your Maker and thank Him for the breath in your lungs and the life in your body.

~Shiney

"Saul died in disobedience, disobedient to God. He didn't obey God's words. Instead of praying, he went to a witch to seek guidance. Because he didn't go to God for help, God took his life and turned the kingdom over to David son of Jesse." 1 Chronicles 10:13-15 (MSG)

Have you ever felt like you were the default?

Yes, you got the job, promotion, or opportunity but was it because they really wanted you to have it? Or because the person they actually chose couldn't, wouldn't or just didn't want to take it?

Sure, it is yours but it kind of feels like a half-win at best.

That's exactly where I was so I vented to my sister, Binu, about it. I told her it was hard to embrace something when you felt like they didn't really want you there to begin with. I acknowledged that I felt like I was the default.

Her response was immediate. *"That's not how I see it at all."* She went on ... *"I see that man didn't choose you for it, but God did."* Then, she reminded me of the story of David.

That changed everything for me.

When God wanted a new king for Israel, He sent Samuel to Bethlehem (that wouldn't be the last time a king would come from there). He invited Jesse and his sons to participate in the sacrifice but for some reason, Jesse forget to include his youngest son, David, who was out in the fields.

Then, Samuel began the selection process. He took one look at Eliab and said, "... *Surely the Lord's anointed is before him.*" (1 Samuel 16:6b ESV)

Samuel was wrong.

Jesse paraded 7 of his sons in front of Samuel. He assumed that God's chosen king of Israel was one of them.

Jesse was wrong.

I wonder what David thought when he heard how the day unfolded ... the fact that he was an afterthought. He probably felt like a default too.

But he would have been wrong. While Saul was still on the throne, God chose David.

David could have approached his role as king with the mindset that man didn't think he should be there. Or he could see that God did. History shows us that David became the greatest king of Israel.

So now, I choose to see myself as chosen, maybe not by man, but by God. Not bad for a default.

~Anu

"But from everlasting to everlasting the Lord's love is with those who fear him, and his righteousness with their children's children—" Psalm 103:17 (NIV)

I was in middle school when my dad bought me my first desk. It was a beautiful cream-colored desk with a nice accordion-type cover to keep all my things private with different sections. I kept it for years.

The desk sat in front of a window that faced a small corner of our backyard, where the air conditioning unit sat. It was almost like a forgotten part of the yard.

Well, Dad brought a beautiful bougainvillea and planted it right there in that lonely space. My mom questioned his decision: why plant it so far back, hidden away?

Dad had good reason. Since that is where my desk faced, he wanted me to watch the plant bloom and grow as I studied. He put it there for me to enjoy. I always remember how thoughtful that was of my dad because he was thinking of me.

Last week, my husband brought home a bunch of flowers that were not quite blooming yet. It stood in a vase with green stems and red bulbs cupped together. It didn't have the beauty of flowers in bloom. As the days passed, we started to see how each flower opened up and flared its petals. Such a magnificent thing to witness.

The Bible says, *"As for man, his days are like grass; he flourishes like a flower of the field; for the wind passes over it, and it is gone, and its place knows it no more." (Psalm 103:15-16 ESV)*

A flower has a life cycle, just like us. As magnificent as it is, it will eventually die. No plant on this earth is eternal.

However, God's Word tells us what *is* eternal in the next verse: *"But the steadfast love of the LORD is from everlasting to everlasting on those who fear him, and his righteousness to children's children," (Psalm 103:17 ESV)*

God's love is eternal, unlike our love or our *life on earth*, for that matter. I am so grateful for a God who loves me, despite my weaknesses and mistakes!

God's love is more breathtaking than a rose in full bloom. When you experience His love, compassion and forgiveness, that beauty arises inside of you. Nothing can compare.

~Elizabeth

May 1 ~ 2 Samuel 5, 1 Chronicles 11-12
"...He also went down into a pit on a snowy day and
killed a lion." 1 Chronicles 11:22b (NIV)

In 1 Chronicles 11, it lists King David's mighty warriors including a man named Benaiah. He was described as *"a valiant fighter"*. Verse 22 goes on to say that *"He also went down into a pit on a snowy day and killed a lion." (NIV)*

That's a lot to process.

First of all, there's a lion. Secondly, there's a lion (I mean, I know I'm repeating myself but there was a lion!!). The icing on the lion cake was the snow.

I'm from Texas. Benaiah was from Israel. One thing we have in common is our lack of experience with snow. If this were me though, I think I would have been happy enough that the lion went into the pit and then proceeded to run in the opposite direction. Not Benaiah. He chose to go down into the pit with the lion.

Benaiah didn't want to just escape this issue. He wanted to defeat it.

My husband and I serve in the marriage ministry at our church. We take our couples through a 16-week curriculum which covers various topics related to marriage like love, forgiveness, and humility. There is a short reading along with questions each spouse needs to answer then discuss together.

After years of doing this, we hear the same thing over and over again: *"We fought when we went through this chapter."*

It sounds bad but it's actually okay. They are likely talking through issues that have been developing for years but have not been addressed. This process allows them to uncover those things that have been swept under the rug for too long. To them, it probably feels like there is a lion in a pit on a snowy day. Maybe you can relate too.

There is a time to watch God shut the mouths of the lions like He did for Daniel. There are other times, God directs us to go after the lion ourselves.

Confrontation, when done the right way, still may not be easy but is necessary in certain situations. And when you are done, that will be one less lion lurking around later.

~Anu

May 2 ~ Psalm 133

"How good and pleasant it is when brothers live together in unity! ...
For there the Lord bestows His blessing ..." Psalm 133:1,3b (NIV)

I remember when my boys were little. There were days I felt more like a referee than a mom.

The younger one was usually the instigator, egging his brother on. But it takes two to tango, right? So, when it looked like there was no end in sight, I'd step in.

"Okay boys. Enough is enough. Repeat after me, 'How good and pleasant it is when brothers dwell together in unity.'"

Yes, I was that mom. I was determined, my kids will get along, whether they like it or not.

Guess what? It worked. They stopped fighting! Of course, they were now annoyed at me instead of each other.

The Old Testament is filled with examples of how NOT to treat your brother: Cain and Abel, Jacob and Esau.

But in the book of Exodus, we come across Miriam, Aaron and Moses... siblings who actually got along. Miriam, waited by the bulrushes to ensure Moses' safety. Decades later, Aaron and Moses work side by side, leading the children of Israel out of Egypt ... together!

Unfortunately, like most siblings, even these three had their moments.

In Numbers 12, Aaron *and* Miriam spoke against Moses. They had an issue with his authority and with his wife's ethnicity.

As a result, God struck Miriam with leprosy. Aaron then cried out to Moses. It would have been the perfect "I told you so" moment. But Moses prayed for his sister instead.

Talk about *choosing* to turn a bad situation into one of restoration and healing.

Centuries later, David mentions Aaron in a beautiful Psalm about brotherly fellowship and the blessing of unity. *"How good and pleasant it is when brothers live together in unity! It is like precious oil poured on the head, running down on Aaron's beard ... FOR THERE THE LORD BESTOWS HIS BLESSING." (Psalm 133:1,3b NIV)*

So, maybe you too have days where you feel more like referee than a mom, or perhaps your kids aren't the only ones at odds with one another ... family drama can last decades.

I won't pretend to understand every crazy situation out there, but I do know what Psalm 133 says. Strive for unity. It's good, it's pleasant and God's blessing is there.

Don't give up. Be THAT mom, THAT sister, THAT girl. Pray Psalm 133 over your relationships.

"For there the Lord bestows His blessing."

~Binu

May 3 ~ Psalms 106-107
"Let the redeemed of the Lord tell their story ..." Psalm 107:2a (NIV)

Since I was young, I have strongly disliked public restrooms, *especially on road trips.* I'm no diva, I just prefer clean bathrooms ... and I have a very strong gag reflex. So, on such family trips, we had a routine. I would have my sister go in first, assess the bathroom situation, then let me know if it was safe to enter.

Weird confession, I know, but I promise I'm going somewhere with this.

There was a comfort in knowing, whatever I was about to walk through, someone else had already been there and survived.

I grew up during a time and in a culture where no one talked about what they were going through. All struggles were hush hush. Even if you made it through and were now on the other side, it was still a secret.

But I believe that God desires something different from us. The Psalmist tells us *"Let the redeemed of the Lord say so." (NKJV)* Another translation states, *"Let the redeemed of the Lord tell their story." (Psalm 107:2a NIV)*

God wants us to tell our story, both the good and even some of the bad leading up to the good. This doesn't mean we should air our dirty laundry for all the world to see. That would be pointless. But I do think we should be open to sharing our story with someone who needs to hear it.

A friend of mine who has been struggling with a particularly painful situation recently told me, 'When I share my story with someone, nine out of ten times, the floodgates open and that person will begin to open up about their struggles too."

Pastor Craig Groeschel says it this way, *"We might impress people with our strengths, but we connect with people through our weaknesses."*[1]

As God prompts you, share your story. Brag. Not on yourself but on the goodness and faithfulness of our God who has delivered you through some tough times. It may help someone feel less alone or give someone the courage to continue their journey.

So, whether it be a dirty public bathroom warning like my sister was kind enough to give me or simply sharing your own life experience, if it will help someone, share your story.

~Binu

May 4 ~ 1 Chronicles 13-16
"... We did not inquire of Him about how to do it in the prescribed way." 1 Chronicles 15:13b (NIV)

Have you ever been so excited about doing something for God, only to find out later, you and God might not have been on the same page?

In 1 Chronicles 13, that's where King David found himself.

King David was excited to finally bring the Ark of the Covenant to Jerusalem. He wanted to establish worship there. David and his fellow Israelites placed the Ark on a new cart and began their trek to Jerusalem. David was pumped. The crowd was hyped. As they traveled along, *"David and all the Israelites were celebrating with all their might before God." (vs 8 NIV)*

Suddenly, something crazy happened. The oxen carrying the cart on which the ark was placed stumbled. In order to save the Ark from falling, Uzzah, one of the men guiding the ox, reached out his hand to steady the ark.

Then, something even crazier happened.

"The Lord's anger burned against Uzzah, and He struck him down because he had put his hand on the ark. So he died there before God." (vs 10 NIV)

David was now angry and afraid of God; so, instead of taking the Ark to the City of David to be with him, the Ark took a little detour to the house of Obed Edom.

What happened? Why was God so harsh? Uzzah was just trying to help!

God is loving, God is merciful, God is kind, but God is also Holy ... and what He says, goes.

In Exodus 25, God commanded the Israelites to carry the Ark on poles, not on a cart pulled by oxen. Consequently, when David did it his way instead of God's way ... God upset the oxcart.

Three months and two chapters later, David must have realized that God was not being harsh, He was being God. In 1 Chronicles 15:13, David admits, *"We did not inquire of Him about how to do it in the prescribed way." (NIV)*

David was ready to try this again, but this time, he would do it the right way, God's prescribed way.

So it is with our own lives. Whatever God has placed on your heart to do, by all means, get hyped and get excited ... but make sure to do it God's prescribed way.

~Binu

May 5 ~ Psalms 1-2,15, 22-24,47,68
"You prepare a table before me in the presence of my
enemies; you anoint my head with oil;
my cup overflows." Psalm 23:5 (ESV)

I was ready to rub it in their face. Maybe I'm the only one who has ever wanted that kind of moment. I wanted a chance to gloat in front of my enemies.

This mentality was intensified in my mind when I read a verse like this:

"You prepare a table before me in the presence of my enemies; you anoint my head with oil; my cup overflows." (Psalm 23:5 ESV)

In my mind, I'm thinking - *"Exactly! Now that's what I'm talking about. Y'all watch while I chill and eat at my banquet."*

As I was daydreaming of that moment, God brought something else to mind. Actually, Someone else. He reminded me of Jesus while He was on the cross.

Talk about being in the presence of His enemies. He had been beaten, spit on, mocked, then crucified.

It's not the banqueting table I had in mind. In fact, in that moment His enemies thought they had won. But while they looked on ... while THE REAL ENEMY looked on ... Jesus was accomplishing what He was sent to do.

Maybe having a table in the presence of my enemies isn't really about me gloating at all. Jesus had that opportunity every single day while He was on Earth. When He could have exalted Himself, He chose to humble Himself instead. He ultimately gave His life, until every drop was poured out.

After the resurrection, He didn't search out the Pharisees or Roman guards who held the hammer in their hand and pushed a crown of thorns on His head. He didn't walk around saying, *"How ya like me now son?!"*

He continued fulfilling His purpose. He took walks with people, encouraging them along the way. He spent time with His disciples providing final instructions for them once He was gone. He finished out the plan of God for Him on the Earth.

I don't need to gloat. I need to live out my purpose without regard for the opposition around me. The REAL ENEMY may try to get a foothold in my life but the fact is, Jesus Christ took care of him once and for all. So now, he is under my feet ... and completely defeated.

Now, that's what I'm really talkin' about.

~Anu

May 6 ~ Psalms 89,96,100-101,105,132
"For the Lord is good and his love endures forever;
his faithfulness continues through all generations." Psalm 100:5 (NIV)

"I promise I'll do it" is a phrase I would constantly repeat in the first year of my marriage. Whether I was referring to washing the dishes or paying a bill, it was one of those things I would just say...and I am usually a woman of my word. If I say I'll do it, I'll do it.

It wasn't long before I realized that what I guaranteed I would do wasn't being followed through. Dirty dishes would stack up in the sink and bills would be left unpaid. Life just got busy, and I realized that I wasn't keeping my end of the deal. I wasn't being as dependable as I had hoped.

I was making empty promises.

So, I confessed this to my husband and made an intentional effort to avoid making vows that I couldn't keep.

Over and over again in our readings today, we see the writers of the Psalms refer to God's faithfulness. He never let them down, and they knew they could count on Him. When God swore an oath to David, that his throne would be established through all generations, that heavenly promise was kept.

It is so easy for us to make empty promises. They are usually stated flippantly, without true consideration of what circumstances may come our way.

It could be a commitment you made to a friend, a co-worker, or a spouse.

Remember God's faithfulness to you, and it will prompt your desire to keep your own vows. David knew God was faithful and he swore an oath to the Lord to build a dwelling for Him. Eventually, it was done through much time and planning by his son, Solomon, as was decided by the Lord himself.

May our praises come from a heart of gratefulness for God's faithfulness. And may we be faithful in return.

~Elizabeth

May 7 ~ 2 Samuel 6-7, 1 Chronicles 17
"... I will celebrate before the Lord. I will become
even more undignified than this, ..."
2 Samuel 6:21b-22 (NIV)

As I was preparing to teach about the spiritual discipline of worship, I discovered a beautiful definition from 1828 in Webster's Dictionary.[1] It says worship is to *"honor with extravagant love."* In order to honor God this way, it begins by recognizing how awesome He is and then, entering His presence with hearts full of thanksgiving.

I now realize how I have had some misperceptions about worship.

I believed that worship was limited to the four walls of the church and to the few hours I was there for service. To stand corrected, worship is something we can do at any time and any place. In fact, I recall there were days I was overwhelmed by God's love as I was driving, that my car really became a place of worship for me. I couldn't help but sing out praises in adoration of God. I was moved by how much He cares for me, especially as I was walking through anxiety about my future at that time.

Lastly, I have allowed what others will say to deter me when worshiping. "What will they think if I raise my hand?" "Will they laugh at me for saying 'Amen'?" "What will they say if I worship on my knees?"

God has revealed to me that our focus must not be on what others will say because God alone is the audience. He is alone is worthy of all glory, honor, and praise. David was overjoyed that the ark of God was finally being brought into Jerusalem. While others shouted and made music, David danced before the Lord with all his might and it embarrassed his wife Michal. But that did not stop him. He was so moved to be chosen by God that he honored God extravagantly.

God is not looking for the most talented or the best performance. All He desires is an offering from the heart. When we read God's Word, when we think of the blessings that He has showered upon us, the mercy He's shown us, the grace He's given us, when we pray and seek Him, these are all times we can worship Him.

May we honor our Lord God with extravagant love.

~Joyce

May 8 ~ Psalms 25,29,33,36,39
*"Who is the man who fears the Lord? Him will he
instruct in the way that he should choose."*
Psalm 25:12 (ESV)

There is a lot about the Israelites journey through the wilderness that sounds difficult but knowing which way to go wasn't one of them.

A cloud by day ... a pillar of fire by night. I wouldn't mind that for my life too.

When I was in my mid 20's, I remember being confused about some major life choices, including marriage. I talked it over with the young adults' pastor at my church and he said something that has always stuck with me...

"Trust more in God's ability to lead than your ability to follow."

"Who is the man who fears the Lord? Him will he instruct in the way that he should choose. His soul shall abide in well-being, and his offspring shall inherit the land. The friendship of the Lord is for those who fear him, and he makes known to them his covenant. My eyes are ever toward the Lord, for he will pluck my feet out of the net." (Psalm 25:12-15 ESV)

This was a psalm of David full of beautiful promises for those who fear the Lord. Then, you get to verse 15 and it's like ... what???

David was just saying how God will lead him and his eyes are on the Lord. So, how did his feet end up in a net?

Doesn't that happen to us sometimes? We think we're doing the right thing. We want to follow the Lord's leading but somehow, we find ourselves tangled up in something we didn't see coming.

God doesn't expect perfection from us. We're not going to always get it right. We're human. But I love that He is right there, ready to get us back on track.

Charles Stanley put it like this, *"God takes full responsibility for the life wholly devoted to Him."*

The Lord is my shepherd ... and I am glad.

~Anu

"... I will surely show you kindness ... I will restore to you all
the land that belonged to your grandfather Saul, and you
will always eat at my table." 2 Samuel 9:7b (NIV)

Since the day I said "*I do,*" I began enjoying the benefits of my mother in law's cooking.

My visits to their home have felt more like a weekend getaway than a trip to the 'in-laws.' I wake up to the delicious smell of my favorite Indian breakfast. After breakfast, the day usually consists of more eating, resting and then of course, even more eating.

The more I eat, the more she cooks. It's awesome!

In 2 Samuel 9, we read the story of Mephibosheth. If you don't know his story, keep reading and you'll see the correlation.

Mephibosheth was the son of Jonathan, David's best friend.

When Jonathan and his father, King Saul, were killed in battle, the family of Saul tried to escape town. In the rush of the moment, five-year-old Mephibosheth fell from the arms of his nurse. He never recovered from the fall and lived the rest of his life crippled.

Years passed and David wanted so badly to keep a promise he made to his best friend. A promise to "never stop showing kindness" to Jonathan's family.

David discovered that Jonathan has a son named Mephibosheth. He lives in Lodebar which literally means, '*without pasture*' or '*a barren place.*'

David tells Mephibosheth, "*... I will surely show you kindness ... I will restore to you all the land that belonged to your grandfather Saul ... you will always eat at my table." (vs 7 NIV)*

Feeling worthless, Mephibosheth initially resists King David's invitation but by the end of the chapter, Mephibosheth accepts the king's offer. Mephibosheth no longer lives in the barrenness of Lodebar; he has now found a home in Jerusalem, a city of peace.

Do you see the correlation? Do you see the common thread? I have a seat at my mother in law's table, Mephibosheth has a seat at King David's table, and we have a seat at Christ's table ... not because we have earned it or even deserve it, but because we are loved.

Whatever you are going through, however physically or emotionally crippled you may feel, our Father's banquet table has a seat for you. Accept His invitation. It's that easy. The King is waiting.

~Binu

May 10 ~ Psalms 50,53,60,75

"Make thankfulness your sacrifice to God, and keep the vows you made to the Most High. Then call on me when you are in trouble and I will rescue you, and you will give me glory." Psalm 50:14-15 (NLT)

Have you ever cried out to the Lord in desperation for something, and in His faithfulness, He answers you? But instead of thanking God right away, you call or text your friends to share the news?

I know I am guilty of that many, many times over.

Don't get me wrong. I don't think it's wrong to share good news with people who have been praying and believing with you for something. But I constantly find myself not spending enough time thanking the one who made it happen.

I find that I'm not too different from the Israelites.

God showed himself faithful to them over and over ... and over again. Their story unfortunately followed the same pattern. They would be faced with insurmountable odds, God would deliver them, but as soon as the next challenge faced them, they longed for the days when they were slaves in Egypt.

In Psalm 50, God tells them that He has no complaints about their sacrifices and burnt offerings, but that is not what He wants from them. He reminds them that He owns all the cattle on a thousand hills...which means He owns EVERYTHING. Whatever monetary gift or sacrifice we can give him pales in comparison to what he already owns.

But what He really desires from us is thankfulness.

"Make thankfulness your sacrifice to God, and keep the vows you made to the Most High. Then call on me when you are in trouble and I will rescue you, and you will give me glory." (Psalm 50:14-15 NLT)

It's that simple. He's not asking for some grand gesture to show Him we love Him. He just wants us to give thanks and to be grateful.

Let's not reserve gratitude simply for Thanksgiving Day. Rather, I pray gratitude can be the very thing our lives are characterized by.

My friend, even if you are in a difficult season of your life, you don't have to look too far to find something to be thankful for.

I know God has been good to me, and I bet you will find, He has been good to you too.

~Vijoy

"... Do you really think these men are coming here to honor your father? No! David has sent them to spy out the city so they can come in and conquer it!" 2 Samuel 10:3 (NLT)

"Did you see the way she looked at me?" "Did you hear how he said that?" "I can't believe she had the nerve to talk to me that way!"

Sound familiar? Have you ever assumed the worst about someone based on your perceived reaction of their words or tone with you? I know I have.

I don't know if it's human nature or pride. It often seems easier to assume the worst of someone's intentions rather than assuming the best.

In 2 Samuel 10, we see how quickly assuming the worst led to death and destruction.

King Nahash of the Ammonites had died, and his son Hanan had become king. David had been loyal to King Nahash, so he decided he would show the same loyalty to his son.

As a gesture of goodwill, King David sent some ambassadors to express sympathy to King Hanan for his father's death. When they got there, Hanan and his commanders *assumed* they were there to spy on the city in order to conquer it.

Instead of receiving the gesture of sympathy with kindness and gratitude, Hanan humiliated David's men by shaving their beards and cutting their robes and sending them back home in shame.

David was insulted and furious. He organized the army of Israel and went to war with the Ammonites. As a result, many lives were lost. I imagine this story could have been vastly different ending if Hanan had not assumed the worst of David's intention.

The dictionary defines assumption as *"a thing that is accepted as true or certain to happen, without proof."* [1]

What would happen if we assumed the best instead of the worst? What if the way that someone is acting has nothing to do with you, but is really about them?

I want to encourage you to approach this with prayer and try not to assume the worst of someone's intentions. You might be surprised to find that God can use you to change a negative situation into a positive one. Your response may even help bring healing to a hurting individual.

~Vijoy

*"Those who live at the ends of the earth stand in
awe of your wonders ..." Psalm 65:8 (NLT)*

Recently, we had the opportunity to travel to Hawaii. After a morning at the beach, we decided to take a drive around the island. Using a guidebook and online maps, we wound around until we reached a dead end. We got out of the car and walked to what seemed like the edge of the Earth.

What lay before us was a breathtaking view in Pololu Valley. Lush, green hills and rolling valleys framed the right side of our view. The sun created shadows behind the clouds that added even more dimension to this canopy of greenery. The trees continued to a dramatic cliff that dropped off into the bluest ocean that I have ever seen. Waves capped with white foam relentlessly pounded the small strip of beach below. The sound of the waves along with the soft breeze made me speechless in reverence. I was in awe of the beauty before me. Pictures could not do it justice.

Right before my eyes was everything that David describes in Psalms 65, especially in the verse above.

My God, the one who listens to my meager words, created all of this beauty. The same God who carved out that cliff and valley carves a path for me every day to travel safely. The same God who dances the sunlight over the trees dances over you and me!

With the same power that created the roar of the waves, he created a roar in you and I. He created beauty in us that far exceeds the beauty that we can behold with our eyes.

You are an invaluable, irreplaceable, reflection of that beauty.

~Shiney

May 13 ~ 2 Samuel 11-12, 1 Chronicles 20
"Then Nathan said to David, 'You are the man! ...'" 2 Samuel 12:7 (NIV)

David was God's chosen king who proved to have an intimate relationship with Him as noted through his songs in the book of Psalms. We remember David as a young shepherd boy, an unlikely choice for a king, yet chosen by God and anointed by the prophet Samuel. While in those fields caring after the sheep, David learned to trust in his heavenly Father and in His faithfulness.

So, it's surprising to see how a man so close to God could fall so hard. While robed in royalty and having favor with God, he gave into temptation, and it's a reminder of how human David was.

Our readings today recount the sin that David committed with Bathsheba, a woman married to Uriah, a Hittite, but also shows his acknowledgement of his sin and the consequences he had to suffer.

When the prophet Nathan came to David to confront him with the words, *"You are the man!" (2 Samuel 12:7 NIV)*, he started off by telling him a simple story that portrayed David as a rich man and Uriah as a poor one.

Uriah was most definitely the victim in the adulterous relationship between the king and his wife, yet his character should be recognized.

Uriah was off at war during the spring...a time when David should have been there too. Uriah was fulfilling his duty appropriately. When he comes home on break, he refuses to lie with his wife although it was suggested by David in an effort to hide the sin that was committed. Uriah refused because he knew the ark and his fellow comrades were out in the open field.

Uriah is sent back to the fields with a letter written by David, one that held his fate. Just as the letter commanded, Uriah was put on the front line of attack and died. It was a ploy by the king to get a faithful man out of the picture so that a secret could be concealed.

But, as we know, there are no secrets with God.

We have been given a charge to remain responsible to our job and serve God faithfully through it. May we never be deceived into thinking we won't fall as David did. Instead, we must be in daily communion with our Father so that we are closing the door to the enemy's strikes.

~Elizabeth

May 14 ~ Psalms 32,51,86,122
"My sacrifice, O God, is a broken spirit ..." Psalm 51:17 (NIV)

One of the qualities that binds people together is transparency.

When I was in college, I had an inclination to put on a smile and hide my shortcomings. It was a way to guard my heart and reputation, but it blocked me from connecting with people. Sure, I *looked* "put-together", but I really wasn't.

It wasn't until my sister and I had one of those uncomfortable "heart-to-heart talks" that I realized I was only hurting myself. She made me realize that once those walls come down, people can relate to me, and I can start to have stronger relationships.

No one wants to look weak, but we *are* all weak, if not for the strength that God gives us. We just need to admit it to *ourselves* sometimes.

David fell flat on his face when he admitted his shortcomings to God in Psalm 51. He had sinned against God and others. When he was confronted with his sin of adultery, he begged God for mercy.

"You do not delight in sacrifice, or I would bring it; you do not take pleasure in burnt offerings. My sacrifice, O God, is a broken spirit; a broken and contrite heart you, God, will not despise." (Psalm 51:16-17 NIV)

God *delights* in a humble heart that looks to him. Why? Because He is a good, good Father, and when we fall at His feet, it shows our humility and brokenness without Him.

When we have tried putting together the complicated puzzle of our circumstances *on our own* and none of the pieces fit, we tend to run to God.

Why not trying to run to Him first? He delights in His child running to Him desperately and saying, *"God, you are all I have, but you are all I need."*

And you know what? He does not despise you for not being perfect.

So, go ahead. Let's get real ... with God and with each other.

You will be surprised at how admitting your weaknesses can bind your heart to another person. It can also draw you closer to God by admitting your need for His perfect strength.

~Elizabeth

"But Amnon had a friend, whose name was Jonadab ..." 2 Samuel 13:3a (ESV)

While attending my nephews' basketball games over the past 10 years, I've noticed an interesting predicament that happens.

There are a lot of voices to listen to: the cheerleaders, parents, fellow teammates and of course, the coach.

One dad is yelling *"Go to the basket"* while a teammate is saying, *"Pass me the ball!"*. The whole time, the coach is wondering why no one is following his play call.

And the kid? He's just confused. Who should he listen to?

In the game of life, who are we listening to?

Abram listened to a frustrated Sarai and a child, not of the promise, was born. Aaron listened to the people and an idol was created. Rehoboam listened to his peers instead of the elders, and God's chosen nation was divided.

"But Amnon had a friend, whose name was Jonadab, the son of Shimeah, David's brother. And Jonadab was a very crafty man." (2 Samuel 13:3 ESV)

(I seem to recall another time the description of "crafty" was used ... in the beginning, back in the Garden of Eden, about a serpent. So, this is already not looking too good.)

Jonadab apparently had quite the reputation but he still manages to be Amnon's choice as a friend and confidant. As a result of following Jonadab's advice, Amnon commits a horrible sin against his sister which tears his family apart.

Jonadab spoke. Amnon listened.

If Amnon had chosen some non-crafty people to surround himself with, this story may have ended differently.

When David inquired about Bathsheba, it seems that David's servant knew what David was thinking and tried to steer him away. Unfortunately, David didn't listen.

Thankfully, David eventually did listen to the prophet, Nathan. He repented but was still punished for his sin.

Do you have people in your life that will help keep you in check like that? More importantly, do you choose to heed their words as well?

"Walk with the wise and become wise; associate with fools and get in trouble." (Proverbs 13:20 NLT)

Choose wisely the voices you listen to.

~Anu

May 16 ~ Psalms 3-4, 12-13, 28, 55
"You have given me greater joy than those who have
abundant harvests of grain and new wine."
Psalm 4:7 (NLT)

If you have lived life long enough, you have probably experienced deep sadness.

A diagnosis, a betrayal. Whatever the cause, you are left engulfed and overwhelmed with sorrow ... so much so, you can hardly move.

You are not alone.

Theologians believe Psalms 3 and 4 were written during one of the darkest seasons of King David's life.

It was a time when his son, Absalom, attempted to steal the kingdom from his hands. Once David was informed of his son's plot, David gathered his men and fled. 2 Samuel 15:30 tells us, *"But David continued up the Mount of Olives, weeping as he went." (NIV)*

Imagine David weeping with each step. He didn't really know where he was going or how things would turn out once he got there. Thoughts of betrayal flooded his mind. He must have wondered how things got this bad this fast.

Then, God does something miraculous. He doesn't change David's immediate circumstance; He changes David's heart. God replaces David's sadness with joy. And not just joy, *greater joy.*

During this trial, David writes, *"You have given me greater joy than those who have abundant harvests of grain and new wine." (Psalm 4:7 NLT)*

Another translation states, *"You have put gladness in my heart." (NASB)*

I love the visual this translation brings. In the middle of extreme sorrow, the Almighty God reaches down from heaven and carefully places joy into David's grief stricken, delicate and fragile heart.

God can do the same for you and I.

No sadness is too deep, no anxiety is too great. When life doesn't make sense and circumstances tell you that it's over ... it's NOT over. Lift your eyes to our Heavenly Father and ask Him to fill your heart with joy ... *Greater Joy.*

~Binu

"He reached down from on high and took hold of me; he drew me out of deep waters. He rescued me..." (2 Samuel 22:17-18a)

In the past few years, my family has been able to attend events, travel on vacations, and not exist in a constant state of worry. There are not enough words to thank and praise God from the bottom of my heart for this time because it hasn't always been like this.

Not so long ago, I would refrain from going to public places during cold and flu season. I lived in a perpetual place of anxiety about someone with a cold interacting with my child. If he grew ill, what would happen had become a familiar place of heartache. I would have to pack our bag and rush to the emergency room with my sick baby. With our doctor's letter on hand explaining the necessity for quick admission, I prayed that things would move smoothly. Watching my child get poked by needles and waiting for lethargy to dissipate was frightening and exhausting. Being away from my family and not knowing the duration of the hospitalization left our lives in limbo. I felt discouraged and sad. Like David, I found myself crying out to God for help and for mercy.

As I shared my heart with God, the words that followed were praise because His sovereignty and presence were real to me even in the cold, lonely hospital room. Before seeing improvement or receiving the discharge papers, I found myself singing aloud and declaring God's faithfulness to us because He is worthy of praise. I knew I wasn't alone and I trusted that God would help us.

The following lyrics from "Never Once" by Matt Redman[1] echo my heart's song:

> *"Standing on this mountaintop*
> *Looking just how far we've come*
> *Knowing that for every step*
> *You were with us*
> *Never once did we ever walk alone*
> *Never once did You leave us on our own*
> *You are faithful, God, You are faithful"*

~Joyce

May 22 ~ Psalms 95, 97-99
"For the Lord is a great God, and a great King above all gods." Psalm 95:3 (ESV)

If you are having a hard time making conversation with someone, just ask them about themselves and discuss topics they are interested in.

Conversation.officially.started.

It's not a bad thing. Conversations happen because two people are talking about various subjects which often include themselves.

I think we would all agree that when the dialogue becomes one-sided is when it gets a little old...right?

Unfortunately, our relationship with God, including our worship, can also turn into a one-sided conversation. Many songs focus on what God is doing in MY life. It was a hard realization when I saw that even this had now become about me.

How do I feel about me after I sing this song? What do I feel like I can get through or overcome? Do I feel empowered to do more or be a better person?

This isn't a bad thing. Even the Psalms, the Bible's own hymnal, includes those types of statements. David spent a lot of time talking about his own experiences with God. Our testimonies are important – people are inspired and encouraged to know what God has done in our lives.

But our worship can't be based solely on our circumstances because they change. The character of God never does.

"Let us come into his presence with thanksgiving; let us make a joyful noise to him with songs of praise! For the Lord is a great God, and a great King above all gods." (Psalm 95:2-3 ESV)

Before David said these famous words *"Bless the Lord, oh my soul and forget not all of His benefits"*, he said *"Bless the Lord, oh my soul and all that is within me, bless His Holy name." (Psalm 103:1-2 ESV)* It's like David was saying ... before I list off everything I'm thankful for (because I really am thankful), I just want to bless Your name. That's it.

Keep singing about how God makes you brave or that you're an overcomer. I know I will.

But let's not forget to turn the tables and talk about Him too.

~Anu

May 23 ~ 2 Samuel 24, 1 Chronicles 21-22, Psalm 30
"So the Lord sent a plague on Israel from that morning until the end of the time designated, and 70,000 of the people from Dan to Beersheba died." 2 Samuel 24:15 (NIV)

For years, I have been writing devotions for our women's group. Every week I pray, read, study, then write as the Lord leads. But every so often, as I hit the submit key, I hear the voice of the enemy. *'Is anyone even going to read what you just wrote? Do you really believe you are making a difference?'*

Perhaps you can relate. You know God has given you a message for His people, but all too often, you hear that same voice.

King David experienced similar moments of doubt. The *'likes'* to his latest tweets must have been declining and the maidens were no longer singing his praises in the streets. So, he did something he knew he shouldn't do. He took a census.

2 Samuel 24 and 1 Chronicles 21 tells the story.

David asks his commanders to go and count the fighting men of Judah and Israel.

"So the Lord sent a plague on Israel from that morning until the end of the time designated, and 70,000 of the people from Dan to Beersheba died." (2 Samuel 24:15 NIV)

What was so bad about taking a census?

Nothing really, if done in the right way with the right heart.

According to Exodus 30, if a census was to be taken, a ransom tax was also to be taken. With David's census, no such tax was implemented.

Secondly, scholars say David's heart wasn't in the right place. The people had been so quick to leave him and follow his son, Absalom. David's ego was wounded. Instead of looking to God for affirmation, David looked to numbers.

But David knew better and eventually repented for his sin.

Seventy thousand people died when David looked to numbers and to man to build his confidence. No doubt, God is serious about this issue. God desires that our worth and confidence come from Him.

Don't allow the taunting voice of the enemy, the number of people in your army or the number of likes on your post dictate what God has called you to do. May our confidence come from the one consistent voice that truly matters, the voice of our Heavenly Father.

~Binu

May 24 ~ Psalms 108-110
"In return for my love they accuse me, but I give myself to prayer." Psalm 109:4 (ESV)

If you ever think the Bible is made up of perfect people with perfect feelings, think again.

David starts out good when he is talking to God about his enemies. He even says, *"In return for my love they accuse me, but I give myself to prayer."* (Psalm 109:4 ESV)

Wow! So noble! What a great guy, right??

Well ...

This prayer isn't exactly what you might expect it to be. He starts it off by asking God to cut his enemy's life short and *"... appoint a wicked man against him" (verse 6)*. He also makes the request that no one would be nice to his enemy ... ever. To top it all off, he petitions God to *"... cut off the memory of them from the earth!" (verse 15)*

Okay David. Tell us how you really feel.

I often wondered why God chose to put this in the Bible. Does it give us a license to pray these kinds of prayers?

There was a time when it was an eye for an eye however, Jesus turned the law and the old statutes completely around. He gives this command regarding our enemies: *"You have heard that it was said, 'You shall love your neighbor and hate your enemy.' But I say to you, Love your enemies and pray for those who persecute you, so that you may be sons of your Father who is in heaven..."* (Matthew 5:43-45 ESV)

That sounds completely different from David's prayer. Not only did Jesus say this, he modeled it for us too. Jesus only uttered 7 statements *while on the cross*. One of them was a prayer asking God to forgive the people who had crucified Him.

There was a time when I had been hurt by some people and held unforgiveness in my heart toward them. I wanted to take a few lines from David's prayer myself. After some time, I sensed the Spirit instructing me to pray blessings over them instead. (He had probably been nudging me for a while about that - I just finally obeyed). When I did that, my heart toward them began to soften. The hurt was still there but the chains that held me captive to those feelings were gone.

A changed prayer. A changed heart. A changed relationship. A changed life.

~Anu

"For David said, 'The Lord, the God of Israel, has given us peace, and he will always live in Jerusalem. Now the Levites will no longer need to carry the Tabernacle and its furnishings from place to place.'"
1 Chronicles 23:25-26 (NLT)

Have you ever been in a position to set someone else up for success? It's never glamorous or easy. In fact, it goes against human nature to help someone else knowing that you won't get credit for it.

King David found himself in a similar position.

From the time of Moses, the presence of God dwelled in the tabernacle. This was basically a tent that would move with the people of God as they made their journey towards the promised land.

Fast forward many years.

The people of Israel have inhabited the promised land. They were now a real nation under the leadership of King David, who himself had some very noteworthy accomplishments. He unified Israel, he established Jerusalem as their capital, and brought the Ark of the Covenant back to Jerusalem from the Philistines.

As he neared the end of his life, his heart was grieved knowing that he lived in a beautiful house of cedar wood, while the presence of God still dwelled in a tent. He determined in his heart that he would build the Lord a temple as a more permanent home for the presence of God on earth.

But David's life was marked by much violence and bloodshed. Although God was pleased that David desired to build a temple, God would not allow David to build it. Instead the responsibility was given to David's son, Solomon.

At this point, David could have just washed his hands of the whole thing because *he* wasn't allowed to build it. But the beauty of David's heart was that he didn't let that stop him from setting up Solomon for success.

He meticulously gathered supplies and appointed the labor needed to take on this huge project. He didn't leave it all up to Solomon. He did what he could to give his son the best chance to complete the project. And Solomon did just that. The temple was eventually finished and God's presence inhabited it.

Is there something that God is asking you to do to set someone else up for success? It might not bring you the credit you may want, but it could have an impact that could far outlive you.

I pray that you will be able to work behind the scenes to accomplish something with an impact far greater than you could imagine.

~Vijoy

May 26 ~ Psalms 131,138-139,143-145
"I praise you because I am fearfully and wonderfully made ..." Psalm 139:14 (NIV)

While going through management changes in the workplace, I was faced with a sea of negative comments day after day. I would hear, *"This wasn't how it was done before!"* or *"Why are they changing things around?"*

None of us had answers, but it was easy to get caught up in all the distrust and antagonism.

I was trying to stay upbeat, but the comments they made and ideas they came up with just seemed to get under my skin.

All around us, people are disillusioned, forgetting to focus on their blessings. You would have to leave your television unplugged and be off social media completely to avoid the hostility that is surrounding us daily. Disturbing comments about our current or potential leaders swirl around us all the time.

I listened to a segment on the radio that addressed this issue recently, and it really spoke to me. The disc jockey mentioned how even believers can get caught up in the negativity, and that we should be careful.

She stated a Bible verse that I love, *"For we are his workmanship, created in Christ Jesus for good works, which God prepared beforehand, that we should walk in them." (Ephesians 2:10 ESV)*

Regardless of our political affiliation or personal beliefs, God created each one of us for a purpose ... even the people you don't agree with. God's word affirms that He is loving to all he has made. We are all *"fearfully and wonderfully made." (Psalm 139:14 ESV)*

We can truly be agents of change and positivity if we love even the most difficult people. It takes patience, compassion, humility, and even keeping our mouths shut at times, to change the tide of negativity.

Let us pray for those around us who seem to pull us down, so that they, too, can appreciate all that they have been blessed with. It's just a better way to live.

I came across this beautiful quote that may speak to you, too, as we face negativity around us:

"It is the Holy Spirit's job to convict, God's job to judge and my job to love." - Billy Graham[1]

~Elizabeth

"And you, my son Solomon, acknowledge the God of your father, and serve him with wholehearted devotion and with a willing mind ..." 1 Chronicles 28:9 (NIV)

As the pastor's daughter, I had the honor to play many roles at our church. Before the congregation would trickle in, our family would set up the pews with the appropriate books, choose the songs for worship, and get the projector ready for Sunday School.

At about 9:45 am, I would sit at the piano bench and help lead songs for praise and worship. Soon after, I moved into teacher mode and taught young children a Bible lesson.

When church service was over, it was clean-up time, making sure the bathrooms looked decent and the books were organized back onto the shelves.

In those times of serving, it would be so easy to lose focus of why I was doing what I did. There were moments I found myself just doing the job but forgetting the REASON for serving.

Have you ever felt that way? Doing all you can to serve God, but your heart's just not in it?

King David knew his time on the throne was coming to an end. God had given him a successful reign, but it was time to pass it onto his son, Solomon. In 1 Chronicles 28, King David gives advice to his son, who is soon to take on the responsibility of kingship and for building the temple of the Lord.

He challenges his son to serve God with *wholehearted devotion* and with a *willing mind*.

I am fascinated by the advice of this king who enjoyed fame, wealth, and wisdom...a "man after God's own heart". He could have told his son anything, like...*gather all the gold and plunder you can from your enemies* ... or *become a great warrior* ... or *make yourself famous*.

Instead he tells his son to serve God wholeheartedly. He knew that if Solomon was WILLING TO SERVE and did it with the right MOTIVE, he would be following God's will for his life.

We do a better job of serving God when we do it wholeheartedly. The next time you are doing something, *anything*, for God, check yourself: Am I doing this with devotion or am I just half-hearted about this?

It may be time for a break and some quiet time with God. You can't hide from Him. He knows your heart.

~Elizabeth

May 28 ~ Psalms 111-118

"He raises the poor from the dust and lifts the needy from the ash heap;
he seats them ... with the princes of his people." Psalm 113:7-8 (NIV)

My family and I have begun a new pastime of watching certain reality shows on television. Before you judge me, let me explain. We have been watching "Shark Tank"[1] and "Undercover Boss"[2]. What has fascinated me about these shows is the story of the successful business person who is able to invest in others. Most of their stories are actually the same: they came from humble beginnings. Some had such a difficult childhood or upbringing, that it's almost impossible to believe where they are today as thriving millionaires. But that just proves the point that your past doesn't determine your future.

I believe if we look around us, there are many who have the same story. Maybe it's the immigrant who achieved the American dream or the one who grew up in poverty and is now wealthy or the one who was abused and now is raising a loving family.

When reading 1 Samuel 16, we first meet David as a shepherd boy. Being a shepherd isn't a glamorous job. Countless hours are spent outdoors herding sheep. It's lonely and one is left quite smelly. Apparently, David's father didn't think much of him either when the prophet Samuel visited their home and asked to meet his sons to decide who would be the future king. But the Lord told Samuel that David was the one and Scripture shows us that he went from being a shepherd to a king of Israel.

God is able to turn our rags to riches, our mourning into dancing, and our sorrow into joy. He can elevate us when it seems that the odds are stacked against us. Thank You, Lord!

But what stands out to me about such stories is that once this exchange has occurred, they don't just forget where they came from. Rather, they use what they have now been blessed with to help others. Whether it's the CEO who gives an employee several thousand dollars to overcome a financial struggle or the abused sharing their story to help others heal from the pain, each one is giving generously.

May we use the blessing of elevation to help those in need and be the hands and feet of God.

~Joyce

May 29 ~ 1 Kings 1-2, Psalms 37,71,94
"When David's time to die approached, he charged his son Solomon, saying, 'I'm about to go the way of all the earth, but you—be strong..." 1 Kings 2:1 (MSG)

Everyone's story will one day come to an end. In today's scripture passage, it feels like we are saying goodbye to a friend. We've spent a lot of time reading about David from his humble beginnings as a shepherd boy. Then, he was the son who was overlooked by man but chosen by God. And now, the final days of his life.

I think what saddens me the most is that this powerful man ... a man after God's own heart ... the one who boldly ran towards his giants began running away from his challenges and responsibilities.

It started with Bathsheba. We saw it in the circumstances surrounding Absalom and Tamar. And now, when it his time to announce his successor, he doesn't confront his son, Adonijah when he tried to position himself as king. In fact, if Nathan hadn't got involved, would Solomon have even been the next king of Israel as God had instructed?

David's legacy will forever be known as the greatest king of Israel but could there have been more to his story in his latter days too?

In my fitness videos, the instructor encourages us to "finish strong". I think that apply to more than just workouts. It applies to life too. I think of men like Joshua and women like Anna - that's how I want my legacy to be: focused in life and finishing strong in the end.

"When David's time to die approached, he charged his son Solomon, saying, 'I'm about to go the way of all the earth, but you—be strong; show what you're made of! Do what God tells you. Walk in the paths he shows you: Follow the life-map absolutely, keep an eye out for the signposts, his course for life set out in the revelation to Moses; then you'll get on well in whatever you do and wherever you go...'" 1 Kings 2:1-3 (MSG)

A father's final words for his son ... and for us.

~Anu

May 30 ~ Psalm 119
"I have hidden your word in my heart..." Psalm 119:11 (NIV)

We were hovering in the pantry the night of the tornado warning.

The alert told us to take shelter so we didn't waste time gathering together in there. As my husband and I prayed, my daughter was hunched over and crying. She was visibly trembling with fear. The thought of a tornado was scary, and she prayed that God would keep us safe.

About twenty minutes passed, and while my husband and I talked and prayed, my young boys were munching on cookies, not completely aware of the situation.

My daughter continued to tremble, then she sat up and started to pray aloud, earnestly, between her sobs. Her prayer sounded something like this, *"Just like you saved Noah in the flood, save us, Lord! Just like you helped Paul, Lord, save us! I bless your name, Jesus!"*

I was in amazement and close to tears. I had never heard her pray like this. She was making a desperate plea, remembering God's faithfulness to His people in the past...and praising God in the middle of the storm.

A few months ago, I talked to my husband about my concern that our daughter wasn't learning Bible stories like I had hoped. I wasn't sure if what she was learning at Sunday School, or even at home, was sticking with her.

But here we were, in what seemed like a terrifying situation in her life, and she was able to call out to Jesus. Jesus was *real* to her. That humbled me, and I praise God that I could witness that in my five-year-old!

Parenting is a challenge, and there are days I wonder if I am teaching my children the things that they will remember. Yet, even when I don't realize it, they are absorbing things they heard or things they witness each day.

Psalm 119:11 NIV says, *"I have hidden your word in my heart that I might not sin against you."* As we go through "calmer" days in life, we should be intentional in memorizing and hiding truths in our heart. That way, when we go through those unexpected storms, we can speak boldly in confidence of God's past faithfulness ... and praise His holy name.

~Elizabeth

May 31 ~ 1 Kings 3-4

"Give me an understanding heart so that I can govern your people well and know the difference between right and wrong ..." 1 Kings 3:9 (NLT)

Last summer, as I was driving the kids to their dentist appointment, I hit a barrier on the side of the highway. It came out of nowhere. (Actually, it's been there as long as the road has existed!) We were all fine, thankfully, but I was incredibly upset. I honestly didn't see what I had hit, which concerned me because I thought that I had been paying attention to the road.

When I called my husband and told him, he was very calm. I dislocated my side mirror and put a heinous scratch down the side of my SUV - all 6 panels. I was upset at how much it was going to cost to fix the mirror and replace the panels. He repeatedly reassured me that it was going to be fine and not to worry about it.

But my husband is a car guy. He loves cars - buying them, selling them and all the stuff in between. He spends hours out in the garage cleaning, buffing, waxing, spraying, wiping, and vacuuming every inch of our cars to keep them looking like they just rolled off the lot. He notices every mark, and there was no possible way to cover this one up.

When he came home later that evening, he brought me flowers. He presented them to me and *said "I know you had a rough day."* That's it. No accusations, no angry words.

A few days later, as I was explaining the flowers to someone, my husband chimed in. He reminded me that he scratched up my car while pulling it out of the garage a few days earlier. When he came in and told me, I said *"It's just a car. It's just a thing. It's not a big deal- it was just an accident."* Those were the exact words he had said back to me. I had forgotten all about that!

I'm not saying this to brag about my husband (although he is pretty amazing). This was just one time that we actually responded to each other in love and grace. If only all of our interactions were this positive!

When God tells Solomon that He will give him whatever he requests, Solomon asks for wisdom. Imagine if we asked God for wisdom, especially in our critical relationships - maybe more of our exchanges would be like this one.

~Shiney

June 1 ~ 2 Chronicles 1, Psalm 72

"Give me the wisdom and knowledge to lead them properly, for who could possibly govern this great people of yours?" 2 Chronicles 1:10 (NLT)

When you pray for something, what is your motivation? To be honest, many of my prayer requests have to do with me or my family. I try to spiritualize it somehow, but at the core they can be pretty self-serving.

I wonder what types of prayer get God's attention?

I stumbled onto something when I read one of the prayers of King Solomon.

When Solomon succeeded his father David as king of Israel, he was young and very inexperienced. Scholars say he was somewhere between twenty and thirty years old. But Solomon did not shy away from what he knew he had to do. He also knew he couldn't do it without God.

Solomon gathers together the leaders of Israel, the generals and captains of the army, the judges, the political and clan leaders. He leads the entire assembly in worship in front of the tabernacle and prepares a sacrifice for the Lord. And that night in a dream, God gives Solomon the opportunity to ask him for whatever he wants.

While most of us would ask for something which might make our lives easier, Solomon did not.

Solomon's response is that of gracious humility. He honors God by telling of His faithfulness to his father David and asks Him to keep the promise He made to David. He then says *"Give me the wisdom and knowledge to lead them properly, for who could possibly govern this great people of yours?" (2 Chronicles 1:10 NLT)*

Solomon had the God of the universe granting him one wish and his request is not for himself. Instead, he asks for wisdom to lead *God's* people.

The scripture says that God was so pleased with his request He granted it. But it was not just wisdom and knowledge that was granted to him, he was also given wealth, riches, and fame like no other king before him and no other king after him had ever seen.

I would like to challenge you and I to focus our prayers on taking care of the things that are important to God, not simply the things that are important to us.

In doing so we just might find ourselves seeing many answered prayers and also tapping into the purpose for which God has put us on this earth to accomplish.

~Vijoy

June 2 ~ Song of Solomon 1-8
"How beautiful you are, my darling! Oh, how beautiful!" Song of Solomon 1:15 (NIV)

I love romantic movies, especially romantic Indian movies. Bollywood really celebrates love. In case you have never seen a Bollywood love story before, let me give you the formula. Guy meets girl. After stealing a glance or after some brief, but witty, encounter, guy falls in love with girl. Girl does not reciprocate feelings right away but is quickly convinced after (literally) a song and dance number. Girl's parents object to the relationship, but girl and guy feel that their love (based on their brief interaction) can withstand the test of time. Insert multiple song and dance routines. Insert some sort of heroic action to overcome aforementioned family conflict. Guy and girl ride off into the sunset for their happily ever after. Love story wrapped up in a bow from start to finish within a 3-hour movie.

The lovers in this portion of scripture demonstrate that same naive, movie love. They are both so enamored with each other and thrill of being together. They can't see anything beyond each other. The challenge that we see in this section of scripture is to take this human love story and turn it into our love story with God.

Real love doesn't work that easily. True love is modeled after Christ's character- one of sacrifice, patience and serving. After the giddiness is gone, there is still a passion that God wants us to maintain. It takes work, effort, sacrifice and commitment. There must be something deeper than the initial enchantment.

God's love for us is unparalleled. We grasp only a slight understanding in this dimension. He longs for us to acknowledge Him in every aspect of our lives. He wants to be your first thought in the morning and your last thought at night. He longs for us to spend time and talk with Him. He can't wait to see your face as you unwrap one of His gifts. His love is unconditional, unending, and unyielding. He wants you to reciprocate- fully devoted, sold out, committed, 100% to Him.

That's the true love of a lifetime. No movie or love story could compare to the one that He has written for His children.

~Shiney

June 3 ~ Proverbs 1-3
*"For wisdom will enter your heart, and knowledge will
be pleasant to your soul." Proverbs 2:10 (NIV)*

I may have made a fashion faux pas today. I went the entire day feeling pretty good about my choice of ankle length pants and heels until I came home.

My five-year-old daughter eyed me as I walked into the garage and said, *"Mommy, heels with those pants and that shirt doesn't look good."*

When did she grow up and learn to appreciate style?

Her comment reminded me of myself when I was young. I am guilty of correcting my parents when they said a word incorrectly or their accent was slightly off. My brother, sister, and I would say, *"Dad! That's not how you say that!"* Then, Dad would say, *"Well, you move to a new country, learn a new language, and earn a degree! I know three languages ...."*

He got us there.

Why do we feel that we know more than our parents? We start learning a thing or two from TV, friends, or school, and then we think we gained a little wisdom and start educating our elders.

Wisdom is an interesting thing.

According to the dictionary, wisdom includes *knowledge, experience,* and *good judgement.*[1]

Do you find it fascinating that Solomon, the wisest man to ever live, made a "wise" choice even *in* asking for wisdom? Before God even granted his request, Solomon showed discernment. He doesn't depend on his own understanding.

I have been dealing with a major decision at work for the past week. What I decide to do can affect many people, and I am at a crossroads. I have sought advice from colleagues and my family, but I know that what gives me the most peace about what I will finally do is God's wisdom.

Is there something you are facing, and you don't know what to do?

James 1:5 NIV says, *"If any of you lacks wisdom, let him ask God, who gives generously to all without reproach, and it will be given him."*

Bury yourself in God's Word and truly seek him. You can't go wrong when you have sought God and his wisdom.

You can depend on his guidance. He will give you the right direction to take *"and make your paths straight." (Proverbs 3:6 NIV)*

~Elizabeth

June 4 ~ Proverbs 4-6
"Don't put it off; do it now! ..." Proverbs 6:4 (NLT)

One of our favorite movies to watch when our children were young is "A Bug's Life."[1] This movie reflects how there is wisdom in working hard and working together.

In the opening, we see ants working systematically to store up food for the winter and boy, were they able to gather up a lot! They lined up from the place where they found food all the way to the place where they stored food. Each one passed the food down until it was securely stored. This process occurred from sunrise to sunset. It may sound tedious and monotonous, but their hard work paid off when winter came and they actually had food to eat because they had stored away during the summer.

In comparison, there were grasshoppers who enjoyed themselves all summer long and expected to feed their bellies by taking the ants supply. However, the movie ends with their demise or departure from the area without any food.

This movie brought to life the verse I've read and heard many times from Proverbs 6: 6-8 (NIV): *"Go to the ant, you sluggard; consider its ways and be wise! It has no commander, no overseer or ruler, yet it stores provisions in summer and gathers its food at harvest."* We can learn a great deal from a tiny creature's actions.

We see that there is wisdom in being diligent. In other words, it is to our benefit to be a hard worker with the earnest desire to do things correctly. The purpose of being diligent is not to become wealthy, but to be prepared.

The reality is that the temptation to be lazy is all around us. "Ehh, I'll get to it tomorrow." But the result of laziness is that *"poverty will come on you like a bandit." (Proverbs 6:11 NIV)* God does not desire that we have such a foolish mindset.

What area of your life do you need to tend to with more diligence? Maybe it's getting your finances in order and making sure you have an emergency fund available for a rainy day. Maybe it's going grocery shopping regularly so your pantry is fully stocked when unexpected weather shows up. When you recognize what the area is, ask God for wisdom to be like the ant.

~Joyce

June 5 ~ Proverbs 7-9
"Give instruction to a wise man, and he will be still wiser..." Proverbs 9:9a (ESV)

How do you feel when someone corrects you?

I'd like to think that I can just take it like a (wo)man and roll with it. But the fact that I feel myself getting hot and my heart rate climbing indicates that is probably not the case.

Maybe I don't take correction as well as I thought.

"Do not reprove a scoffer, or he will hate you; reprove a wise man, and he will love you. Give instruction to a wise man, and he will be still wiser; teach a righteous man, and he will increase in learning." (Proverbs 9:8-9 ESV)

This verse seems counterintuitive. Why would a WISE man need reproof or instruction? Doesn't a wise man have it all figured out? Apparently not.

My husband and I recently got electric toothbrushes. I've been a regular (aka non-electric) toothbrush girl my entire life so this was a change for me. When my husband saw me brushing my teeth, he actually came over to me and suggested I slow down because I was using it wrong.

Lucky for him, I still had my toothbrush in my mouth so I couldn't say anything but my facial expression along with the eye roll conveyed my thoughts pretty well. Honestly, I was embarrassed. *"Wow! Someone has to tell me how to use a toothbrush?!"*

It seems easier to listen to advice when you are unsure about something because they are providing clarity. It's when you are sure ... when you are confident ... when you know that you know how to brush your teeth. That's when correction can rock your world.

I can't tell you how to avoid that initial feeling of wanting to tell someone where they can put their toothbrush – God is still working on me about that. I may feel foolish but if I am wise, I will heed my husband's advice. After all, who benefits from it? Me.

A wise woman knows that she doesn't know it all. We all want to be wise but a part of that is listening to others who are wise too. It won't always feel good but their thoughtful correction could be used for our good. So, don't brush it off.

~Anu

June 6 ~ Proverbs 10-12
"... whoever refreshes others will be refreshed." Proverbs 11:25b (NIV)

Yesterday I was blessed to receive bright pink roses. They were beautiful and breathtaking. However, I had not gone home immediately after receiving them. In fact, the flowers had to sit in my warm car for a few hours until the celebrations of the day finally drew to a close. By the time we arrived home, the roses didn't look as lively or vibrant. Sadly, they seemed to be wilting.

Nevertheless, I found a vase, filled it with water, and placed the roses in. When I awoke this morning and went out into my breakfast room, the roses were there to greet me. They had perked up and looked just as lovely as when I first received them. My husband's immediate observation was, *"Look what some water did for those flowers!"*

What happened to those flowers reminds me of relationships. If you are attentive to the person by speaking words of affirmation and spending quality time with them, then that person and that relationship will thrive. If, however, you neglect it by not doing those things, then you will see that relationship begin to wilt a bit.

A few months ago, my husband and I had a lightbulb moment. Even though we are together 24-7 (he works from home and I'm a stay at home mom homeschooling our kids), we became so busy with a plethora of activities that we actually were not spending quality time together. We began to feel a "wilting" as we were just passing each other by, rather than being intentional to converse and just have some fun together.

Thankfully, we sat down and talked about it. We both agreed we had to be intentional about spending quality time together. As we began scheduling regular times to have coffee together, go out for dinner or watch a movie, we immediately found ourselves happier, not only as individuals but as a couple. And our kids noticed too! In fact, they're pushing us out the door these days for a date night!!

Life is always going to be busy dear Friend, but as the famous quote says, "Stop and smell the roses." My two cents in addition to that is "water them, too!" The example I shared about my flowers illustrates no matter how the relationship appears, it's not too late.

~Joyce

June 7 ~ Proverbs 13-15
"A soft answer turns away wrath, but a harsh word
stirs up anger." Proverbs 15:1 (ESV)

Recently I found myself in the middle of a minor road rage incident in the Chick-Fil-A drive thru.

Another car who I didn't see, was apparently in the line already when I drove up. She was not directly in the line, so I got in front of her.

Her response to me was one of anger and rage.

I motioned for her to go around me and get in front of me, but she rolled her eyes and just motioned for me to stay there.

I'll be honest, I was angry. In my mind, what I did to offend her was completely unintentional. I even did my best to correct what I had done.

Almost immediately, I felt a prompting to pay for her meal. Really God? After what she just did to me, I have to bless her? But I decided to obey the prompting and I told the cashier that I'd like to pay for the lady behind me.

I never waited for her reaction to my "kind" gesture. To be honest I was hoping it would make her feel bad for yelling at me. I guess you can see that I have some work to do in this area as well. As I drove away that day, I felt God gently remind me of the verse *"A soft answer turns away wrath, but a harsh word stirs up anger." (Proverbs 15:1 ESV)*

I had a choice in this situation. Do I respond in anger or do something to diffuse the already tense situation? The truth is I know that this woman's anger at me had nothing to do with her getting her chicken sandwich before me.

I have no idea what she is walking through in life. Maybe a difficult marriage, a bad diagnosis, or the loss of a loved one. Once I was able to calm down, I found the strength to pray for her, and even asked the Lord to bless her.

I don't know who the difficult or angry people are in your life. Is it your boss, a coworker, your spouse, or even a stranger on the road who cuts you off while driving? I want to encourage you to not respond in anger. Let God's love flow through you so that God can begin to do a work in their life and in yours.

~Vijoy

"... An offended friend is harder to win back than a fortified city." Proverbs 18:19b (NLT)

Walls are a good thing. Can you imagine your house without them? Walls create distinct boundaries and separate spaces. In ancient times, they were built around cities to provide protection from attack.

Sometimes, walls exist that we can't see but we know are there. These walls are not built with stone, brick or even by human hands. Instead, they are formed by our thoughts. And it will take more than a bulldozer to tear it down.

"... An offended friend is harder to win back than a fortified city." (Proverbs 18:19b NLT)

It's easy to build a wall in our minds. For most of us unfortunately, it's our natural default.

They didn't say hi to me. Brick

They think they are better than me. Brick

They never call or text me. Brick

This happens in our marriages, work, friendships and even ministry. In other words, this happens all the time. You've probably noticed that adding a brick to a wall is easier than removing it. Everything in me wants to say that this is their issue...this is their fault.

"So then let us pursue what makes for peace and for mutual upbuilding." (Romans 14:19 ESV)

The word, *pursue,* in the Greek means to "aggressively chase, like a hunter pursuing a catch."[1] I've talked to people that hunt and it is a process. They get up early. They wear a particular type of clothing. They purchase equipment. They load up their car. Then, the hunter goes and finds the thing they are wanting to catch.

Did you notice that? The hunter doesn't wait to be found by what they are pursuing ... they go find it. So, if I want to pursue peace and for the walls to come down, it's going to require some effort on my part. Where do I even start?

Putting down my pride. Brick removed.

Responding in love. Brick removed.

Giving them the benefit of the doubt. Brick removed.

Praying for me, them, and our situation. Brick removed.

The wall may not come tumbling down, but as each brick is removed, we can see the other person on the other side more clearly. From brick-layer to brick-slayer.

Sometimes, not having walls is a good thing too.

~Anu

June 9 ~ Proverbs 19-21

"Fathers can give their sons an inheritance of houses and wealth, but only the Lord can give an understanding wife." Proverbs 19:14 (NLT)

A new roll of toilet paper on top of an old one ... it's an all too common occurrence as I walk into my bathroom. In the early years of my marriage, this sight would have caused a myriad of negativity -annoyance, nagging, annoyance ... did I mention annoyance?

Decades into marriage, God reminds me...it's not a big deal. So, I laugh and put the new roll of toilet paper on properly.

Years of marriage have also taught me that my husband and I each have our own set of strengths which we bring into our marriage and in maintaining our home. Fingerprints on our appliances don't bother me, but they bother him. Toilet paper rolls - I guess that's my area of expertise.

Proverbs 19:14 states, *"Fathers can give their sons an inheritance of houses and wealth, but only the Lord can give an understanding wife." (NLT)*

My sister, Anu Abraham explains.

"Sometimes, we work so hard to make sure that we are understood that we forget, our husbands need to be understood too. He wants us to understand that he is human and will mess up. He hopes that we understand that he sees the world differently but that doesn't make him wrong ... it just makes him different. The world we live in doesn't always take the time to understand us but I can make my home a place where my husband feels understood."

A wise friend once reminded me that marriage isn't 50/50. Divorce is. Marriage is 100/100.

Each of us selflessly giving our all. Working through our differences and asking God to give us a greater understanding of one another.

I've heard it said that *"Marriage wasn't meant to make us happy; it was meant to make us holy."* Hopefully, with God's gift of *understanding* poured out on each of us, we can be both. Happy and holy.

~Binu

June 10 ~ Proverbs 22-24
"Train up a child in the way he should go [and in keeping with his individual gift or bent]..."
Proverbs 22:6 (AMPC)

Sometime around the first or second grade, a significant gap began to form in the center of my smile.

My father's advice, *"Molé (daughter), in your free time ... try and close that gap."* He gave me instructions on how I could use my thumb and index finger to squeeze my teeth together. I guess it was an old school Indian version of braces.

I wasn't always the most compliant kid, but in this case, I did what he asked and somehow my teeth eventually came together. Perhaps my dad's advice worked or maybe my permanent teeth naturally shifted together.

Proverbs 22:6 states *"Train up a child in the way he should go [and in keeping with his individual gift or bent]..."* (AMP)

My teeth had a natural bent to go the wrong direction. My dad took note of this and wanted to steer them in the right direction.

The truth is, we all have bents. Both good and bad. Certain quirks, strengths, weaknesses. It's how God made us.

Proverbs 22:6 instructs us to keep our children's bents in mind as we train them. Some bents, like my teeth, may need a little pressure to be reset in the right direction. Other bents may need a whole lot of prayer to be reset in the right direction.

God has gifted each of us, and our children, uniquely. We all have a bent towards something. God created us that way. Does this mean we allow our children, or ourselves, to just be lazy or just go wild because that is the way God made us? Of course not. That's where the training comes into place, and training isn't easy.

Do you see a strong willed, determined spirit in your child? *Father, use it for good and not harm. Allow that strong will to be channeled to do great things for God.*

Do you see a child who is overly sensitive? *Oh Father, please steer this sensitivity in the right direction. Let this child be ever so sensitive to your voice. May it be a strength in my child's life, not a weakness.*

Bents aren't all bad. Each of us have them and God gave them to us. But as my dad advised me, continue to *"apply the right kind of pressure in the right direction"* and let's see what God can do.

~Binu

June 11 ~ 1 Kings 5-6, 2 Chronicles 2-3

*"Now I am about to build a temple for the Name of the Lord my
God and to dedicate it to him ... The temple I am going to build will
be great, because our God is greater than all other gods."*
2 Chronicles 2:4a & 5a (NIV)

Did you know that when God created us, He designed each of us for something specific and unique?

Mother Teresa was designed to be a humanitarian. Billy Graham was designed to evangelize. Darlene Zschech was designed to sing and lead worship. C.S. Lewis was designed to write. Not one is like the other. I am so thankful for what God designed them to be. Their gifts have blessed countless and pointed many to our Creator.

I think of how Anu, our visionary of this ministry Whispers and Fringes, was designed to empower women. Through various avenues, she has not only empowered our leadership team but also countless women across the globe to use our gifts for the glory of God.

Solomon was the son of King David. He became king of Israel and was known as the wealthiest and wisest king. I'd say he had a lot going for him. Not many could boast that they had accumulated as many riches or even possessed half of the wisdom he had. But that was not what Solomon was solely designed for. These chapters show that this great leader was designed to build the temple of God.

We see that King Solomon had vision, passion, and confidence to build the temple. He was committed to this project, but moreover, he was committed to honoring God. Solomon's faithfulness to God is evident in the amount of materials, laborers, and detail invested in this process. I can only imagine how marvelous it must have been to look at and worship in. What glory and honor the Lord must have received. All because King Solomon fulfilled what he was designed to do.

Whatever it is that we are designed to do, I pray that the vision and passion for it would be stirred deep within our hearts. May we look to the Lord for confidence and seek His help to be committed through the countless hours. Let's make a great impact for the kingdom of God by doing what we are designed to!

~Joyce

June 12 ~ 1 Kings 7, 2 Chronicles 4

"Solomon also built a palace for himself, and it took him
thirteen years to complete the construction."
1 Kings 7:1 (NLT)

Have you noticed that with certain food, sometimes a microwave just doesn't cut it? Yes, it will heat up your food quickly but you may compromise on taste. If you use an oven instead, it may take longer but the food will likely taste better.

It just depends on what is more important to you at that time.

It took Solomon 7 years to build the house of God. This was where the ark of the Covenant would be kept, the holiness of God proclaimed and His name praised. Offerings would be given and sacrifices made there. The glory of God would fill this place.

Solomon also built another house. This time it was his own home which took 13 years to build.

Commentators disagree on why it took much longer to build Solomon's house versus the temple. Some say the temple took less time because King David had already gathered the supplies and plans for its construction. There was also an urgency for the people to have a place to worship.

Others say it was Solomon's selfish indulgence that led him to devote more time to his home than the temple. This is a possibility based on the response of the people after his death, who stated that Solomon was a *"hard master"* (1 Kings 12:4 NLT).

Regardless, there is lesson for all of us: We take the time to invest in what is important to us.

If we kept a log of our time, what would it show? Did we catch up with the latest reality show or with our own families? Did we have time to scroll on social media but didn't have our quiet time?

When we establish what is important to us, our time should reflect that as well.

~Anu

June 13 ~ 1 Kings 8, 2 Chronicles 5
"'When the priest withdrew from the Holy Place, the cloud filled the temple of the Lord. And the priests could not perform their service because of the cloud, for the glory of the Lord filled his temple."
1 Kings 8:10-11 (NIV)

I'm not one for large crowds or detailed planning, but since Indian weddings are massive by nature, I had to just smile and go with it. So, with the phone book in hand, and a guest list of about 800, the planning began (keep in mind, this was before the internet).

There were lots of decisions to be made and even more details to be ironed out. Throughout the planning process, it was easy to get distracted and lose sight of what the day was all about.

In 1 Kings, we read about the planning of another major project, the construction of God's temple. And King Solomon was the man God appointed to the task.

Interior walls lined with cedar boards, planks of pine covering the floor, pure gold covering the inside of the temple ... every inch of the temple was filled with detail. And when the work was finally done, Solomon summoned the priests to bring up the ark of the Lord to its place in the inner sanctuary.

"When the priest withdrew from the Holy Place, the cloud filled the temple of the Lord. And the priests could not perform their service because of the cloud, for the glory of the Lord filled his temple." (1 Kings 8:10-11 NIV)

I wonder if at this point, Solomon breathed a sigh of relief. All of that hard work would have been in vain if God failed to show up.

The Psalmist says, *"Unless the LORD builds the house, the builders labor in vain." (Psalm 127:1a NIV)* Moses said, *'Lord, I'm not going, unless you go with me.' (my paraphrase Exodus 33:15)*

In other words, we can do it all, we can build the most magnificent buildings, we can put together the most beautiful weddings, every detail in place...but at the end of the day, God's presence is what matters most.

Needless to say, after ten months of planning, my wedding day came and went. Not everything went exactly like I had planned, but that's okay. My husband and I were married, and God was there. Mission accomplished.

Father, whether we are planning an event or simply planning out our day, I pray we become so keenly aware of Your presence. And like the priests, may we stop and acknowledge that You are with us.

~Binu

"... His love endures forever." Psalm 136:1 (NIV)

Repetition is a powerful tool. We use it to teach simple concepts - shapes, colors, life skills. You pair the repetition with a melody and it embeds, especially for kids. When my kids were younger, these little songs were like earworms. I couldn't shake them out of my head.

Psalm 136 uses this concept of repetition to ingrain an important thought to us: *God's love endures forever.*

The repetition of that phrase is so simple but compelling. Placed within the context of Solomon's beautiful prayer in the dedication of the temple and God's powerful response, it rings truer than ever. Solomon was humbled by the fact that he was chosen (over his father, David) to complete this incredible task. In spite of all of his efforts and the beauty of the result, he knew that God could not be contained in an earthly building. Solomon's prayer recounts the struggles and victories of the Israelites, and each repetition of this phrase supports the truth that God's love endures forever.

I used to rarely listen to Christian radio; I really disliked it. A few years ago, my mentality changed. I was going through a struggle that was weighing on me very deeply. I was in a bad place and would cry when I was alone. I couldn't eat or sleep. On my drive to work one day, I was singing along to a secular song on the radio and realized I was only reinforcing the state of depression I was swimming in.

I needed to hear something, anything, that would give me some hope. I needed to build some positive pathways. I needed to be reminded that God could use me in my brokenness. I had to change what I was listening to and change what I was speaking over myself and my situation. I needed to build some faith. I changed what I was listening to and it changed what was coming out of my mouth. I began playing some of those songs on repeat and began to believe what they said about me, about God and about His love for me. My situation changed and so did my mentality going forward.

"Jesus loves me, this I know."

"Yes, Jesus loves me."

Sometimes we need to sing those simple songs again, just as a reminder.

~Shiney

June 15 ~ Psalms 134,146-150
"Blessed are those whose help is the God of Jacob,
whose hope is in the Lord their God." Psalm 146:5 (NIV)

Every four years, there is an election for the presidency in the United States.

No doubt, during that time, your news feed is infiltrated with posts that include criticisms and praises of the election and the candidates. It would take months before we could enjoy pictures of our friends on social media again without being interrupted by political banter.

How did we get past all the noise during this time? It seemed like we were consumed by the election. There are three things we realized we needed to do.

Vote - it is both a privilege and a responsibility. Your vote counts. Find out where a voting station is in your area and cast your ballot.

Pray - Your prayers count. Do you remember what Nehemiah did as soon as he heard that the walls of his hometown, Jerusalem, had broken down? The Bible says that for some days he mourned, fasted and prayed. (Nehemiah 1)

What happened? God opened a door for him to return to his homeland and repair a wall so that the city would be kept safe from enemy attack.

Jonah is inside the belly of a big fish (that still amazes me sometimes) and what does he do? He prays. God saves his life and he was able to minister to a people that had turned against their creator.

Trust - Our trust is in the Lord our God. That should not change during an election year.

Let's pray that God will use our president and our local leaders to lead this country in His ways. Your prayers matter to God.

Would you commit to praying for your country and its government officials? God has moved the hearts of people and leaders in the past, and we serve the same God today. He never changes.

"Troubles surround me, chaos abounding. My soul will rest in You ..."[1]
(Lyrics from "Always" by Kristian Stanfill)

~Elizabeth

June 16 ~ 1 Kings 9, 2 Chronicles 8
"... I have heard the prayer and plea you have made before
more; I have consecrated this temple, which you have built,
by putting my Name there forever..." 1 Kings 9:3 (NIV)

I am a football fan. From September to February each year, much of my week centers around games being played and scores or highlights of said games. We celebrate the Super Bowl as though it's a national holiday.

The 2017 Super Bowl consisted of the Atlanta Falcons playing the New England Patriots. As a non-Patriots fan, I sat and watched with glee as the Falcons outplayed the Patriots in the first half. I was ecstatic. The Patriots were down 28-3 at the end of the second quarter. We went into halftime thinking that the game was over. OVER. No team in history had ever come back from a deficit that great.

No team until this Patriots team. The Falcons did not score again in the second half of the game, and the Patriots went on to win.

Later that year, when the New England Patriots unveiled their new Superbowl rings, they did something unique to commemorate this game. The ring was rumored to have 283 diamonds to remember the 28-3 deficit which they overcame.

In this reading, Solomon completes the temple which is built on the threshing floor of Araunah. This place has significance because of Solomon's father, David. Due to David's disobedience, a plague was sent on the land. The angel of God who was spreading death was at the threshing floor of Araunah when David saw him (2 Samuel 24). The angel relents and David wants to build an altar there - at the spot where death was being spread. David purchases the land and Solomon uses it later as the place for the temple.

We don't like to commemorate our 'threshing floors'- the places in our lives of pressing, crushing, pain, or sacrifice. These are often the memories that we would like to forget. However, it's usually at your threshing floor where you have a life-changing moment with God. It's usually from these moments that we mount our greatest comebacks.

Solomon built an altar here. The Patriots designed their ring around it. Honor your comeback. Commemorate your story. When you look back months or years from now, you will be able to distinguish this time and the path that it carved out for you. You may not be able to see God in that moment, but as you look back, you will see His presence all over it.

~Shiney

June 17 ~ Proverbs 25-26
"Like an earring of gold or an ornament of fine gold is the rebuke of a wise judge to a listening ear." Proverbs 25:12 (NIV)

I was lying flat on my OB-GYN's exam table when I noticed the sign taped up on the ceiling that read, "I HATE THIS!"

I chuckled as I read the words that most women feel but are afraid to voice aloud when they're about to be examined. Fortunately for me, it was only a quick "measure-my-belly" pregnancy visit that day.

It's the same sentiment I feel when I make that routine visit to the salon.

I wish I could say I'm going there for highlights or a facial, but when I climb onto her chair, I know I'm in for a literal tear-jerker as the sweet lady threads my face.

Not a visit I look forward to, but trust me, it's a necessity.

Recently, I was going through a rough time, feeling alone and overwhelmed. At the time I didn't realize it, but I was putting more expectations on the people around me, but as for me?

I was doing everything just fine. Or so I thought. It took a bit of counseling for me to realize that I had things mixed up. I had a counseling session with my Father. Recently, I was reminded that the Holy Spirit is our Counselor.

After Jesus left the earth, the Holy Spirit came to reside in the hearts of the believers and took the role of our Comforter and Counselor.

When you think of a counselor, you think of a person who will listen for long periods and then, will impart wisdom. I can tell you that I vented to God, and He listened to me. He also convicted me, and I needed that to move forward and ask for forgiveness.

We all go through situations where we want to throw up our hands and say, "I hate this!" I get it. Sometimes, we need to seek counseling from a licensed professional, depending on our experiences. Trained counselors can help us in ways friends cannot. That is okay, too.

Just know that you can trust your Father, who has sent the Holy Spirit to bring complete healing and conviction to your soul. Trust him with your deepest thoughts and longings, and start talking to Him.

Watch the healing begin.

~Elizabeth

June 18 ~ Proverbs 27-29
*"As a face is reflected in water, so the heart reflects
the real person." Proverbs 27:19 (NLT)*

I have found myself in unchartered territory lately: enjoying time for a hot shower, to style my hair, apply my makeup, AND coordinate a pretty outfit.

Perhaps it's not the riveting answer one may have imagined. But allow me to explain.

Since I became a mom, having time for myself became a thing of the past. It's just one of the perks of early motherhood and besides, it's not a permanent situation. Or so I thought.

When faced with the unexpected and for an extended period, caring for myself literally sank to the bottom of my to-do list. T-shirts and sweats became my go-to outfits pretty much everywhere I went. Anything nicer would have required time and energy I didn't have. And you know what? I didn't care.

My primary focus was on my children's health and keeping myself afloat while shuffling to appointments, making mad dashes to the hospital, and keeping track of all the medical history. I just wanted to be comfortable, I told myself.

The truth is I wasn't happy. I was saddened by how much life had changed, how I tired I was, and how I had no control over what happened.

Then one day, I observed my friend whose child was quite ill. In the midst of the frenzy of packing for the hospital and making arrangements for the children at home, my friend was dressed beautifully, accessorized, and putting her makeup on. I stood shocked and I asked her about it.

Her response was advice once given to her: dress yourself to look like how you want to feel, even if you don't feel like much at the moment. Besides, she said her girls were watching her and she wanted to set an example to them of how to carry yourself in spite of the circumstances. How inspiring!

I felt convicted and challenged by what she shared. God impressed upon my heart that this is about being a reflection of His beauty. I have to walk in confidence that God is my strength. I must be rooted in His abundant joy.

Whatever circumstances you may find yourself in, I pray that God's love, peace, and joy would flow from your heart causing your appearance to radiate with His light.

~Joyce

June 19 ~ Ecclesiastes 1-6
"There is a time for everything, and a season for every activity under the heavens:"
Ecclesiastes 3:1 (NIV)

Dirty diapers. Frequent feedings. Sleepless nights. When preparing for parenthood, does anyone mention how exhausting it is? I honestly felt as if I was a walking zombie during those times while lugging around half of my house in a diaper bag to appointments and shopping. When covered in spit up and listening to incessant crying, my weariness would make me wish for the next stage of childhood when things would be "easier".

It's funny though because as much as I struggled during those early years, I find myself now thinking those days were a walk in the park! Dealing with choices that children make as pre-teens and teenagers, along with their "lovely" attitudes, I feel as if gray hairs have been sprouting like weeds. My days are now filled with discussions about foolish versus wise decision making and attitude adjustments.

What I wouldn't do to sterilize some bottles right now! My parental responsibilities seemed much simpler when my children were babies. But who am I kidding? Every season of parenting has its own challenges, so I need to quit despising the present one I'm in.

When I think about my kids as babies, their precious smiles, first words, and meeting their milestones brightened my days instantaneously. Likewise, as I reflect on my children in their adolescent years and their love for God and others, I am left in awe.

Whatever season we find ourselves in, the temptation is to focus on the challenges and struggles rather than the joys and gladness we experience. The reality is that while we may feel exhausted, it's not permanent.

Before we know it, this season will pass and we'll be in the next one. So, we can either wish away each stage we're in, missing out on the blessings before us or we can enjoy each moment with hearts full of gratitude for each blessing.

Ecclesiastes 3:11 (NIV) (my favorite!) reminds us that *"He has made everything beautiful in its time."*

Wherever you find yourself today, choose joy for the present moment through the good, bad, and ugly. Next season will have its own good, bad, and ugly so may our hearts be filled with praise today and see His beauty all around us. Today is a gift.

~Joyce

June 20 ~ Ecclesiastes 7-12
"Do not be hasty in your spirit to be angry, for
anger rests in the bosom of fools."
Ecclesiastes 7:9 (NHEB)

"It's your turn! I washed the last set of dishes!"

If I had a dollar every time I heard my boys make that statement to one another!

My kids are great, but they are kids ... and sometimes they forget. Not only is the roof over their head at no cost to them, so are their meals and every other living expense you can think of. Why are they keeping track of a few dirty dishes?

Even the best of us have a tendency to keep track of things we shouldn't be keeping track of.

In Matthew 18:21-35, Jesus tells a story of a king who wanted to settle accounts with his servants.

A man who owed the king millions of dollars was brought before him. The servant pleaded with him and the king had pity on him and cancelled his debt. Then, this same servant went out and found one of his fellow servants who owed him just a few dollars. He grabbed him, choked him and insisted he pay him. That servant pleaded with him but instead of being merciful like the king was to him, he threw him in prison until he could pay back his debt. The king was furious when he heard this and turned him over to the jailers to be tortured until he could pay him all that he owed.

"That is how My Heavenly Father will treat each of you unless you forgive your brother from your heart." (Matthew 18:35 BSB)

Jesus didn't mince words.

Forgiving others isn't easy, but Jesus knew keeping a record of wrongs can imprison you ... physically, emotionally and spiritually. In fact, medical research has found that unresolved conflict may be negatively affecting your heart rate, blood pressure and immune response.

On the flip side, resolved conflict (forgiving others) can help your body heal.

In Ecclesiastes 7:9, Solomon states, *"Do not be hasty in your spirit to be angry, for anger rests in the bosom of fools." (NHEB)*

Solomon understood - it is the foolish who harbor anger and refuse to let it go.

So, whether it's the annoyance because of dirty dishes left in the sink from this morning or the hurt of something much deeper from years ago ... for our own emotional, physical and spiritual well-being, let us ask the Lord for the strength to let things go.

~Binu

June 21 ~ 1 Kings 10-11, 2 Chronicles 9

"For when Solomon was old his wives turned away his heart after other gods, and his heart was not wholly true to the Lord his God, as was the heart of David his father." 1 Kings 11:4 (ESV)

We hear it too often.

A moral failure. Another pastor resigns.

That isn't just a 21st century problem. It was an Old Testament problem too.

Solomon started out so strong. He had the legacy of David in his veins. When given the opportunity for riches or long life, he instead asked God for wisdom. He built the temple of God for the people of God. People everywhere admired him. He lived well. He led well.

And then he fell.

God warned Solomon that these foreign women he was marrying would be the beginning of the end for him. As wise as he was, he ignored the voice of God and what he knew was right. Instead, he *"clung to these in love." (1 Kings 11:2b ESV)* Then, things unraveled, just as God said it would.

"For when Solomon was old his wives turned away his heart after other gods, and his heart was not wholly true to the Lord his God, as was the heart of David his father." (1 Kings 11:4 ESV)

For many of us who live in Western society, the concept of idols is far removed from us. However, I have visited friends' homes who practice other religions and seen their "god" in their living room.

It's easy to say, *"Well, I've never worshipped other gods. I should be okay."* But not all "gods" have to look like idols.

Anything we cling to more than God will eventually turn our heart away from Him.

Maybe it's a person or a career. It could be something intangible like greed or fame. Even seemingly innocent things like comfort or wanting to be accepted can stop us from being wholly devoted to God.

What is it for you?

If you have found yourself in a place similar to Solomon, where the God you once served is no longer the God you serve now, it isn't too late. Even though your heart has turned, His heart hasn't.

As a wise man once said, *"Trust in the Lord with all your heart, and do not lean on your own understanding. In all your ways acknowledge him, and he will make straight your paths." (Proverbs 3:5-6 ESV)*

If only Solomon had followed his own counsel.

~Anu

June 22 ~ Proverbs 30-31
"When she speaks her words are wise, and she gives instruction with kindness." Proverbs 31:26 (NLT)

The woman described in Proverbs 31 sounds like a rockstar. She is smart, industrious, financially savvy, and honored by her husband and children. She dresses in fine clothes and extends her hands to the poor. She has no fear of the future and she laughs at the days to come.

What an amazing woman! She sounds like a woman I wish I could be.

With all her admirable qualities, something that stood out to me is that the scripture says *"When she speaks her words are wise, and she gives instruction with kindness." (Proverbs 31:26 NLT)*

Kindness.

In today's world, kindness seems like a lost art.

The dictionary defines kindness as the *quality or state of being gentle, caring, and helpful; considerate [of others].*[1]

Sometimes instruction or correction can be hard to take from someone. If we are on the giving end of instruction to someone, say our children, we might be inclined to bark orders at them, or feel that because we have the authority over them, that we can say whatever we want.

But what if we could do this with kindness? Can we share what we need to say with gentleness and consideration of the person we are speaking to? Can we take into consideration their feelings without being hurtful and unkind?

John Gottman, world renowned psychologist and researcher, says kindness is the key to lasting relationships. Kindness makes people turn towards each other in a way that connects them. It makes them feel like we care enough that we consider their feelings and interests.[2]

Whatever role we play in life, whether a wife, mother, sister, or friend, we can always give instruction or correction with kindness. It doesn't take much on our part, but it could mean a world of difference to the person on the other end. I hope that our kindness can be the catalyst to making a just *okay* relationship into a *great* relationship.

~Vijoy

June 23 ~ I Kings 12-14

"I have been told by the word of the Lord: 'You must not eat bread or drink water there or return by the way you came.'" 1 Kings 13:17 (NIV)

Several years ago, I was invited to a ladies' night out with a group of women. This was not my usual crew; I knew several of the ladies but didn't know all of them. I was excited at the opportunity of getting to know some of them a little better.

After several weeks of planning, the night of our outing arrived. I arrived a little late and eager to join in and enjoy the evening. I had been there just a few minutes when one of the ladies made several comments indirectly directed towards me. They were innocent enough, but it made me realize that I was the outsider in this clique of friends. They spent every weekend together, and I was just a guest for this event. I tried to enjoy the rest of my evening, but in my mind, I kept replaying these comments over and over again, reminding myself of how I didn't belong.

But I did belong. I was invited to be there that evening just as much as those other women. My place at the table was just as important as anyone else's.

Insecurity is a sneaky weapon. It just takes one lie to cause self-doubt. The old prophet gave the man of God one lie that caused him to doubt his own word from God and eventually caused his death. If only he had held on to the truth that God had given him directly!

As women of God, we must hold fast to the word that God gives us. He has strategically placed us in spheres of influence and will equip us with what we need to accomplish His goals in these areas. He will even surround you with people who will speak into your life, but we must be careful who we listen to. Those outside voices can even seem louder than the voice of God. People around you will always be speaking, ready to give you their opinion, but we must discern which voices are in line with what God has already spoken to us. Allow God to confirm His message to you. Shut out the voices that are not in line with what God has told you. Let Him be your confidence and security.

~Shiney

June 24 ~ 2 Chronicles 10-12
"So the king did not listen to the people, for this turn of events was from God ..."
2 Chronicles 10:15 (NIV)

My boss for a few years was a woman I would call a servant leader. She directed our organization with high expectations and was firm, but was very compassionate.

I recall a meeting one afternoon in which someone confronted her about major changes that had been recently rolled out. It was a touchy subject that many were in disagreement with, and she was put on the spot. I held my breath for her response.

She gracefully answered the difficult question by acknowledging what information she knew, then reassured us that she was doing the best she could to prevent any significant impact to our organization.

I was impressed with how she dealt with the question on the table. Her facial expression was calm and she spoke kindly, with resolution.

Our reading today takes us to the palace of Rehoboam, King Solomon's son, who has taken over his father's kingdom. He is faced with a challenging situation in which the people are crying out for mercy. He needs to decide whether or not to continue the harsh labor that his father imposed on the people.

The young king turns to two groups of people for advice.

Older and wiser group: Be kind, please them, give the people a favorable answer. The reward: they will always be your servants

Younger peer group: Tell the people that their labor will be even heavier and the punishment harsher.

The Bible says that young King Rehoboam rejected the advice of older men even BEFORE he asked his friends their thoughts. Sounds like he already knew what he wanted to do.

When the people came to realize that their cry for help fell on deaf ears, they revolted. It was at this time that Israel was divided into two: Kingdom of Judah and Kingdom of Israel. His unjust ruling lead to division.

At the end of his life, the Bible says of Rehoboam that God was not important to him; his heart neither cared for nor sought after God.

There is something attractive about kindness. When you are in a leadership role, and you display an attitude of confidence mixed in kindness, you've got yourself some willing followers.

Regardless of your personality type, compassion will not cost you anything. The grace that exudes will make you a more powerful and effective leader and will draw people into unity.

~Elizabeth

June 25 ~ 1 Kings 15, 2 Chronicles 13-16
"... be strong and do not give up, for your work will be rewarded." 2 Chronicles 15:7 (NIV)

My family and I enjoy going on road trips across the United States. Being entrusted with the joy of packing our family's belongings for our trips, I have mastered the craft of folding and packaging so that everything we need fits ... somehow. So, imagine my dilemma when my children received beautiful, yet bulky gifts from friends for us to take home. What's a girl to do??

The task seemed insurmountable. I tried rearrangements in each piece of luggage. No luck. Each attempt left me with a pile of clothes that still needed to go somewhere. What if I opened the gifts and packaged the toys alone? Maybe I should ship the gifts instead? Neither were viable options. As far as I was concerned, this became mission impossible.

I voiced my worries to my husband. He expressed his vote of confidence in me that I would be able to pack it somehow. His comment empowered me. So, I decided to put the gifts aside temporarily and just start packing. Before I knew it, everything was in its place and then, voila! I realized I could stack some things on top of each other and fit the gifts in after all. What a relief!

When King Asa began his rule of Judah in 2 Chronicles 14, he was faced with quite an undertaking. Removing pagan altars. Commanding the people to seek the Lord. Building up the city so it is fortified. Fighting enemies. Keeping the peace. Where does one begin? How does one get it all done?

We find the answer in verse 11 (NIV) when he called on God and said, *"Lord, there is no one like You to help ... Help us, O Lord our God, for you we rely on you"*. Then, we see how King Asa was encouraged by the words from the Spirit of God. The rest of this chapter reveals how he was courageous and accomplished every task set before him.

What impossible assignment is on your plate today? Take heart, my friend, because His Word assures us that "With God all things are possible." You can accomplish your tasks by:

- Asking God for help.
- Trusting in Him.
- Being still to hear God's voice.
- Being empowered by His truth and strengthened to make it mission possible.

~Joyce

June 26 ~ 1 Kings 16, 2 Chronicles 17
"The Lord was with Jehoshaphat, because he walked
in the earlier ways of his father David ..."
2 Chronicles 17:3 (ESV)

Plato said, *"The measure of a man is what he does with power."*

In these particular chapters, we read about men who were given the highest position in all of the land - they were kings.

In 1 Kings 16, it lists some of the evil kings of Israel. Men who led the people of God astray. Men who committed murder, caused chaos and concocted altars for idols. Men who used their power for harm instead of good.

In 2 Chronicles 17, the story is told of Jehoshaphat who was also a king, but reigned in Judah. He was not perfect but his reign was very different from the other kings. He used his power for good.

Jehoshaphat strengthened the land of Judah and avoided following after idols, *"but sought the God of his father and walked in his commandments...". (vs 4 ESV)* He also appointed officials and Levites to teach the people the Book of the Law.

And the result was peace.

"And the fear of the Lord fell upon all the kingdoms of the lands that were around Judah, and they made no war against Jehoshaphat." (2 Chronicles 17:10 ESV)

A woman (or man) who knows how to handle power benefits herself and the people around her.

Back in 2nd grade, we were "forced" to take a 20-minute nap at our desk. During that time, my teacher would assign someone to stand at the front of the class to make sure everyone kept their heads down. One day, I was given that assignment.

I wasn't sure what I was going to do if someone dared raised their head but I did know for those 20 minutes, I was in charge. It was my first taste of power ... and I liked it.

Now, that I am a supervisor in my department, what I've come to understand is how I can use that power to affect the environment of the people I lead. I can create chaos like the evil kings or help foster an atmosphere of peace like Jehoshaphat instead.

We all have power as a mom, wife, career woman or leader in the corporate world or ministry. Use it wisely. Keep your heart turned towards God and allow Him to use you to accomplish His good work.

~Anu

June 27 ~ 1 Kings 17-19
*"For the jar of flour was not used up and the jug of
oil did not run dry ..." 1 Kings 17:16a (NIV)*

Think back to your old school days. Did a teacher ever use your test paper as a positive example in front of the class? If so, did you light up inside? I know I did.

In Mark chapter 12, Jesus was sitting in the temple opposite to the offering box. He watched as the rich threw in large amounts of money to the temple treasury, but what caught His attention was an unassuming widow who gave two small copper coins. She was the prized student. Jesus told the crowd, *"They all gave out of their wealth; but she, out of her poverty, put in everything - all she had to live on." (Mark 12:44 NIV)*

It's a recurring theme we see throughout scripture: less is more.

Another widow, this time in the Old Testament, gave the little oil she had left to make a meal for the prophet Elijah. She did as God commanded and guess what happened next? In a time of famine, *"... the jar of flour was not used up and the jug of oil did not run dry." (1 Kings 17:16a NIV)*

Jesus fed four thousand with seven loaves and a few small fish, but fed five thousand with five loaves and two fish. He fed more with less.

Perhaps you feel as if you have nothing to offer God. No talents, no gifts. I bet you have two coins. I bet you have a couple drops of oil. It's okay if it's not much. God seems to do quite well with less.

Your assignment: Search deep in your pockets, deep in your pantry, deep in your heart. God will show you something, something you can give to Him. Give Him what you have and His Word reveals, He will multiply it.

We aren't told much more about the widow who Jesus saw in the temple that day. Maybe she walked out of the temple and found two more coins in her pocket (or knowing God, maybe she found four more coins). Either way, I am certain, God took care of her every need. I also believe she left the temple that day, the same way I would leave class, with her countenance lifted inside.

Do you think you have nothing to offer God? Think again. God specializes in empty pockets and empty vessels.

~Binu

"'Have you noticed how Ahab has humbled himself before me? Because he has humbled himself, I will not bring this disaster in his day..." 1 Kings 21:29 (NIV)

Turning points. We have all had them at various stages in our lives - in our marriages, in our careers, in our personal thoughts. The funny thing about turning points is that you may not know that you were in one until it's over.

A close friend of mine has been struggling with infertility. After 2 years of a painful struggle, she was blessed with a beautiful baby boy. She desperately wants to have another one and has begun the stages of treatment again. The emotional rollercoaster has been trying for her. Even now, in the early stages, she has already experienced high hopes and low disappointments.

She asked me point blank one day, *"Do you think that I should do this again?"* She was standing at a turning point in her life and needed some support. After a long pause, I reinforced the behavior that I knew she had been doing already. I told her to continue to pray about it and seek God's direction. No matter what she chose, as long as she was seeking God in it, she would not be disappointed.

Ahab found himself in negotiations with a maniacal warrior, and he knew very clearly that his victory was coming from God. As God was handing him his second victory over the same enemy, Ahab faced a turning point. He could have killed Ben-Hadad's men and demonstrated God's might. Instead, he went his own way and decided to make a treaty and set King Ben-Hadad free.

Brother or not, this man attacked Ahab twice - what would make him stop short of trying a third time? It seems foolish to strike a treaty with such a crazy ruler. I wonder what the rest of Ahab's reign would have been like had he listened to the prophet and completed the battle as God had directed.

Later, when Ahab humbled himself and mourned over his punishment for obtaining Naboth's vineyard, God changes his mind and spares Ahab's life. God clearly had a heart for the king of Israel and was waiting patiently for Ahab to turn to him.

God has a heart for each one of us, and he is waiting patiently as we stand in our turning point. He is waiting for us to turn to Him and seek His plan and presence in our lives.

~Shiney

June 29 ~ 1 Kings 22, 2 Chronicles 18
"An Aramean soldier, however, randomly shot an arrow at the Israelite troops and hit the king of Israel between the joints of his armor..." 1 Kings 22:34 (NLT)

Does it sometimes seem like evil prevails while good people get the short end of the stick? Although it may appear so at times, God watches over all and when the time is right, evil is always punished.

In the scripture we see this so clearly in the life of King Ahab. Ahab was one of the evil kings of Israel. His wife Jezebel was even more wicked than him. She influenced Ahab to bring pagan worship and idolatry to Israel. She also wasn't afraid to kill anyone who stood in her way.

Ahab longed for a piece of land near his palace to plant a garden for himself. The land belonged to a man named Naboth who refused to sell, no matter what the price. You see, Naboth's land was an inheritance from his family and it was clearly not for sale.

Jezebel stepped in and devised a plan to have people lie about Naboth, and eventually have him killed. Once Naboth was murdered, Jezebel gave Naboth's land to Ahab. God was so grieved by this injustice, that He sent Elijah to give Ahab a strong warning of what was to come.

Fast forward several years. God had not forgotten and He was about to act.

King Ahab convinces King Jehoshaphat of Judah to make an alliance with him and to go to war with him against Ramoth-Gilead. In this battle, Ahab decides he wants to trick the enemy into thinking he is just a common soldier and not the King of Israel by not wearing his royal wardrobe.

Then, it happened. An Aramean soldier *randomly* shoots his arrow towards the troops of Israel and hits King Ahab between the joints of his armor. This injury mortally wounds Ahab, who dies by the end of that day.

Ahab tried to escape God's judgement by disguising himself on the battlefield. But God directed a *random* arrow to hit the mark.

This story reminds me ... there is no randomness with God. Although we live in a world filled with sin and evil, God always prevails.

Whatever you're walking through today, I pray you find peace and comfort in knowing your life is in the hands of the Almighty God. He knows and sees all.

~Vijoy

June 30 ~ 2 Chronicles 19-23
"You will not need to fight in this battle. Stand firm, hold your position, and see the salvation of the Lord on your behalf..." 2 Chronicles 20:17 (ESV)

Life can be stressful. Most days, we can roll with the punches. Other days, not so much.

Recently, I woke up feeling like there was a weight on my chest. I had been dealing with a particular situation and it was beginning to consume me. I had done everything I could. I talked to the people involved. I was respectful but firm. I had been gracious. Now, my heart and mind were heavy.

There are some battles we were meant to engage in. We can't just stand still...we have to walk through the parted Red Sea. We can't just hide in the camp...we have to run towards our giant with the stones in our hand.

But every now and then, we see this: *"You will not need to fight in this battle. Stand firm, hold your position, and see the salvation of the Lord on your behalf, O Judah and Jerusalem. Do not be afraid and do not be dismayed. Tomorrow go out against them, and the Lord will be with you." (2 Chronicles 20:17 ESV)*

This time, they didn't have to fight. This time, they simply stood firm and watched God move. I finally realized that this was one of those situations for me. I had done all I could do. I couldn't change the people or the situation... but God could. And He could change me too.

I'm not going to tell you that I immediately felt better because that was not the case. Releasing it to God for me was a process. Thankfully, the more I kept praying and simply recalling who God is, the better it got. The next day, I encountered the same situation but I wasn't the same. My heart wasn't heavy – the burden wasn't there but God's peace was.

We serve a God who specializes in freedom. Freedom from our sins. Freedom from our heaviness. Freedom from carrying our burdens alone.

Stand firm and see what God will do.

~Anu

*"The day of the Lord is near for all nations. As
you have done, it will be done to you;
your deeds will return upon your own head." Obadiah 1:15 (NIV)*

"Mommy, have you ever lied?"

I cringed. I tried to avoid answering, but not giving my son an honest answer would make me a hypocrite.

"Yes, I have..." How difficult to admit wrongdoing to our very own children! Yet, how teachable those moments can be.

One of my earliest memories of receiving a consequence for my actions was when I was on the ride home after school with my dad one day. He had just picked me up from my friend's home and he heard the sound of coins in my hand. When he found out I had taken the coins from my friend's pencil box, he turned the car around and made me walk up to her home and apologize.

How tall her father seemed to me that day as I stood and admitted my fault! I was ashamed.

The Bible says, *"Godly sorrow brings repentance that leads to salvation and leaves no regret, but worldly sorrow brings death." (2 Corinthians 7:10 NIV)*

That memory has stuck with me as a reminder that because I realized my wrongdoing, it brought shame, which led to repentance.

Obadiah, a prophet bold enough to hide 100 other prophets in a cave from the evil tactics of Queen Jezebel, was chosen to call out the nation of Edom.

Edom was hostile to Israel and their pride would eventually lead to their destruction. Edom is actually another name for Esau and Israel was the name given to Jacob. This ancient nation was committing violent crimes to his brother nation.

Obadiah reminded its people, *"The day of the Lord is near for all nations ... your deeds will return on your own head." (Obadiah 1:15 NIV)*

Wow. Talk about justice. We serve a God of mercy ... and justice. God will defend the cause of the weak, and will not allow wickedness to prevail. Praise God for that, because without His justice, this world would be chaotic.

Yet, we also praise God for the sorrow that will lead us to have a change of heart. We all mess up but thankfully have the opportunity to receive forgiveness from our Father. There's no need to live in condemnation.

I received the due consequences from my father the day I was found out, but I also learned the valuable lesson of not taking what doesn't belong to me.

Is there a lesson God is teaching you through a similar experience? Don't be overtaken by guilt and shame. Let God's forgiveness wash over you. Know that you get to start fresh and walk in the abundant life He promises you today.

~Elizabeth

July 2 ~ 2 Kings 1-4
"... Your servant has nothing here at all ... except a small jar of olive oil." 2 Kings 4:2b (NIV)

Do you ever feel like your circumstances have IMPOSSIBLE written all over them?

That's how my husband and I felt when we decided to move from New York to Texas. Although my husband had a great resume, not one company in Texas expressed an interest in him as long as the address was from New York. So began the process of praying, applying, and waiting ... repeat ... for TWO years.

Fear and doubt began to rear their ugly heads: Did we hear God correctly? Were we really supposed to leave our family, our friends, and all that was familiar to us? How were we supposed to move across the country without a job secured?

Suddenly, the whole idea just seemed impossible. However, we decided, *"Do or die, we're going to believe that God will make a way and start packing."*

The book of 2 Kings shows us someone who may have felt that way, too. In Chapter 4 from verses 1 through 7, we read about the widow who not only lost her husband but was also facing poverty and the prospect of her sons being taken as slaves by a creditor. I can only imagine how embarrassing it must have been for this widow to share this situation with the prophet Elisha and then, admit that she had nothing "except a little oil."

To add insult to injury, she was instructed to go ask neighbors for jars. But it's clear she was desperate and she did as she was told. Her *willingness to put her pride aside*, to be *transparent*, and to *trust* Elisha's word took her situation from the impossible to POSSIBLE. These verses show us the miracle of every jar she had being filled with oil, so she could sell it to repay the debts and still have enough for her family to live on what was left.

After the time span I mentioned earlier, my husband was called into the office by his employer and given a promotion. Instead of simply accepting it, my husband was empowered by the Holy Spirit to step out of his comfort zone and openly share our desire to move to Texas. Then, he proceeded to boldly request permission to work remotely. Glory be to God; his employer granted his request and that job was the bridge which finally brought us from New York to Texas!

~Joyce

July 3 ~ 2 Kings 5-8
"But Naaman went away angry and said, 'I thought that he would surely come out to me and stand and call on the name of the Lord his God, wave his hand over the spot and cure me of my leprosy.'"
2 Kings 5:11 (NIV)

Appam, chicken curry and a cup of tea. Now that's my kind of comfort food.

For those readers who are not familiar with South Indian cuisine, let me explain.

Appam is a type of pancake made with fermented rice batter and coconut milk. Its light sweet flavor goes perfect with spicy chicken curry and a cup of sweet hot Indian tea. This meal puts me in my happy place.

Making appam isn't a quick process. It involves soaking uncooked rice, pureeing that rice, adding a little bit of yeast to that rice and then waiting for the yeast to do its thing.

Like most good things in life, there is no shortcut. You must submit to the process in order to get what your heart and stomach desire.

2 Kings 5 tells the story of the army commander, Naaman who suffered from leprosy. Naaman sought God's prophet for healing and was instructed by the prophet Elisha to go and dip in the Jordan river seven times to receive his healing.

"But Naaman went away angry and said, 'I thought that he would surely come out to me and stand and call on the name of the Lord his God, wave his hand over the spot and cure me of my leprosy.'" (2 Kings 5:11 NIV)

Can you blame Naaman for his negative response?

Sure, his healing was coming but imagine the pain he would experience as his open wounds are exposed to the Jordan River? Naaman had heard about Elisha's God. Naaman knew God could do anything, instantly. Why the process? And the painful process at that.

Because God said so.

It was a process of obedience. A process of discomfort. A process of perseverance. So much of what God is asking of me lately also involves a process. And I am not just talking about my appam craving.

I am referring to deeper dreams and desires which require that I too submit to the process. God's process. On His terms, *not mine.*

Do you have a dream, goal or desire that you are waiting on God for? Maybe you feel as if you are on your sixth painful dip into the Jordan River, open wounds and all.

Be faithful to the process. Be faithful to the creator of the process.

Your dreams are worth it!

~Binu

July 4 ~ 2 Kings 9-11
"As for Jezebel, dogs will devour her on the plot of ground at Jezreel ..." 2 Kings 9:10a (NIV)

In reading through the Old Testament, I'm reminded that God's plans take time. His stories are often years in the making.

The story of Naboth, Jehu and Jezebel proves this to be true.

In 2 Kings 9 and 10, a man by the name of Jehu was 'sitting around' with his fellow army officers when a prophet, sent by Elisha, arrived to the scene. The prophet pulled Jehu aside, poured oil on his head and anointed him as king over the Lord's people.

He then gave Jehu his assignment: destroy the house of Ahab, your master. *"As for Jezebel, dogs will devour her on the plot of ground at Jezreel ..."* (2 Kings 9:10a NIV)

A few verses later, the Bible tells us Jehu drove his chariot like a madman in pursuit of overthrowing Joram, the current king of Israel (and son of King Ahab). Jehu drew his bow and shot Joram between the shoulders piercing his heart.

One down, one to go. Jehu is off to see the wicked Queen Jezebel.

When Jezebel heard Jehu was coming, she fixed her hair, applied her eye makeup and looked out her window. Upon Jehu's request, two eunuchs threw her off the balcony, and dogs devoured her flesh.

In chapter 10 there is even more bloodshed. It leaves your stomach queasy and your head spinning.

What's the point? Was all this bloodshed even necessary?

Keep in mind, these events didn't just happen, this story was over ten years in the making. Turn the pages of your Bible back a bit and you'll see.

In 1 Kings 21, an incident had occurred involving a vineyard belonging to a man named Naboth. King Ahab wanted to purchase his land but Naboth declined his offer. Queen Jezebel wasn't used to hearing the word 'no,' so she had Naboth murdered. After the death of innocent Naboth, Elijah prophesied disaster upon King Ahab.

Now, more than ten years and several chapters later, Elijah's prophecy is fulfilled. Justice is served. Finally, more than ten years later, it's all starting to make sense.

Maybe you're reading this today and life doesn't make sense. Be patient with God and with life. This isn't your life's final chapter. It may take time but as Romans 8:28 reminds us, God will work out all things for your good when you choose to love Him.

~Binu

July 5 ~ 2 Kings 12-13, 2 Chronicles 24

"Then the Spirit of God clothed Zechariah the son of Jehoiada the priest, and he stood above the people, and said to them, 'Thus says God, 'Why do you break the commandments of the Lord, so that you cannot prosper? Because you have forsaken the Lord, he has forsaken you.'" 2 Chronicles 24:20 (ESV)

Have you ever listened in on an accountability conversation between women? There may be exceptions but here's what I've heard...

"Oh girl, you deserve that ice cream after what you've been through this week!"

"Of course, you are too tired to work out! You work all day so you don't have the energy to do it."

"I'm sorry to hear that you've missed your quiet time all week. It's okay. God knows your heart."

Women tend to be nurturers so it is outside of our nature to hurt someone's feelings, even when we are trying to help them. Having hard conversations is hard.

In the assigned readings today, we come across various conversations that could be labeled as hard.

Jehoash, the king and Jehoiada, the priest seemed to have that type of relationship. Whatever Jehoiada was saying, Jehoash listened and followed through with it. But it was just a matter of time before the roles were reversed in a particular situation. This time, Jehoiada heeded the king's command and implemented a new system for the temple repairs.

Sounds good so far. Iron sharpening iron.

Once Jehoiada dies, his son Zechariah steps in as an advisor to Jehoash. Unfortunately, Jehoash doesn't take too kindly to Zechariah's words and has him killed.

Why Jehoash chose to listen to Jehoiada and not Zechariah, we don't know. But the fact is that both spoke the truth into his life but he decided who he wanted to listen to.

We are called to be discerning. Not everything that is said to us is necessarily right or true. However, we can't dismiss the message because of the messenger, especially when that person has a particular place in our lives. The first year of our marriage, my husband's biggest frustration was that I would take advice from other people even though he had been telling me the same thing.

In the book, The Daniel Dilemma, Chris Hodges said this:

"Truth without grace is mean. Grace without truth is meaningless. Truth and grace together are good medicine."[1]

It's great to have an accountability relationship as long as we are actually keeping each other accountable. Give instruction in love and receive it with an open heart and mind. You will both be better for it.

~Anu

July 6 ~ 2 Kings 14, 2 Chronicles 25
"Amaziah did what was pleasing in the Lord's sight, but not wholeheartedly." 2 Chronicles 25:2 (NLT)

The story of the Old Testament shows me one thing. People are disloyal, self-seeking, and filled with envy and pride but God is always faithful.

God is faithful to His word. He is faithful to His covenant with Abraham. No matter how ugly the story gets, God does not waiver in keeping His covenant with us.

In 2 Kings, we read the story of King Amaziah of Judah and King Jehoash in Israel.

Amaziah follows God's commands *partially*. He neglected to destroy the pagan shrines, and still allowed people to offer sacrifices and continue pagan worship in Judah. He conquered many of the enemies of Judah, but then these victories get to his head.

Amaziah's pride leads him to challenge King Jehoash of Israel to come and fight him. King Jehoash tells him that he should just stay where he is at or he will be crushed. Instead of heeding the warning, Amaziah fights the King of Israel and is utterly defeated.

Amaziah's defeat allows Israel to destroy 600 feet of Jerusalem's wall, carry off all the gold, silver and articles from the temple, plunder treasure from the royal palace and even take hostages back to Samaria.

King Amaziah's life eventually ends as part of an assassination plot by his enemies.

Even so, God's faithfulness continues as Amaziah's son, Uzziah, was crowned king after the death of his father. Under Uzziah's reign Jerusalem's wall was reconstructed, towers were built, and the nation was generally prosperous as Uzziah sought to follow the Lord's commands.

The story of Judah and Israel is a continued cycle of faithfulness and unfaithfulness on the part of God's people. Through it all, God's promise to them never wavered. He always remained faithful to the covenant He made with Abraham, even when His people were unfaithful.

God's promise for us doesn't change even when we do. The life He promises us through the death of His son is always available if we will receive it.

My friend, I pray you will know that even when you stumble, our God is always waiting to receive you back. He is always faithful.

~Vijoy

July 7 ~ Jonah 1-4
"To the roots of the mountains I sank down; the
earth beneath barred me in forever.
But you, Lord my God, brought my life up from the pit." Jonah 2:6 (NIV)

One important lesson my daughter learned this past Christmas was how to be grateful.

When she first opened the puzzle that we got her, she showed no excitement. In fact, she looked disappointed. My husband and I were thrilled at the opportunity to give her a puzzle that taught her the capitals of the 50 states.

Not so fascinating for a five-year-old. She was hoping for Barbie and a dollhouse.

After teaching her about gratefulness, we started putting the puzzle together and she realized how fun it could be. In fact, the puzzle made me a little smarter, too!

As our kids are growing, we have realized the need to teach them how to be thankful for what they have, instead of *expecting* something better every time.

On New Year's Eve, we came across a homeless gentleman requesting money. It was an opportunity, again, to show her how to be grateful for the things we do have. The gentleman happily received our gift and bid us a happy new year. We showed our daughter where we believed he had set up his home, and it was interesting to see her start to understand how other people live.

Jonah lived in a very different time, but he also had a lesson in how gracious our God is. He was swallowed by a big fish due to his disobedience to God, and out of God's awesome and miraculous grace, the big fish spit up Jonah onto dry land.

Jonah survived being swallowed by a fish. That is nothing short of amazing. I think I would be grateful each. day. of. my. life. after an encounter like *that*!

Jonah finally obeys God and speaks to the wicked people of Nineveh. Guess what happens? The Ninevites believed God and they turned from their evil ways! *"When God saw what they did ... he relented ..." (Jonah 1:3 NIV)*

Jonah's reaction was anger and displeasure that God would have compassion on the people of Nineveh. Wait ... didn't Jonah *just* experience an amazing and awesome miracle when he was spit out of the belly of a great fish?

Remember what a gracious God we serve - *El Channun (The Gracious God)*. When things don't go *your* way, remember our God is gracious. That is part of His nature.

May we be daily reminded of God's grace in our lives and never forget even the smallest of blessings.

~Elizabeth

July 8 ~ 2 Kings 15, 2 Chronicles 26
"... As long as he sought the Lord, God gave him success." 2 Chronicles 26:5 (NIV)

What are you known for?

Do you have a certain skill, like playing an instrument or a sport that people recognize you for? Are you an excellent public speaker that can engage an audience within minutes? Do you drive a noticeable car or have a prominent career?

One of the kings in our readings, Uzziah, was known for amassing a well-trained army and for having extensive farmlands. He built towers (in the desert!) and won wars. Wow - what a legacy he could leave behind!

As a result, He became famous and powerful. During this time, he sought God and followed the advice of Zechariah, who instructed him.

Yes, he was successful, but only AS LONG AS he sought God.

While he was enjoying success and fame, something started to creep in ... pride. This ultimately led to his downfall and the tarnishing of a legacy. His pride led him to enter the sanctuary to burn incense when not being qualified to do so. Instead of leaving a stellar legacy, he was later known for the leprosy he developed due to his disobedience. Not for his army, successes in war, or the majestic towers.

The story could have ended so differently had he continued to seek God throughout his achievements.

God does not desire that we live as unsuccessful paupers in the name of religion. No - we are called to do great and mighty things. It is okay to achieve fame and power, but not for our own glory. When we seek God and remain faithful to Him, whatever success we achieve is for His fame and renown.

So, what are you known for?

Take that talent and ability to a new level by seeking God daily. Seek counsel from godly men and women of God. God has positioned you in places where help is available to lift you up and point out areas that you may be weak in.

You may be confronted by people around you like Uzziah was when he was unfaithful. Seek God in those times too. Be grateful for those who care enough for our well-being that will only point us to success instead of failure.

May our hearts be eager to rise to the top with our giftings, and may God be glorified in our achievements.

~Elizabeth

July 9 ~ Isaiah 1-4
"If you are willing and obedient, you will eat the good things of the land; but if you resist and rebel, you will be devoured by the sword ..." Isaiah 1:19-20 (NIV)

As I was entering my teen years, I became consumed with anger. It began when we had moved and left all that was familiar. I became the new person in school while everyone else appeared to know each other and I felt alone. I was unhappy with my appearance and wanted to look different because I didn't think I was pretty.

All this anger ultimately led to rebellion. Suddenly, I felt I knew better than my parents. I didn't care for their rules and I wanted to do whatever I felt like doing. Sadly, I became disrespectful and began talking back to my parents. I heard a lot of foul language in school and I felt it was also alright for me to express myself using such words.

I can only imagine how hurt and infuriated my parents must have been with me. They had moved us to a new town because it had an excellent school system. All they desired was to give my siblings and me the best opportunities.

My decision to be rebellious wasn't ignored as I found myself being punished by my parents. It wasn't any fun having privileges removed. But as a foolish young person, I didn't learn from my mistakes quickly. I continued in this rebellion for a few years until I yielded to the prompts of the Holy Spirit and realized I was wrong. I repented of my poor behavior. As I began to improve how I spoke to my parents, I found that I could share my feelings and that we could actually have reasonable conversations.

The nation of Israel decided to sin and rebel against God. He was a loving Father Who had provided for all of their needs and helped them through each challenge. But they strayed from His ways and decided to do what was right in their own eyes. Like my parents, we read how God doesn't disown them as His children (even though the thought may have crossed their minds.)

Friend, we always have a choice in the decisions we make. We must understand that our choices yield either blessings or consequences. What will you decide?

~Joyce

July 10 ~ Isaiah 5-8
"In the year that King Uzziah died, I saw the Lord ..." Isaiah 6:1 (NIV)

What is it you see when the unexpected happens? Isaiah saw the Lord...and so did my brother-in-law, Lance.

Life changed for my family when my husband's parents were involved in a serious car accident.

About a month after the accident, Dad was still in the ICU, and mom was moved to a rehabilitation facility for more extensive physical therapy. During mom's rehab stay, I sent picture updates of mom and dad's progress to my sister and her husband. One picture in particular was that of mom with my two boys.

I loved Lance's response. *"Mom's pic made me smile, but seeing you guys thrive in the fire makes me smile more. I see an extra man in there with you."*

In case you are unfamiliar with the *"extra man,"* Daniel chapter 3 tells the story.

Three men, Shadrach, Meshach, and Abednego refused to bow to the god of King Nebuchadnezzar. Because of their refusal to bow, they were cast into a burning fiery furnace. Guess who showed up in the fire with them?

I'll let King Nebuchadnezzar tell you.

"Then Nebuchadnezzar the king was astonied, and rose up in haste, and spake, and said unto his counsellors, 'Did not we cast three men bound into the midst of the fire?' They answered and said unto the king, 'True, O king.' He answered and said, 'Lo, I see four men loose, walking in the midst of the fire, and they have no hurt; and the form of the fourth is like the Son of God.'" (Daniel 3:24, 25 KJV)

God showed up. He was the fourth man.

It isn't always easy to recognize the Lord in the midst of difficult circumstances, but I am grateful for God appointed people who see the Lord as Isaiah did ... and remind me to do the same.

"In the year that King Uzziah died, I saw the Lord...." (Isaiah 6:1 NIV)

~Binu

July 11 ~ Amos 1-5
"The words of Amos, one of the shepherds of Tekoa-
the vision he saw concerning Israel..."
Amos 1:1a (NIV)

Amos. As I read through the Bible, I feel an immediate connection with this minor prophet. He wasn't a priest; he wasn't a king. Amos was a shepherd and a fig farmer, a man with no high and mighty position of authority. He was a layman just like me and perhaps like you too. His book is found in the Old Testament.

"The words of Amos, one of the shepherds of Tekoa—the vision he saw concerning Israel." (Amos 1:1a NIV)

Amos was born and raised in Tekoa, a little town in Judah. Insignificant and unpopular, Tekoa literally means "camping ground." Nevertheless, God sought out this man from this insignificant city in the Southern Kingdom of Israel to deliver a powerful message to the Northern Kingdom of Israel. God gave Amos ears to hear the heart of God.

The book of Amos is a plea for justice regarding the oppressed as well as a warning that God will judge the apathy of the land. Imagine telling people today, *'The reason your gardens aren't growing isn't because you got a bad batch of miracle grow. It's because of you. God is trying to get your attention.'* In chapter four, Amos does just this. He reminds the people of the numerous chances God has given them to repent. God withheld rain from them, God struck their gardens, God sent plagues. Despite these multiple chances, the people failed to return to their God.

It wasn't an easy message to deliver, but Amos delivered it (and he didn't sugar coat his words). Remember, Amos wasn't a priest, Amos wasn't a king. Amos hardly even considered himself a prophet. He was an ordinary guy, willing and yielded to the Spirit of God.

I believe God desires to do the same through us.

Father, keep us aligned to Your Word and to Your Spirit. Like Amos, give us ears to hear your heart and the boldness to share your message.

~Binu

July 12 ~ Amos 6-9
*"Then he showed me another vision. I saw the Lord standing
beside a wall that had been built using a plumb line. He was
using a plumb line to see if it was still straight."*
Amos 7:7 (NLT)

In physical therapy school, we spent several lab sessions learning about posture. We learned techniques to evaluate and fix postural stresses. One particular day, we walked into our lab and there were several plumb lines dangling from the ceiling. The lines consisted of thick thread anchored at the bottom with a small weight. We divided up into groups of twos and took turns measuring ourselves against the line.

If my posture was textbook perfect, the line would pass through several anatomical landmarks simultaneously as I stood next to it. My earlobe, shoulder, hip, portions of my knee and ankle joints should align perfectly against the line. It served as a great visual reinforcement of what parts of my posture needed work. A slight adjustment of the head, straightening of my back, or a relaxation of my shoulders would get me back into alignment.

I don't have a plumb line in my clinic, but I often use this illustration to educate patients on how to get themselves back into alignment after they've been in precarious postures for extended periods of time.

Life often puts us into precarious positions. Before you know it, you sense that your situation is out of whack. Maybe you can't figure out exactly what it is... so, maybe you just need to get up against the plumb line to adjust yourself.

The plumb line is weighted so that it doesn't sway to the left or right. Similarly, we need to be anchored to the something that is solid. My suggestion is to line up with the word of God. Check your alignment points. What are you hearing? Is it positive and uplifting or negative? Is it reflective of God? What does the work of your hands look like? Is it futile or productive? Where are your struggles? What are you pushing and pulling away from or towards? Where have your feet been taking you?

Get up against your plumb line. Fix your posture. Get back into alignment.

~Shiney

July 13 ~ 2 Chronicles 27, Isaiah 9-12
*"King Jotham became powerful because he was careful
to live in obedience to the Lord his God."*
2 Chronicles 27:6 (NLT)

I think it took a long time for me to understand the power of obedience. The laws of the land in their intent are always meant to protect us. Without laws, civil unrest would break out and anything would go.

While laws are put in place to keep things fair and in order, sometimes they are painful to follow. But when followed, these laws can be powerful to help us succeed.

God's laws are like that too. Whether we like the law or not, there is a reward for submitting to it.

King Jotham of Judah was a great example of that. Jotham was the son of Uzziah, a king who had a very prosperous reign...until pride and disobedience led to his downfall.

But Jotham was different from his father. The scripture says that he didn't do those things that displeased the Lord like Uzziah had done.

By obeying God, Jotham experienced many great accomplishments. He rebuilt the upper gate of Jerusalem; he built towns in the hill country of Judah, and constructed fortresses and towers in the wooded areas of Judah. He victoriously fought against the Ammonites. As a result, he received an annual tribute of silver, wheat and barley to the treasury of Judah from the Ammonites.

I would say that is a fairly great accomplishment for the 16-year reign of King Jotham.

The Bible so beautifully states that *"King Jotham became powerful because he was careful to live in obedience to the Lord his God." (2 Chronicles 27:6 NLT)*

How different would our lives be if we were careful to live in obedience to the Lord our God? With the God of the universe on our side, can you imagine what we could accomplish in our lifetime on this earth?

If you're not sure where to start, then do what Pastor Kathy Hayes would often say: *"Go back and recall the last thing God asked you to do ... and obey it.!"* And from there on, continue to obey what He tells you to do.

~Vijoy

"And he will stand to lead his flock with the Lord's strength, in the majesty of the name of the Lord his God.... for he will be highly honored around the world. And he will be the source of peace ..."
Micah 5:4-5 (NLT)

I love Easter eggs.

That phrase brings to mind a certain image, right? You're probably thinking about chocolate or jelly beans right now. You may be imagining the little plastic eggs that you hide and hopefully find before the treat inside melts.

While I do love those little treats, the Easter eggs I am actually referring to are those little extra scenes in movies. For example, in some movies, during the credits sequence, they'll play outtakes from the movie that they caught while filming. Sometimes, they will even show scenes of future movies or sequels.

Other times, the Easter egg consists of a picture or an object of some sort in the background of a scene that is meant to be a hidden message. Their purpose is to wet your palate, leaving you wanting more, and waiting excitedly for what is to come. It's like an inside joke between you and the directors.

Micah gives us an Easter egg in this book. It was so well-veiled to me that I had to read another version to find it. In the midst of the bleak judgment and punishments that Micah is delivering from the Lord, he gives us a sneak peek of what is coming...a small taste of a future scene. In chapter 5, Micah briefly mentions a promised ruler from Bethlehem. He gives a quick description in a few lines of a powerful leader who will provide security and peace to his followers (verses 1-5).

A little light in the middle of the darkness. A small ray of hope in an otherwise desperate situation.

(Then, we continue on to more destruction and punishment.)

You may be struggling in a desperate situation. You may find yourself surrounded by darkness. You may be in the middle of what feels like an indefinite punishment. Let this be an Easter egg for you - there is hope. There will be peace and stability. This will not last forever. Your Savior is still saving.

~Shiney

"... Unlike David his father, he did not do what was
right in the eyes of the Lord his God."
2 Kings 16:2 (NIV)

The weeks leading up to our wedding were peaceful ... for me.

I jokingly say that my husband was the "bridezilla" because he planned most of the wedding. He likes the details. So, my role was to agree or disagree, and honestly, I preferred it that way.

There was one day, I was left to make one decision. It should have been simple.

I was visiting the florist with my future sister-in-law to decide on my bouquet and the table arrangements. The florist showed me so many different possibilities that I was getting dizzy.

"Yes, that arrangement looks gorgeous ... let's go with that. No, this one looks classier...oh, but look! That one goes with our color theme."

Y'all...I could not wait to get out of there.

It's funny how much time and effort go into planning one special day, and then it's all just a memory, captured by a photographer who you spent hours researching.

The venue, the flowers, the videographer, the linen ... but, what about the vows ... the covenant?

One of my favorite memories of our pre-wedding period was sitting in the car with my fiancé and praying over the *other* details...our future, our families, our guests, and that our marriage would be an example to others. We even prayed against anything that would come between us.

That day in the car, we could never have imagined what our marriage would look like in ten years. But we knew the gravity of our decision and didn't take it lightly.

Our readings today take us to the downfall of King Ahaz. His error? Forgetting the covenant that was made and forsaking God. His poor leadership led the Israelites to be taken captive by Assyria.

The Lord commanded the Israelites to fear Him and made a special covenant with them that He would be their God. Instead, they bowed down and sacrificed to false gods. They carved images, practiced witchcraft, and even had their sons and daughters walk through fire!

They didn't grasp the seriousness of the covenant and had to pay the consequences.

We make decisions every day that involve family, a career, or finances. Don't "major on the minors"[1] as one pastor says. In other words, don't get caught up in the details. Make sure that God is glorified in whatever decision you make.

~Elizabeth

July 16 ~ Isaiah 13-17

"The Lord will have compassion on Jacob; once again he will choose Israel and will settle them in their own land..." Isaiah 14:1a (NIV)

Unlike most people, learning how to drive was not exciting to me. In fact, it was pretty stressful. I was nervous every time I sat in the driver's seat. I held my breath when driving. I attempted every skill with great trepidation. Just knowing the value of my parents' car and how much any damage to it would cost them had my stomach in knots.

Then, as I drove more often and became comfortable, I began to relax and breathe easier. Before I knew it, my mantra became *"Put the pedal to the metal!"* because as it turns out, I have a lead foot. I mean, I'm a New Yorker and there's just no time to waste!

One afternoon as I was driving home, I went to change lanes but I did not check my blind spot. Then, it happened: my first car accident. And I was in a complete panic. I cried so hysterically that the driver of the car I hit was actually comforting me. (Yes, you read correctly.) The only thoughts that were running through my mind were that I was careless and now it was going to cost my parents a fortune. I was riddled with guilt and shame. I expected to be met with anger and disappointment when facing my parents.

However, our conversation unfolded quite differently. My father calmly asked me to tell him what happened. Tears were streaming down my cheeks and I was blubbering as I tried to explain. I don't even know if he actually understood a word I said. I began to apologize profusely and weep uncontrollably.

To my surprise, my father's countenance remained exactly the same. He didn't raise an eyebrow or raise his voice. My father just said he was glad the other driver and I were both okay and he assured me that the car could be repaired.

When my dad forgave me, I felt undeserving of such compassion and mercy. I mean, I messed up! But what I experienced that day reminds me of the key verse. In spite of His children's decisions to wander away from Him more than once and disobey Him, God forgave them, had compassion on them, and kept His promise to them.

What a good, good Father we serve!

~Joyce

July 17 ~ Isaiah 18-22
"at that time the Lord spoke by Isaiah the son of Amoz..." Isaiah 20:2 (ESV)

Yesterday, I was taking a walk in our neighborhood and happened to see a woman working on her yard.

Her landscape was beautiful. I couldn't help but admire her seemingly green thumb.

Then, I felt a nudge to tell her that.

I had a lengthy conversation in my head about it. *"Well, that's just weird. She's going to wonder why is this random stranger telling her that from across the street? What if she is mean and yells at me? I'll just say something if she turns around."*

She never turned around and even if she did, if I'm being honest, I probably wouldn't have said anything anyway.

Has God ever asked you to do something that seemed ... weird? Or say something that was ... hard?

Isaiah dealt with both.

I know Old Testament times were different but this was a new one...

"at that time the Lord spoke by Isaiah the son of Amoz, saying, 'Go, and loose the sackcloth from your waist and take off your sandals from your feet,' and he did so, walking naked and barefoot.' Then the Lord said, 'As my servant Isaiah has walked naked and barefoot for three years as a sign and a portent against Egypt and Cush...'" (Isaiah 20:2-3 ESV)

Weird. Check. Hard. Check.

God is God and He can do whatever He wants and can ask us to do whatever He wants. When it doesn't fit in the right box according to our standards, we may want to back away.

I've had these nudges from God before. Sometimes, I've obeyed. I'm not proud of this but sometimes I haven't.

We don't know why God chose certain people as prophets but with Isaiah, I think it is safe to say this: Isaiah could be trusted to do what God asked him to do.

No matter how weird or hard it was.

I don't know why God nudged me about that woman in her yard. Maybe she was having a bad day and needed to hear something positive. Or she could have had been working really hard on it and hoped someone would notice.

Either way, she didn't get to hear it from me ... and now, I regret it. Hopefully, someone else came along who was willing to go outside their comfort zone and tell her. Hopefully, next time, I will be the willing one.

~Anu

July 18 ~ Isaiah 23-27
"You will keep in perfect peace those whose minds are steadfast, because they trust in you." Isaiah 26:3 (NIV)

Recently, I came home after an extremely busy day at work. I was hungry and exhausted and admittedly, could have displayed a more pleasant attitude. I blamed the sour mood on my day.

The next day, my poor attitude still weighed heavy on me, and I developed a headache that lingered for some time. I knew that stress probably had something to do with it.

A few months ago, my husband developed a small infection on his finger. With the appropriate treatment and prayer, his skin started healing well. During that time, he mentioned how his mind was also affected.

Isn't it interesting how our body and mind are intertwined? When one part of us malfunctions, the other part suffers, too.

Genesis 2:7 (NIV) says we are more than just body and mind, *"Then the LORD God formed a man from the dust of the ground and breathed into his nostrils the breath of life, and the man became a living being."*

God made us unique from other creatures in that we have a soul that is eternal.

It should come as no surprise that without rest, *both* body and mind can be weakened. We are attacked with discouraging news daily and our newsfeed gives us little to smile about. Our health takes a beating with poor food choices and lack of exercise.

How do we combat this and find time to revive ourselves? The prophet Isaiah says to trust in God.

"You will keep in perfect peace those whose minds are steadfast, because they trust in you." (Isaiah 26:3 NIV)

I have noticed my mind wandering off when I am not focused on God.

Solomon says, *"Do not be wise in your own eyes; fear the Lord and shun evil. This will bring health to your body and nourishment to your bones." (Proverbs 3:7-8 NIV)*

Even our physical bodies will be nourished by fearing God. Time spent focusing our eyes on Jesus gives us overall good health: body, spirit, and soul.

Are you tired? Weak? Aching? Discouraged? Find comfort in God's Word. He will give you rest. (Matthew 11:28 NIV)

~Elizabeth

July 19 ~ 2 Kings 18, 2 Chronicles 29-31, Psalm 48
*"Have the gods of any other nations ever saved
their people from the king of Assyria?"*
2 Kings 18:33 (NLT)

Hezekiah was on a roll. He had cleansed and rededicated the temple. He organized the priests for temple worship and planned the Passover celebration. He gave offerings and required the people to do so as well.

In spite of all that Hezekiah had done right, because of the sins of the people, he couldn't avoid trouble completely. The Assyrians came against Judah and captured some of the fortified cities.

And the trash talking began. The Assyrians boldly asked the leaders of Judah, *"Have the gods of any other nations ever saved their people from the king of Assyria?" (2 Kings 18:33 NLT)*

The enemy's tactics haven't changed.

He's been playing this game since the Garden of Eden. We all give Eve a hard time for conversing with the enemy but aren't we guilty of the same? We know what God said but we choose to listen to the enemy instead.

When God came *looking* for Adam and Eve, He basically said ... *Who have you been LISTENING to? Because if you had listened to what I said, we would be walking together right now. Instead, you are hiding.*

How many of us have found ourselves there? I have.

Years ago, I felt God calling me to start a Bible study with a group of girlfriends. It has expanded in different ways but we have also experienced a lot of disappointments. I wanted to quit, more times than I can count. The enemy began to whisper to me, *"Did God really say that you should do this?"*

What is the enemy saying to you? Where is he planting doubt?

The enemy speaks through our circumstances. He comes into agreement with us when we are feeling discouraged. What the enemy is saying often matches what our eyes can see.

The Assyrians were talking to the people of Judah. The enemy was talking to Eve and still talks to us. When we can finally stop looking down at the serpent on the ground and turn our eyes back up to God, then we are back in the right conversation.

That was the case for me. I didn't quit and that is one reason why you are reading this devotional right now.

The Assyrians had the ear of the people temporarily, but they would not have the final word.

~Anu

July 20 ~ Hosea 1-7

"... Go, show your love to your wife again, though she is
loved by another man and is an adulteress..."
Hosea 3:1a (NIV)

I'm not sure what part of *"Thou shalt have no other gods before Me"* (Exodus 20:3 KJV), did the Israelites not understand. But they just didn't get it.

Over and over again, through His prophets, God conveyed how much He loved His people, how grieved He was by their worship of other gods, and how all they had to do was turn back to Him and He would turn to them. But their hearts remained hardened.

So, the Lord asked His prophet, Hosea, to participate in a little object lesson.

God asks the prophet Hosea to *"go and marry a prostitute."* (Hosea 1:2 NLT). Hosea obeyed. He chose Gomer as his wife. Some scholars believe Gomer hadn't exactly retired from her profession in harlotry.

Three kids into their marriage, Gomer goes back into her old lifestyle.

God then asks the prophet Hosea to go find her and take her back. *"... Go, show your love to your wife again, though she is loved by another man and is an adulteress."* (Hosea 3:1a NIV)

If I were Hosea, I think I would've changed professions by now.

But Hosea obeys God.

Hosea took to the streets looking for his wife. I wonder if he trembled as he turned each corner, afraid of what he might see. The Bible tells us he found her, the woman who had not only left him, but also abandoned their three kids.

He bought her back for fifteen shekels of silver and one and one-half homers of barley.

Hosea purchased what was already his.

The name Hosea means salvation. Hosea is a picture of God. You and I are a picture of Gomer.

I don't even know half of what God has done in His pursuit for me. How many streets did He have to walk down...how many corners did He have to turn? But He did. In my sin, He purchased me with a price far more valuable than fifteen shekels of silver and some barley. He purchased me with the blood of His Son, Jesus Christ.

If you have ever wondered if you've gone too far, crossed God's line or done too much for our Savior to love you...can I assure you? You haven't.

As Hosea loved Gomer, so God loves you and me.

~Binu

July 21 ~ Hosea 8-14

*"They have planted in the wind and will harvest
the whirlwind ..." Hosea 8:7 (NLT)*

My morning routine generally unfolds like this: wake up, exercise, make coffee, drink coffee and have my quiet time simultaneously. Quiet time is spent in my closet, with my dog, coffee, Bible, journal, and pen. I read my portion for the day, write in my journal, and pray. All of this usually happens before the rest of my family is awake.

I have learned that once another pair of feet are up and running around, this routine will crumble quickly. During the week, I set my alarm early to get all in. There are times that I skip the workout but not the quiet time. On the weekends, I sleep later and the routine may change a little, but I know that before I start the bulk of my day, I have to get in the word and have some face time with my Father.

This is what works for me. Before I got into a good groove, though, there were days that I would skip it. I would rush through my entire day in a frantic pace as if I was chasing something, but I could never quite figure out what it was that I was chasing.

I was spending time in traffic with my fellow frustrated commuters. I was spending time at work and with my family, but it wasn't filling the space. Occasionally, I felt like I was bowing to the traffic God, work God and even societal God without taking time to spend with the true God - the One who could recharge and refresh me.

I felt like I was literally *"planting in the wind"* and *"reaping the whirlwind"*. I would watch my day spin out of control, right along with my attitude. I felt helpless to stop it. All of it seemed empty and useless without the actual true God starting the day alongside me. I could feel my stress snowballing. I knew that something had to change.

God wants to be priority number one in your life. He wants to fill that space and walk alongside you through your day. Give Him the time. Invite Him in to walk through your day with you.

~Shiney

July 22 ~ Isaiah 28-30
"Yet the Lord longs to be gracious to you; therefore
he will rise up to show you compassion.
For the Lord is a God of justice. Blessed are all
who wait for him!" Isaiah 30:18 (NIV)

Indian chai is my drink of choice. In fact, I just had a cup of it, and it was delightful.

The blend of cardamom and ginger mixed in with tea leaves evolves into a taste and aroma that is unmatched, in my opinion.

Take a sip and the calm slowly creeps into an otherwise chaotic day.

I realized over time that there are several ways to concoct chai, using any variety of natural spices. However, unless you are using a simple tea bag, you need a strainer. Without that filter, your cup of tea is a grainy, lumpy, liquid mess.

I have been in a season at work that has been challenging. At dinner this week, I vented to my husband, and ever-so-gently he said, *"You may be too emotional right now. Be careful."* He was reminding me to remain calm and stay reasonable.

This morning, I woke up an hour before my alarm was set. My mind mulled over what was going on at work. I looked up into the dark and asked God how He wanted me to handle things. I felt that I was at a crossroads.

He reminded me that despite the changes we were going through, I needed to treat my colleagues with love and that *"love is kind ... it is not proud, not arrogant, not rude ..." (1 Corinthians 13: 4-5 ESV)*

How often I have heard those words ... yet how difficult to live out.

I went to work today, knowing God was well aware of what I was going through, and He was developing His character in me.

Today's reading reminds us that whatever adversity we face, God is there and leading us.

Have you heard that quote that states that whatever happens to us as believers is filtered through the loving hands of our Heavenly Father? What a visual!

God is sovereign. He knows our pain and sees our tears, and He allows it to transform us into the loving, kind, and patient child that He desires us to be. He is refining us, sharpening us, and molding us through our circumstances.

So, the next time you pull out your strainer to create a savory, aromatic, perfectly light brown cup of tea, let it remind you of God's sovereignty over your life. He is making you into the beautiful woman He intends you to be.

~Elizabeth

July 23 ~ Isaiah 31-34

"... the eyes of those who see will not be blinded, And the ears of those who hear will listen attentively. The ... (mind) of those who act impulsively will discern the truth," Isaiah 32:3-4 (AMP)

Over the years, I have experienced a hurt or two. During each experience, I cried and vented, but eventually, I dismissed it. I'd tell myself that I was fine, that I forgave the person who hurt me, and I would leave the situation in God's hands.

The only thing is that as soon as I had an encounter with that person, a whirlwind of negative emotions would overtake me. It's almost as if I was reliving the entire experience and as if I never extended forgiveness.

For a while, I really didn't think anything was wrong with this vicious cycle. I actually thought it was just a normal part of life ... but it wasn't. My husband tried to tell me that several times. I wouldn't listen to him. I decided I knew better. After all, I'm a social worker. I know a problem when I see one. I know the value of seeking out help. And I decided I didn't have a problem.

This continued for years until we met with two pastors to pray for our child's health. I had hardly warmed up to the seat I was in when the Lord revealed to them that I had been harboring bitterness and unforgiveness. I knew the presence of God was there and that something life-altering was about to happen.

My husband's prayers from the key verse had been heard.

For the first time in my life, I began to see how hurt I was. I began to listen to how bitter I had become. I began to understand that unforgiveness was residing in my heart and spilling over in my relationships, especially in my marriage. I walked through healing and deliverance that day as I forgave aloud those who hurt me and truly released them into God's hands. I literally walked away feeling lighter and free ... unlike anything I had known my entire life and I am so grateful.

If you care for someone who has been struggling to see God's truth about themselves or a situation, I encourage you today to pray this Scripture over them. Believe that they will receive the revelation they need in God's perfect time.

~Joyce

"... 'Be strong, fear not! Indeed, your God will come with vengeance [for the ungodly]; The retribution of God will come, But He will save you.'" Isaiah 35:4 (AMP)

Moms (and the Bible) know best.

Popular blogger/vlogger Kristina Kuzmic challenges her kids to follow up any negative statements with a *"Yeah, but..."*[1] and find the positive in it.

This isn't a new idea. The Bible has much to say about the thoughts we think and the words we speak. Paul told the church in Philippi (and us) to dwell continually on things that are *"... true ... right ... of good repute ... and anything worthy of praise ..." (Philippians 4:8 NASB)* When we think on these things, we will speak accordingly.

My dad was hospitalized recently. While there have been many points of frustration, we have had our own *"Yeah, but ..."* moments too.

He had to be rushed to the ER ... yeah, but my mom was with him and able to drive him there.

He has been in the hospital ... yeah, but they are fixing the problem.

He has had some setbacks ... yeah, but at least they have caught it early enough.

As I reflected on my own experiences, I realized quickly that I would add one word to the "Yeah, but ..." phrase.

"YEAH, BUT GOD ...".

The encouragement of Isaiah 35 comes between a word of judgment and threats from Assyria. Isaiah had to remind the people of their own, "Yeah, but God ..." situation.

"Say to those with an anxious and panic-stricken heart, 'Be strong, fear not! Indeed, your God will come with vengeance [for the ungodly]; The retribution of God will come, But He will save you.'" (Isaiah 35:4 AMP)

There have been countless "Yeah, but God ..." moments in my life. I bet you could say the same.

Scripture shares more of these with us too:

"... With man this is impossible, but with God all things are possible." (Matthew 19:26 ESV)

"My flesh and my heart fail; but God is the strength of my heart..." (Psalm 73:26 ESV)

"... You meant evil against me; but God meant it for good ..." (Genesis 50:20 ESV)

What situation are you in that is challenging? What is your "Yeah, but ..." statement?

Better yet, what is your "Yeah, but God ..." truth?

~Anu

"At that time Merodach-Baladan son of Baladan King of Babylon sent Hezekiah letters and a gift, because he had heard of his illness and recovery." Isaiah 39:1 (NIV)

Have you ever begged God for a miracle and God answered your prayer?

If you are anything like me, you were initially super excited and ready to tell anyone who would listen what God did for you. But before you knew it, the excitement of the miracle wore off and you began living life as if nothing ever even happened. Unfortunately, this happens to the best of mankind. And it happened to one of the most faithful kings of Judah, King Hezekiah.

The Bible tells us that there was no one like him among all the kings of Judah for he held fast to the Lord and kept God's commands. During King Hezekiah's reign, God reversed the shadow of the sun ten steps as a sign that He would deliver him and his city. God also sent an angel and killed 185,000 Assyrian men on his behalf.

In the later years of his life, King Hezekiah became gravely ill. *"The prophet Isaiah son of Amoz went to him and said, 'This is what the LORD says: Put your house in order, because you are going to die; you will not recover.'" (Isaiah 38:1b NIV)*

"Hezekiah turned his face to the wall and prayed to the Lord." (2 Kings 20:2 NIV) God heard his cry and added fifteen years to his life. *Fifteen Years!* You'd think Hezekiah would not let a day go by without telling the world what God did for him.

Right? Wrong.

Shortly thereafter, the King of Babylon paid King Hezekiah a visit (he had heard about his illness and his miraculous recovery). What a perfect opportunity for King Hezekiah to testify and be a witness of Jehovah God to this visiting king. But what does King Hezekiah do instead? King Hezekiah showed off his stuff, not his God. *"There is nothing among my treasuries that I did not show them" (2 Kings 20: 15b NIV)*, Hezekiah told Isaiah.

We don't know why King Hezekiah did what he did (or didn't do what he was supposed to do) but we know God took it personally. *"The time will surely come when everything in your palace ... will be carried off to Babylon" (2 Kings 20:17 NIV)*, the prophet Isaiah sadly told King Hezekiah.

What has God done for you? If given the opportunity, tell of His goodness and give God praise for what He has done. May we finish strong and remain faithful until the end.

~Binu

July 26 ~ Isaiah 40-43
"Forget the former things; do not dwell on the past. See, I am doing a new thing! ... I am making a way in the wilderness and streams in the wasteland." Isaiah 43:18-19 (NIV)

Do you find yourself making decisions based on the past?

Thanksgiving and Christmas are my favorite times of the year. I love to host large groups of people at my home. Decorating, cooking, and organizing gift exchanges are some of my favorite things! Yet, that all changed the year one of my children became ill Christmas morning. I had to painstakingly call each guest to cancel the event before heading off to the hospital.

Since then, I have hesitated to plan a similar event due to the disappointment of what happened. I mean, all those hours of preparation just went up in smoke. Bags of groceries and prepared dishes had gone to waste. Tons of folks suddenly had no plans on such a special day. Presents which had been purchased had to be returned.

Would I risk all of that happening again? NO THANK YOU!

Maybe you were in a close relationship with someone. You probably spent a lot of time getting to know one another, made yourself vulnerable, and trusted each other with things you wouldn't tell just anyone. Unexpectedly, rejection rears its ugly head and this relationship is severed. When given the opportunity to connect with a new person, you remain as superficial as possible to avoid getting hurt.

Why would you go through all of that hard work again only to be left feeling alone and broken? NO THANK YOU!

The underlying theme in these situations is fear. Fear is driving decisions of the present and future based on what we experienced in the past.

God reminds us that as painful and difficult as those situations were, we don't need to let those experiences dictate our present day or future decisions. After all, yesterday is gone. "Today is a gift. That's why it is called the present."[1]

Can we put our hope and trust in God, rather than in our experiences? Can we believe that God is good and that the best is yet to come?

~Joyce

July 27 ~ Isaiah 44-48
"I am the one who made the earth and created people who live on it. With my hands I stretched out the heavens. All the stars are at my command." Isaiah 45:12 (NLT)

Recently, I was overcome with fear and anxiety about a very difficult situation in my life. What I had hoped and planned for was suddenly in question. My stomach was in knots and I barely slept. I woke up the next morning still feeling the heaviness of the uncertainty of what was going to happen.

I couldn't take it anymore. I called up my friend and prayer warrior. I explained the situation to her and just asked her if she could pray.

And pray she did! Through her prayer, I was reminded of God's great faithfulness in my life. He formed and fashioned the galaxies, and yet He cares enough about the things in my life.

I was reminded that God is not only faithful, but He is the God of the impossible.

After her prayer, I immediately felt my stomach start to relax and the heaviness begin to lift. The anxiety began to diminish and I felt even a fog lift off of me. It was one of the most immediate waves of peace I've experienced in my life.

Max Lucado references this peace of God in his book "Anxious for Nothing". He says *"God bestows upon us the peace of God...this is not a peace from God, [but] the very peace of God. He downloads the tranquility of the throne room into our world, resulting in an inexplicable calm."* [1]

This God, who knows all and sees all, holds me in the palm of His hands.

In Isaiah, God tells the people *"I am the one who made the heaven and earth and created people who live on it. With my hands I stretched out the heavens. All the stars are at command." (Isaiah 45:12 NLT)*

Yes, this very BIG God is also my friend. He is my defender. He is my source.

People will come and go. Money will come and go. Security will come and go.

But God is faithful to stay with us through it all.

As I was reminded of the power of prayer this week, don't forget that you have access to this big God too. He is right there. You just have to turn to Him and ask Him to help you. He is near and He will be there for you.

~Vijoy

July 28 ~ 2 Kings 19, Psalms 46,80,135
"Be still, and know that I am God ..." Psalm 46:10a (NLT)

Waiting. If there is one thing I don't do well, it's that.

Even long, drawn out stories make me antsy. I want to know the end...now!

So, imagine me in a critical care waiting room for five days. Life changed one Monday morning for my family when we received a call from a care flight nurse. My husband's parents were involved in a major car accident.

So, there we were...waiting. But we weren't alone. So many others were also waiting. Each with their own story.

On day three of waiting, I began to speak with an elderly woman who had been sitting next to us since day one. She told me about her husband's accident and the critical state he was in, but then she did something unusual. She got out of her seat and squeezed herself into mine. She then began explaining how, despite all of this, *God is still God.*

For over an hour she went through scraps of paper from her purse. She read aloud all the scriptures the Lord had been bringing to her remembrance since her husband's accident.

For over an hour she sat IN MY CHAIR with me.

Anyone who knows me, knows how much I appreciate my personal space. But she didn't know me and God had a plan. I could've made up an excuse to scoot myself over and onto another chair, but I didn't. Her radiant countenance spoke volumes to me.

God knew the scriptures I needed to hear that day. When I didn't have the strength to read the Bible for myself, He read it to me.

Perhaps you are also in a waiting room, going through a critical time and enduring a situation which is completely out of your control.

God is there. I promise. Not just in the waiting room sitting a few feet away from you, but I believe God is invading your personal space as He did mine. And He wants you to know, you are not alone. He is sharing a seat with you and He is in control. For He is still God.

"Be still and know that I am God." (Psalm 46:10a NLT)

~Binu

"... Before I was born the Lord called me;
from my mother's womb He has spoken my name." Isaiah 49:1 (NIV)

My daughter was about to be voted in as the leadership representative from her class. I could feel it in my bones.

The campaign preparation included an attractive poster, which contained glitter, of course. We spent hours putting it together. And the speech was engaging, likening leadership qualities to items at a grocery store...easy for any second grader to understand.

She even dressed the part on voting day, donning a floral dress with a strand of pearls.

My daughter just fit the part, and I was proud of her. Those other kids didn't stand a chance.

That evening when I got out of work, I eagerly asked her about the competition.

She looked at me with sad eyes and said, "I didn't win ...."

What?? There is no way!

She then went on to talk about another topic, while my mind was still spinning. My competitive side kicked into gear and I was trying to analyze how things could go wrong.

She should have won!

After day #3, I moved into self-comfort mode, and reminded myself of her soccer game that was coming up. She was going to win that game!

We received word the morning of the game that it was cancelled due to rain. I was so bummed ... this was going to be her opportunity to win!

As a parent, it is so tempting to push our ideals onto our children and set expectations for them that may, at times, be unreasonable. God has designed each one of them with certain strengths and abilities but they also have weaknesses. Our job as parents is to embrace them just the way they were created.

In his book, Grace-Based Parenting, Dr. Tim Kimmel states, *"Grace-based parents spend their time entrusting themselves to Christ ... they understand their own propensity toward sin."* [1]

Our kids may not work at the job we want for them or win the awards we'd like for them, but may they never need a trophy to earn our love.

May God give me the grace to raise them up to walk in His wisdom regardless of their weaknesses, and that they would know in their Father's eyes, they are always winners.

"See what great love the Father has lavished on us, that we should be called children of God! And that is what we are!" (1 John 3:1 NIV)

~Elizabeth

July 30 ~ Isaiah 54-58
*"As the heavens are higher than the earth, so
are my ways higher than your ways
and my thoughts than your thoughts." Isaiah 55:9 (NIV)*

The first year of our marriage had humble beginnings.

My husband picked up his whole life, leaving a business behind, to live in a new city with me while I was training for my career. It wasn't easy for him to leave the home he always knew.

Being apart from parents and close friends, we encroached on a new season of life.

One afternoon, I came home to our sparsely furnished apartment after the first day of work since becoming a wife. The lights were dim, and it just looked depressing. My husband was laying on our futon in the living room, looking exhausted.

He had been trying to work from home, but missed a webinar because the internet was not set up correctly. He even had to borrow the laptop of our apartment manager, a woman we barely knew!

I could see that he was frustrated, and everything seemed so overwhelming to me in that moment.

I began to wonder if he was happy, not only with the job, but with this apartment, this new city, and ... with me. And this was just the first day of our reality! The wedding and honeymoon were over and now, we were in the thick of things ... marriage.

I didn't want to be the reason for his unhappiness, and I remember crying. It's amazing how doubt starts creeping in when reality hits.

I knew God had brought us together, and I knew that we were in the right place. But, in that moment, I felt the weight of my husband's happiness and our future happiness, on my shoulders.

We sat in the dark that day, and he told me about how he had problems with the internet, and yes, it was hard to leave home, but that he loved me and he was happy. I felt reassured after that talk.

Everyone's story is different, but looking back, living away from our families was one of the best things that could have happened in our first year of marriage.

We learned how to communicate and how to trust each other, all without anyone to run to. Yes, we loved our families and maintained a close relationship with them, but ultimately, we only had each other to rely on.

You may be going through a similar season in life in which you feel the weight of someone's happiness on your shoulder.

Keep trusting Him, and things will turn out to be better than what you ever anticipated.

~Elizabeth

July 31 ~ Isaiah 59-63
*"The Spirit of the Lord God is upon me, because the
Lord has anointed me ..." Isaiah 61:1 (ESV)*

Texas born and raised. And I have a t-shirt to prove it.

I often wonder what people think when I wear that shirt. After all, I don't look like your "average" Texan. I just happen to be an Indian, born in the Lone Star State who says y'all ... a lot.

Sometimes, things just aren't what you expect.

Jesus dealt with that too.

"The Spirit of the Lord God is upon me, because the Lord has anointed me to bring good news to the poor; he has sent me to bind up the brokenhearted, to proclaim liberty to the captives, and the opening of the prison to those who are bound; to proclaim the year of the Lord's favor ..." (Isaiah 61:1-2 ESV)

In my opinion, this may be one of the most beautiful passages of scripture. In the midst of Isaiah's prophetic words of judgment, there is a promise of hope.

When Jesus began his earthly ministry, He read this passage from Isaiah in the synagogue and ended it with, *"... Today this Scripture has been fulfilled in your hearing." (Luke 4:21 ESV)*

If you recall, God had been silent for 400 years until Jesus came on the scene. Now, here comes the carpenter's son claiming to be the one they had waited for. Can anything good come from Nazareth, much less the promised Messiah?

Maybe the story of Jesus wasn't what you expected either. A baby born in a manger. He lived in obscurity for 30 years then ministers for 3 years along with 12 other men. He performed miracles, including raising people from the dead. And if that wasn't enough, they crucified Him but He resurrected and is alive.

This man who washed feet and touched the leper may not seem like the King of Kings and Lord of Lords. The story may be strange to some but the fact is that same Jesus is our Messiah too. He has good news for us and wants to bind up our broken hearts. He is here to set us free and to give us life, and that more abundantly.

Jesus may not have been what they expected but He sure was what they needed ... and what we need too.

~Anu

"... These are the ones I look on with favor: those who are humble and contrite in spirit, and who tremble at my Word." Isaiah 66:2b (NIV)

If you're a woman over the age of forty, then you know, the struggle is real.

It was that time of year again and there I was, standing in the corner of the room as the technician adjusted the large X-Ray machine. She looked over at me, *"Oh honey, you look cold. Can I get you a warm robe?"*

I wonder what gave it away? Perhaps she noticed my lifted shoulders or my crossed arms. But I just wanted to get this appointment over with, so I declined her offer. *"No, it's okay ... I'm good. I'm always cold."*

Despite what I said, she grabbed a robe from the warmer and put it over my shoulders.

No exaggeration, the warm robe made me feel as if I had just exited the Women's Imaging Center and entered a spa. *I said no to this?* And then it hit me. How often do I do this with God?

God is always accessible but do I always access Him the way I should? He is right there. His word tells me so.

"He who dwells in the shelter of the Most High will rest in the shadow of the Almighty." (Psalm 91:1 NIV)

"Draw near to God and He will draw near to you." (James 4:8a ESV)

"These are the ones I look on with favor, those who are humble and contrite in spirit, and who tremble at my Word." (Isaiah 66:2b NIV)

God wants to give me a robe straight out of His warmer (figuratively speaking, of course) but how often do I do what I did at my appointment? *'No thanks God. I'm good"*, when I'm clearly not. Five minutes of Bible reading and thirty minutes of scrolling through my news feed might not be what God had in mind when He asks me to *'dwell in His shelter,' 'draw near to Him'* or *'tremble at His Word.'*

God doesn't just love me; He likes me and wants to hang out with me. He desires to be near me and warm my soul.

He wants to be near you too.

We may not always have an attendant offering us a robe straight out of a warmer ... but we do have a Heavenly Father who desires to surround us with His presence and warm our soul.

Now, why would we ever say no to that?

~Binu

August 2 ~ 2 Kings 20-21
"Hezekiah listened to and welcomed them and [foolishly]
showed them all his treasure house..."
2 Kings 20:13a (AMP)

Another one bites the dust.

Hezekiah was another good king whose reign wasn't so good in the end.

With all that God had accomplished through him and for him, in his final days, he seemed to forget who really deserved the credit.

Remember that he started out great. When faced with the threat of the Assyrian army, I love Hezekiah's response. He takes the letter, and "*... spread it before the Lord." (2 Kings 19:14 ESV)* He acknowledged that it was God who would give him the victory: "*So now, O Lord our God, save us from his hand, that all the kingdoms of the earth may know that you alone are the Lord." (Isaiah 37:20 ESV)*

The last verses about Hezekiah portray a different man. When he had an opportunity to testify of God's power, he testified of himself instead. Obviously, God was not pleased and issued a punishment for Hezekiah's descendants.

His response to the prophetic warning of the future was very telling. "*Then Hezekiah said to Isaiah, 'The word of the Lord that you have spoken is good.' For he thought, 'Why not, if there will be peace and security in my days?'" (2 Kings 20:19 ESV)*

This good king was now more concerned with himself than his children or His God.

How did he get from the man he was to the man he became?

When Hezekiah humbled himself, God honored him. When Hezekiah honored himself, God humbled him.

"*Pride ends in humiliation, while humility brings honor." (Proverbs 29:23 NLT)*

Humility is a funny thing. Most of us think we are humble and overall, we probably are. But it doesn't take much for me to realize that I've got a little more pride lurking in there than I'd like to admit.

We can try to be humble and do external things that appear that way but true humility is a heart issue. When Hezekiah was pressed, the "pride of life" that was in him came out. We've all been there when we say or do something that surprises even us and we'll ask ourselves, "*Where did that come from?".*

The answer isn't something we want to admit it. Unfortunately, it was in us all along.

Praying for a humble spirit for myself ... for all of my days.

~Anu

August 3 ~ 2 Chronicles 32-33

"But while in deep distress, Manasseh sought the Lord his God and sincerely humbled himself ...and when he prayed, the Lord listened to him and was moved by his request ..." 2 Chronicles 33:12-13 (NLT)

Do you know of a person seems too far gone that it appears to be no hope for them?

Manasseh, the son of King Hezekiah, comes to my mind.

Hezekiah is remembered as a good and honorable king who on his deathbed, pleaded with God to extend his life. God granted his request and added 15 years to life. He honored God and was faithful before the Lord.

But his son Manasseh is often described as one of the most evil kings of Judah. He rebuilt pagan shrines, constructed altars for Baal, and set up Asherah poles for worship. He built pagan altars inside the Temple of the Lord. He practiced sorcery and divination. He even sacrificed his own sons in the fire to the pagan gods he worshiped.

It's safe to say, this guy was as wicked as they come.

God warned him that judgement was coming but Manasseh did not listen. It came in the form of an invasion from the Assyrian army. Manasseh was carried off from Jerusalem, bound in chains and thrown in a Babylonian prison with no hope of ever being free again.

But something happened to Manasseh in that prison. The scripture says *"while in deep distress, Manasseh sought the Lord his God and sincerely humbled himself ... and when he prayed, the Lord listened to him and was moved by his request." (2 Chronicles 33:12-13 NLT)*

Manasseh spent 12 years in that prison. But when he turned his eyes towards God and asked for help, God not only freed him from prison, God restored him as King of Judah!

Once restored to the throne, Manasseh went to work rebuilding the walls of Jerusalem, removing the pagan gods and idols from the Lord's temple, and tearing down altars he had built in Jerusalem. He offered sacrifices to the Lord and encouraged the people of Judah to worship the God of Israel. (2 Chronicles 33:14-16 NLT)

Manasseh's life started off one way (evil), but ended in a way that honored God.

Maybe you've also had a rough start in life. It's not how you start, but how you finish that truly counts. I pray you will not let your past determine the course of your destiny. I pray you would turn your eyes to God for He is the one who can and will help you to finish strong.

~Vijoy

*"... Celebrate your festivals, O people of Judah, and
fulfill all your vows..." Nahum 1:15 (NLT)*

Identity. It's something that we are born with but spend our whole lives searching to define.

Our creator maps us out in such great detail to the point that no two people have the exact DNA or the exact fingerprint. Our uniqueness reflects His beauty.

We search for our identity starting at a young age, clinging to the things that make us similar; girls will play with the girls and boys will play with the boys. As we grow, we divide ourselves into cliques based on sports, hobbies, likes or dislikes; all in hopes of finding a group of people who share the same ideology with us.

The Israelites lost their identity. They were the chosen people of God; His blessed nation. All of God's favor and love was to be lavished on them, but somewhere along the way, they wandered away from this recognition. They began searching in other cultures and with other gods to fulfill this lack that they were now experiencing. This led to their downfall and captivity.

A big part of Israel's culture was their celebrations. They had festivals throughout the year to commemorate significant times in their religion, and through the years, these had been forgotten as well.

In the first chapter of Nahum, the people are encouraged to celebrate their festivals...a small step to recovering their identity once more. Taking the time to prepare and reflect on what these festivals meant demonstrated that God was still present in their lives.

It can be a challenge in this culture to maintain our identities as Christians. We can get lost in the things that this world dictates we identify with. I would encourage you to celebrate God in your life. Celebrate who He is and what He has done. Celebrate the big and the small things. Celebrate the close parking spot and celebrate the healing with the same zeal.

God takes pleasure in you and we must never forget that our identity is in Him.

~Shiney

"While they were bringing out the money that had been taken into the temple of the Lord, Hilkiah the priest found the Book of the Law of the Lord that had been given through Moses."
2 Chronicles 34:14 (NIV)

There was a small closet in the narrow hallway of my house when I was a young girl. The hallway led to the living room from the bedroom that I shared with my sister. You would open the closet at your own risk because you never knew what would fall out. Sheets were stuffed into a few shelves along with odd objects, like Dad's typewriter.

But way down on the floor of the closet was a cardboard box that was bursting at the seams. It contained a white album that gingerly held pictures from my parents' wedding.

I treasured looking through it as I sat on the wooden floor of that hallway. I carefully turned the pages, as not to drop any of the cherished photos. The glue from the album was drying out. I would imagine being there and loved seeing my mother as a beautiful bride, beside her dashing groom with a wide smile.

What a sweet treasure among what otherwise seemed like just a cluttered closet.

King Josiah was probably one of the wisest eight-year-olds you would ever meet. Forget the fact that he was KING at EIGHT, but he happened upon a treasure himself.

He had been king for 18 years when he wisely decided to rebuild the Lord's Temple. As they were working among the timber and beams, the Book of The Law was discovered and brought to the attention of King Josiah. This discovery was a game-changer. When he realized that the Israelites would be cursed for not following the law as instructed, he sprang into action.

This young king read the Book to the elders, made a new covenant to follow the laws, and had everyone pledge to follow it, too.

He treated the Book of the Law like treasure.

In a sermon, John Piper described the Bible like treasure. Imagine that in your backyard you discovered a chest with one million dollars, how ecstatic would you be?[1]

You have a treasure IN YOUR HOME worth FAR MORE! We should treat God's Word like it is the most valuable thing you own.

"Take my instruction and not silver, And knowledge rather than choicest gold. For wisdom is better than jewels; And all desirable things cannot compare with her." (Proverbs 8:10-11 NIV)

~Elizabeth

August 6 ~ Zephaniah 1-3
"The Lord your God is in your midst, a mighty one who will save; he will rejoice over you with gladness;..." Zephaniah 3:17 (ESV)

With young children, it takes effort to stay connected with my husband.

The morning rush tests our patience. We hunt for matching socks, grab school snacks, and scramble to get everyone in their car seats before heading out of the garage.

My husband and I are off to work, and when we finally make it home, we are exhausted. Oh, but no time to nap. It's time for dinner, clean up, and the eventful bedtime routine.

Trying to reconnect after a long day is no easy task.

I got out of work early today, so in between my husband's schedule, we took a few hours to chat and spend time at a local bakery. It was a nice quiet moment in the midst of our chaotic day.

I spoke with a friend who had recently received a gorgeous bouquet of roses from a gentleman friend who was interested in her. She mentioned that though a "nice guy", he was asking her restrict time spent with her family and had made other negative statements.

While it is nice to receive flowers, the real mark of a person's character is how they treat you through actions and words. If my husband sent me flowers but didn't treat me with respect and didn't seem interested in my company, I am not sure how much I would value the gift.

We received the gift of salvation when Jesus shed his blood on the cross; it was a gift backed by love and time. He loves you and desires your time.

Os Hillman, in his book, Today God Is First, states, *"When we begin to lose the relationship, we are susceptible to becoming rebellious, going our own way. Invest your life in this relationship so that you may continue to hear His voice and sustain the weary ones around you."*[1]

Will you commit to find a quiet moment in the chaos of your day?

Sustaining a meaningful relationship takes time and effort.

If it is your quiet time that you would like to work on, you will be surprised at how much you will enjoy your time with Jesus. And the Bible says he delights in you too! *"The Lord your God is in your midst, a mighty one who will save; he will rejoice over you with gladness." (Zephaniah 3:17 ESV)*

~Elizabeth

August 7 ~ Jeremiah 1-3
"Before I formed you in the womb I knew you,
before you were born I set you apart;
I appointed you as a prophet to the nations." Jeremiah 1:5 (NIV)

One of my favorite things to do while I was pregnant with my first child was settle in and read about how she was developing inside me. The book would describe my baby week by week, and would even use tangible, descriptive words to give me a better idea of how big she was:

Week 7: your baby is the size of a pumpkin seed

Week 10: your baby is the size of a grapefruit

I found these portrayals a bit amusing, but it really *did* give me a better idea of her size and what organs were developing. Of course, my thoughts would drift off to the unpredictability of motherhood and the excitement of holding her soon.

I felt, in some sense, that just by carrying her, I knew her.

What I knew so far about my baby was that she kicked more to party music on our television than classical music, to my surprise. I knew she was going to be loved, would have a purpose and would be taught to love Jesus.

I knew all this *while* she was being formed.

Do you want to hear something incredible I heard this week that struck me?

God had a purpose for my baby even *before* she was formed! God *knew* her, God *set her apart*, and God *appointed* her! (Jeremiah 1:5 NIV)

BEFORE ... not WHILE.

That means, even before the formation of any heart valve, eyelid, or limb, God had a purpose for *you.* Don't ever let circumstances determine your purpose or your motivation. You have been set apart. God not only knew you, but has determined your path, and it is for good!

Oswald Chambers said, *"As Christians we are not here for our own purpose at all -we are here for the purpose of God, and the two are not the same."*[1]

How will you fulfill God's purpose for your life? Live a life of purpose, because if you don't live the abundant live that Jesus died for you to have, you will miss out on the blessings of this short time here on earth.

If you are struggling to know what your purpose is, simply ask God to reveal it, and He will. He has already appointed you for something significant even before you were formed!

"The greatest tragedy is not death, but life with no purpose." (Rick Warren[2])

~Elizabeth

August 8 ~ Jeremiah 4-6

"... I, the Lord, define the ocean's sandy shoreline, as an everlasting boundary that the waters cannot cross. The waves may toss and roar, but they can never pass the boundaries that I set."
Jeremiah 5:22 (NLT)

I love the beach and the ocean. The sound of the waves does something to reset my soul.

I usually get to the beach once a year, and collect shells from each trip. I wish I could tell you that I do something creative with them. I don't. They are all sitting in labeled, plastic bags somewhere in my home.

On a recent trip, I walked along the sand and caught a glimpse of a few shells, but they looked like ones that I already had in my bags at home. There was nothing really special about any of them. This time, I wanted a treasure different from what I already had.

As I walked out away from the beach, towards the water, I noticed different colors and different shapes of shells at the shoreline. I walked farther into the water, eager to explore, and I started to see more of these unique shells washing up.

As I ventured deeper, the waves hit me harder, but when the waves would subside, the water was clearer than it had been at the shore. I could see larger, whole shells stuck in the sand, waiting to be plucked by my greedy little hand. I excitedly grabbed as many as I could. They were completely different than ones that I had collected on previous trips. Varying shapes, colors, and patterns.

These particular shells didn't just sit in a bag. I have them on display where I can see them daily as a reminder. So many times in my life, I just hang out at the shoreline, content with what I see there. But I have noticed that if I am willing to go deeper, willing to be patient...if I am willing to take a little battering by the waves of life, the treasure is more special. God's voice gets a little clearer. My focus changes and I can see things better.

He knows the waves that are battering against you. They, too, have a limit. I know that they are rough, but if you can keep walking through them, your treasure will be worth it.

~Shiney

August 9 ~ Jeremiah 7-9
"They offer superficial treatments for my people's mortal wound ..." Jeremiah 8:11 (NLT)

A wound is an insult or injury to the body. Be it a physical wound or an emotional one, there is usually trauma and pain associated with it. The healing process is a slow, tedious one. It takes time to heal a wound completely, especially if it is a deep one. Band-Aids are enough coverage to protect a surface cut, but for a deeper wound to heal properly, it often needs ointments and more complicated dressings.

For tissue to heal properly, especially if the wound is deep, the tissue needs something to attach itself to. It has to heal from the inside out. If the surface of the wound heals before the inner tissue, you can develop an abscess which could turn into an infection that could affect your entire body.

Our body is so beautifully connected that one cut could turn into something dangerous to your entire system.

When I performed wound care on my patients, we were careful to pick the correct ointments and dressings that would create a proper healing environment for each patient. We picked dressings that had the proper surfaces for tissue to attach itself to without being too invasive in the body. These would often be embedded with ointments that would promote tissue growth.

Even after picking all the right things, it would still be a process for the wound to heal.

In the key verse, the Lord expresses His disgust with His prophets and priests.

For our wounds to heal, we need to attach ourselves to something that will promote proper healing. We need to find something that will encourage us to heal from the inside out. God's word is a living, healing tool that we need to attach ourselves to for complete healing. It contains the right treatments and fosters the perfect environment for our healing to take place.

Let Him heal you from the inside out.

~Shiney

August 10 ~ Jeremiah 10 -13

"But afterward I will return and have compassion on all of them. I will bring them home to their own lands again, each nation to its own possession." Jeremiah 12:15 (NLT)

The love that a good Father has for his children surpasses human understanding.

It's the kind of love that would make him risk his own life to save his child. It's the kind of love that, without thinking or considering the consequences, would step in and take a bullet or step into harm's way to protect his child from injury or death.

And no matter how far away from home the child has gone, a good Father still hopes and believes for the best ... continuing to love that child over and over again until their prodigal returns home.

The book of Jeremiah is a heart wrenching portrait of this kind of selfless, unconditional love of God to His children. The children of Israel have gone so far away from the Father. They have broken His heart with sin and disobedience. And still, He continues to offer them a way back to Him.

He doesn't let them off the hook for their sin, but He does warn them that punishment is coming. He also tells them that after their time has been served in exile, He has a plan to bring them back home.

Over and over again, Israel refuses God's offer and continues to sin. But that doesn't stop God from continuing to believe the best for them.

This love of God is beyond anything I can understand. His love is so wide and deep, the vast expanse of the ocean or the stars in the galaxies cannot capture how big His love is for His children.

God loves you and I more than our minds can comprehend.

Has sin and disobedience have kept you from Him? Know that He still offers a way home for you. And He won't give up until you have come back home to Him.

"The overwhelming, never ending, reckless love of God! Oh, it chases me down, fights 'til I'm found, leaves the ninety-nine. I couldn't earn it, and I don't deserve it, still, You give Yourself away. Oh, the overwhelming, never-ending, reckless love of God..." [1]

~Vijoy

August 11 ~ Jeremiah 14-17

"... It does not fear when heat comes; its leaves are always green. It has no worries in a year of drought and never fails to bear fruit." Jeremiah 17:8 (NIV)

In my life, I have experienced many faith-building events. Getting accepted into graduate school. Getting married. (Once I was married, my faith had to grow on a much higher level!) Unemployment, losing my dog, having children, family problems, work issues. All of these events involved me stepping out in faith and believing for something that I could not see. I had to relinquish control and submit to God to do the rest.

When my faith starts to waver in respect to the new stressors around me, I can look back at these previous events and remember how God brought me out of a desperate place and placed me in a place with hope. A place of peace and happiness that I know I would not have been able to reach on my own.

Life brings each one of us circumstances to build our faith. A chance for God to show up and help us build our faith muscle.

In Jeremiah 16:14 (NIV), Jeremiah introduces the idea of captivity as a faith-building event for the Israelites. Instead of the Israelites being known as the people that God had delivered out of Egypt, He says they will now be known as the people brought *"out of all the countries where He had banished them."*

A new identity comes with a new deliverance.

In the next chapter, Jeremiah encourages us again by saying *"But blessed is the one who trusts in the Lord, whose confidence is in Him."* He continues to paint the picture of a tree, situated near the water, with strong roots, leaves that are always green and always bears fruit *(17:7-8 NIV).*

I want to be that like that tree but for that to happen, I have to go through some stuff - particularly, some heat, wind, and rain. To be situated where God wants me, bearing fruit and with strong roots, I must clench my teeth and walk through life ready to exercise my faith.

What faith building events has God brought you through? I encourage you to make a list and keep it in a place where you can be reminded daily.

~Shiney

August 12 ~ Jeremiah 18-22

"But if I say, 'I will not mention His word or speak anymore in His name,' His word is in my heart like a fire, a fire shut up in my bones. I am weary of holding it in; indeed, I cannot."
Jeremiah 20:9 (NIV)

At the start of summer, my thirteen-year-old son began to *play around* on the piano. He would hear a song at church or on the radio, then come home and attempt to figure out the keys. The more he played, the better he played. And I was pleasantly surprised.

"Wow, Caleb...that's sounds really nice."

His response, *"Thanks. I feel like God is moving my hands."*

From the moment I heard him say those words, I heard God say - *"I'm moving in you too."*

Now you have to understand, any musical gifting my son has, did not come from me. So, when God said He was moving in me ... it wasn't my fingers on a piano. The creative methods in which God chooses to move and minister are limitless.

That same summer, I attended a small women's fellowship meeting. The leader of the fellowship had such a sweet, quiet and gentle countenance. After the meeting, she and I began to chat. I couldn't help but ask what inspired her to start this beautiful fellowship. She explained, *"God was moving in my heart. It was like a weight on me. A weight I could not resist."*

The prophet Jeremiah had a similar encounter with God. God not only touched Jeremiah's mouth; God also infused His words into his mind. From that moment on, Jeremiah had no choice but to speak out for he could not resist the weight of God's Word.

"But if I say, 'I will not mention His word or speak anymore in His name,' His word is in my heart like a fire, a fire shut up in my bones. I am weary of holding it in; indeed, I cannot." (Jeremiah 20:9 NIV)

Perhaps God is doing something similar in you. You feel a weight in your heart, you feel a fire in your bones and you feel God moving in you.

Like my son, like the humble leader of the women's fellowship, and like the prophet Jeremiah, God moves in us, so that through us, His glory can be seen.

~Binu

August 13 ~ Jeremiah 23-25

"'The days are coming,' declares the Lord, 'when I will raise up for David a righteous Branch, a King who will reign wisely and do what is just and right in the land. ... This is the name by which he will be called: The Lord Our Righteous Savior.'" Jeremiah 23:5-6 (NIV)

When I first moved to my new home state, a cooking catastrophe led me to the emergency room. After the visit, it was quite late when I drove home. I was by myself and so upset that I drove slowly.

To my surprise, I saw lights flashing behind me. When I pulled over to the side of the empty road, I was told that this state's law is to pull over to an area off the road. I then headed into a parking lot and fear overwhelmed me as I saw that the vehicle blocked the exit of the parking lot.

What was going on?? It was the middle of the night, it was dark, I was alone, and I was miserable from the pain of my injury. When I asked why I was pulled over, I was not given a reason, but only told to provide identification. After waiting for what seemed like an eternity, I was told I could go home and there was no explanation provided.

Needless to say, that left quite a terrible taste in my mouth about the local law enforcement. How could I feel safe after such an incident or believe that I could be protected?

Years later, we became acquainted with the officers on duty at our church. We are grateful for each and every one who clearly are proud of their job and work with integrity. They have demonstrated how much they value people and protecting them. My hope in local law enforcement was restored.

Jeremiah chapter 23 refers to leaders who were entrusted to take care of, protect, and lead God's people. Sadly, they neglected their responsibility and it infuriated God. These leaders drove His people away with violence and oppression. How could anyone have hope in leadership after such lack of care?

We can have hope because the greatest Ruler of all is God. He is just and He is fair. God keeps His promises. He loves His people and sent His only Son that we might live under the authority of our Savior.

Thank You, Lord!

~Joyce

August 14 ~ Jeremiah 26-29
"Also, seek the peace and prosperity of the city to which I have carried you into exile. Pray to the LORD for it, because if it prospers, you too will prosper." Jeremiah 29:7 (NIV)

Have you ever felt like you were in a place of exile?

Maybe not a literal deportation from your homeland to a foreign country, but you find yourself in a place or situation you would rather not be in.

You have moved to new city or a new school and now you long for close friendships. You are in a struggling marriage and you long for your relationship to be better. Or maybe you are in a season of waiting. Waiting for that new job, for admission into the right school, or for your life partner.

Whichever end of the spectrum you find yourself in, Jeremiah 29 offers clear instructions as to what God desires for His children living in exile.

"... Seek the peace and prosperity of the city to which I have carried you into exile. Pray to the LORD for it, because if it prospers, you too will prosper." (Jeremiah 29:7 NIV)

God wants you to pray.

Pray, not just for yourself to find friends in your new city or school, but pray for your city and for your school ... because if it prospers, you too will prosper. Pray for your broken marriage, not just that your spouse will understand you more, but that you will understand him more and that in the end your marriage will honor and glorify God.

We often have little control of our present situation, but we do have control of what we choose to do while there.

After seventy years of being faithful in exile, Jeremiah 29:11 declares God's glorious promise to His children.

"'For I know the plans I have for you,' declares the LORD, 'plans to prosper you and not to harm you, plans to give you hope and a future.'" (Jeremiah 29:11 NIV)

As you wait for the fulfillment of Jeremiah 29:11, I pray God will give you the strength to pray and may He give you eyes to see His hand of faithfulness, even in your very place of exile.

~Binu

August 15 ~ Jeremiah 30-31
*"... I have loved you with an everlasting love; I have
drawn you with unfailing kindness."
Jeremiah 31:3b (NIV)*

Chloral hydrate. Just the mention of it makes me cringe.

When my son was nine months old, his body was affected by what doctors believed to be a virus. This virus affected his heart.

After his initial hospitalization stay, our son would need to have an echocardiogram performed every few months to ensure his heart was healing properly. The echocardiogram visit required our son lay still. Try telling that to an eleven-month-old! And that's where chloral hydrate comes into the story.

What is chloral hydrate? It's a sedative commonly given to young children. It is very bitter and probably the worst tasting stuff you can imagine.

It took both my husband and I, to hold our son down and force this liquid into him. My eleven-month-old gurgled, gagged, and wailed. While holding him down, I told him over and over again that I loved him. It broke my heart.

And so it was with Jeremiah. The message God asked him to deliver was a bitter one. Exile is coming. Jeremiah's voice trembled, his eyes were filled with tears and his heart was broken for the people. Jeremiah was indeed the weeping prophet.

In Jeremiah chapter 30, Nebuchadnezzar's Babylonian army stood right outside Jerusalem's city walls. Exile was no longer an empty threat; exile was literally knocking at their door. But in the midst of this dark hour, Jeremiah proclaims the word of the Lord *"... I have loved you with an everlasting love; I have drawn you with unfailing kindness." (Jeremiah 31:3 NIV)*

The New Testament says it this way, *"For God so loved the world, that He gave His only begotten Son ..." (John 3:16a KJV)*

From Genesis to Revelation, God's message is consistent. His love is deep, His love is unconditional, His love is everlasting. Even in our darkest moments, when nothing makes sense.

Maybe you are there. Depression, loneliness, divorce, sickness ... whatever your chloral hydrate looks like, however bitter it may taste ... you are not alone. I pray you feel the arms of our Father, holding you and whispering these words in your ear: *"I have loved you with an everlasting love; I have drawn you with unfailing kindness." (Jeremiah 31:3 NIV)*

~Binu

August 16 ~ Jeremiah 32-34
"... They did nothing of all you commanded them to do. Therefore you have made all this disaster come upon them." Jeremiah 32:23b (ESV)

There are some days I am very disciplined when it comes to my diet. And many other days that I am not.

With much fear and trembling, after the "many other days", I will get on the scale, and hope for the best.

It's not the best. In fact, it reflects the choices I have made. The extra fries, the dessert after every meal, the lack of exercise ... it all comes screaming back at me in the higher than desired number on the scale.

That happens in other areas of our lives too. The choices we make impact the life we have.

The Israelites knew all about this. Jeremiah reflected on it:

"And you gave them this land, which you swore to their fathers to give them, a land flowing with milk and honey. And they entered and took possession of it. But they did not obey your voice or walk in your law. They did nothing of all you commanded them to do. Therefore you have made all this disaster come upon them." (Jeremiah 32:22-23 ESV)

It's easy to read verses like that and feel like God did this to them but Israel was suffering due to the choices they had made. God was now *allowing* them to experience the consequences of their sins.

God is just and rightly so. Thankfully, He is also *"... compassionate and gracious ... abounding in love." (Exodus 34:6 NIV)*

He displayed that with Israel time and time again. In the midst of judgment, there is assurance of the plans He has for their future.

'"For thus says the Lord: Just as I have brought all this great disaster upon this people, so I will bring upon them all the good that I promise them." (Jeremiah 32:42 ESV)

Some of my choices cut deeper than a few extra pounds on the scale. While I understand the natural cause and effect of those choices, I have seen God's hand of grace come and lift me *"out of the pit ... He set my feet on solid ground and steadied me as I walked along." (Psalm 40:2 NLT)*

The consequences of my sins have taught me valuable lessons about the choices I should make.

The grace of God has covered me through it all and assured me that He isn't done with me yet.

~Anu

*"Therefore, this is what the Lord of Heaven's Armies, the
God of Israel, says: 'Jehonadab son of Recab will always have
descendants who serve me.'" Jeremiah 35:19 (NLT)*

When I was a child, I remember my parents telling me about other kids who obeyed their parents and were good examples of how children should act. Even though I hated the comparison, deep down inside, it made me want to be a little more like those children.

God seems to make a similar comparison toward a group of people called the Rechabites.

God tells Jeremiah to go and find the Rechabite people and invite them into the temple and offer them wine to drink. He does so, only to find that they refused to drink it. You see, their ancestors instructed them never to drink wine and to live in tents as nomads.

Although hundreds of years had passed since they were given these rules, they still adhered to these laws.

And God was impressed with their faithfulness.

God used them as an example to Jeremiah and to Israel. He pointed out that these people respectfully obeyed the laws and traditions of their forefathers ... in contrast to Israel who continued to disobey.

Because of the Rechabites' faithful obedience, God promises to give this people group, a special place in Israel. God tells Jeremiah that there will always be one of their descendants who serve God.

I love how God tries so hard to help His people understand just how important it is to obey Him. He doesn't say it in a demanding and dictatorial kind of way. God lovingly tries to help them understand how obedience to His laws are there to benefit them as well. I pray that I will obey this loving God who only wants what is best for me.

Help me Lord to understand that your ways are always better and higher than mine.

~Vijoy

August 18 ~ Jeremiah 38-40, Psalms 74, 79
"... They lowered Jeremiah by ropes into the cistern; it had no water in it, only mud, and Jeremiah sank down into the mud." Jeremiah 38:6 (NIV)

Right out of graduate school, I was blessed with my dream job. I got to work with patients in the hospital who weren't healthy enough to return home yet. I loved my patients and had a great team. Gradually, our team split up. Other issues began cropping up, and I started looking for another job.

After much prayer and conversation, I left the job that I loved for another opportunity that I believed would be better. It was closer to home and had potential for growth.

My first day started with orientation in the morning and patient care in the afternoon. By the end of that day I realized that I had stepped out of one mess and into another. I wanted to quit that same day but knew that I couldn't until I found another job.

I stayed at that job for 4 months. I worked 45-60 hours a week. I was exhausted and miserable. *During that time,* I ran into a friend who worked at my previous job, but in a different department. There was an opening in her area, and she wanted to know if I was interested. I had limited experience in that skill set and was horribly intimidated at the thought of learning, but I was desperate to leave my situation. Within a few weeks, I gave my notice and started a new job.

Jeremiah was imprisoned in a dungeon and then moved to the palace prison where he was provided with a loaf of fresh bread every day. Then he was moved into a cistern with mud at the bottom. The scripture says that Jeremiah sank down into the mud. He was rescued, not by his own people, but by an outsider who knew his value. He was led back to the prison where he stayed until the fall of Jerusalem. He was given food and money and allowed to return to his broken, destroyed home. He was finally free for good.

In prison, Jeremiah was saved from the ransacking of Jerusalem.

No matter what it looks like around you ... dungeon, prison or well ... God is with you. He always has a plan. God may even send a rescuer that doesn't look like what you expected. Stay strong in your darkness and allow the Lord to complete His work in you.

~Shiney

"But they mocked God's messengers, despised his words and scoffed at his prophets until the wrath of the Lord was aroused against his people and there was no remedy." 2 Chronicles 36:16 (NIV)

I was sitting in the optometrist's office when I got the news. *"Glasses"*, he said. Tears filled my eyes, and I leaned into my mother. I felt silly, crying as a teenager over something as simple as glasses. But I was devastated, and the struggle was real at an age when image mattered.

My mom comforted me, and then we turned to check out the options for my frames. I was doomed. Our insurance only covered a collection of the thickest, most hideous frames. Why, oh, why did I need glasses!

The day came, and I went to pick up the frames I had chosen - the thinnest pair I could dig up. A few hours later, I remember being high up on the swings when suddenly something caught my eye. My new lenses showed me something I hadn't noticed before ... leaves ... on the trees.

Sure, I knew where leaves came from, but there they were, as clear as day! How did I miss such beauty? My crystal-clear, newly corrected vision allowed me to see things I had missed before.

Many of the kings of Judah failed to lead righteously. Jehoiakim, Jehoiachin, Zedekiah ... their failed leadership led to the people being unfaithful to the Lord.

So, God sent His people messengers to warn them to change their ways. Their vision was dim, and God was giving them an opportunity to look through clear lenses. But they scoffed and despised these messengers until God's wrath was aroused. They desired to remain blind and rejected the chance to see things God's way.

Due to their disobedience, many Israelites were killed by the Babylonians, and those who escaped the sword were taken into exile to Babylon until seventy years were fulfilled as prophesied by Jeremiah.

Often, we get comfortable living with blurry vision, going about our days in a fog. Maybe it's a broken relationship or harbored hurts that we can't let go. While there may be people in our lives offering clarity through advice or prayer, we are reluctant to move forward.

Friend, it is time to see things more clearly. Take a step of faith and ask God to reveal areas where you need clarity, whether it's a relationship, a job, or even a health issue.

You'll start to see things in whole new way.

~Elizabeth

August 20 ~ Habakkuk 1-3
"yet I will rejoice in the Lord, I will be joyful in God my Savior." Habakkuk 3:18 (NIV)

After our son was diagnosed with a metabolic disorder and was hospitalized numerous times, I made a decision. We were not going to have any more children. I didn't discuss this with my husband. I didn't pray about it. I was just overwhelmed and I couldn't handle another child. Or so I thought ... until the Holy Spirit revealed that I made that decision based on fear. I sought the Lord for forgiveness and asked for His will to be done.

Before I knew it, we were expecting a baby. But I was terrified. What if she was born with the same disorder? I began to pray really hard. I asked those in my support network to pray for our baby. My faith arose. My fear disappeared. I trusted God to provide us with a healthy child.

Everything about my newborn was perfect and I couldn't have been happier ... that is until we received a call two days later. Test results showed that she had the same metabolic disorder.

As the tears poured down my cheeks, I was quite honest with God. In frustration and sorrow, I asked how this could happen when we believed and when we trusted Him. Then, my husband received a word from God that it wouldn't be the same with our daughter. She would not suffer the way our son had.

I struggled at first to receive that word in my broken state, but I trusted God and I thanked Him. And I have seen that word come to pass. Our daughter's journey with this disorder has been milder and indeed, different. I am incredibly grateful to God.

In the book of Habakkuk, evil was thriving in Judah. The prophet Habakkuk's prayers reveal how he was quite honest with the Lord as he questioned God's silence and doubted His wisdom. But God's unexpected response in chapter 1:5b (NIV) says, "... *be utterly amazed. For I am going to do something in your days that you would not believe."* While Habakkuk voiced his frustration, he concluded by praising God.

Friend, whatever it is you are walking through know that God can handle your honesty as you pray. But don't just make it a griping session. In the midst of the confusion, praise Him because His plans are good.

~Joyce

August 21 ~ Jeremiah 41-45
"Whether it is good or bad, we will obey the voice of the Lord our God ..." Jeremiah 42:6a (ESV)

The story reads like a soap opera. There is betrayal, murder, rebellion and of course, the wise old sage.

Gedaliah has been appointed the governor of Judah but is assassinated by Ishmael and his band of rebels. As if that wasn't enough, they also killed a group of men who had come to the temple to worship.

Ishmael escapes and the people of Judah are left wondering what they should do next. They consult Jeremiah with the assurance that *"whether it is good or bad, we will obey the voice of the Lord our God..." (Jeremiah 42:6a ESV)*

Spoiler: they didn't.

God commanded them to stay put. If they chose to go to Egypt, disaster would surely follow. It was so predictable what happened next. They accused Jeremiah of lying and went to Egypt anyway.

Jeremiah reminded them of the punishment awaiting them. What happens next though wasn't as predictable.

The women responded.

Did anyone else feel hopeful at this point? Oh surely, the women will talk some sense into these men who chose to rebel against God! Maybe they will talk them down off the ledge like Abigail did with David or Esther with King Xerxes.

Unfortunately, that was not the case. They were proud of their sins almost to the point of bragging about it. In fact, they claimed, that their husbands were right there with them as they prepared offerings for the idols. It was one disobedient act after another, with the final nail in the coffin delivered by the women.

With all that has happened, it seems like this isn't anything. But it is.

It's easy to think that in the midst of darkness, a small match can't do anything. But it can. No matter how small the flame, it provides light. A light that can easily be spread. But it takes one person to choose to strike the match.

These women chose to the fan the flame of sin instead.

What situations have we found ourselves in where the same choice is offered to us? It happens more often than we think. A girlfriend calls you to gossip - what do you do? Your co-workers take longer lunch breaks than allotted - what do you do?

We have the match in our hands. Do we fan the flame of sin or shine a light? The choice is ours.

~Anu

August 22 ~ Jeremiah 46-48

"Fear thou not, O Jacob my servant, saith the Lord: for I am with thee; for I will make a full end of all the nations whither I have driven thee: but I will not make a full end of thee, but correct thee in measure ..." Jeremiah 46:28a (KJV)

I love to talk, read and write about God's love. The warmth He brings us, the forgiveness He offers us and the joy of the Lord that fills our souls. All are definite perks of being His child!

But what about the corrective aspects of our Heavenly Father's love. Proverbs 3:12 reminds us, *"... The Lord disciplines those he loves, as a father the son he delights in." (NIV)*

In reading through the later chapters of the book of Jeremiah, we see clearly the *corrective* side of God's love.

God gave His people multiple chances and spoke through multiple prophets, begging the people to repent and turn to Him. But time after time, chance after chance, the people did not listen. Discipline was a long time coming. Discipline in the form of Babylonian captivity.

Even so, God wanted His children to understand that He still loved them.

In Jeremiah 46:27-28, God speaks to a certain remnant who bypassed the first round of captivity. This group eventually fled to Egypt in hopes of escaping all rounds of captivity.

God tells them, *"Fear thou not ... for I am with thee ... but I will not make a full end of thee, but correct thee in measure." (vs 28 KJV)* In other words, you can run but you cannot hide from God's discipline. They might have bypassed round one but correction was coming. And God was right. Nebuchadnezzar eventually made his way down to Egypt.

As a Father, God Almighty *had* to discipline them. He had to *"correct them."* God loved them too much to let them slip away from Him.

It's what a loving Father does.

Father, thank you that you 'correct us in measure,' not to destroy us but to refine and restore us. May our hearts, our minds and our eyes be open to see your love ... in all aspects of our lives.

~Binu

August 23 ~ Jeremiah 49-50
"... They will come and bind themselves to the Lord in an everlasting covenant that will not be forgotten." Jeremiah 50:5 (NIV)

Jeremiah delivers a very specific message to each of the aggressors against the Israelites. Destruction is coming for them! There is so much destruction, anger and wrath contained in these two chapters. Why is all of it even necessary?

In the midst of Jeremiah's prophecy against the enemies of Israel, he gives a glimmer of hope. While he is warning of impending destruction and annihilation, in the verse above, he predicts that this will cause the Israelites to return to the Lord.

God knew that He could only bring His people back using drastic measures. He gave them many chances to repent and return to Him, but they did not listen. He allowed everything to be taken from them - their homes, their families, their identities - so that they could give birth to a new identity in Him.

The word covenant implies something stronger than just a promise. In Biblical times when a covenant was made, blood was generally spilled or exchanged. In an exchange, the blood of one person was mixed with another's. In some respects, they became one. In the spilling of blood, we find ourselves weaker, unable to attack or face our challenges alone. Our strength is found in the person that we have or made the covenant with.

Sometimes in tragedy, we find ourselves face to face with God in a way that changes our lives. I know that I have fought this change tooth and nail. I don't want to go through the struggle. But in this change, we receive a hope for the future - the hope of a new covenant with God.

It will change the makeup of who we are into the person that God is wanting us to become.

~Shiney

August 24 ~ Jeremiah 51-52

*"In the thirty-seventh year of the exile of King Jehoiachin of Judah,
Evil-merodach ascended to the Babylonian throne. He was kind to
Jehoiachin and released him from prison on March 31 of that year.
He spoke kindly to Jehoiachin and gave him a higher place than all
the other exiled kings in Babylon." Jeremiah 52:31-32 (NLT)*

Is there still a plan in the midst of chaos? In the thick of it, it never seems so. But once the dust settles and we look closely, we can see the divine hand of God guiding us all the way.

In scripture, we read about how Jeremiah spoke for years of the coming judgement of God. But his warnings seemed to fall on deaf ears.

Eventually, the sin of Israel reached a tipping point, and God had to respond.

It was during the reign of Jehoiakim, the son of King Josiah, that Nebuchadnezzar marched into Jerusalem and laid siege to it. The people of God were now forced to pay tribute to Nebuchadnezzar, and many, including some of the best and brightest of Israel were taken as captives to Babylon.

King Jehoiakim rebelled against God and was eventually killed. He was succeeded by his son King Jehoiachin. Jehoiachin's reign lasted only 3 months before Nebuchadnezzar marched back into Jerusalem and carried him and his family off to Babylon. Jehoiachin was imprisoned, thus fulling the prophecy of Jeremiah that no one from Jehoiachin's his family would ever sit on the throne of Judah again.

Though it seemed that Israel's sin and rebellion brought punishment and hopelessness, God still had a plan. But how could this be if neither Jehoiachin or his descendants would sit on the throne again?

What we see is that even in captivity, God preserved Jehoiachin and his family. After 37 long years in prison, Jehoiachin was set free when a new Babylonian king ascended the throne and showed kindness to him.

Even though Jeremiah's prophecy to Jehoiachin came true and his descendants never ruled on the throne again, God still used them to do His good work. It was Zerubbabel, the grandson of Jehoiachin, who was allowed to leave Babylon and return to Jerusalem to rebuild the temple that was destroyed by Nebuchadnezzar.

And when you read the genealogy of Christ in Matthew chapter 1, you see Jehoiachin, his son, his grandson and their descendants in the lineage leading up to Jesus Christ.

You see, even when it seemed hopeless, God had a plan.

I hope you are encouraged in knowing that even though things may seem out of control around you, God's plan for you remains. Trust Him and He will see it through.

~Vijoy

August 25 ~ Lamentations 1-2

"... Is any suffering like my suffering that was inflicted on me, that the Lord brought on me in the day of his fierce anger?" Lamentations 1:12 (NIV)

When I became a parent, I knew nothing. (I would argue that I actually still know nothing!) I watched parents around me and took silent lessons. I listened to advice and tested things out on my own kids.

One particular piece of advice that always stuck with me was in regards to punishment.

My friends advised me that when I threatened my kids with punishment, I needed to carry it out, no matter how difficult. We all threaten our kids with phrases that start with *"If you do [or don't do] this [insert action here], then I will [insert consequence here]."*

As a rookie, I would throw out consequences that were over the top:

"I'll never help you again." That was a lie - there's no way that my kids could make it through the day without my help.

"I won't ever take you out to eat again!" Woah, that was actually punishing myself and knowing how much I dislike cooking, I knew that was a lie also.

I remember one time my husband advised my son, *"If you don't take a nap, we aren't going to go over to your friend's house tonight!"* It didn't work. He didn't take a nap, and we still went to the friend's home.

I knew that kids would call our bluff on things, but I didn't realize that they learned at such an early age whether the threat was empty or real. I finally learned after several failed punishments that I needed to sharpen my threats to something that I could actually carry out.

In Lamentations, we see the Israelites facing their punishment. Four of the five chapters in Lamentations were written as an acrostic poem where the first word of each line follows a successive letter of the Hebrew alphabet. Lamentations itself means *"How?"*

I am sure that's what the Israelites were asking as this book describes the beginning of their punishment and downfall. The threat of their punishment, once so vague, was becoming a reality. God wasn't playing around. He does everything He says He will - good or bad.

What can we learn from this? Well, if you're like me, it's the ultimate parenting lesson. Say what you mean and mean what you say. But, the beauty of God's love is that He gives us chance after chance to make things right with Him.

~Shiney

August 26 ~ Lamentations 3-5
"The Lord is good to those who wait for him, to the soul who seeks him." Lamentations 3:25 (ESV)

Waiting can be hard and sometimes we don't understand the reason. It was a part of the process in the search for my husband. I just couldn't find the right person to share my life with. I wondered why it seemed so easy for some women to find their spouses, and how for me, it was such a struggle.

Then, I prayed and cried to God. He heard me. I was at a prayer meeting one night and decided that I would focus my prayers on this special need. On my way home from that meeting, I listened to a voicemail my mom had left me. She said knew of someone I should meet.

This turned out to be my future husband.

God hears us. He listens.

God was preparing me in the waiting even though I didn't realize it ... even though I didn't want it. He knows best. What I have learned is He wants me to trust Him in that pause that seems to never end ... because honestly, that is all I can do.

The word, "wait" in other translations refers to depending or trusting.

We don't know why, but God asked many people to wait, and for different reasons:

Sarah waited.

Joseph waited.

Joshua waited.

Elizabeth waited.

Mary and Martha waited.

In all of their stories, God was ultimately glorified. They could do nothing more than trust and depend on their Father.

May God be glorified in our lives, even while we wait, because He is preparing our hearts for more than we could *ever* imagine.

"The Lord is good to those who wait for him, to the soul who seeks him." (Lamentations 3:25 ESV)

~Elizabeth

August 27 ~ Ezekiel 1-4
"... Do not be afraid of what they say or terrified by them ..." Ezekiel 2:6b (NIV)

My son grew gravely ill when he was just five months old. We found ourselves in the emergency room on Thanksgiving not knowing what was happening to him. Due to the holidays, we had to wait to get an MRI done. Once it was finally done, we received a phone call from our pediatrician weeks later. She said that the images showed that our son had suffered from a stroke. In my shock and disbelief, I vehemently denied that such an event could have happened to our son. I was so angry as I told our doctor that she was mistaken, I actually hung up on her!

The doctor was just the messenger. She didn't do anything to make this happen to our son. Yet, I reacted adversely to her because I was angry and unwilling to accept the truth of what our child had experienced.

Can you imagine how many times she has to make difficult calls like that? What if she chose not to because of such negative reactions? Ultimately, patients would not know the truth of their medical issues and the doctor would not be faithful to doing her job well.

In the book of Ezekiel, we see that God knew that there were Israelites who would respond adversely when they were corrected. This is evident as He spoke to His prophet Ezekiel. God repeatedly encouraged Ezekiel in chapter 2 not to be afraid of how the people reacted or responded. His admonition to Ezekiel was that he speaks the words that He was going to give him.

Doing what God instructs us to do will not always find us surrounded by people who care to hear what we have to say. That can be quite a terrifying place, but we see that as believers, we cannot be afraid of men. We are reminded of such in 2 Timothy 1:7 (NKJV) which says, *"For God has not given us a spirit of fear, but of power and of love and of a sound mind."* Luke 11:28 (NIV) states, *"Blessed rather are those who hear the word of God and obey it."*

"Trust and obey,
For there's no other way,
To be happy in Jesus,
But to trust and obey."[1]

~Joyce

August 28 ~ Ezekiel 5-8
"...They will recognize how hurt I am by their unfaithful hearts... "(Ezekiel 6:9b NLT)

Can you remember when you first committed a sin?

It's certainly not something we want to think about. Of course, there were the things our parents told us about: the terrible two tantrums and refusal to share with our siblings. But when is the first time you actually realized that you had sinned?

For me, I was in the 2nd grade and at the grocery store with my mom. She didn't oblige my request for candy which wasn't a surprise. She usually said no. My typical response was to whine but eventually move on. For some reason though, this day was different. I took the piece of candy and slipped it into my pocket without anyone seeing what I had done.

Or so I thought.

I got home and had to figure out a way to enjoy my candy without my parents wondering where I got it from. I devised what I thought was a clever plan (at least according to my 7-year-old brain). Long story short, my parents figured out what I did. Not only was I immediately punished and rightly so, I had to go back to the store to return the candy.

Back then, I realized what I did was wrong. I knew I went against what my parents had taught me and even what I learned in church. What I didn't realize was that my sin hurt more than myself or my parents.

It's easy to see the ramifications of our sins on the people around us. They express hurt or tears ... sometimes, it looks like outrage and anger. We also feel the guilt of our wrong doing and try to quickly put things back together.

But it goes beyond the people we can see. We hurt the heart of God too.

Regarding the children of Israel, He said, *"They will recognize how hurt I am by their unfaithful hearts..." (Ezekiel 6:9b NLT)*

When David committed adultery with Bathsheba, there were many who were impacted by this. But the cry of David's heart was towards God, *"Against You, You only, have I sinned ..." (Psalm 51:4 ESV).*

When we sin, we should be repentant to the people around us and to our Heavenly Father.

~Anu

August 29 ~ Ezekiel 9-12
"And I will give them singleness of heart and put a new spirit within them. I will take away their stony, stubborn heart and give them a tender, responsive heart." Ezekiel 11:19 (NLT)

Our kitchen trash reached its max capacity. So, my eldest son, being the responsible guy that he is, tied up the trash bag and took it out.

Weirdly enough, the trash was now out of the house, but a horrible trash smell (which wasn't there before) was now inside the house. Where could it be coming from?

I cleaned and sanitized the now empty trash can. I retraced my son's steps from the kitchen to the garage and mopped up a few smelly droplets that must have leaked out of the bag during the transit. I lit candles, sprayed air freshener, and opened the doors. But the smell was getting worse!

What in the world?

Then, my other son noticed the smell had made its way up the stairs...at the same time that his brother had made his way up the stairs.

Bingo! My son must have unknowingly stepped in the smelly droplets, and now his socks reeked like trash juice. Wherever he went, there went the smell! Mystery solved. We've all experienced situations like this. But it isn't trash we smell.

No one can do anything right; people are annoying us and life just stinks. We try to get away... but wherever we go, annoyance follows us around like the stench of my son's socks.

God has a solution.

In the book of Ezekiel, God offered a heart reset to the most negative, disobedient group of people you can imagine: *"And I will give them singleness of heart and put a new spirit within them. I will take away their stony, stubborn heart and give them a tender, responsive heart." (Ezekiel 11:19 NLT).*

If God can transform these folks, He can surely transform you and I. We just have to ask.

People will disappoint us, and we will disappoint people. It stinks, but it's life ... and it's often inevitable.

Clean what you can around you, but don't forget to look within. We may be the ones who need to change our smelly socks.

~Binu

August 30 ~ Ezekiel 13-15

"And you, son of man, set your face against the daughters of your people, who prophesy out of their own hearts. Prophesy against them..." Ezekiel 13:17 (ESV)

My job is centered around collecting data from the local county hospital. A couple of years ago, that hospital moved into a new building.

Well, the move obviously involved lots of changes. We were desperately trying to get all of it sorted out so we could collect our data accurately. I reached out to various people and after speaking with one employee in particular, I was 100% sure I finally found the answers I needed. She seemed knowledgeable and was very confident in the information she was sharing with me.

Well, within 12 hours, I found out that she was very wrong. How did I find this out? I received an information sheet that had been created by the department itself.

I got it straight from the source.

In our continued pursuit of God, this is key as well. I love listening to podcasts and reading devotionals (like this one we have created for you!) but it is crucial to go to God ourselves.

Ezekiel was encountering this very thing ... and over 2000 years later, we do too. People who claim to be from God but speak things that do not line up with who He really is.

"Instead, they have told lies and made false predictions. They say, 'This message is from the Lord,' even though the Lord never sent them. And yet they expect him to fulfill their prophecies! Can your visions be anything but false if you claim, 'This message is from the Lord,' when I have not even spoken to you? Therefore, this is what the Sovereign Lord says: 'Because what you say is false and your visions are a lie, I will stand against you', says the Sovereign Lord." (Ezekiel 13:6-8 NLT)

How do we know if something is truly from the Lord or not? Because we have spent time in His word and with Him. We are going straight to the source so if others give us wrong information, we know the truth.

What amazed me was how confident this girl was - that's what sold me. But confidence doesn't equal truth. Be careful who you listen to. People can be very convincing but if it contradicts the Word of God, it's not true.

Keep reading books that encourage your faith. Listen to sermons from good Bible teachers. And continue making the time to seek God for yourself.

~Anu

August 31 ~ Ezekiel 16-17
"Yet I will remember the covenant I made with you when you were young,
and I will establish an everlasting covenant with you." Ezekiel 16:60 (NLT)

The book of Ezekiel is not an easy read. And definitely not for the faint of heart.

Ezekiel 16 starts off with the imagery of a baby girl right after birth being carelessly tossed into a field and left to die. The baby is rescued, cleaned up and raised by the caregiver.

Once the child has grown to adulthood, the caregiver takes her as his wife and forms a covenant relationship with her. He gives her fine clothing, jewels, and the best of foods.

She is now a beautiful woman and other men begin to notice her. She forgets her humble beginnings and lets the attention get to her head. She enjoys the attention of men to the point that she becomes a prostitute. She even takes the gold and jewelry given to her by her husband and turns them into statues of men that she worships.

She continually gives herself over to adultery and idolatry while her heartbroken husband looks on. This depiction poignantly describes God's relationship with the people of Israel. He brought them back from death, cared for them, and made a covenant with them. And yet, they reject Him. They follow after other gods and are unfaithful to the God who loves them and is in covenant with them. He vows to bring judgement upon them, stripping them of His protection and allowing other nations to destroy them.

But in this passage of unfaithfulness and judgement, we still see the love of God shine through.

God tells them that even though they will get the judgement they deserve, He will still honor the covenant He made with them when they were young. And He makes a promise to restore them.

Right there in the in the middle of darkness, we see hope.

We also see love. God's amazing and reckless love for his people.

In the middle of your difficult circumstance, I want you to know that your story isn't finished. Our loving God works in the darkest of places and always brings life and hope. He is the God of redemption and restoration. Stay the course, my friend. God is bringing it all together for your good and for His glory.

~Vijoy

September 1~ Ezekiel 18-19
*"... I will judge each of you according to your own
ways, declares the Sovereign Lord ..."*
Ezekiel 18:30 (NIV)

Last night, we went to church and sat together as a family. During worship, I looked down at my 5-year-old and saw her mimicking the same movements that I was doing. If I lifted one arm, she lifted the same one. If both of mine were raised, both of hers would slip into the air. She even tried to mimic my facial expressions.

As much as I loved to see my daughter imitate my worship posture, I couldn't help but wonder what the future would look like for her. I pray that she would worship like that forever, but I know that life doesn't stay so simple. It was a small demonstration of how she looks to me as a role model. I hope that I can set a positive example for her in what I do, but I know that I have my own faults and slip ups. In the end, I know that she will be judged based on what she does. Copying my works won't save her.

In chapter 18, God's word to Ezekiel tells the Israelites that the sins of the father won't bring judgement to the son. Contrarily, the righteousness of the father won't save the son, either. We each stand on our own.

Later in the chapter it says that if an evil man turns away from his sins and starts to live right, he will live and not die (vs 21-22). If you start off righteous and then turn the other way, you die in your unrighteousness (vs 24). God isn't necessarily concerned with how we start this race but more so how we finish it.

Flash forward into the New Testament, in John 9, where the disciples ask Jesus why a man was born blind. They ask if it was because of the man's own sin or the sin of his parents. Jesus very plainly tells them that neither is the case, but the blindness is present so that the work of God can be shown (John 9:3).

The trials in our lives aren't meant to expose our sins, they are meant to reveal the work that God is doing in our lives.

God has a specific work in each of us that he wants to complete. Run your race and finish strong!

~Shiney

September 2 ~ Ezekiel 20-21
"This is what the Sovereign Lord says: 'Take off the turban, remove the crown. It will not be as it was: The lowly will be exalted and the exalted will be brought low.'" Ezekiel 21:26 (NIV)

We were a family of six growing up, so a station wagon made sense. To Dad, though, having TWO station wagons made even more sense.

I can still picture the back door of the blue wagon, plastered with what seemed like a hundred bumper stickers. Dad was the pastor of our church, so it served as a ministry tool. *"NO Jesus, NO Peace; KNOW Jesus, KNOW peace!"*

We made use of those cars, enjoying long road trips and making hundreds of memories along the way. One particular time, my sisters and I were in the back of the car, and in a station wagon, when you sit in the back, you are facing the rear.

We were entertaining ourselves by waving at the drivers behind us. One such driver kept waving back frantically. We giggled and continued the exchange. He was having fun with us.

I then noticed his facial expression was serious, he was pointing at our car, and trying to say something. I suddenly realized that he wasn't waving for fun, he was trying to get our attention because there was something wrong!

When we finally pulled over, Dad discovered that there was a gas leak, and fortunately, it was an easy fix.

God used Ezekiel, a man from royal lineage, to be His prophet. Ezekiel was a bold man called to perform different tasks that were symbolic to warn the Israelites of their coming destruction. Their disobedience was stirring God's judgements.

He was met with opposition.

The Israelites desired to live like the other nations. They did not heed the warning signs and continued keeping vile images, worshipping them. They desecrated the Sabbaths, and devoted their hearts to idols.

They completely missed the red flags.

Has God sent you a person or a situation as a warning sign that you have completely missed because you're "having fun"? Is there an area of your life or a behavior pattern that God is prompting you to change so that your walk with Him can be more authentic?

The Lord wants to bring you into covenant with Him and purge you from defilement, so that you can become His bride. Get rid of those things that are hindering you from enjoying this love relationship. And just like that bumper sticker says, once you know the love of Jesus, you will know His peace.

~Elizabeth

September 3 ~ Ezekiel 22-23

"I looked for someone among them who would ... stand before me in the gap on behalf of the land so I would not have to destroy it, ..." Ezekiel 22:30 (NIV)

Having grown up in New York, I drove on several bridges. These massive structures carry a road across a large body of water. Therefore, vehicles can commute easily to their destination. There were days that traffic would be unusually heavy on my way home from work. Upon further inspection, I observed that a portion of the bridge had been raised up so that large boats could pass under it. While waiting for this process to be completed, I have wondered what would happen if there was a mechanical failure and the raised part did not come back down. How would we cross? How would we get to where we need to go? Thankfully, every time I was on that road, the gap was bridged and all the commuters were able to continue on their journey.

This made me think about how there are times when God is looking for people to stand in the gap and be intercessors, those who would pray and petition for others.

Do you remember how God wanted to destroy Sodom and Gomorrah, but Abraham stood in the gap as he asked the Lord to spare anyone who was not evil? Thus, his nephew Lot and his family were saved.

There was also the instance when Moses pleaded with God not to destroy the Israelites for worshipping the golden calf. We can't forget the time when Haman wanted to destroy God's people and Esther, after fasting and praying, intervened by approaching King Xerxes.

When Peter was imprisoned by King Herod, the fervent prayers of the believers were heard as an angel appeared to Peter and he was set free! The Greatest Intercessor of all is Jesus Who helps bridge the gap between us and God the Father.

Is there someone in your life in need of your intercessory prayers? Whether they are in need of a job, healing or for a relationship to be repaired, you can stand in the gap for them by praying on their behalf and believing that the Lord will make a way for them. "*...The prayer of a righteous person has great power as it is working." (James 5:16 ESV)*

~Joyce

September 4 ~ Ezekiel 24-27
"... the next morning I did as I was commanded." Ezekiel 24:18b (ESV)

"... This is very hard to understand. How can anyone accept it?" (John 6:60 NLT)

Those words were uttered by people who had been following Jesus, to the point that they were called disciples. In this particular passage, He spoke to them about being the bread of life and how they must partake of his flesh and blood.

If I'm being honest, I understand why they thought it was hard.

But I think I am feeling the same way after reading this passage in Ezekiel.

It's bad news after bad news. God continued to punish Jerusalem because they strayed from His ways. Also, being punished and deservedly so were Ammon, Edom, Philistia and Tyre for what they did to the children of Israel. God made a promise to Abraham that He would "... *bless those who bless you, and whoever curses you I will curse." (Genesis 12:3 NIV)* God was making good on that promise.

It's not fun to read about people being punished but at least they had it coming, right?

Well, nestled between the punishment for Israel and its enemies was more bad news. But not for someone who deserved it. This time, it was for Ezekiel.

"Then this message came to me from the Lord: 'Son of man, with one blow I will take away your dearest treasure ...'" (Ezekiel 24:15-16 NLT)

Ezekiel's dearest treasure was his wife. She died the next morning.

God used this and Ezekiel's response to it as an illustration to the people. They were about to experience a similar tragedy and God wanted them to respond just as Ezekiel did.

Couldn't God have just told the people, "Respond like this...?" Did Ezekiel's wife have to die for them to understand?

Only God knows the answer to that and one can surmise that it was going to take something extreme for the people of Israel to understand. It wasn't the last time God would pay such a high price for a group of people who seemed to have turned their backs on Him.

Remember, it wasn't just Mary who lost a son on Golgotha. God did too.

Sometimes it seems like what God expects of us is hard ... but don't forget what He has also endured for us.

~Anu

September 5 ~ Ezekiel 28-31
"You regard yourself as wiser than Daniel and think no secret is hidden from you." Ezekiel 28:3 (NLT)

I loved high school chemistry. My teacher, Mr. Snyder, had a way of explaining Avogadro's number, moles and the periodic table like no one else. I entered college as a science major and felt like I had a pretty good grasp on the subject matter.

Until College Chemistry came along. Let's just say, I didn't do so well and had to retake the course over summer. I felt as if my dreams were about to come crashing down.

Throughout the Old Testament, we see king after king who thought they had a *pretty good grasp* on success. And sure enough, we see king after king whose dreams *and kingdom* came crashing down.

In Ezekiel chapter 28, God warns the King of Tyre that his downfall is coming.

'You think you are wise ... by your wisdom and understanding you have gained wealth ... by your great skill in trading, you have increased your wealth." *(vs 2-5 paraphrased NIV)*

God desires that we be good stewards and work hard, but He wants to make sure we know what He knows: Whatever success we have, ultimately comes from Him.

It's a lesson we learn as life forces us to take a few bites of humble pie; it's a lesson I learned through my freshman chemistry class. God showed me the 'D' I was capable of achieving on my own, and the 'A' that I was able to achieve through Him the following summer.

It was in that summer (when I retook the course) I understood what Paul meant when He said, *'I rejoice in my weaknesses.'* For it is in our weaknesses, we get to see firsthand, God becoming strong in us.

Whether you're the King of Tyre, a freshman just starting out in college, or a seasoned veteran of whatever it is you do ... we all have a freshman chemistry story ... and may we never forget it.

Whatever success we have, ultimately comes from God.

"For it is [not your strength, but it is] God who is effectively at work in you ..." *(Philippians 2:13a AMP)*

~Binu

"As for you, my flock, this is what the Sovereign Lord says:
'I will judge between one sheep and another, and between
the Rams and the goats.'" Ezekiel 34:17 (NIV)

In Ezekiel 34, Ezekiel prophesies against the shepherds of Israel. Instead of leading and caring for their sheep (their people), they have been negligent and allowed them to wander away from the flock. God promises to bring them back and care for them, and in verse 17, it says that He will judge between rams and goats.

As I read, I wondered why there would need to be division among these animals. Aren't they all basically the same?

Here's a quick zoology lesson for you: Sheep are stocky, cud-chewing animals. Rams are male sheep with horns. Both are raised for their fleece, wool, milk, and meat[1]. Goats are intelligent, social, and often difficult to herd. Their coats are similar to sheep, and they are also raised for their meat and milk[2]. I found their diet habits interesting. Sheep and rams both prefer grazing on the grass that is short and tend to graze closer to the root. They graze in flocks and are more selective about what they eat[1]. Goats will eat a variety of things and are 'top down' grazers; they start at the top of the plant and work their way down. Goats are very curious and tend to explore by sniffing and nibbling[2]. They learn about their environment by tasting and eating things, even though that may not be the best thing for them.

In Matthew 25, Jesus returns to this analogy of dividing the sheep from the goats. In verse 34 (NIV), Jesus says for the sheep (on the right) to "*take your inheritance, the kingdom prepared for you since the creation of the world.*" The 'sheep' fed Him when He was hungry, gave Him something to drink when He was thirsty, and invited Him in when He was a stranger.

The goats, however, did not recognize Jesus when He came to them as a hungry and thirsty stranger.

Are you a sheep or a goat? Are you eating at the root or just sampling the world around you? One has tremendous benefits that the others could not even begin to offer. The sheep see God in the people around them while the goats are preoccupied with other things.

God wants us honed in and focused on His word and plans for our life, not foraging for sustenance in a depraved world without Him.

~Shiney

September 7 ~ Ezekiel 35-37
*"... Prophesy over these bones, and say to them, 'O dry bones,
hear the word of the Lord. Thus says the Lord God to these bones:
Behold I will cause breath to enter you and you shall live.'"*
Ezekiel 37:4-5 (ESV)

Are you staring at a situation in your life that is dead? I mean there is not even a glimmer of life left. It is as dead as dry bones. Can anything good come from it?

Well, with God, that's actually a great place to start.

In the book of Ezekiel, God took the prophet in the spirit to a valley of dry bones. The scene sounds very morbid. It was a large valley with only skeletal remains. A place that was undoubtedly filled with hopelessness.

But God had another story in mind.

He asks Ezekiel *"Can these bones become living people again?"* And Ezekiel rightly answers *"O Sovereign Lord ... you alone know the answer to that." (Ezekiel 37:3 NLT)*

Then God tells Ezekiel something interesting. He says *"Prophesy over these bones, and say to them, 'O dry bones, hear the word of the Lord. Thus says the Lord God to these bones: Behold I will cause breath to enter you and you shall live" (Ezekiel 37:4-5 ESV)*

Now why would God, who has the power to bring these bones to life, ask Ezekiel to call them to life?

I believe it is because God wants us to see an example of being an *active* participant in the miracle. In doing so, we get the privilege of taking the step of faith, speaking the words, and then watching the miracle unfold right before our eyes.

Ezekiel prophesies to the bones ... and the bones came together to form a complete skeleton. Then flesh and skin covered the skeleton. Ezekiel then prophesied that the breath of God would come into them. Finally, he commands them to breathe.

And breathe they did! What was once just a pile of bones, was a now a great and mighty army before him.

Are you facing a lifeless situation today? I want to encourage you that even from the most hopeless of situations, life can still come.

I pray that you will allow God to use you to be an active participant in the miracle that He wants to do in your life.

~Vijoy

September 8 ~ Ezekiel 38-39
"... I will show my greatness and my holiness and I will make myself known in the sight of many nations. Then they will know that I am the Lord." Ezekiel 38:23 (NIV)

We have an incredibly abysmal depiction of the wrath of God in these readings. God is astonishingly descriptive and specific on the massacre that He plans to unleash on Gog and the people of Magog.

God is also clear on His intentions and His reasons: *"I will execute judgement ... I will show my greatness and my holiness and I will make myself known in the sight of many nations. Then they will know that I am the Lord." (Ezekiel 38:22-23 NIV)*

Everything the Lord does, whether we deem it good or bad, is to reflect His glory.

As the reading continues into chapter 39, the word says that the Israelites will use their weapons for fuel and burn them up. They will have no need for them. Not even to cut down trees for lumber. Verse 10 (NIV) states that *"they plunder those who plundered them, loot those who looted them."* God promises a time of rest after a strenuous battle.

Gog will have a burial place in Israel to serve as a constant reminder of God's victory on behalf of His people. This was a battle so destructive that there was no way they could have completed it on their own without the intervention of God.

Are you facing a battle like that? Are you facing a struggle that is taunting you? Are you facing a battle so severe that you cannot handle it on your own?

Take heart in God's plans that are written at the end of this chapter. (My translation appears in the brackets!)

I will display my glory and all the nations will see [Your story will speak to the nations]. I will bring them back [I will restore my people]. I will have compassion [I will show you mercy]. I will be zealous for my holy name. I will show myself holy. I will gather them [You won't be alone anymore]. I will no longer hide my face from them [You will have a real, authentic encounter with God]. I will pour out my Spirit on the house of Israel [You will have my powerful Spirit on the inside of you].

Your battle and your deficiencies are there to display the glory of our God. What a beautiful promise awaits us after our time of struggle.

~Shiney

September 9 ~ Ezekiel 40-41

"The man said to me, 'Son of man, look carefully and listen closely and pay attention to everything I am going to show you, for that is why you have been brought here. Tell the people of Israel everything you see.'" Ezekiel 40:4 (NIV)

I remember walking into a small bridal boutique to look for a wedding dress. It was a two-room quaint structure that had all the appearances of a little home. This location had been recommended by a friend, and it happened to be the right place for me. The dress I had imagined with its lace bodice and A-line skirt was among the gorgeous gowns.

The seamstress measured me to get the size to perfection. She was a small, kind lady that pulled out her tape measure while listening to my requests for the neckline, cap sleeves and train. Her patience showed me how much she understood the importance of each detail.

Ezekiel was given a vision by the Spirit of God involving the courts of the Temple. The details were so specific that even the measurements of the door hinges were explained. The carvings of the cherubim and palm trees on the walls were among the minute details. How intricate each aspect of this temple was for our Lord!

Bible commentators believe that the Temple described to Ezekiel during the captivity of Israel was a vision of a future Temple, perhaps to be built for the millennium. When you think about it, Ezekiel is given this vision *while* the Israelites had been in captivity for 25 years!

The day would come when God would dwell with His people again in a temple with sophisticated measurements specified by God Himself. The people were not forgotten!

Why do the details matter? Without the seamstress, my wedding gown would not have fit in such a way that would make me feel like confident. Yet, because of her thoughtful measurements, I was able to walk down the aisle like a princess, knowing that every stitch was in place.

What was the purpose of the specifications for the gates, courtyards, and furnishings in Ezekiel's vision? God was preparing a place for His people, and He wanted it to be done to perfection.

God is in the details.

Your Father has an intricate plan for your life which includes particulars you would otherwise consider minutiae. Nothing is haphazard or vague. What area of your life do you need God's direction? Ask your Father in Heaven for guidance, and you will be surprised at how elaborately He has worked everything out for your good.

~Elizabeth

September 10 ~ Ezekiel 42-43
*"Then the Spirit lifted me up and brought me into the inner court,
and the glory of the Lord filled the temple." Ezekiel 43:5 (NIV)*

When reading through the Old Testament, we learn about the history of the Israelites, God's chosen people. We see how God miraculously led them out of slavery and bondage in Egypt. His presence was with them through a cloud by day and by a pillar of fire at night.

Under Moses' leadership, a tabernacle was built which the glory of God filled. The people of God were keenly aware of His presence. Years later after Solomon built the temple, the glory of God filled it reminding people that His presence was with them. What a beautiful history!

Sadly, the Israelites grew far away from the Lord by forsaking His Word, disobeying His commandments, and engaging in activities that God considered to be disgusting. He sent prophets to warn them of their foolishness and to turn away from their sins, but unfortunately, His people rejected them. As a result, we learn that the prophet Ezekiel saw the glory of God leave the temple. What a devastating tragedy!

Thankfully, their history didn't end there. In Ezekiel 43, the prophet saw the glory of the Lord returning to the temple. Can you imagine how overwhelmed he was with awe and joy? Ezekiel was instructed to tell the Israelites to put away their detestable practices so He would live with them forever.

Dear Friend, maybe you find yourself relating to the Israelites' history. You invited the Lord to live in your heart, your temple. You read His Word, you prayed, and you grew in relationship with Him. It was a beautiful journey. Then, one day came when you engaged in sin. It seemed harmless at first, but before you knew it you had grown further and further away from God.

The Lord desires to commune with you. Confess your sins to the Lord and ask Him to forgive you. Allow His presence to usher into your temple once again.

The Psalmist David reminds us that *"In Your presence is fullness of joy."* (Psalm 16:11 ESV)

~Joyce

September 11 ~ Ezekiel 44-45

*"But the Levitical priests, the sons of Zadok, who kept the
charge of my sanctuary when the people of Israel went astray
from me, shall come near to me to minister to me..."*
Ezekiel 44:15a (ESV)

I had just walked off the stage at one of the largest speaking events of my life. I was greeted by people patting me on the back and telling me what a good job I did. Then, I came face to face with the person I admired most in that entire room.

"Thank you for being faithful."

Faithful?? It was nice but not exactly what I was hoping to hear. I wanted to be in the "That was amazing" category or "Let me sign you up to speak again next year!".

Anyone can be faithful, right? All you have to do is keep doing what you are supposed to be doing and you get the faithful label. But even though it isn't complicated doesn't mean it's easy. In fact, being faithful may be the hardest thing we do.

In Ezekiel 44, God was doing some housekeeping. The people had defiled the temple and the Levites contributed to it too. God had enough and decreed they would be punished and could not minister as priests ... except for one group.

"However, the Levitical priests of the family of Zadok continued to minister faithfully in the Temple when Israel abandoned me for idols. THESE MEN WILL SERVE AS MY MINISTERS. They will stand in my presence ... They alone will enter my sanctuary and approach my table to serve me. They will fulfill all my requirements." (Ezekiel 44:15-16 NLT)

When God needed people to do His work, He wasn't looking at who had the best turnout at Sabbath school class. He didn't ask who was quoted most around the water cooler (aka the well). Instead, He recalled the faithfulness of the sons of Zadok during a time when other priests had turned their backs on Him.

Their faithfulness was the key to their future.

Being faithful isn't glamorous. It's showing up when you feel like backing out. It means staying committed even when the luster and shine have faded. It is consistently doing your part.

Mother Teresa said, *"I do not pray for success, I ask for faithfulness."*[1]

Now, when another big day comes, and I'm standing before the One who gave His life for me ... I hope He says, *"Well done good and faithful servant."* And I know that is all I will need to hear.

~Anu

September 12 ~ Ezekiel 46-48
"He asked me, 'Son of man, do you see this?'..." Ezekiel 47: 6 (NIV)

Just when we think it's over. It's not.

In the later chapters of the book of Ezekiel, the Israelites were at their lowest point in history. They were not only exiled to Babylon; their sacred temple had also been destroyed. In the natural, things looked bleak.

But in Ezekiel chapter 47, God gives Ezekiel a vision of a new temple. In the vision, an angel serves as Ezekiel's tour guide.

"Son of man, do you see this?" (vs 6 NIV) the angel asks Ezekiel.

A small trickle of water was streaming from under the south side of the new temple. As Ezekiel and his tour guide went eastward, the water went from ankle deep to knee deep to water so deep you could not walk through it.

This water from the temple eventually made its way into the Dead Sea, a sea with no life. Then, Ezekiel saw something strange happening.

Instead of the Dead Sea contaminating the fresh water from the temple, the fresh water from the temple transformed the Dead Sea. The Dead Sea was now teeming with life. A once destroyed temple now had life coming out of it and hope began flowing in a sea of hopelessness.

A few years ago, my husband received a call from a care flight nurse. His parents were involved in a serious car accident. Both mom and dad were in critical condition and on life support.

Talk about bleak.

The weekend following the accident, as we sat in the waiting room, one of our friends had an idea:

It's Sunday. Why not bring worship into the waiting area? After all, who better to comfort the downcast than the downcast?

We sang, we prayed, and like the river in Ezekiel's vision, hope began to flow in a hopeless waiting area.

John 7:38 tells us, *"Whoever believes in me, as the Scripture has said, streams of living water will flow from within him." (NIV)*

That's good news!

As the angel asked Ezekiel, so I ask you... *"Son of man, do you see this?"*

Do you see that no matter how hard life gets, even in your darkest moments, rivers of living water can still flow from within you?

Whatever your situation is, I pray you see what I see. I pray you see hope.

~Binu

September 13 ~ Joel 1-3
"... your old men shall dream dreams..." Joel 2:28 (ESV)

Yesterday, I turned another year older. The wiser part is still to be determined.

Birthdays will get you thinking a lot about your life in general.

I look back at my past and think of the kind of person I was and the decisions I made. Some were good ... some were not. Because of those "not good" decisions, I ended up hurting others and myself.

I look around at my present and recognize that even after 40 plus years of living on this earth, I still don't get things right.

I look ahead to my future and become more aware that I truly have no idea what is ahead for me.

Well...I found some reassurance in this familiar passage of scripture:

"*I will restore to you the years that the swarming locust has eaten ... which I sent among you.*" *(Joel 2:25 ESV)* Christians quote the restore part all the time but those 5 words at the end are also key: "*... which I sent among you.*"

The reason? God was administering punishment on Israel. This time, their hardships weren't the result of big bad Egypt or even the giant Philistines picking on little Israel. This was more about what Israel had done to themselves.

Unfortunately, I can relate. Some of my "locust" seasons weren't caused by anyone else or even by the enemy. It was me doing it to me.

In spite of this, there is also hope provided for Israel, you and me. While God gave Israel what they deserved to teach them a lesson, this same God also gave Israel what they DIDN'T deserve because He loved them. He gave them restoration.

It gets better.

"*And it shall come to pass afterward, that I will pour out my Spirit on all flesh; your sons and your daughters shall prophesy, your old men shall dream dreams, and your young men shall see visions.*" *(Joel 2:28 ESV)*

Logistically, it seems dreaming is for the young but that's not how it is presented here. The middle-aged and old folks, including yours truly, are still meant to dream.

My past? Restored. My present? Satisfied. My future? Dream away.

I was looking back at my past, looking around at my present and looking ahead to my future ... and all I could say is God is good.

~Anu

September 14 ~ Daniel 1-3
"He reveals deep and mysterious things and know what lies hidden in darkness..." Daniel 2:22 (NLT)

A few years ago, as I was driving my father in law's car, I noticed the clock had not been updated for daylight savings time. So, I decided to take it upon myself to fix the time while I was in the car.

It was evening at the time, and the only light in the car was the backlight which illuminated the car's dashboard and radio.

Because this wasn't my car, I was unfamiliar with how to change the time. Once I stopped at a traffic light, I pushed the buttons to try to change the time on the car. I tried several times, doing what logically seemed correct, but nothing seemed to work. So, I gave up.

I remember saying out loud to myself, *"How can changing a clock be THIS difficult?"*

A few days later, I was in my father in law's car again. This time, it was during the day. I looked over and the clock was still not updated. Instinctively, I started the process to change the time in the same sequence I had done a few nights earlier. But because it was daytime, I could now see something I had not seen before.

Right there, in plain sight, I saw small letters signifying which button to press to change the hour and the minutes of the clock. With the light of day, the solution was right in front of me. It was there all along!

In the book of Daniel, we read *"He reveals deep and mysterious things and knows what lies hidden in darkness..." (Daniel 2:22 NLT)*

The longer I live, the more I realize how much I need the light of God to illuminate what is right in front of my eyes. God knows what I do not ... and only He can shine a light on what I cannot see.

For the problem that is frustrating you today, I pray you will lean in and ask God to reveal the missing piece ... the piece which will be the key to unlocking the solution to your problem.

You might be surprised what is revealed as the light of God begins to illuminate your path.

~Vijoy

September 15 ~ Daniel 4-6
*"I want you all to know about the miraculous
signs and wonders the Most High God
has performed for me." Daniel 4:2 (NLT)*

What difference could just one person make in the lives of others?

In these chapters, the story of Daniel continues. We read King Nebuchadnezzar's recollection of Daniel interpreting his dream and the circumstances of this dream coming true.

We read it in a letter he has written which includes *"the miraculous signs and wonders that the Most High God has performed." (4:2 NIV)* Nebuchadnezzar's letter went out *"to people's, nations and men of every language, who live in all the earth." (4:1)* His letter is bookended by praise to God and ends with a very definite declaration of a changed life.

When Nebuchadnezzar's son, Belshazzar, becomes king and has his own crisis, Daniel is called up to interpret again. Quick exit for Belshazzar and now enters our third king, King Darius.

Daniel survives his night in the lion's den and King Darius writes a similar letter declaring praise, honor, and omnipotence to God. We will never know how far reaching these letters were or how many people were inspired by this story, but we know from them that Daniel's influence changed two powerful kings and their kingdoms.

Daniel's life of discipline and prayer caused him to affect the reigns of three kings and change the lives of two of the most notorious kings in the Bible. He was a believer, situated in worldly kingdoms, ready to enact change at the right time. I dare say that if he hadn't lived his life of steady prayer (chapter 6 tells us that he prayed three times a day) he would not have been prepared when his time came. Daniel may never know the influence that he had on people outside of his own territories, but we know he was effective.

You can make a difference. Your sphere of influence is not a random thing. God has placed you there for a reason. You are the agent of change that He wants to work through. Your prayer life can make a difference. Be disciplined and be ready to change the world.

~Shiney

September 16 ~ Daniel 7-9
"At the beginning of your pleas for mercy a word went out, and I have come to tell it to you, for you are greatly loved..." Daniel 9:23 (ESV)

Joyce Meyer's first public message was about the love of God. The back story is that it wasn't her preferred topic. She thought it was too simple but she knew it was what God wanted her to share. God revealed to her that if people really knew how much He loved them that they would act much differently.

When I walk into a room and my husband is there, even if I don't know anyone else, I know him. What makes it even sweeter is that I know I am loved by him. That changes how I feel in that space.

But the fact is my husband is not going to be in every room I walk in. Thankfully, God is there! That changes everything.

You live life differently when you know you are loved.

Daniel is a character in the Bible whose life seemed to be without reproach. (If you've seen one too many Veggie Tales like I have, you may be picturing a cucumber right now but that is not the case.) From the very first moment we are introduced to him, he shows himself to be a man of integrity who honored God even when it was risky.

He was consistently a solid guy with solid faith but even he grew weary at times. With all of the visions and revelations he was having, along with everything that was going on with his people, he was burdened.

So, Daniel prayed (as he often did) and received a message from an angel:

"At the beginning of your pleas for mercy a word went out, and I have come to tell it to you, for YOU ARE GREATLY LOVED." (Daniel 9:23 ESV)

Imagine that! Above all else, that was the first thing this angel, who was on direct assignment from God, was instructed to say.

God wants us to know it too.

"And may you have the power to understand, as all God's people should, how wide, how long, how high, and how deep his love is. May you experience the love of Christ, though it is too great to understand fully. Then you will be made complete with all the fullness of life and power that comes from God." (Ephesians 3:18-19 NLT)

In other words, you are greatly loved.

~Anu

September 17 ~ Daniel 10-12

"I ate no choice food; no meat or wine touched my lips; and I used no lotions at all until the three weeks were over." Daniel 10:3 (NIV)

At the beginning of each year, my church does a 21 day fast. During the first one I participated in, I realized I had not understood fasting and prayer very well. I mistakenly equated it with checking off a box as a good Christian.

Daniel set an example of abstaining from choice foods that were commonly associated with feasting. For him, fasting wasn't about checking off a box. This choice revealed his heart to remove himself from anything that would distract him from hearing God clearly.

In Daniel's mourning for three weeks in chapter 10, we understand that he was praying fervently and regularly as there were many adversaries who wanted to destroy his people. In fact, verse 13 reveals that the man in Daniel's vision, who came on the twenty-fourth day, had been trying to reveal himself earlier but had opposition for twenty-one days.

When my husband was laid off, I was devastated initially. It was unexpected and I found myself feeling afraid as his income is the sole income for our family. I knew saying a quick daily prayer would not be enough during this period of the unknown. I decided to fast and pray during the entire season of layoff. I discovered that I trusted in an income as a provision more than in God as my Provider. My eyes and ears were opened to see and hear what God wanted to reveal during this time. And I earnestly waited in His presence for my husband to receive the right opportunity at the right time with the right company.

Jesus instructed the following in Matthew 6:16 (NIV): *"When you fast, do not look somber as the hypocrites do, for they disfigure their faces to show others they are fasting,"* Lisa Bevere says, *"Fasting changes your perception by changing your focus. Fasting positions you to acknowledge God's provision in your life."*[1]

If you are looking for a way to *"disconnect from the world and connect to God"* as Pastor Stephen Hayes said[2], then I encourage you to enter a time of fasting and prayer.

~Joyce

"... And all the people shouted with a great shout when they praised the Lord, because the foundation of the house of the Lord was laid." Ezra 3:11b (ESV)

"I wish there was a way to know you're in the good old days before you've actually left them."[1]

That profound quote is courtesy of Andy Bernard, on the TV show, "The Office."

There is a lot of truth there for us ... and for the people of Israel.

The exiles have returned from Babylon to a city that has been destroyed, including the temple. As they began rebuilding, there were mixed emotions.

"But many ... who had seen the first house, wept with a loud voice when they saw the foundation of this house being laid, though many shouted aloud for joy, so that the people could not distinguish the sound of the joyful shout from the sound of the people's weeping ..." (Ezra 3:12-13 ESV)

The older men who had seen the grandeur of Solomon's temple were grieving what had been.

And who can blame them? So much time and effort had gone into the original temple ... there wasn't any way this temple could compare to the former temple.

Or could it?

Shea Sumlin from the Village Church said this, *"... eventually, this is going to be the temple that a little boy named Jesus is going to be sitting in when His parents are coming to look for Him. This is going to be the temple that Jesus is going to drive the money changers out of. That's this very temple. This is going to be the temple where Jesus is going to be put on trial before His sentence of death and ensuing resurrection. That's this temple."[2]*

This temple may not have perfectly selected stones but it would have the Chief Cornerstone.

This temple may not have beautiful cedar beams but the man who would die on a wooden cross for our eternal salvation would visit this temple.

This temple may not have the gold and opulence of Solomon's temple but the King of Kings would be there.

This temple would be greater than the former temple.

Maybe you can relate to what they were feeling. What has passed seems better than what is to come. The same God who brought glory to the latter temple can do that in our lives too, because we are His workmanship ... and His temple.

~Anu

"... They finished building the temple according to the command of the God of Israel and the decrees of Cyrus, Darius and Artaxerxes, kings of Persia." Ezra 6:14b (NIV)

From the time our sons were old enough to ask questions, my husband's response to hard and controversial topics has not changed.

"Boys, it's not about what I say or think about a particular issue or what you or your friends say or think about that issue. Let's see what the Bible says about the issue."

It's important to know why we do what we do and why we believe what we believe. And the Bible has always been my family's reference guide.

In the book of Ezra, after seventy years of captivity, King Cyrus of Persia gave the Israelites a thumbs up to leave captivity and go back to Jerusalem to rebuild the temple.

But as quickly as the building project began, so did the opposition to this project.

False accusations were spoken against the Israelites, and after much debate, the building project ceased.

So, God rose up two prophets, Haggai and Zechariah, to encourage the people to not give up. The people took heed to the prophets' words, and the building project resumed...but of course, so did the opposition. This time around, the new King of the land, King Darius, wanted to get to the bottom of things.

What did King Cyrus actually decree?

The archives were dug up and King Cyrus' decree was read. *"Let the temple be rebuilt ... And the expenses of these men are to be fully paid out of the royal treasury." (Ezra 6:3,8 NIV)* Despite the opposition, at the end of the day, the King's decree was all that really mattered. The Israelites now had the fuel *and the money* they needed to stay on task and continue doing what God purposed them to do.

In Ezra 6:14, the temple project was finally completed!

We live in an ever-evolving world. Much has changed since Jesus walked this earth. It's easy to get discouraged and lose sight of why we do what we do, and why we believe what we believe.

But just as King Cyrus' decree had not changed over the years, so our King's decree has not changed! And as my husband tells our boys, *"The Word of God, our King's decree, is all that really matters."*

Let God's Word be the fuel we need to complete whatever task He has given us to do.

~Binu

September 20 ~ Haggai 1-2
"Then Haggai, the Lord's messenger, gave the people this message from the Lord: 'I am with you, says the Lord!'" Haggai 1:13 (NLT)

Every year, I start off with a verse or theme for the year. This year was no different. God spoke to me about what this year would entail. His words were very clear: hard work. There were things that I wanted to accomplish personally, professionally, in my marriage and in ministry, and I knew it would take work. Not just regular work, but hard work. It's scary when God tells you that it will take 'hard' work- what exactly does *hard* entail for our God?

I wanted to lose weight, and I knew that my usual fitness and diet routine would not work. I had to step up my game in both of those areas; I needed to be healthier all around. I wanted advancement in my career, and I knew this would mean taking extra classes and putting my nose back into a book. I wanted a marriage that would thrive, not just survive, and I knew this would take immense time, patience, and sacrifice. I wanted to collaborate in writing this amazing devotional, and there was no way I could accomplish this with my own skills. I needed face down, floor time; I needed to be in-taking the right things so that I could produce something of value.

In Haggai, the Lord charges his people to finish the work of building the temple. He tells them to go up the mountain and bring the timber down to build the temple. Let's be clear here: Hike up a mountain. Chop down trees. Bring them safely back down. Then build. That sounds exhausting; it sounds like hard work.

But the people obeyed, and this beautiful thing happened.

In verse 13 of chapter 1 (NIV), the Lord says *"I am with you."*

A few months into my season of work, I remember feeling frustrated and worn out by thinking that I had taken on more than I could handle. I re-read this chapter and submitted myself to it again. I am still in the process of accomplishing my goals, but at some point, my goals became more tangible. God met me in my obedience. The impossibility of your task shouldn't stop you. God expected his people to do the work, and He met them in their obedience. God will meet you in your challenge - stay obedient and keep doing the hard work!

~Shiney

September 21 ~ Zechariah 1-7
"Do not despise these small beginnings for the
Lord rejoices to see the work begin ..."
Zechariah 4:10 (NLT)

What is my life's purpose? What was I put on this earth to accomplish?

This is likely the most asked question by every human being on the planet at some point in their life. But what if the answer to that big question isn't one big purpose?

In the book of Zechariah, we see how something seemingly small, was a part of something great.

Towards the end of the Babylonian exile, some of the Israelites were allowed to go back to Jerusalem to rebuild the temple. The project was a huge undertaking and they were met with naysayers who tried to discourage them.

To top it off, the temple they were building was going to be much smaller than that of Solomon's temple. It would have been easy for them to just give up.

But the word of the Lord came to Zerubbabel telling him, *"Do not despise these small beginnings." (Zechariah 4:10 NLT)* He was being encouraged to keep doing what he was doing, even though it looked small in comparison to the former temple.

What Zerubbabel might not have known is that the rebuilding of the temple was a big part in the nation of Israel coming back from exile and being re-established in their home country.

Are you tempted to stop what we are doing because it seems insignificant in comparison to what others have done? It's easy to look at the accomplishments of those around us and think what we are doing does not matter.

But it does.

Do not be discouraged by how small your part in the story seems. It is being carefully weaved by God to bring about a beautiful masterpiece for His glory.

~Vijoy

September 22 ~ Zechariah 8-14

"... See, your king comes to you, righteous and
victorious, lowly and riding on a donkey,
on a colt, the foal of a donkey." Zechariah 9:9 (NIV)

The evening before the birth of my second child, I went into a "nesting" phase, that time of urgency to clean and organize to prepare for my new baby.

I had decided that our bedroom needed a splash of character, so I had bought a few frames and pictures to put up on the wall. My husband pulled out the measuring tape and nailed them up carefully in their precise positions.

About three hours later, I went into labor.

We rushed to the hospital as my labor was intensifying. The pain was indescribable.

The doctor who came into the room was one we had never met, but he had compassionate eyes and such a tranquil demeanor. He asked us the intended name for our son as he gowned up. When he heard that it was the name of a Biblical prophet, he mentioned, *"Oh! From the Bible."*

Then, as he calmly helped to deliver my son, he said, *"A prophet is among us!"* What a sweet finale to such a painful time of labor and a long nine-month period of waiting ... of anticipating.

Here he was, our special little guy.

The Old Testament of the Bible recounts the time of punishment of the Israelites due to their persistent disobedience to God. Over and over, God reminds his people that only He should be worshiped, but they continued to follow other gods.

Numerous prophets warn them of the destruction that will come. *"Repent and obey!"* they plead. But, to no avail.

We see, however, tiny slivers of hope through a few prophets like Zechariah, who says, *"Rejoice ... Shout ... See! Your king comes." (Zechariah 9:9 NIV)*

Then...400 years of silence. Not a sound.

All of a sudden, hope is born as a tiny little babe in the unlikeliest of places ... a lowly manger.

God is here!

"The Word became flesh and made his dwelling among us. We have seen his glory, the glory of the one and only Son, who came from the Father, full of grace and truth." (John 1:14 NIV)

Just as labor pains end as a new life begins, God can come and bring hope to your situation.

"May the God of hope fill you with all joy and peace as you trust in him ..." (Romans 15:13 NIV)

~Elizabeth

September 23 ~ Esther 1-5

"... This young woman, who was also known as Esther, had a lovely figure and was beautiful. Mordecai had taken her as his own daughter when her father and mother died." Esther 2:7 (NIV)

Have you ever looked at someone else and wished you could live like they did? Like, maybe a celebrity or someone you personally know? They seem to dress right, know the right people, and live with fame.

At work today, a colleague mentioned how she wanted to be best friends with a particular celebrity couple just for those reasons: *beauty, fashion, fame.*

It's hard to admit it, but I've fallen into that trap many times. Over time, though, I have learned to appreciate *my* life and what God has given *me.*

While it seems that they live a glamorous lifestyle, those who earn front cover photo opportunities also care about safety, privacy, and about a sense of fulfillment ... just like us. At the end of the day, we are all nothing without Christ.

Just ask the lottery winner who just went bankrupt. Money doesn't buy everything.

Hadassah, also called *Esther*, lost her mother and father. If it not for her older cousin, Mordecai, or *God's grace* in her life, she may not have been elevated to queen and able to save the Jewish people from a massacre.

Nehemiah, a Jewish man and a cupbearer for a Persian king, living far from home, hears about his native city being destroyed. Were it not for a kind king and God's grace, he may not have been able to take a bold step to rebuild the wall and ensure safety for his homeland.

These two people were not born in a castle to a royal family to be used by God. They beat great odds.

J. Hudson Taylor, a British missionary and pioneer to China, said, *"All of God's greats have been weak men who did great exploits for God because they reckoned on His being with them."*[1]

Where God has placed you is no accident. When you are aware of who you are and to whom you belong, it should thrill you!

Remember God's destiny for your life is just that ... yours.

"I have been crucified with Christ and I no longer live, but Christ lives in me. The life I now live in the body, I live by faith in the Son of God, who loved me and gave himself for me." (Galatians 2:20 NIV)

~Elizabeth

September 24 ~ Esther 6-10
*"... This is what is done for the man the king
delights to honor!" Esther 6:11 (NIV)*

What is your motivation when you decide to do a good thing? Is it because you know it's the right thing to do or because you want people to notice and recognize you?

In Esther 6, we read that when Mordecai discovered that two of King Xerxes' officers had planned to kill the king, he exposed them. Sounds to me like he was just doing what he knew to be right. It seems that sparing a king's life is a pretty big deal. He definitely should have been awarded a medal of honor or something commendable.

But what do you do if your good deed goes unnoticed without any mention? Do you become bitter and question what was the point? Do you resolve not to do the right thing again?

Before you answer, know this: God notices. Hebrews 11:6 (NKJV) says that *"He is a rewarder of those who diligently seek Him."* Furthermore, Ecclesiastes 3:11 (NKJV) reminds us that *"He has made everything beautiful in its time."*

We see how these verses came to fruition for Mordecai. During a restless night, King Xerxes requested that the history of his reign be read aloud. When he heard what Mordecai had done, he wanted to know how Mordecai had been honored. After King Xerxes realized that recognition was never given, he saw to it that it was done expeditiously. Mordecai was entrusted with a royal robe and a royal horse, which he rode on through the streets, while a royal proclamation was made. Wow! Talk about honor!

Dear Friend, maybe you find yourself in a position like Mordecai who seemed to be forgotten. Keep doing the right thing. Remember what the Word of God says, *"And we know [with great confidence] that God [who is deeply concerned about us] causes all things to work together [as a plan] for good for those who love God, to those who are called according to His plan and purpose." (Romans 8:28 AMP)*

~Joyce

"... For the gracious hand of His God was on Him. For Ezra had devoted himself to the study and observance of the Law of the Lord, and to teaching its decrees and laws in Israel." Ezra 7:9b-10 (NIV)

About a month after my husband and I moved into our first home, we purchased a pool table. My husband was passionate about the game and quite convincing about the need for a pool table. He couldn't wait to enjoy his favorite pastime in his own home.

Once our kids were old enough to understand right from wrong, and could see above the table, my husband implemented a few house rules.

Rule #1: The pool table is not a coffee table. We don't place our drinks or toys on it.

Rule #2: The pool table is not a chair or a bed. We don't sit or lay down on it.

With these rules in place, my husband was excited to teach our children the basics of billiards. He even shared a few insider tips and some cool trick shots he had learned over the years. By the time our boys reached kindergarten, they were both little pool sharks and my husband was one proud daddy.

If my husband, an earthly father, couldn't wait to engage with his boys over his favorite pastime, how much more does our Heavenly Father beam with excitement when we take an interest in what interests Him. His Word.

In Ezra 7, Ezra is described as a *"ready scribe in the law of Moses". (vs 6 KJV)*

Ezra had a passion for the Word of God and because of this, the Bible tells us, the Lord showed favor towards Him.

"For the gracious hand of His God was on Him. For Ezra had devoted himself to the study and observance of the Law of the Lord, and to teaching its decrees and laws in Israel." (Ezra 7:9b-10 NIV)

God's Word is the very heart of God. John 1:1 states, *"In the beginning was the Word, and the Word was with God, and the Word was God." (NIV)*

As we dive into the Word of God, we will deepen our understanding of Him and grow in our intimacy with Him. It's inevitable.

Like Ezra, may we be *"ready scribes"* in the study of God's Word. Our Heavenly Father can't wait to share His heart with His children. Who knows what kind of cool insider tips and deep revelation awaits us!

~Binu

September 26 ~ Nehemiah 1-5

"... Remember the Lord, who is great and awesome, and fight for your brothers, your sons, your daughters, your wives, and your homes." Nehemiah 4:14b (ESV)

A common occurrence on our elementary school playground was the game, Red Rover.

It starts with 2 teams facing each other. The members of each team hold hands to form a type of human chain.

The first team yells for a member of the opposing team to come to their side, *"Red Rover, Red Rover, let _____ come over."* If that person can break through the opposing chain, they go back to their own team along with one other person. If they don't break through, they are forced to stay with the opposing team.

Years ago, my husband and I were in a situation where it seemed like we kept running into the opposing team and couldn't break through. We felt completely defeated.

At the point of wanting to give up, my husband felt God say to him.... *"If you quit, he (the opponent) will still be there but there will be one less of you... then what?"*

When we face opposition, quitting is often our go-to response...but just because it is our first thought doesn't make it the right one.

In the Old Testament, Nehemiah was heartbroken over the destruction of Jerusalem and felt the call to do something about it. Before he even started, he was met with opposition. The easy thing would have been for Nehemiah to go back to his day job but he doesn't do that.

"So we built the wall...for the people had a mind to work...From that day on, half of my servants worked on construction, and half held the spears, shields, bows, and coats of mail. And the leaders stood behind the whole house of Judah ..." (Nehemiah 4:6,16 ESV)

Nehemiah continues with the plan, equips the people to build the wall and arms them to fight if needed. His approach may have changed but his focus stayed the same...build.

I don't know what God has called you to do but facing opposition doesn't change that call. Nehemiah reminded the people (and us), *"...Do not be afraid of them. Remember the Lord, who is great and awesome, and fight for your brothers, your sons, your daughters, your wives, and your homes." (Nehemiah 4:14 ESV)*

The enemy will taunt you and at times you may have to fight. But when you do, remember you never fight alone. Stay focused and keep building. Your team needs you.

~Anu

September 27 ~ Nehemiah 6-7
"...I am engaged in a great work, so I can't come.
Why should I stop working to come and
meet with you?" Nehemiah 6:3b (NLT)

The concept became popular in the 20th century but it seems like Nehemiah understood boundaries. While he was working on a literal boundary, the wall around Jerusalem, he also understood the necessity of the not so tangible kind.

What can we learn about boundaries from this former cup-bearer turned wall-builder?

1. Know who you are dealing with - Sanballat and his buddies had been harassing Nehemiah since the beginning of this project ... and now they want to meet with him? He knew they were up to no good and actually were plotting to harm him. Boundaries protect you from others.

2. Know your purpose - His response to them was telling: *"I am engaged in a great work, so I can't come. Why should I stop working to come and meet with you?"* (Nehemiah 6:3b NLT) When you say no to something, you are really saying yes to something else. Taking the time to meet with these men would mean taking time away from the work God had called him to. More than his protection, he was concerned about his purpose so he refused to meet them. Boundaries guard your time and your purpose.

3. Know who you are - When Sanballat couldn't get Nehemiah to budge, he tried another method. He had a letter written that accused Nehemiah and the people of rebellion and went so far to say that Nehemiah was trying to be king. Nehemiah's response again was sure and strong: *"I replied, 'There is no truth in any part of your story. You are making up the whole thing.' They were just trying to intimidate us, imagining that they could discourage us and stop the work. So I continued the work with even greater determination."* (Nehemiah 6:8-9 NLT) Nehemiah wasn't shaken by their lies because he knew the truth. Boundaries define who you are and who you are not.

To some, boundaries seem self-serving but this story demonstrates that is not the case. Thousands of exiles who returned home were now also safe in their city thanks to Nehemiah's boundaries that he built for the city and for himself.

~Anu

September 28 ~ Nehemiah 8-10
"All the people assembled with a unified purpose ..." Nehemiah 8:1a (NLT)

Have you ever had one of those amazing cleaning days? The kind where the whole family gets involved in the work. Folding laundry, mopping floors, vacuuming, cleaning bathrooms. Like little elves, everyone does their part. And voilà, within hours, your home is clean.

What would have taken you all day is done before lunchtime.

There is just something about unity. And no other story displays the power of unity better than the story of Nehemiah.

Nehemiah was a cupbearer to the King of Persia. His heart was broken when he discovered the walls of his hometown were torn down and his city was now susceptible to enemy attack. When Nehemiah prayed, God made it clear. He was the man God had chosen to rebuild the wall. But he couldn't do it alone. Nehemiah needed favor from the king and favor from the people. God granted him both. The people stood behind him and were willing to do whatever it took to rebuild the wall.

Everyone got involved. Everyone did their part. From perfume makers, to goldsmiths, both men and women worked day and night to rebuild the wall.

And the wall was rebuilt in 52 days.

Psalm 133:1-3 states, *"How good and pleasant it is when brothers live together in unity...For there the Lord commanded His blessing..." (ISV)*

Where there is unity, the world will be able to see God.

For once the wall was complete, Nehemiah's enemies were afraid. They realized such work could have only be done with the help of God. God could have miraculously built the wall by himself, but He chose to use the miraculous power of unity to accomplish His work.

If that wasn't enough, after rebuilding the wall together, the people wanted to do more together. There is a momentum found in unity. In Nehemiah 8:1a, we read, *"all the people assembled with a unified purpose." (NLT)* They asked Ezra to read God's Word, they confessed their sins, they even worshipped together.

So, not only do homes get clean quicker and walls get rebuilt faster, people are drawn to the things of God when His people are united.

~Binu

September 29 ~ Nehemiah 11-13, Psalm 126
"Those who sow with tears will reap with songs of joy. Those who go out weeping, carrying seed to sow, will return with songs of joy, carrying sheaves with them." Psalm 126:5-6 (NIV)

A few years ago, we traveled out of town to attend a funeral. We arrived early and watched as the priests were setting up for the mass. We sat down and watched them prepare all of the elements that were needed for the service. One priest lit the candles around the altar and throughout the church.

On either side of the altar were two golden candelabra. Several individual candles outlined the altar and stage area. Once the priest had lit the candles on the stage, he moved to light the candles on the candelabra. He lit each wick and adjusted the position of the candelabra so that everything was symmetrical. It was beautiful. The church looked like it was glowing. It was so peaceful- just the perfect environment for the service that would be starting in a few minutes. Once he finished lighting all of the candles, he took out glass covers and covered each flame to protect it for the duration of the service.

I thought that everything looked perfect as it was. I was disappointed to see the glass covers over the flames, but then I noticed something interesting about those particular lights.

The glass cover did not hide the beauty of the flame. Instead, it created a reflective surface. One flame now reflected off the glass and created the illusion of three flames. Those that were covered produced a stronger light than those without covers. The glow was now even more intense than before.

The beauty of the key verse is that it's about intention. In verse 6, the action isn't even complete, but the end result is already predicted.

Sometimes we feel like life is covering our flame ... things like shame, divorce, disability, abuse, and guilt. Don't be discouraged. Under these kinds of covers, your flame is not extinguished, but instead, it shines brighter. Keep sowing your seed. Keep plugging forward and let God magnify it.

~Shiney

September 30 ~ Malachi 1-4

"'On the day when I act,' says the Lord Almighty, 'they will be my treasured possession. I will spare them, just as a father has compassion and spares his son who serves him.'" Malachi 3:17 (NIV)

Before we were married, my husband and I would meet over meals and have long, meaningful conversations about our future. One day, I kindly asked him to refrain from saying the words, "I love you" until he was ready to ask for my hand in marriage.

I knew how fragile my heart was, and I didn't want to hear those words from someone who was not genuine. For me, love meant fulfilling a lifelong promise. It wasn't just flowers and a nice dinner.

It had been about 100 years since Israel returned home from captivity. The temple had been rebuilt and routines such as sacrifices and festivals were being resumed, but there was a hardness in the peoples' hearts. They did not regard God as they should.

In comes the prophet Malachi with words of reassurance that God still loves them and words of instruction on how He should be honored and respected. This book starts out like a love letter, with the words, *"I have loved you..."*

The rest of the book of Malachi outlines the requirements God had for the people He truly loved in regards to many areas of their life, including sacrifices. The people were bringing in blemished animal sacrifices, which was completely against God's desire for a first-born, unblemished animal. The love they had for God was not genuine, and it showed in their actions.

The priests were not following God's ways, husbands were being unfaithful to their wives, and the Israelites were not bringing the tithes into the storehouse as they should have been.

This was not acceptable to God. There would be consequences for their lack of respect, but for those who revered him, they would be treated as His treasured possession.

The condition of your heart is an open book in front of your Father in Heaven. God knows all things, and He is aware of the motive behind your actions. He is asking us for our complete reverence. Will you honor Him today through your time and worship? He is waiting to shower you with so many blessings that you won't even have room to store it.

When He says, "I love you", He means it, and demonstrated it by sacrificing His first-born, unblemished Son to die so that you can have a genuine relationship with Him. There is no greater display of pure love.

~Elizabeth

October 1 ~ Luke 1, John 1
"I am the Lord's servant...may your word to me be fulfilled." Luke 1:38 (NIV)

I got married a bit later than I had always imagined. I remember days of wondering where and when I would meet a godly man...or even if I would be a wife at all.

When I met the man who would be my husband, and we finally got engaged, it was a time of excitement and anticipation for the future. We paid attention to small details regarding our wedding day and would share the wonder with our friends and family.

Mary was a young woman, betrothed to be married, as well. What a wonderful season of dreaming of married life with her fiancé and sharing those special moments with her family, who were probably just as thrilled as she was.

This engagement season for Mary was unexpectedly and indescribably transformed when God sent the angel Gabriel to her to reveal that she, a virgin, would be with child. She would give birth to a son, and he would be called the Son of the Most High. Mary was confused...how could this be?

Have you ever been in the middle of making major plans when circumstances shift suddenly and you have no idea how to respond? Mary, a humble woman, was faced with this reality. Her world changed one day when she was given the news that she would bear a child much earlier than she anticipated.

Her response? *"I am the Lord's servant...may your word to me be fulfilled."* (Luke 1:38 NIV)

Mary realized that there would likely be embarrassment from the ridicule she would receive. She likely knew there would be questions from Joseph, her family, and the community. Yet, she was willing to take on this responsibility because she knew it was an assignment from God.

Mary's obedience and willingness are amazing examples to those of us who prefer to sit in our comfort zone and resist any major change that may rock our world. Is there something God is asking you to do that makes you feel uneasy because of the fear of rejection or ridicule? If it is truly God speaking to you, He will make a way and make everything beautiful in its time...just as the birth of Jesus came at the perfect time when the world needed a Savior the most.

~Elizabeth

October 2 ~ Matthew 1, Luke 2
*"... she began to give thanks to God and to speak
of him to all who were waiting for
the redemption of Jerusalem." Luke 2:38 (ESV)*

Sometimes, life doesn't turn how we thought it would.

The marriage that never happened. The marriage that ended in divorce.

A barren womb. A prodigal child.

Financial challenges. Physical illness.

In Luke 2, we encounter Anna who likely felt that her life didn't turn out exactly how she thought it would either. Her story is summarized in just 3 verses of scripture.

She was a widow after only 7 years of marriage. There was also no mention of any children or that she ever remarried. During that time period, being a wife and mom was everything. Even in our society today, it is a big deal. Many women would have let their lives stop there.

But not Anna.

Sheryl Sandberg[1] alluded to this concept after the sudden loss of her husband. She talked about living out Option B - the life you didn't want but currently have. After some wise counsel from a friend, she realized the choice was hers on how she was going to handle it.

I think we would all agree that it's one thing to say this, and another thing to live it. We all want option A - that's why it's option A. But when life presents us with option B as our only option, then what happens?

Anna showed us that while option B may not be our first choice, our lives can still find fulfillment and purpose beyond what we ever imagined. Anna spent her days at the temple. She worshipped. She fasted. She prayed. Her faithful service there positioned her to receive another promise - meeting the Messiah. Then, she spent her days telling people about Him.

"... she began to give thanks to God and to speak of him to all who were waiting for the redemption of Jerusalem." (Luke 2:38 ESV)

From wife to widow to witness.

If you are currently living in Option A, praise God for that. But if you are one of many who are in the Option B camp, know that God still has plans for you. Great plans. He has a way of making our lives exceedingly, abundantly above all we could ask or think ... even if it wasn't what we initially imagined.

~Anu

October 3 ~ Matthew 2
"So Joseph got up and returned to the land of Israel with Jesus and his mother." Matthew 2:21 (NLT)

When the name *Joseph* is referenced in the Bible, who comes to mind? Usually, it's the guy with the coat of many colors, the dreamer who became a big deal in Egypt.

However, there is another Joseph in scripture - the husband of Mary and the earthly father of Jesus. That's a pretty big deal too.

Scripture doesn't say a lot about him but he is described as a good and faithful man who was devoted to Mary and God.

In Matthew 2, we read how Joseph took care of his family, traveling to Bethlehem along with his very pregnant wife for a census registration, fleeing to Egypt after being warned in a dream, then eventually settling in Nazareth.

One of the final passages in which Joseph is mentioned occurs much later in Jesus' life, when He had returned to His hometown. *"... When he taught there in the synagogue, everyone was amazed and said, 'Where does he get this wisdom and the power to do miracles?' Then they scoffed, 'He's just the carpenter's son...' (Matthew 13:54-55 NLT)*

The acknowledgment of Joseph in scripture ended pretty much as it started. Not the star. Simply a supporting role, even to the point of being discredited as "just a carpenter".

This is the tale of 2 Josephs. One was the #2 guy in all of Egypt – he was popular among the rulers and the people. The other was just a guy in the background, taking care of his family and doing his thing without much recognition. Both fulfilling their God-appointed roles.

Which one can you relate to more?

Honestly, the characteristics we see in Joseph of the New Testament aren't necessarily exciting. This regular guy submitted himself to the plan of God and just did regular things. As ordinary as that may seem, extraordinary things happened: prophecy was fulfilled and the Son of God was raised.

Jesus thrived under the care of Mary ... and Joseph.

There is something to be said about a person who may not be the most popular one but is good, just, faithful, responsible, devoted to people and submitted to God. A person who can be trusted in the small things that won't get a lot of attention but will keep doing them anyway.

An ordinary person doing ordinary things but part of an extraordinary plan.

~Anu

October 4 ~ Matthew 3, Mark 1, Luke 3
"Come, follow me, and I will make you fishers of men." Mark 1:17 (NIV)

There is a problem in my household.

I will ever so sweetly tell my kids to do something- pick up their trash, put their shoes up, or put their markers away. I will come back ten minutes later, and the chore hasn't been done. I come back ten minutes after *that*, and it STILL hasn't been done. Then, I start to get annoyed.

"GUYS! I said to pick up your stuff! This is the second time I am telling you!" I will say, in my not so sweet-sounding voice. Thirty minutes will go by, and things are still where they left them. At this point, there are usually consequences which involve me picking up the item and tossing it into the garbage. But, if it's something that I know they really love, like valuable Lego pieces or newly purchased markers (or shoes!!), I will tell them for the third time.

"GUYS! PICK UP YOUR STUFF!!!!" (And then they usually ask me why I'm so mad!)

One particular day, I had been telling my kids to get ready so we could leave the house. I had given them an hour warning and then a 30-minute warning. With 15 minutes left, they finally got up to go get ready, whining the whole way, *"Aww, but we wanted to color before we left!"* I said *"If you guys would have just gotten ready the first time that I had asked you to, who knows what you could have done with all the time that you had!"*

I stopped right there with this thought: How many times has your (mine) delayed obedience cost you something?

I could feel my stomach churning at the thought. I will never know.

Immediate obedience. That's what Jesus requires of us. No delay, no negotiations. Just do it.

In Mark 1, Jesus begins his ministry and gathers his disciples. He saw Simon and Andrew casting their nets and simply asked them to come. Every version of the story says that they immediately dropped their nets and went with him. No questions asked. Their lives were changed forever because of this one, non-debated, non-delayed decision.

Don't put off what God has been telling you to do. The blessing will always outweigh the cost.

~Shiney

October 5 ~ Matthew 4, Luke 4-5

"When the devil had finished tempting Jesus, he left
him until the next opportunity came."
Luke 4:13 (NLT)

Do you ever doubt that God is who He says He is and that His word is true?

I do. And often.

I also believe this is the number one strategy of the enemy. He whispers in our ear trying his best to get us to doubt our creator.

He even tried this on Jesus.

In the gospels of Matthew, Mark, and Luke, we find the story of Jesus being led into the wilderness by the devil. He tried to use God's very own word against Jesus. But Jesus was prepared and able to defeat the him.

The devil's tactics haven't changed since the Garden of Eden. He succeeded at getting Eve to doubt what God had told her. And today he's still playing the same game. He tries to twist what God says in order to bring doubt in our hearts and minds of who God is and what He is really saying to us.

If God is good, why is there war and poverty, and death and disease?

If God's word is filled with promises, why does it sometimes seem to not work for me?

I have lived long enough to have seen many highs and many lows in my walk of faith. Through all of it, I can confidently say, God's ways are higher and better than mine. Even through the pain, God shows me that He is still a good and loving Father.

Is the enemy whispering doubt in your ear today? Fill yourself up with the word of God and with the help of God through prayer, you can shut out the doubt.

And because our Savior Jesus defeated the enemy, know that you can defeat him too.

~Vijoy

October 6 ~ John 2-4
"Come, see a man who told me all that I ever did.
Can this be the Christ?" John 4:29 (ESV)

We all have a story. Some of it ... we may be proud of. Other parts may have left some scars.

The Samaritan woman in John 4 knew more about the "other parts" - the stuff she wasn't proud of. She had made some bad choices. She had a reputation and it wasn't a good one.

Jesus met this woman on a not so random walk through Samaria. Scripture records that He *"had to go through Samaria." (John 4:4 NIV)* However, this wasn't the usual route for Jews. In fact, they tried to avoid Samaria and Samaritans all together.

But not this particular day or this particular Jew. Jesus had to meet with this woman.

He talked to her about her life. She tried to change the subject but Jesus persisted. He explained to her that what she was using to satisfy her thirst was only temporary. She needed the living water so she would never thirst again.

He then reveals to her that He is the Messiah.

In scripture, we read several times where Jesus basically says, "Don't tell anyone who I am or what I've done" but to this woman, he reveals Himself as Messiah! Why would He entrust such an important revelation to her, the most unlikely of people?

Maybe that answer is revealed by what she did with the information.

"Come and see..." was her declaration. (John 4:29 NLT)

She came out of hiding and went to where everyone else was. She was so excited to tell the people about Jesus that she left her water jar behind which was the very reason she went to the well to begin with. She wasn't afraid to say that Jesus talked to her about her life. She didn't hesitate to tell them that she met the Messiah.

She used her story to entice her village to meet Him.

Do you think your story disqualifies you from sharing the good news of the Gospel? Think again. The scars in our story serve as a reminder to us and others that a wound that once was open is now closed. It displays healing from our hurt.

Do you know who else used their scars to help a doubting friend? Jesus.

Tell your story, the good and the bad. Tell others about the One who changed your life. Tell them to come and see for themselves.

~Anu

"*... they were all amazed and glorified God, saying, 'We never saw anything like this!'" Mark 2:12b (ESV)*

True story. People have told me that I ask too many questions.

It happened once at a wedding reception and again at a department lunch at work.

I thought I was just making conversation. Apparently, they didn't take it that way.

I have also been complimented for being easy to talk to.

It has happened with friends and strangers.

I thought I was just making conversation. Apparently, they were glad I did.

One person's compliment of you may be another person's criticism.

Same you. Different reaction.

For you, people may ask why you started that blog or ministry. Is it because you think you have it all together? Some may see it that way. Others may just be encouraged and inspired.

Same you, different reaction.

Maybe you have chosen to be a stay-at-home mom instead of working outside the home. Some may say you are wasting your education. Others will see the value of a mom who has chosen to pour her time in being with her kids.

Same you, different reaction.

In Mark 2, Jesus encountered this very thing. When a paralyzed man was brought to Jesus for healing, the man gets what he came for and then some. He walks away (literally) healed and his sins forgiven. Some people were praising God, other people began accusing Jesus of blasphemy.

Same Jesus, different reaction.

You are going to come across people who misread, misunderstand and mistake you for being a certain way. You're going to come across other people who acknowledge, appreciate and applaud you for being that exact same way.

That's when you have to ask yourself ... why? Why am I doing this? When we do things with a right motive, we can rest assured that our Heavenly Father is pleased even when people aren't.

Mother Theresa gives us a beautiful reminder that when we do what we do, "*... in the end, it is between you and God; It was never between you and them anyway.*"

And what a beautiful reaction God has for you: "*Whoever pursues righteousness and kindness will find life, righteousness, and honor.*" *(Proverbs 21:21 ESV)*

~Anu

October 8 ~ John 5
"Then Jesus said to him, 'Get up! Pick up your mat
and walk.' At once the man was cured; ..."
John 5:8-9 (NIV)

Have you ever been in a tough situation for so long you just lose hope that it will ever change?

My journey with allergies began when I was ten years old. I sneezed every single day. I subjected myself to shots for a decade with little change. On the particularly bad days, asthma would flare up and I was taking additional medications just so that I could breathe.

Finally, I decided that I was done with all medications because nothing appeared to help. Then, sinus infections became a regular occurrence. I was miserable. In desperation, I tried a procedure that left me traumatized and I finally gave up hope of ever having relief from allergies. I didn't want to hear anyone's suggestions or try any more alternatives.

Then, I met a doctor who was empathic and gentle. When we realized that surgery was my only option, I reluctantly agreed. I had to follow up with him regularly for the next three months and follow a strict regimen for my sinus health. I began noticing some changes. I sneezed less. I had much fewer sinus infections. And I slept way better because I could finally breathe through my nose correctly!!! I couldn't believe it. My hope has been renewed ever since the Lord connected me with this wise doctor.

I imagine this is similar to how the man near the pool called Bethesda felt. John 5:1-8 (NIV) shows that after laying there like an invalid for thirty-eight years, it seemed all hope of getting better was gone. When Jesus asked if he wanted to be well, his response was that no one ever helped him into the pool. In fact, it seems that every time he tried, someone else would go ahead of him. It sounds like he was plain ol' tired and frustrated. But his story didn't end there. Jesus saw him and spoke life into him. Praise God!

"Now all glory to God, who is able, through His mighty power at work within us, to accomplish infinitely more than we might ask or think." (Ephesians 3:20 NLT)

Dear Friend, no matter how hopeless your situation seems, I pray you are encouraged today to know that God is the Source of all hope. He sees you and He will help you.

~Joyce

October 9 ~ Matthew 12, Mark 3, Luke 6
"Love your enemies! Do good to them ..." Luke 6:35a (NLT)

So, there's this person that I don't like. As a Christian, I probably shouldn't feel that way but it's true. I don't know if this makes it any better but I am about 99% sure, they feel the same way about me.

If you are a Christian, your likely response to me is to pray. You are right. I have prayed about it and know that God can change my heart in an instant. But that hasn't happened. Yet.

So, now what? Keep praying. I agree.

Have you noticed that it is the rare occasion that our hearts are changed instantly? We'd like that much better, wouldn't we? No drama...just poof! *I like you now! Let's go have lunch!*

God has heard my request for a heart change and now He asks me...

"What are you going to do?"

Me: "Lord, isn't there a verse that says if I am kind to my enemies, it will feel like burning coals to them? I like that burning coals thing. I'll do that."

Of course, I know that's not what the verse had in mind but the instruction is clear.

We are called to show kindness to people who are unkind to us and love people who aren't so lovable.

"Love your enemies! Do good to them. Lend to them without expecting to be repaid. Then your reward from heaven will be very great, and you will truly be acting as children of the Most High, for he is kind to those who are unthankful and wicked." (Luke 6:35 NLT)

Throughout scripture, God demonstrates this time and time again. From the children of Israel to the religious leaders who arrested and crucified Jesus. He was always kind and loving even when it wasn't deserved.

God isn't asking me to do anything He didn't do Himself ... back then and now ... to others and to me.

Loving our enemies isn't easy but we may never have a greater opportunity to demonstrate God at work in us. So, we keep loving. And keep praying.

~Anu

October 10 ~ Matthew 5-7
"Blessed are the peacemakers, for they will be called the children of God." Matthew 5:9 (NIV)

Are you a peacemaker or a peacekeeper?

I've been thinking about this question recently, especially in light of the racial tension and tragedies we've been experiencing as a nation.

After doing my own research I found some key differences between the two.[1] Peacekeepers work to keep tensions from rising. They pretend that nothing is wrong and avoid conflict at any cost. Peacekeepers believe that pursuing peace means to keep quiet and not speak the truth or not share how they really feel.

Even though we think this is helping, it's actually causing a deeper wedge in our hearts and minds ... between us and the other person.

But Jesus calls us to be *peacemakers*.

A peacemaker wants to understand and is willing to listen. They try to see things from the other person's point of view. They speak the truth in love. They pursue reconciliation at the risk of their own comfort. A peacemaker calls out tension for the ultimate purpose of resolution.

Who are you today? To be completely honest, I've been a peacekeeper most of my life. I hate conflict and confrontation. I've spent a lot of my energy to keep the peace in many of my relationships.

But I have come to understand, peacekeeping is ultimately a selfish response. A peacekeeper operates out of fear and self-preservation instead of working towards the difficult task of pushing through the hard stuff...in order to have a real and honest relationship.

Wherever you find yourself today, I pray that Jesus' word will challenge you to push through the tension in order to bring about true peace. It won't be easy, but I believe it will be worth it.

~Vijoy

October 11 ~ Matthew 9, Luke 7

"Therefore I tell you, her sins, which are many, are forgiven—for she loved much. But he who is forgiven little, loves little." Luke 7:47 (ESV)

It's easy to get distracted. Most of the time, it is pretty harmless. Sometimes though, it can really get the best of us.

At a recent conference I attended, there was a woman in the row in front of me who stood during worship when the others around her were sitting. She raised her arms while they held onto their notepads.

But as she expressed her worship, they experienced distraction.

I watched the whole thing play out. Someone behind her asked this particular woman to sit down. I'm not sure what all was said but immediately, her countenance changed from joyful worship to disheartened spectator.

I was immediately reminded of the woman in scripture whose worship distracted a few folks too.

"And standing behind him at his feet, weeping, she began to wet his feet with her tears and wiped them with the hair of her head and kissed his feet and anointed them with the ointment." (Luke 7:38 ESV)

Simon, the Pharisee – yes, the religious leader – watched it happen but all he could see was a sinful woman touching a man (Jesus) Who should know better. Simon didn't vocalize his thoughts but Jesus chose to publicly acknowledge it anyway. Jesus chose to publicly acknowledge her.

Simon saw it as an unfortunate distraction. Jesus recognized it as exceptional worship.

I can't judge Simon too hard. It's easy to get flustered when the person next to you at church is waving their arms so freely that they have now entered your personal space. It can throw you off when the person behind you is singing off-key or clapping off-beat.

We can't always help being distracted but are we going give in to it? Are we going to force our idea of what worship should look like in that moment on someone else? Someone who possibly has been forgiven of their many sins or maybe they are simply very grateful? Their praise may look different from ours but maybe it's because their story is different.

Honestly, it could be distracting but are we going to see it like Simon did ... or Jesus?

By the way, remember that woman at the conference who was told to sit down? She moved to the aisle, and continued her worship there. She didn't let the distracted person distract her from her worship.

~Anu

October 12 ~ Matthew 11

*"And Jesus answered them, 'Go and tell John what you hear and
see: the blind receive their sight and the lame walk, lepers are
cleansed and the deaf hear, and the dead are raised up, and the poor
have good news preached to them.'" Matthew 11:4-5 (ESV)*

Don't you just love encouraging people?

Unfortunately, some days your cheering section is busy and there are no pats on the back to be found.

The story of John the Baptist's time in prison reminds me of this very thing. He had been teaching, prophesying, baptizing, fasting, rebuking sin and proclaiming the Messiah had come. He was busy. Then, he ends up in prison because he offended Herod, the current ruler.

While he is in jail, the ministry of his cousin, Jesus, takes off. He was busy too. But no one had arrested Him (yet).

So, John sends his disciples to Jesus in search of some answers. Jesus responds then sends those disciples back to John to tell him what He said. Once they left, Jesus tells the crowd, "*... among those born of women there has arisen no one greater than John the Baptist...*" (Matthew 11:11a ESV)

You have to wonder – why wouldn't Jesus tell John's disciples that stuff too? I'm sure John would have been happy to hear that Jesus was bragging about him to the crowds and that all the people there agreed. It could have reminded him that even though he was in prison, it didn't mean he was off track.

When we get words of encouragement, it's great. We feel good about ourselves and what we are doing. But what about when we don't? What about those times when it's just you and God and it seems like that even He is a little quiet?

For John, it was while he was in prison. For us, it could be at work, home or church ... there's no applause and sometimes not even a thank you.

Have you noticed that God will sometimes do the opposite of what we think we need? When I feel like I need a shout out, the world around me grows silent. God knows if I get a "You're awesome" then, I'll look for it again the next time. And thus begins His fatherly attempt at weaning me from something I shouldn't be relying on anyway.

So, enjoy the encouragers when they are around. I know I do. But also remember that Jesus is always cheering you on even if you don't hear Him say it.

~Anu

October 13 ~ Luke 11

"And I tell you, ask, and it will be given to you; seek, and you will find;
knock, and it will be opened to you." Luke 11:9 (ESV)

We play a lot of hide and seek at my house. It's one game that we can all play together with no drama. The kids really enjoy finding new places to cram themselves into and fool the grown-ups.

I have a four-legged child along with my two, two-legged children. He is my first child and sticks closer to me than my shadow. So, we play hide and seek and the dog gives away my location EVERY time! I hide in the pantry, and he stands right outside the door. I hide in the living room, and he comes and lays right where I am. Find the dog and you'll find me.

The last time that we played, I had hidden in the kids' bathtub, behind the curtain, in the dark. The dog was laying inconspicuously at the end of the hallway, so he didn't give away my location. I was the last to be found. Next round, I hid in my walk-in shower. I huddled on the ground in the shower, and the dog came and laid on the bath mat, right outside of the shower. (For the record, this is his usual spot when I am in the shower.) They came in the bathroom, saw the dog and looked around the closets, bathtub and toilet area. They stepped over the dog and looked through the frosted glass of the shower but still didn't see me in there. I could hear my 4-year-old say, *"I know you're here, but I just can't find you!"*

I know that there are times in my life where I felt like I have been playing spiritual hide and seek with God. I see no signs of Him in the middle of my chaos. Like my daughter said, I know He's there, but I just can't find Him. I need a big sign to point out His whereabouts, just like my dog signals it to my family. We are all looking for Him in the midst of our issues.

Luke 11:9 puts it very simply. Ask. Seek. Knock. That's it. Seek and you will find. There's no condition. No stipulation. You will find Him or He will find You.

Just keep looking.

~Shiney

October 14 ~ Matthew 13, Luke 8
"... As Jesus was on his way, the crowds almost crushed him." Luke 8:42b (NIV)

For over 40 years, my dad took a peanut butter and jelly sandwich to work for lunch. The only exception was when the local Mexican restaurant had an enchilada special. Now that he is retired, he still has a daily routine.

So, the fact that I am a structured person shouldn't surprise you. It is part of my DNA.

Case in point: My husband and I had lunch plans so I asked him what time he wanted to leave so I could plan my morning accordingly. We finalized a time and I proceeded to carry on with the stuff on my to-do list.

Then it happened.

He said, "Hey babe".

"Yeah?"

"What time are we leaving?"

"11:15" (which was the time we discussed just 2 hours ago).

"Oh..." (his voice sounding very disappointed).

"Why?" I ask nervously because I know what this usually means.

"Can we leave a little earlier?"

Silence because I am screaming on the inside.

Doesn't he know that I have strategically planned every single thing to the minute so I would be ready at 11:15 and not a second sooner?

There was a workout to be done, dishes to be washed, laundry to be folded ... plus it would be really nice if I showered and brushed my teeth.

See? This apple didn't fall too far from the peanut butter and jelly eating tree.

Structured is good. Structured people get important things done. However, I'm recognizing that there's more to life than getting things crossed off my to-do list.

What about what's on God's to-do list for me?

I think about the life that Jesus lived. Was there ever anyone with a greater mission on earth? In spite of that (or maybe because of that), He still MADE time for the children who just wanted to be with Him and for the woman at the well whose life needed some guidance. In the eyes of the people, the woman with the issue of blood wasn't on the agenda at that moment ... but she was a part of His plan all along.

Being structured is who I am. But being God's servant is also who I am.

My prayer is that I live life according to His plans, not mine.

~Anu

October 15 ~ Mark 4-5

*"When she heard about Jesus, she came behind Him in the crowd
and touched His garment. For she said, "If only I may touch
His clothes, I shall be made well." Mark 5:27-28 (NKJV)*

Is there a need you have been praying about for a LONG time? Maybe there are days you feel as if you may not receive the answer any day soon. Perhaps all of the waiting is choking any hope you have left.

I think that's what my husband may have felt like in the early years of marriage. Let's just say it didn't look like the happily ever after we expected. As much as I hate to admit it, that had a lot to do with how I communicated with him.

My husband began to pray and wait. Months of such eventually became years. Seeing the light at the end of the tunnel grew more difficult and almost felt impossible. Then, one day as I was talking to folks possessing wise counsel, it was evident I had been struggling with bitterness and unforgiveness. The time had come for me to LET GO AND LET GOD.

I did and my communication in our marriage has improved drastically since with God's help and grace. Boy, am I grateful that my husband kept praying and had faith, even though the waiting seemed like an eternity.

I'm reminded of the woman with the issue of blood found in the Gospels. We read that she had been bleeding for *12 years*, suffered a great deal, and progressively grew worse. How awful! After all those years, seeing doctor after doctor, and spending lots of money, who would blame this woman if she gave up believing that she would be healed?

But that's not her story.

This woman had faith and Jesus said it was her faith that healed her and freed her from all of that suffering!!!

I don't know what you've been praying for, but whatever your need is I understand that after a while of waiting you may lose faith and hope. I realize that day after day of not seeing a change in your struggle is wearisome, but *"Cast your cares on the Lord, and He will sustain you; He will never let the righteous fall." (Psalm 55:22 NIV)*

God loves you, my dear Friend. He sees your tears and hears your cries.

~Joyce

October 16 ~ Matthew 10

"Whoever receives you receives me, and whoever
receives me receives him who sent me."
Matthew 10:40 (ESV)

I sat across from my petite friend as we ordered dinner at the Italian restaurant.

She told the waiter, *"I'd like some soup..."*, then I waited for her to announce the pasta of her choice but instead she said, *"... and some asparagus."* Then, I proceeded to order my dish that contained the words cheese and mashed potatoes.

Looking at my friend, the payoff of her food choices is evident. She takes good care of herself and it shows.

As I mentioned how much I admired her discipline, she said something that caught me by surprise... *"It's hard!"* She recognized in order to be the person she wanted to be that it was going to come with some challenges too.

She made it look easy but her words reminded me - there is a cost.

I can't imagine what the disciples felt when Jesus chose them to join Him in ministry. These were regular guys who lived regular lives, until Jesus called them.

The plans He had for them probably blew their minds: *"... Heal the sick, raise the dead, cure those with leprosy, and cast out demons ..." (Matthew 10:8a NLT)* From fishing and tax collecting to this? Their lives were on a completely different trajectory than they likely ever envisioned.

But with the calling of discipleship was also a cost. It was going to be hard. Jesus warns them that they will face difficult situations along the way. But in order to be the men that they were destined to be, they had to walk through that too.

Thankfully, they did not have to do this alone. The same God who equipped them to do the miraculous in His name, would also empower them as they encountered opposition.

"When you are arrested, don't worry about how to respond or what to say. God will give you the right words at the right time. For it is not you who will be speaking—it will be the Spirit of your Father speaking through you." (Matthew 10:19-20 NLT)

Our challenges as followers of Christ now may look very different than what the apostles faced back then. Regardless, there may be times when we find ourselves saying, "It's hard."

But the payoff will be worth it. We will look like our Savior.

~Anu

October 17 ~ Matthew 14, Mark 6, Luke 9
"For Herod had seized John and bound him and put him in prison for the sake of Herodias, his brother Philip's wife..." Matthew 14:3 (ESV)

With a name that includes "Herod", Herodias was off to a bad start.

Herodias was married to, you guessed it, King Herod. From today's scripture reading, we see that John the Baptist had informed Herod of God's displeasure with their current family arrangement. Even though it bothered Herod that John called him out like that, he still held John in high regard.

Herodias did not share in that sentiment and was ready to take care of Herod's offense herself. She worked out a plan and recruited another member of the family - her daughter.

Her daughter was able to manipulate King Herod to the point of promising to give her anything she asked for. She went to her mother to find out what she should say.

This was the chance Herodias had been waiting for. She wanted the head of John the Baptist. Her daughter conveyed the request, and Herod had to oblige her.

An offense led to a grudge, ended in revenge and ultimately the death of John.

How should we respond when we have been offended?

1. Look at yourself. Sometimes, the offense has nothing to do with who the offender is or even what was done. Instead, it could have everything to do with us. Is this about an insecurity or a trigger from the past? Check your heart.

2. Look at the other person. On the flip side, the offense may have nothing to do with you and everything to do with them. You've probably heard the saying, "Hurt people hurt people." As challenging as this may be, Jesus modeled this, even at the point of His greatest suffering, the cross. He asked God to forgive the people who had done this, *"... for they know not what they do"*. (Luke 23:34 ESV)

3. Look closely at the situation. In the book, The Peacemaker: A Biblical Guide to Resolving Conflict[1] by Ken Sande, he offers some guidelines: *"Is the offense dishonoring God? Has it permanently damaged a relationship? Is it hurting other people? Is it hurting the offender himself?" If you can answer no to those questions, this may be an opportunity to 'overlook the offense'."*

Pastor Steven Furtick said, *"Offense is an event ... offended is a choice."*[2] What will we choose?

~Anu

October 18 ~ John 6
"Another of his disciples, Andrew, Simon Peter's brother, spoke up." John 6:8 (NIV)

Sometimes it starts with just a feeling...

John chapter 6 tells the familiar story. Jesus was teaching. Crowds were listening. It was getting late. And instead of sending the people home like I would have done, Jesus suggested they all eat dinner together. All five thousand of them.

It gets better. Jesus also suggested that He and His disciples take care of the bill.

John 6:7-9 picks up the story from there.

"Philip answered him, 'It would take more than half a year's wages to buy enough bread for each one to have a bite!' Another of his disciples, Andrew, Simon Peter's brother, spoke up, 'Here is a boy with five small barley loaves and two small fish, but how far will they go among so many?'" (NIV)

I have read this story countless times, but for the first time, a different character caught my attention.

Andrew.

Sure, the little boy was sweet for his willingness to share his lunch. But what about Andrew, the adult?

It takes boldness and faith for a practical adult to even make mention of such a small lunch. By doing so, Andrew was suggesting something. *Maybe, just maybe, Jesus could do something big with something so small and insignificant.* Andrew's feeling was right.

"Jesus then took the loaves, gave thanks, and distributed to those who were seated as much as they wanted. He did the same with the fish." (vs 11 NIV)

And they all had enough! God takes the little we have, but are willing to offer up, and He does the miraculous.

It may start with just an idea or a feeling of what you believe God can do ... but don't let it end there. Be bold like Andrew and mention it to Jesus! Put it in the hands of the only one who can take it, bless it, break it and multiply it.

Mention it to Jesus. What have you got to lose?

~Binu

October 19 ~ Matthew 15, Mark 7
"But the things that come out of a person's mouth
come from the heart, and these defile them."
Matthew 15:18 (NIV)

Have you ever felt a pit in your stomach after you've shared something you shouldn't have... or said something too quickly?

Gossip often feels good because it can be pleasant to hear or share. Often, we even feel a sense of momentary satisfaction when speaking maliciously, talking sarcastically or giving a rude comment. In the Christian community, it is easy to gossip under the umbrella of sharing to pray. It doesn't take much to spread hurtful words.

However, if our conscious pricks us in our spirit, we feel regret and shame. Today's passages remind us that our words actually expose our heart. Where is your heart?

It is difficult to undo the damage of gossip or a hurtful word, but there are ways we can prevent making this mistake and ways to fix the damage if it's already been done.

Here are some practical ways to watch our words:

- *Slow Down:* Think before you speak. The Bible has much to say about guarding our lips and speaking rashly.
- *Talk Less:* The Bible advises us to avoid people who gossip and says that we are considered wise when we hold our tongue. We can save ourselves a lot of embarrassment and regret when we know how to be quiet. Sometimes listening is more valuable than talking.
- *Damage Control:* What do you do when your words have hurt someone? Humble yourself and ask for forgiveness. You release yourself from being imprisoned by your own words. Don't wait too long. The sooner you deal with the hurt caused by those words, the sooner you will free yourself.
- *Hide God's Word in your Heart:* Having disciplined quiet time with God allows you to stay in tune with His Word. God deposits his wisdom in you so that you can avoid gossip and be an encouragement through your words.

The next time you are tempted to share some juicy details with someone, ask yourself: Is it kind? Is it helpful? Is it necessary? If the answer is no, then it is safer to stay silent regarding the matter.

Our words expose our heart. May our lips speak truth and kindness to those around us so that others can see the Christ who rules our heart.

~Elizabeth

October 20 ~ Matthew 16, Mark 8

"Jesus took the blind man by the hand and led him out of the village. Then, spitting on the man's eyes, he laid his hands on him..." Mark 8:23 (NLT)

One rainy morning, as I opened my garage to take my son to school, we noticed a bunch of worms rolling around on our driveway. We had been experiencing several days of rain, and it seemed as though every worm in the city was hanging out on our patch of concrete.

My son started asking about them and as any good "boy mom" would do, I indulged the conversation. *"Mom, would you ever want to be a worm?"* (Keep in mind that he was about 5 at the time!) I told him no because I didn't see how worms really contributed to the food chain other than being eaten.

The topic soon shifted to other creepy, crawly things and eventually caterpillars. It led to this question: *"Would you suffer as a caterpillar if you knew that you would eventually turn into a butterfly?"*

He quickly and resolutely said no. I said, *"What if you were going to be the most beautiful butterfly in the world, but you had to wait as a caterpillar until then?"* His answer did not change. I continued, *"So, you're telling me that you wouldn't temporarily suffer even if you knew this amazing thing was coming soon?"* Temporary suffering for a delayed gratification was not something that his 5-year-old brain could grasp.

Sometimes it's not something that my 40-year-old brain can grasp either.

The blind man at Bethsaida wanted to be healed. I can only imagine his excitement as Christ led him outside of the village. He must have been thrilled to know that his disability was about to disappear! The Messiah himself was holding his hand, leading him ... and putting spit in his eyes?!

The Bible does not tell us the reaction that he had when he was spit on by Jesus. My brain tells me that it would be extremely difficult to not recoil from another human spitting on me, even if it was Jesus. But this man trusted that his healing was on the other side of that spit.

Temporary discomfort for a permanent blessing.

As you read this, I want to challenge you today to be patient in your struggles. Be patient in your annoyances and grievances. These temporary discomforts are nothing compared to the blessing that awaits you once you have passed through them.

~Shiney

October 21 ~ Matthew 17, Mark 9

"Sitting down, Jesus called the Twelve and said, 'Anyone who wants to be first must be the very last, and the servant of all.'" Mark 9:35 (NIV)

I was a bossy big sister.

With three younger siblings, I felt a sense of authority over them and would have them get things for me, feed me, and blackmail them if they didn't do what I asked. I distinctly remember jumping on my trampoline and saying that I was queen of the house.

As the eldest sibling, it's easy to develop a small chip on your shoulder. All of the first-borns out there probably agree. You learn your letters first, so obviously you're the smartest. You had your parents' attention first, so of course, you're the favorite, and you're taller so obviously, you're more powerful.

I quickly lost in the height department, and soon after, my sister shined in academics. Then, I learned that parents don't have favorites, so all my reasons to be arrogant had no foundation at all.

Fortunately, my bossy demeanor was a short-lived phase, which my parents have forgotten about, and for which my siblings have forgiven me. What a relief!

In our reading today, Jesus gives us gives us a formula for greatness, one that defies all logic. Most secular blogs today on professional success would challenge us to fight our way up the ladder, no matter the cost. Jesus says the *"first must be the very last, and the servant of all." (Mark 9:35 NIV)*

How is that even possible? It goes against everything we were taught! We make it to the top and people serve us! While there is merit to doing your best and having a heart for excellence, what Jesus is saying is that we need to examine our hearts and our position.

The King of Heaven stooped down to wash the feet of His friends. The Son of God left Heaven's glory to save us "while we were still sinners". We need to remember whose we are and who we represent.

Growing up, my mother would constantly remind me of the example I needed to be for my siblings. In time, I began to realize the influence I had over them. That chip on my shoulder started to slowly crumble as I began helping them more as a big sister and deciding that my bossy attitude needed to change.

May we lead today with a servant's heart, and may we see God widening our borders and opening up doors because of our humility.

~Elizabeth

October 22 ~ Matthew 18

"... your Father in heaven is not willing that any of these little ones should perish." Matthew 18:14 (NIV)

When I was in my early teens, my family had gone on a road trip with family friends. Two cars packed to the brim and filled with energy. We played games. We sang songs. We laughed a lot. The most memorable stop was at an amusement park. We were all excited to eat delectable treats and looked forward to the adrenaline rush from the rides.

We moved rapidly keeping an eye on the person ahead of us as there were a lot of people all around us. After walking for a bit, one of the adults asked us all to stop. We moved away from the crowd and when we did a headcount, there was the realization that one kid was missing. He was nowhere to be found. Panic set in. Where could he be? The park was huge. There were hundreds of people. How would we ever find him? (Mind you, this was before cell phones were around).

The adults came up with a plan of who would spread out to search for our missing friend while the rest of us remained in one location. His parents frantically searched and shouted his name as they pushed through the crowds. We stood praying and waiting for what seemed like an eternity. It was a frightening time. Worry set in as we wondered if he was okay.

I couldn't tell you how much time passed by during the search. But the moment is crystal clear when our friend was found by his father and they came running towards us. Oh, what a relief! Thank You, Jesus! We were so grateful that he was safe and sound. Tears of joy streamed down as everyone hugged him. I was reminded of Luke 15:6 (NIV) which says, *"Rejoice with me; I have found my lost sheep."*

Recalling this incident pointed my attention to a wall hanging in our home. It depicts the parable of the lost sheep with our Good Shepherd reaching out to the one sheep who had been lost.

What a comfort that God will literally go to the ends of the earth to find us and bring us to safety. May this encourage each of us today of our Father's love and care for us. He is good.

~Joyce

October 23 ~ John 7-8

*"Jesus stood up and said to her, 'Woman, where are
they? Has no one condemned you?'"*
John 8:10 (ESV)

We have all felt the sting of shame when our sin has been discovered by others and when we have caused pain by our own actions. You want to hide until things have settled and memories begin to fade. The last place you want to be is in the public eye to avoid the possibility of your secrets being discovered.

That is the story of one woman who encountered Jesus when he was teaching in the temple. This woman caught in adultery is brought before Him by some Pharisees and teachers of the law.

She is forced to stand before the group, and her crime is publicly announced. Oh, the humiliation and rejection she must have felt! She was probably holding back tears as her head hung down in shame in front of the Teacher. The group of people with accusing eyes ask Jesus His thoughts on her punishment.

She does not hear what she expects, but instead there is silence. Then, more questioning. They are ready to stone her, punish her and kill her for this very deed. She is waiting for the first blow...but then, she hears a voice.

Jesus is speaking to them and not to her. Strange...as it appears all eyes turned from her to the men. She feels a shift in the air. Jesus leans down to write on the ground, and slowly the group begins to dissolve.

Except Jesus stays. Despite the accusation, ridicule, and embarrassment, He never leaves her. She is not alone. Jesus now asks her a question for the first time since her arrival, *"Where are they? Has no one condemned you?" (John 8:10 ESV)*

Her accusers are gone! How did things shift so quickly? She was about to die and now she hears the sweet words of Jesus to her, *"...neither do I condemn you." (John 8:11 ESV)*

Yes, the Pharisees knew the law, but they could not see the fulfillment of the law standing right in front of them! The law of sin and death was abolished through the work of Jesus Christ on the cross, which gives anyone a chance to live a life of freedom.

If you are living in condemnation for something you have committed, acknowledge your sin and receive the forgiveness Jesus offers you. No more shame or condemnation.

You are free.

~Elizabeth

October 24 ~ John 9-10
*"...Whether he is a sinner I do not know. One thing I do
know, that though I was blind, now I see."*
John 9:25 (ESV)

"A man with an experience of God is never at the mercy of a man with an argument." Although the exact source of the quote is questionable, it could have been said by someone in scripture over 2000 years ago.

This particular young man had an experience with God like few did at that point. He had been blind since birth, until Jesus came along and healed him. Instead of celebrating a miracle, the Pharisees were fixated on the fact that it was the Sabbath. Because that was all they could *see*, they accused Jesus of being a sinner.

The healed man's response – *"...Whether he is a sinner I do not know. One thing I do know, that though I was blind, now I see." (John 9:25 ESV)*

This man didn't know theology; in fact, he barely knew Jesus. He just knew what he had experienced.

I don't get massages as often as I'd like but when I do, I have a massage therapist (Manda) whom I absolutely love. Not only is she my friend, but she also gives AMAZING massages. I've told other people about her and just recently, another friend tried her out – she loved her too.

I can tell people all day about the training Manda had but when I tell them about my experience and what she did for me ... that seals the deal.

Time and time again, we see in scripture how God used people including a demon possessed man, a woman with relational struggles, and now this formerly blind man...to share their stories and bring people to Him. All from different situations but all with the same experience – Jesus touched me.

Maybe there is someone around you who has heard about Jesus but doesn't know Him as their friend and Savior. Let them see Him in you. Let them experience Him through you. Let them hear you talk about what He has done in your life. Then, hopefully their story will be like the blind man, yours and mine.

"I was blind but now I see."

~Anu

October 25 ~ Luke 10
"But Martha was distracted by all the preparations
that had to be made ..." Luke 10:40 (NIV)

I love being a hostess. Showing hospitality and making others feel welcome in my home matter a great deal to me. However, I have been guilty of focusing so much more on serving, that I miss out on enjoying time well spent with my family and friends.

It seems that Martha and I have a few things in common. She was known as a doer, so it doesn't come as a surprise that she was serving Jesus during His visit to her home. However, she complained when her sister Mary didn't help her, but rather just sat at the feet of Jesus. Jesus' response to Martha was to not focus on her worries and concerns, but rather to concentrate on what was important.

Martha was not doing anything terrible. Taking care of her guests was commendable. The problem was that she allowed the busyness of life to distract her from what was really important. Her priorities were a little mixed up. Maybe you're like Martha. You love God and really want to serve Him, yet you struggle.

Ask yourself the following questions:

- Do I have my priorities in order?
- Am I distracted or worried about many things or am I focused on Jesus?
- Have I put devotion to Christ and His Word first or am I more concerned about serving?

How many times in our lives do we get so caught up in doing ministry or trying to do God's work that we forget that it's all about the relationships – our relationships with others, but more importantly, our relationship with God.

To refocus your priorities on relationships:

- Spend time with God in prayer and read His Word. Include some quiet time as well, listening for the message He has for you.
- Be intentional about spending quality time with others.

As you draw closer to God, your devotion will be deepened and your desire to serve will be strengthened ... less stress and more joy!

~Joyce

October 26 ~ Luke 12-13

"And he said to them, 'Take care, and be on your guard against all covetousness, for one's life does not consist in the abundance of his possessions.'" Luke 12:15 (ESV)

"Did you hear that they're having a sale that ends today?"

"You've got to buy this...you'll be so happy you invested in it!"

"They're running out of this style...get it right away!"

Phrases like these put a fire under our feet, and if we can't get our hands on the latest and greatest that the store has to offer, we feel let down.

It's so easy to get blinded by the false sense of security of possessions. Have you ever given in and spent a small fortune on the trendiest pair of shoes, just to see it at the bottom of the shoe pile a week later?

While there is absolutely nothing wrong with wearing the latest brands or sporting trendy styles, if you allow things to determine your happiness, it can steal your joy.

In today's reading, we are introduced to the parable of a rich man who tore down his barns and built bigger ones to store his material things. God told him to watch out because it was foolish to store up earthly wealth, but not have a rich relationship with Him. We are reminded to "watch out" when it comes to greed.

Why does greed lead us the direction of a false sense of security? We make the mistake of putting our security and satisfaction in what is temporary and not what will last. It removes our focus on the Provider, our Father God. He is the giver of good things and knows what we need before we even ask.

While the rich man seemed happy when he stored up all his goods, he didn't realize that his life might soon come to an end and how short-lived that happiness would be. What good is a storehouse full of possessions when you are not around to enjoy it?

However, when we are rich in good works and give generously, we are storing up treasure as a *"good foundation"* for the future to take hold of eternal life. (1 Timothy 6:19 ESV)

Our joy comes from being rich toward God because we gain so much more when we invest in what is eternal, like time in God's Word and prayer.

When we do that, our perspective changes. We discover that our contentment isn't about what is going on around us, rather what is going on in us.

~Elizabeth

October 27~ Luke 14-15

"Instead invite the poor, the crippled, the lame and the blind.
Then at the resurrection of the righteous, God will reward you for
inviting those who could not repay you." Luke 14:13-14 (NLT)

A few weeks ago, we went out for my sister in love's birthday. We were at a long table with 7 kids and 10 adults. The wait staff brought the kids colors and coloring pages to keep them entertained and seated. Towards the end of the evening, the kids started getting restless and began wandering around our table. They weren't being disruptive; they were just being kids and playing with each other. I got up as well and moved to talk to some family seated at the opposite end of the table.

A few minutes into my conversation, I felt a tugging on my shirt. It was my daughter.

"Mama, can I ask that girl to come color with me at our table?"

She pointed to a little girl, about her age, at a table near us. The girl was sitting at the end of the table by herself. Her table was filled with women and a few other little girls, but for some reason, she was alone, at the end of the table, with a few extra chairs. She was wearing a blue princess costume, and she just looked sad. (Sad princesses are just the worst!)

I told her that she could ask, but I warned that her mom might say no since we were strangers. She went over to ask, and the answer was no. She came back to our table, picked up 2 sets of crayons and coloring sheets, and marched back over to sit at their table to color with the little girl.

The frown on the princess' face dissolved and soon the two were chatting as if they'd known each other their whole lives. When we left, my daughter gave her a huge hug.

I take no credit for this compassion that she exemplified, but I did take note. She knows nothing about comfort zones or boundaries; she acts on her heart alone. My daughter had left her table, full of cousins and family, and reached out to a stranger to make her day brighter.

Jesus instructs us twice in this reading to reach out the poor, crippled, lame and blind. If He says it twice, I think it's pretty important. He's encouraging us to reach beyond our comfortable areas and do some physical work to bring His love to those who may not be reached otherwise.

~Shiney

October 28 ~ Luke 16-17

"He replied, 'If you have faith as small as a mustard seed,
you can say to this mulberry tree, 'Be uprooted and planted
in the sea,' and it will obey you.'" Luke 17:6 (NIV)

The following is an excerpt from my prayer journal written last month:

"Dear God,

I have been having stomach pain for the past 3-4 days. Everything I eat is causing me discomfort. So, I'm hungry because I am afraid to eat anything as it will lead to discomfort.

I decided to call in sick at work, which was a big decision. There were a lot of rearrangements that needed to be made at work due to my absence. I rested today, and it was good. While I was resting, around 10:15 am, my husband came to the room I was resting in and he prayed over me. He said, "She is healed in Jesus' name."

Then he asked me, "Do you believe you are healed?"

I was surprised that he asked me that. It was expected that I should believe it ... but did I truly believe?

About an hour later, I got out of bed. As I was walking toward the kitchen, I repeated, "I am healed. I am healed. I am healed."

I ate noodles for lunch, and it's been 2 hours with no discomfort.

I can say with confidence: Jesus healed me! I just texted my manager to let her I know that I will be back at work [tomorrow].

Thank you, Jesus, for your healing power, at work in me! I love you!"

I share this testimony from my journal not only to give praise to God, our healer, but it also makes me realize that I need to believe in my own prayers.

In a story in Mark 9, a boy was possessed by a spirit that caused him to have seizures. His father came to Jesus and asked for healing ... and help to overcome his own unbelief.

As the apostles said to the Lord, my prayer to God is, *"Increase our faith!"* *(Luke 17:5 NIV)*

"Spirit lead me where my trust is without borders. Let me walk upon the waters wherever You would call me."[1] (lyrics from Oceans by Hillsong United)

~Elizabeth

October 29 ~ John 11
"But I know that even now God will give you whatever you ask." John 11:22 (NIV)

Have you ever walked through a dark time in your life when you felt forsaken by God? Even though you prayed and you trusted Him, you did not see the prayer answered and you felt as if God didn't care about you.

I've been there and done that. One of my heart's desires was for my husband and maternal grandmother to meet. Growing up, I was very close to my grandmother. She was loving and kind and I just adored her. Being that she was elderly and lived overseas, she wasn't able to attend our wedding. So shortly after we were married, my husband and I planned a trip with my family to visit her. I couldn't wait!

However, two months before our trip, my mom fell ill and was hospitalized. Soon after, she began her road to recovery but we knew that traveling would have to be postponed until she was fully better. To our dismay, we received the unexpected news that my healthy grandmother had a heart attack and passed away immediately. I was in utter shock and my heart was broken.

How could this have happened? My husband didn't meet my grandmother. I didn't get to see her one more time. I was so frustrated as I asked the Lord why we didn't have the opportunity to just see her. As I grieved at the funeral, my faith was renewed that her time had come and I trusted that God's plan was better than mine.

In the midst of Martha's grief and sorrow after her brother Lazarus died, her first reactionary comment to Jesus was *"if you had been here, my brother would not have died." (John 11:21 NIV)* Interestingly, this moment of weakness was followed by the faith that she had in spite of what happened. She knew Who she was talking to and was confident in His power.

These accounts illustrate that we all are capable of having a moment of weakness when things don't go as we expect. My prayer is that such will be followed with faith in God and His plans. *"Those who know your name trust in you, for you, LORD, have never forsaken those who seek you." (Psalm 9:10 NIV)*

~Joyce

October 30 ~ Luke 18

*"But the tax collector stood at a distance. He would not
even look up to heaven, but beat his breast and said, 'God,
have mercy on me, a sinner.'" Luke 18:13 (NIV)*

We have been training our three-year-old son to sleep in his own bed. Over time, he has gotten used to snuggling in our bed, so we decided it was time to make a change.

This is no easy task.

There are nights he cries and sneaks back into our room. Out of sheer fatigue, I pull him into bed and he's asleep in no time.

But this doesn't help with the training.

So, we decided that no matter how tired we are, we will put him back in his bed so that he knows that *his* bed is where he sleeps. We even prayed about this during our family prayer.

The other day, we had our first victory! He slept in his bed the entire night. For another family, it may be a small feat, but for us, it was a huge deal. We celebrated our "big boy" with big cheers.

Okay, so it's a simple example of answered prayer, but it's *real* for us.

In the parable of the Pharisee and the tax collector, Jesus tells us the simple prayer of the tax collector. He was explaining this particular parable to those who looked down on others.

While the Pharisee had a longer prayer that criticized others, *"the tax collector stood at a distance. He would not even look up to heaven, but beat his breast and said, 'God, have mercy on me, a sinner.'" (Luke 18:13 NIV)*

How simple, yet *poignant*, were his words. There is a sense of humility and earnestness in his prayer.

It doesn't matter what words you use. It is the belief that God will answer your prayer in due time.

Our leadership team at work recently had a meeting. A few people were randomly asked their values. My heart was warmed when I heard my supervisor boldly say her values included serving others and serving God.

I later emailed her to express my appreciation. She responded by telling me that as a leader, she prays for those working for and with her. I was surprised and amazed. My boss *prays* for me.

Prayer opens up the doors to heaven. We are praying to a living God who loves you and *hears* you. Your prayer doesn't just dissipate into the air. There is power in those words.

Pray. Believe. Wait.

Your answer is coming.

~Elizabeth

October 31 ~ Matthew 19, Mark 10
*"... a man leaves his father and mother and is joined
to his wife, and the two are united into one."*
Matthew 19:5 (NLT)

I had always wanted to be married. Once I finished college, it was the next logical step. I didn't need to find myself. I didn't want to travel. I just wanted to be married.

After several years of waiting and praying, it finally happened.

Unfortunately, our first year was not fun at all. If anyone asked me how married life was going, I simply responded, *"It's hard!"* By our 2nd year of marriage, we had worked through a lot of our issues but still had our moments.

One day in particular, we had gotten into yet another fight. This time, it was over the phone while I was driving home from work. I was so upset that I ended up running a yellow (or was it red?) light and hitting another car.

Thankfully, both myself and the other driver were okay but my car was totaled. We arrived at the dealership and the salesman asked why we were looking for a new car. My husband's response was *"We totaled our car."* What was he saying? I totaled my car, not him. Once I clarified that with the salesman, he responded:

"Well, that's how you know you have a good marriage!"

Really? Us?

My husband had proven before that he would defend me but this went beyond that. He took my mess up as his own. I will never forget that moment when I realized that he was for me, not against me. It wasn't just about a shared living space or bank account. My battles had become his battles and my totaled car had become our totaled car.

Isn't this one of the greatest things we can do for our spouses? Proving to them that when we said our vows, specifically the I TAKE YOU part, we agreed to TAKE it all – the good, the bad and all the stuff in between.

"... a man leaves his father and mother and is joined to his wife, and the two are united into one." (Matthew 19:5 NLT)

On our wedding day, we became one. That day at the dealership just reminded me of it.

~Anu

November 1 ~ Matthew 20-21
"So the last will be first, and the first last." Matthew 20:16 (ESV)

We've been told since we were kids that life isn't fair. We understand that in certain situations ... kind of ... maybe.

There are other circumstances which seem so black and white that anything else would be more than unfair. It would seem to be wrong.

In the parable of the laborers, the workers who had been there all day struggled with those feelings. The master had paid everyone the same wages, even those who had just been there an hour.

This story relates well to those of us who are seasoned Christians and have been around a while. I don't know about you but in the past, I've struggled with feeling like things are not fair, especially when it came to "new laborers", even in the church.

I've served in the choir longer and never got the solo like she did.

I've been a volunteer in this department and they moved her up to lead volunteer before me.

I've been at this church for so long and I never got to hang out with the pastor like those people did.

We may be on the same team but it can still feel like a competition. I think the master's response in the parable is indicative of God's response to us when we grumble, out loud or in our hearts.

"Take what belongs to you and go. I choose to give to this last worker as I give to you. Am I not allowed to do what I choose with what belongs to me? Or do you begrudge my generosity?" (Matthew 20:14-15 ESV)

As it so often is, this is a heart issue which is rooted in envy and leads to bitterness. Maybe that's one reason why *"The harvest is plentiful, but the laborers are few ..." (Matthew 9:37 ESV)*

God is good all the time, even when we don't understand His ways. So, for this laborer and all of my fellow laborers out there, it is time to get to work on keeping our hearts right, trusting the Master and bringing in the harvest.

~Anu

November 2 ~ Luke 19

*"...To those who use well what they are given, even more will
be given. But from those who do nothing, even what little
they have will be taken away." Luke 19:26 (NLT)*

What have you been entrusted with today?

Is it a room in your parents' house? A home or car? A relationship? A job?

In Luke 19, Jesus tells a parable of ten servants who were each given a sum of money to manage while their master was away. When the master returned, each servant told their master what they had done with the money they had been given.

One was able to make ten times the amount he was given. The second was able to make five times the amount he was given. And finally, there was one who did not make anything off of the amount given to him.

What he gave his master instead was an excuse. Instead of taking responsibility for his failure or even asking for help, he blamed his master for him not making any money.

Just like the servants in this story, we have all been entrusted with something. How have you taken care of what has been entrusted to you? Have you stewarded it well?

If you haven't done this so far, then start today. Start right where you are.

Keep the home or car that God has given you clean and well maintained. Nurture and cultivate the relationships God has given you. Be an excellent employee at the job you have. Be a good steward of the finances you've been given.

You will soon see that God is faithful to His word. When He sees that you are faithful in the small things, He will trust you with so much more.

~Vijoy

November 3 ~ Mark 11, John 12
"On reaching Jerusalem, Jesus entered the temple courts and began driving out those who were buying and selling there..." Mark 11:15 (NIV)

I recently read *Made to Crave* by Lysa TerKeurst[1]. Lisa makes a phenomenal case for a direct relationship between food and God. We often use food to fill an emptiness that only God can fill. She explains chapter by chapter, with scriptural examples, that we are meant to crave something deeper than food. We are meant to crave a deeper relationship with our creator.

It was during this time that I re-read the passage of scripture where Jesus clears out the temple. He comes in hot after seeing how His holy place has been defiled. His angry reaction is how any of us would feel after seeing something we love to be used for something so far from its intended use.

We are the temple of God, and we let ourselves become defiled by things we take in, including what we eat. What we eat plays a direct correlation in how we physically feel. Are you putting things in your body that give you the fuel to fulfill His purpose or things that just get you from one crash to the next crash?

Would God be angry at how I am taking care of the temple that He has entrusted me to care for?

It challenged me to clean out my temple. It forced me to think about my weaknesses. I know that when I am tired, I start reaching for sugar or caffeine. Those are the moments that I should be relying on God to give me energy.

I know how I feel the next day after I eat too much sugar or have too much caffeine; I am miserable. I feel sluggish and achy, and sometimes I end up with a migraine. God has given me a very physical sign that I needed to pay more attention to.

I want to challenge you today to clean out your temple. What's that thing separating you from a deeper relationship with God? How do you feel after you indulge in it? What do you turn to when you should be turning to God instead? Don't allow that thing to try to fill you up. Give God control over that and let Him fill you up.

~Shiney

"... Love your neighbor as yourself." Matthew 22:39 (NIV)

Great times with great friends. How could it get any better?

In our time together, my friend shared how much she appreciated the various hats I wear. She imagined it was not easy based on watching others in similar situations.

That sweet friend's words truly lifted my spirits. I didn't hear that she felt sorry for me or pitied me. Rather, she sensed that it isn't an easy journey I travel. The truth is that there are days when I'm plain ol' tired and question if I'm cut out for the job.

My friend's words impacted me because she had EMPATHY. Even though she doesn't face the same struggles, she was able to PLACE HERSELF IN MY SHOES. I shared how refreshing it was to hear those words because women can be pretty tough on one another without even realizing it.

Maybe you've heard "harmless" comments like these in passing:

"I laugh so hard when a woman with no kids says she's tired."

"As a working mom, I don't have the time to run my kids everywhere like stay at home moms."

In such moments, do we pause to think: What if a woman can't have a child? Isn't she still allowed to be tired? What if the stay at home mom made such a sacrifice because her children needed the extra attention? Maybe her time is just as limited as the working mom.

Regardless of where we find ourselves in life, we're all women and we all have our fair share of ups and downs. No matter how pretty our smiles are on the outside, we have moments of feeling pain and sadness on the inside.

So, we have to decide whether we're going to judge or show empathy. Jesus commands us to love others.

Albert Einstein said, *"Empathy is patiently seeing the world through the other person's eyes. It is not learned in school; it is cultivated over a lifetime."*[1] *"Empathy is the key that can unlock the door to our kindness and compassion."*[2]

The best model of empathy we can ever find is Jesus. Though He is perfect, Matthew 9:36 (NIV) shows us *"when he saw the crowds, . . . (He) had compassion on them, because they were harassed and helpless, like sheep without a shepherd."*

Place yourself in someone else's shoes today and see how God can help you be sensitive to them.

~Joyce

November 5 ~ Matthew 23, Luke 20-21
"Truly I tell you … this poor widow has put in more than all the others." Luke 21:3 (NIV)

When my children were young, they had the opportunity to earn "cash" at Sunday School. Every time they brought their Bible, recited their memory verse, or provided a correct answer to a question, they were rewarded with this currency. Then, they could use this reward to purchase items from the store set up for children ranging from pieces of candy to toys.

My husband and I used this as an opportunity to teach our children about saving and spending when we realized how eager they were to spend their rewards immediately. What they learned was the more they had saved, the more they had to put toward small gifts available for purchase during Christmas for family members.

One of my children, who loves to give, couldn't have been happier. This child could be seen perusing the display cases weeks in advance with a pen and pad to note the items available, cost, and who to purchase them for. Then, this child discussed those findings and the budget with their siblings to have a plan in motion by the time Christmas arrived.

However, another one of my children wasn't so enthused by this process. This child wanted to spend their money immediately each week on what they wanted. Therefore, during the sibling discussion, this child could be heard asking if these purchases were necessary, if the recipient would really use the gift, and complained that the cost was too much. Ultimately, this child would give, but grudgingly because they wanted to be a "team player".

When we read about the widow's offering in Luke 21:1-4, we see how she was commended by Jesus for giving two small coins, while the rich were not. Rather than looking at the amount they gave, Jesus was looking at their hearts.

He saw that as this widow gave all she had, she did so from a cheerful and willing heart. 2 Corinthians 9:7 (AMP) reminds us *"Let each one give [thoughtfully and with purpose] just as he has decided in his heart, not grudgingly or under compulsion, for God loves a cheerful giver [and delights in the one whose heart is in his gift]."*

What is the condition of our hearts when we give? I pray that it is positioned with cheerfulness as we observed from this widow.

~Joyce

November 6 ~ Mark 13
"Be on guard, keep awake. For you do not know when
the time will come." Mark 13:33 (ESV)

When something is hard, it's nice to know if there is an end in sight.

Right before the nurse gives us a shot, she says, *"You will feel a little pinch."* No one likes to be pinched but we can handle that. In one of my fitness videos, the instructor says, *"You can do anything for 60 seconds!"* It's hard to believe because 60 seconds of intense cardio feels like 59 seconds too long.

But knowing it's temporary does bring some relief.

In Mark 13, the disciples questioned Jesus about what is to come. He shared some of the hardships that await them but He also offers them hope:

"Then everyone will see the Son of Man coming on the clouds with great power and glory. And he will send out his angels to gather his chosen ones from all over the world..." (Mark 13:26-27 NLT)

It's interesting to hear people talk about the second coming. Some old-time saints will utter the phrase, *"Come quickly Lord"*. When my nephew was younger, he prayed that Jesus would come back before the new school year started. Paul refers to the second coming of the Lord and ends with this... *"Therefore encourage one another with these words." (1 Thessalonians 4:18 ESV)*.

Honestly, for others, the idea of it is so mysterious that it feels a little scary.

Whatever way you look at it, the return of Jesus Christ is guaranteed. And there may be a lot about it that we don't understand. Regardless, we weren't intended to feel unsettled by it. In fact, if anything, it should comfort our hearts to know this experience on earth is temporary. Our Savior will return to gather His people to their eternal home.

C.S. Lewis said, *"If I find in myself a desire which no experience in this world can satisfy, the most probable explanation is that I was made for another world."*[1]

We must live with eternity in mind but never forget that we are on assignment. Let us be found faithful in doing every good work He intended for us to do, including sharing the good news of the hope we have.

Life on earth may not always be easy ... but hang in there, it's just temporary.

~Anu

November 7~ Matthew 24

"Who then is the faithful and wise servant ... It will be good for that servant whose master finds him doing so when he returns." Matthew 24:45a,46 (NIV)

Years ago, as my family and I were on our way to church, we stopped at a nearby convenience store. My husband's parents were with us and my father-in-law needed to run inside and buy some mints (a must have for before and after church fellowship).

Before my father in law could get both of his feet out of the car, my youngest son yelled from the back of our van, *"Appacha (Grandpa), please don't tell anyone in there about Jesus or else we will be late to church."*

It was a funny *and ironic* statement.

Funny, because my son simply verbalized what the rest of us were thinking. Ironic, because ... well, isn't that what church is all about? Jesus.

My boys had taken enough walks and gone to enough stores with their grandfather. They knew, if God prompted his heart, he would not miss out on an opportunity to introduce someone to Jesus. It didn't matter that his English was limited, he knew enough to share the gospel. He would either tell you about Jesus, invite you to church or give you a Bible ... or he may do all three.

My father-in-law doesn't see color or race, he sees souls. And if that soul has not met Jesus yet, he sees an opportunity.

In Jeremiah chapter 1, the Lord appointed a very hesitant Jeremiah to be *'a prophet to the nations.'* Despite Jeremiah's 'But Lord...this isn't my thing,' rebuttal, the Lord continued. *"You must go to everyone I send you to and say whatever I command you. Do not be afraid of them, for I am with you." (vs 7b-8a NIV)*

You and I have the same mandate.

In Matthew 24, Jesus ends His lengthy discourse on the end times with a challenge to every believer. *"Who then is the faithful and wise servant ... It will be good for that servant whose master finds him doing so when he returns." (vs 45a, 46 NIV)*

In other words, our Master has given us a job to do. Are we doing it?

We may not have the boldness of my father-in-law ... *just yet,* but we can pray and ask the Lord to open our eyes for opportunities to share His love. I have no doubt He will hear our prayer!

The harvest is plenty, the laborers are you and I.

~Binu

November 8 ~ Matthew 25

"To those who use well what they are given, even more will be given, and they will have an abundance..." Matthew 25:29a (NLT)

In Matthew 25, Jesus tells the parable of the talents which is a story most of us are very familiar with. We hear a lot about the 5-talent servant because he was the bigger deal. The 1-talent servant also gets a lot of press for not doing anything with his talent except burying it.

We tend to forget about the middle child - the 2-talent servant. He was just as much a part of the story and probably someone who a lot of us can relate to.

It's easy to get caught up in the 5-talent servants around us. We admire their fruit but notice when the master returned, he didn't talk about that. As much as we see fruitfulness, the master saw faithfulness. The 2-talent servant received the same response as the 5-talent servant.

"His master said to him, 'Well done, good and faithful servant. You have been faithful over a little; I will set you over much. Enter into the joy of your master.'" (Matthew 25:23 ESV)

Praise God for the 5-talent servants of our generation. In worship, the impact of groups like Hillsong and Bethel have been experienced all over the world. Then, there are preachers like Andy Stanley, Tim Keller or Steven Furtick whose messages have gone beyond the walls of their churches to countless listeners. And who can forget teachers like Beth Moore and Priscilla Shirer, empowering women in their walk with God.

But they are not the only ones who the Master is pleased with. He proclaims "Well done" to the 2-talent servants as well.

The worship leaders who lead their local congregations in songs of praise to Him. The pastors who prepare relentlessly and teach enthusiastically, no matter how many people are there. And the women who lead Bible studies or mentor younger women in their living rooms.

You may wonder where you fit on the talent scale but that's not the important part. It's what you do with what you've been given that counts.

~Anu

"So, leaving them again, he went away and prayed for the third time, saying the same words again." Matthew 26:44 (ESV)

We had seen Jesus walk in complete authority on Earth. He told the dead to wake up. When He commanded demons to leave, they did. They had no choice.

After 3 years of ministry and just a few days after being hailed as "Hosanna", the time had finally come. The very reason why He came to earth was to be a sacrifice...once and for all.

So, what did He do? He prayed.

This isn't shocking. Jesus prayed a lot but this prayer was different from most. He wasn't praying for someone else's situation. He was praying for His.

How He prayed might surprise you.

"If it is possible, let this cup of suffering be taken away from me. Yet I want your will to be done, not mine." (Matthew 26:39b NLT)

In this case, there was no rebuking, no binding or loosing although Jesus demonstrated there is a time and place for that. This time, it was a single request with one simple condition: *"Your will...not mine."*

In some circles today, this kind of prayer could be perceived as a lack of faith. It can feel like a cop out.

Could it be that a prayer of submission is also an acknowledgment of faith? We can express our desires but when we submit them to His will, we are saying what God wants means more than what we want. In other words, we trust His plan.

Jesus proceeded to pray three times that this cup be taken away. Each time, He also sought the will of the Father above His own request.

Jesus was our perfect example. Throughout His ministry, He didn't pray the exact same way every time but there was a common theme: God's will be done and His glory revealed. Oftentimes, it was manifested through healing or deliverance. In the case of our Savior that night, it was on a cross.

But it didn't end there. The beauty of the submitted life is even when there is suffering, there is always redemption. Three days later, His resurrection brought hope and eternal life to our world.

Thank you Jesus for doing the will of Your Father and dying ... so that we could live.

~Anu

"... Then he began to wash the disciples' feet, drying
them with the towel he had around him."
John 13:5 (NLT)

When my husband started traveling for work many years ago, it was really hard. I wasn't used to being alone in the house and not seeing him every day.

Eventually, I did get used to it and actually started to enjoy some of the perks of it.

(Um ... Maybe I should clarify.)

Of course, I would prefer to have my husband home but his frequent trips have entitled him to some benefits. We don't have to take off our shoes at security or wait in long lines for a rental car.

So, when I travel with my husband, his status becomes my status. Basically, I tag along and he announces, *"She's with me"*. And I'm in. No questions asked.

Knowing your position changes everything.

"It was time for supper, and the devil had already prompted Judas, son of Simon Iscariot, to betray Jesus. JESUS KNEW that the Father had given him authority over everything and that he had come from God and would return to God. SO he got up from the table, took off his robe, wrapped a towel around his waist, and poured water into a basin. Then he began to wash the disciples' feet, drying them with the towel he had around him." (John 13:2-5 NLT)

There are a million reasons to love Jesus and to want to be like Him. This is one of them.

How in the world could Jesus wash the feet of the men who would abandon him and the man who had betrayed him?

It could be summarized like this: *Jesus knew ... so He ....*

He knew who He was. He knew who His Father was. Jesus knew that one day, He would be with His Father again. His identity wasn't based on what Judas was about to do. It was based on His place with the Father.

The same could be said of us.

Our position as children of God doesn't elevate us to a superior status, but to a higher service.

We don't react to others according to who they are or what they've done. Instead, we respond because of Whose we are and what God has done.

Rather than retaliating or proving ourselves, we wash feet.

Now, we know ... so we...

~Anu

November 11 ~ John 14-17
"... In this world you will have trouble. But take heart! I
have overcome the world." John 16:33 (NIV)

I remember when my oldest son first began taking piano lessons, I loved to hear him practice, but I couldn't wait for him to advance to the good stuff ... something with a little more substance. There's only so much beginner piano music even a mama can handle.

Thankfully, his next piano book incorporated more of the sharp and flat keys which brought a whole new level of depth to the music. The ivory keys, if played alone, sound too simple and childlike. The black keys, on their own, sound too harsh and unpleasant.

And so it is with life. Beauty is found in the balance of life's trials and life's triumphs. The mountaintop experiences as well as our time in the valley.

Trust me, no one enjoys coasting through life more than me, but according to John 16:33b, trials are inevitable, *"In this world you will have trouble. But take heart! I have overcome the world." (NIV)*

The Bible also tells us that trials are necessary for the growth of our character.

James 1: 2-4 states *"Dear brothers and sisters, when troubles come your way, consider it an opportunity for great joy. For you know that when your faith is tested, your endurance has a chance to grow. So let it grow, for when your endurance is fully developed, you will be perfect and complete, needing nothing." (NLT)*

Trials are the refining fire which purify our soul. Trials teach us what sermons can't. Trials force us to discern what is truly important in life and what isn't.

When you face difficulties, who do you reach out to? I seek counsel from those whom I know have gone through stuff and endured, for there is a depth to their counsel which I long to hear.

If you are currently in the middle of a trial, if you can only hear the harsh sounds of the black keys ringing in your ears, take heart. The simplicity of the ivory keys will soon be heard. The two sounds played together will, in time, create a God given song and form the beautiful story of your life.

~Binu

November 12 ~ Matthew 27, Mark 15
*"The curtain of the temple was torn in two from
top to bottom." Mark 15:38 (NIV)*

I made it through car line yesterday morning in the nick of time.

It was raining, and I was late getting out the door. I made it to the back of the long car line, and as we inched closer to the school building, I kept my eye on the clock.

The school has a strict tardy policy. So, naturally, parents are scrambling and competitive when it comes to car line.

We finally made it to the front of school, and...success! My daughter was out of the car at the last acceptable minute. What a morning!

Why such strict rules? Why cause parents such stress? Ultimately, to allow school to start in time, but also to build discipline.

The book of Leviticus gives specific laws and regulations regarding worship and ceremonial cleansing. And when we say specific, we mean, "pay-attention-to-every-detail-or-you-will-be-excommunicated", kind of specific.

For example, when a member of the community sins, he must bring a female goat without defect, lay his hand on the goat's head, and slaughter it. The blood is placed by the priest on specific parts of the altar. (Leviticus 4:27-28 NIV)

This allows for atonement of the person's sins.

It made me wonder why the Lord did not make an easier, less complex way to atone for sins.

Ultimately, it is because we serve a holy God.

Parenting experts agree that healthy bonding requires both love and limits.

Could it be that God allowed for those laws because he loved the Israelites and wanted to set limits on their actions? Rules and laws are in place for safety, discipline, love and even holiness. God's laws in Leviticus were in place to establish the Israelites as God's holy people.

Welcome to the Age of Grace. We don't follow the same laws and regulations because Jesus was the sacrificial Lamb, and when He died on the cross, "*... the curtain of the temple was torn in two ...*" *(Mark 15:38 NIV)*

What a relief to know that when I mess up ... and I know I will ... that I serve a loving and forgiving God who made a way for me to Him through Jesus Christ. Because of His sacrifice, I can approach God's throne with confidence as His loved daughter. (Hebrews 4:16 NIV)

~Elizabeth

November 13 ~ Luke 23, John 18-19

"The servant girl at the door said to Peter, 'You also are not one of this man's disciples, are you?' He said, 'I am not.'" John 18:17 (ESV)

When we discuss conflict in our marriage small group, my husband will ask each spouse, *"What are your 'trigger words'?"* The reason it is referred to as a trigger word is because of its ability to initiate an argument.

No matter who you are, married or not, we all have them. They may not start a fight on the outside but something still hits us on the inside.

I have my own set of words that are probably insignificant to most people. To them, it's just another word.

But for me, my heart immediately drops. If I think about it long enough, I may tear up. Certain words remind me of a part of my life that didn't turn out how I thought it would. It is a constant admonition of how I have disappointed the people closest to me.

Everyone's trigger is different.

Peter was one of the closest disciples to Jesus but also the one who betrayed Him. Jesus even warned Peter that he would deny Him. Not just once but three times.

"Peter again denied it, and at once a rooster crowed." (John 18:27 ESV)

If you live in the suburbs of America like I do, you are not likely to hear a rooster crowing. In rural Israel, it may have been a more common occurrence.

Can you imagine what Peter must have felt every time he heard a rooster crow? He was the one who said he would be with Jesus until the end. Each morning, when the rooster woke up the sleeping town, did his heart drop when he remembered how he disappointed his Lord?

Days after the resurrection, Jesus had a one-on-one conversation with Peter, instructing him to *"feed My sheep". (John 21:17b ESV)*

God still had plans for Peter.

Then, in Acts 2, Peter returns to the scene except this isn't the same man who ran away. Instead, he stood boldly and proclaimed the gospel.

As he spoke, I wonder if he heard a rooster crow in the distance, suggesting to him that he was the last person in the world who should be doing this. If he did hear it, he didn't show it. He kept on that day ... and the day after that ... and for many days to follow.

That moment the rooster crowed didn't define Peter. The moments with Jesus did.

~Anu

"But when they looked up, they saw that the stone,
which was very large, had been rolled away."
Mark 16:4 (NIV)

I am a *practicalist.* I don't know if that's even a real word but it seems to describe me pretty well.

Life has to make sense and I like to have all the details ironed out before I take a single step forward in a new or different direction. But the more I read my Bible, the more I realize - God's ways are a lot less practical than my ways.

Think about it.

God had Elijah ask the poorest of widows for food. Why not ask someone who is financially more stable? And what about Moses. He hated public speaking, but who does God choose to lead a nation out of slavery?

Then, there is a story which caught my attention this past week. It involves three sweet women heading toward the garden tomb to anoint Jesus' body. As they were on their way, the question was asked, *"Who will roll the stone away ...?" (vs 3b NIV)*

For these women, it was a passing statement. For me, it would have been an important detail to iron out before heading over to the tomb.

I can hear myself now.

"Listen ladies. I think we should wait. After all, that stone is heavy. Why don't we ask Peter, James and John to meet us there whenever they are free? They can help us move the stone."

I literally would have talked myself (and the others) out of an encounter with God.

God doesn't always give us details, and for a *practicalist* like myself, that's scary!

But my friend, James Mathews, encourages us to do it anyways. *"The cost of sitting still will haunt you later in life. Whisper a prayer and breathe into a paper bag if you must, but face your fears with action..."* [1]

About that stone? God took care of it. *"But when they looked up, they saw that the stone, which was very large, had been rolled away." (Mark 16:4 NIV)*

Maybe you are a *practicalist* like me and maybe there is a *"stone"* blocking your way, holding you back from doing what God has asked you to do. Like the ladies heading towards the garden tomb, take a step and head in the direction God has asked you to go.

"Breathe into a paper bag if you must," but don't talk your practical self out of an encounter with God.

~Binu

November 15 ~ Luke 24, John 20-21
"At dawn Jesus was standing on the beach, but the disciples
couldn't see who he was." John 21:4 (NLT)

When the disciples were called by Jesus, we read that they threw down their nets and followed him without hesitation. In this passage, however, Jesus is gone, and we find that the disciples have returned to their pre-disciple employment. After His death, it seems that they returned to fishing as something familiar and comfortable to fill the void.

This particular night they aren't having much luck. The familiarity of the fishing boats, texture of the fishing nets, and smell of the sea now do not offer them anything of value - until Jesus shows up on the scene. Simon Peter and his crew didn't recognize Jesus from afar but once He made their barren nets full of fish, they knew right away who it was.

They meet Jesus on the shore, and He serves them breakfast. He knew they were hungry after working all night. He nourished them physically and then spiritually.

This story is so simple yet so telling of Christ's character. I am no Bible scholar, but I am pretty sure that these disciples were not where Jesus intended for them to be. I'm fairly confident that they weren't doing the work that He had commissioned them to do. They had not become fishers of men; they had returned to being just fishermen.

But Jesus met them where they were. He blessed the work of their hands, and fed them. Jesus doesn't gripe or question them; He serves them with love. He commissions them once more.

I am so grateful that God meets us where we are, even if it is that familiar place that we were once called out from. I am so thankful that He meets us in our mess.

Maybe that's you today. Maybe you're not where God intended for you to be and you know it. Maybe you've returned to something that's comfortable and familiar instead of fulfilling His calling on your life. Let God in. Let Him meet you right where you are. Invite Him in. Let His love cover you and direct you out of this place and back into His plan for your life.

~Shiney

November 16 ~ Acts 1-3
"And they prayed and said, 'You, Lord, who know the hearts of all, show which one of these two you have chosen...'" Acts 1:24 (ESV)

There are certain passages of scripture that make you wonder if you read them right.

"So now we must choose a replacement for Judas from among the men who were with us the entire time we were traveling with the Lord Jesus ...So they NOMINATED two men: Joseph called Barsabbas (also known as Justus) and Matthias. Then they all PRAYED, 'O Lord, you know every heart. Show us which of these men you have chosen as an apostle to replace Judas in this ministry, for he has deserted us and gone where he belongs.' Then they CAST lots, and Matthias was selected to become an apostle with the other eleven." (Acts 1:21-26 NLT)

For the disciples, it was an important decision with an interesting strategy. The plan seems to start out well but ends with them casting lots. To bring it up to more modern times, it may be like rolling the dice or shaking the magic 8 ball.

They knew they had to move forward but were unsure of the details. This is a common occurrence in the faith journey. Sometimes, it is hard to decipher exactly what God's will is but I think we can take a clue from the disciples.

1. They gathered the facts - they chose men who fit the criteria.
2. They prayed - they wanted direction from God so they asked for it.
3. They made a decision - once you've done your due diligence, trust God is leading you ... and go for it.

"By faith Abraham, when called to go to a place he would later receive as his inheritance, obeyed and went, even though he did not know where he was going." (Hebrews 11:8 NIV)

Oswald Chambers said, *"Faith never knows where it is being led, but it loves and knows the One who is leading."*[1] He is a good Shepherd. Even if I wander in the wrong direction, He can lead me back.

That's something you can bet your life on.

~Anu

November 17~ Acts 4-6

"The members of the council were amazed when they saw the boldness of Peter and John, for they could see that they were ordinary men with no special training in the Scriptures. They also recognized them as men who had been with Jesus." Acts 4:13 (NLT)

In this reading, Peter and John have just healed a man who had been lame "from his mother's womb." They are taken captive, testify and then pray for courage to continue to preach with boldness.

They were not educated men. We don't know if they were particularly good looking or charismatic; their popularity remains unknown. We don't know if they were rich or had a large social circle. Acts 4:13 tells us that the council was amazed when they saw their boldness. They were regular guys who had been with Jesus.

They were just like you and me, but they healed a lame man and gave a message that saved 5,000 people.

When it comes to having a place in ministry, many people often feel inadequate. Sometimes we think we need a degree in theology or need to be prepared with all the right answers to be an effective witness for Christ. Maybe you think that you need to have read the whole Bible, cover to cover, to feel like you are an adequate Christian. These men show us that is not the case.

Our experience with Jesus serves as a powerful witness. It is a compelling instructor. It cannot be disputed. Don't ever doubt the power of your testimony.

There are many things that I don't know, but there is one thing that I do know: Jesus saved me. He brought me out of a pit and set me on a rock, in a place of abundance. That is my experience, and no one can argue against it. I want to be an ordinary woman who has been with Jesus. I want His light to shine so strongly through me that it's indisputable.

Don't be discouraged by the lack that you feel. Be bold in your faith. Be willing. Be obedient. Spend time in God's presence and then walk as if you have been with Jesus. Let Him shine through you.

~Shiney

November 18 ~ Acts 7-8
*"Those who had been scattered preached the word wherever
they went. Philip went down to a city in Samaria and
proclaimed the Messiah there." Acts 8:4-5 (NIV)*

I had an acquaintance in college that I would converse with in the campus dining room. Our schedules happened to converge during mealtimes, and we would talk when we met with each other. He was an intelligent student, and we had stimulating conversations during our time there.

During one particular lunch, I remember sitting down with another friend along with this student and having a passionate discussion about religion. He didn't believe that Jesus was the Savior like I did, but he gave compelling evidence for why he believed what he did.

I stood my ground because I knew what I believed, and while he had a great argument, it wasn't convincing. At one point, I disagreed with him, and then he made the following statement, *"I really feel sorry for you because you don't know or accept the truth."*

Deep down inside, I felt the same for him. Sorrow, really, because he REALLY didn't know THE TRUTH.

It was interesting to witness how firmly he believed what he did and how deep his faith was ... in a false religion. After some time, I didn't converse with him as much regarding religion. I could see that he was steadfast in what he believed and honestly, I had run out of fuel.

The apostle Philip was in a similar situation. After the devout believer, Stephen, was stoned for his faith, persecution broke out in the church, and many were scattered to different cities.

Philip was one of those believers who ended up moving but the Bible says he proclaimed the good news there! The persecution of the church didn't stop him. He didn't go into hiding or avoid non-believers. He was bold and continued to spread the news of salvation wherever he went.

That is a lesson in courage!

The persecution the early church endured included being dragged in the streets, stoned, and yelled at. Nothing like what I had to go through in my lunchroom. We were having a civil conversation! Why did I shy away? Because I didn't like confrontation. Was it the right solution? *No.*

It is when we are obedient and courageous, we experience joy as there was when Philip persisted in sharing in Macedonia. May the Holy Spirit give us wisdom and open doors so that we are courageous to share the good news of Jesus Christ.

~Elizabeth

November 19 ~ Acts 9-10
"... Do not call anything impure that God has made clean." Acts 10:15 (NIV)

Were you raised to believe something your entire life only to learn later on that it was not correct?

For as long as I can remember, I would say "draw-yer" when referring to the drawers, which held my clothing, in my dresser. That's how it was pronounced by my family and so that's how I would say it. That is, until the day I was corrected and taught the proper pronunciation in school.

Let's just say that it was mind-blowing for me. It was hard for me to say it correctly at first because I had been accustomed to saying it my family's way for so long. Eventually, I learned to drop the extra syllable and correctly sound it out.

It may seem like a silly example, but I think each of us can recall a word, action, or belief that we thought was right, but eventually realized was wrong.

Jesus' disciple Peter can relate to this regarding what he believed to be true about the Gentiles. We read in Acts chapter 10 how he had a vision of eating something unclean and the Holy Spirit revealing the truth to him. Although the connection was not obvious at first, he realized what God was correcting as he, a Jew, was brought to the Gentile Cornelius' home.

In verse 28 (NIV), *"He said to them: 'You are well aware that is against our law for a Jew to associate with a Gentile or visit him. But God has shown me that I should not call any man impure or unclean."* Not only did God correct Peter's incorrect way of thinking that day, but he also received divine revelation. In verses 34 through 35 (NIV) he states, *"I now realize how true it is that God does not show favoritism but accepts men from every nation who fear him and do what is right."*

It can be quite earth-shattering when you discover that what you believed is not how God views a particular situation. Thankfully, He is able to open our eyes and ears to see and to hear from His perspective. I pray that not only our hearts desire such revelation, but that we would be willing to take a leap out of our comfort zone in embracing His truth.

~Joyce

November 20 ~ Acts 11-12

"When the others heard this, they stopped objecting and began praising God. They said, 'We can see that God has also given the Gentiles the privilege of repenting of their sins and receiving eternal life.'"
Acts 11:18 (NLT)

Recently, a Christian musician has gained mainstream notoriety. She has even been featured on a couple of popular talk-shows where she also had the opportunity to sing.

The songs she chose were from her most recent album and were encouraging and uplifting. She sang about the Savior.

And people criticized her. Christian people.

Why did she go on that talk show? Doesn't she know what kind of person the host is? Her clothes weren't conservative enough.

Her fellow believers were concerned that she was falling to prey to the lures of the world.

She wasn't the first one to deal with this...Peter encountered it in Acts 11.

"Soon the news reached the apostles and other believers in Judea that the Gentiles had received the word of God. But when Peter arrived back in Jerusalem, the Jewish believers criticized him. 'You entered the home of Gentiles and even ate with them!'" they said. (Acts 11:1-3 NLT)

In spite of the fact that the Gentiles had received the word of God, the believers were still critical. Instead of celebrating what God had done, they chastised Peter for congregating with non-Jews.

Believe it or not, the same thing was said about Jesus.

"But when the Pharisees saw this, they asked his disciples, 'Why does your teacher eat with such scum?' When Jesus heard this, he said, 'Healthy people don't need a doctor—sick people do.'" (Matthew 9:11-12 NLT)

It made me wonder ... what about me? Would people accuse me of hanging out with people who don't act, talk or look like me? Unfortunately, I don't think they would.

Scripture is clear that we should be wise in choosing our friends but Jesus also said that He is sending us out. We are His ambassadors, His light, His hands and His feet. There are people everywhere who have never heard His name. So, when we enter their lives, whether it's from a talk show or as a neighbor, may they recognize that there is something different about us. When they meet us, may they see Him.

If anyone is critical, that's okay. We are in really, really good company.

~Anu

November 21 ~ Acts 13,14
"Now when David had served God's purpose in his own generation, he fell asleep ..." Acts 13:36a (NIV)

Call it a midlife crisis, but the past few months have been different for me. Not bad different. Just different.

I celebrated a birthday recently and so did my son. He turned seventeen! Earlier this year, that same son got his driver's license. How fun and exciting ... for him.

So, for the first time in seventeen years, my Uber services are no longer needed. You'd think this would be a welcome reprieve for me, but I'm finding, I enjoyed being a chauffeur more than I realized. It was part of my routine and as odd as it may sound ... part of my purpose.

Which leaves me asking myself and God one simple question.

Now what?

What do we do when our primary roles and responsibilities have been outsourced? What do we do when a new season of life begins, but we were still enjoying the old one? What do we do when the enemy makes us question our purpose or if we even have one anymore?

We turn to God's Word and find ... if we still have a pulse, we still have a purpose!

In Acts 13:22b, we read, *"He (God) testified concerning him (David). I have found David son of Jesse a man after my own heart; he will do everything I want him to do."* (NIV) Verse 36a goes on to say, *"Now when David had served God's purpose in his own generation, he fell asleep ..." (NIV)*

Purpose isn't just a cute buzzword. Like the air we breathe, purpose keeps us going.

It doesn't begin if or when we get married nor does it end when our children get their driver's license. Our God given purpose begins when we say yes to Jesus and ends when we breathe our last breath.

Whether we are forty-six, seventeen, still trying to figure out a career or nearing retirement ... as cliché as this may sound, God has placed a unique purpose inside the heart of each one of us!

It isn't mystical or even complicated. According to the life of King David, it involves simple everyday obedience. It's being someone God knows He can count on.

So, now what?

As it was said of King David, I pray it will one day be said of me (and you), *"She did everything I asked her to do. She served God's purpose in her generation."*

That's what.

~Binu

November 22 ~ James 1-5

"If you claim to be religious but don't control your tongue, you are fooling yourself, and your religion is worthless." James 1:26 (NLT)

Have you ever felt like you were *dying* to tell someone about what someone else did to you? I was armed and ready. I even thought I could start it out with "Girl, pray for me" and then proceed to tell her my sob story.

The story was a good one but I knew it would make the other person not look so good.

So, I held back. And I'm glad I did.

The temporary relief I may have found from "getting something off my chest" may have permanent ramifications and wouldn't have done anyone any good.

"It only takes a spark, remember, to set off a forest fire. A careless or wrongly placed word out of your mouth can do that. By our speech we can ruin the world, turn harmony to chaos, throw mud on a reputation, send the whole world up in smoke and go up in smoke with it...With our tongues we bless God our Father; with the same tongues we curse the very men and women he made in his image. Curses and blessings out of the same mouth! My friends, this can't go on..." James 3:5-10 MSG

I am not against "sharing" for the sake of getting wise counsel but if we know there is no counsel to be gained, what is the point?

It's ironic because I have heard that this particular person has said some unkind things about me...so, how would I be any different from her?

As Christ followers, we are called to a higher standard. This same chapter in James reveals a hard but hopeful truth – it is HUMANLY impossible to tame the tongue but thankfully, we don't have to rely on ourselves. When our hearts and our minds are submitted to God, it can drastically change what comes out of our mouth because what's inside of us has changed.

Also, being reminded of the fact that this person is made in the image of God, just like me...well, that helped me see her for who she really is...not who I've made her to be in my mind.

I'm reminded of the words of the great sage – Smokey the Bear: Only you can prevent forest fires...only you.

~Anu

November 23 ~ Acts 15-16

"... Paul and Silas were praying and singing hymns to God, ..." Acts 16:25 (NIV)

Can I be brutally honest for a moment? Today has been one of "those" days. Maybe you've had one of them, too. Allergies have been aggravating and all I've wanted to do is crawl under the covers. But a girl can't just do that ...not with a house to run, kids to teach, appointments to keep, and meals to make.

As the sinus pressure and congestion weighed me down, do you know what I was tempted to do? COMPLAIN.

"It's not fair I have to go through this. When will this ever improve?"

As the temptation crept up though, I actually diffused it pretty quickly this time with GRATITUDE. I had to remind myself of truth from God's Word.

"I am victorious through Christ Jesus." "God shall renew my strength."

I reached that conclusion by thinking about Paul and Silas in Acts 16. Those servants of God didn't commit a crime. In fact, they were imprisoned for setting a girl free from a demonic spirit.

I imagine how easy it must have been for them to be confused and feel sorry for themselves. Instead, *"they were praying and singing hymns to God"*, maybe about His amazing grace or how great is His faithfulness. Let's just say my complaints didn't stand a chance after such a powerful reminder.

Please understand my heart. What you and I walk through is not meant to be minimized. Our struggle is real whether it's a health issue, broken marriage, or dealing with financial pressure. Those things can just wreck a person's day.

BUT God is with us and helps us through it all.

If today is one of those days or maybe these past few weeks and months have felt as such, remember we have a choice. We can choose to be a PRISONER to our woes or PRAISE our Savior for His love and faithfulness.

Even when we don't understand the details, we can always trust our Source, the One Who is in control. His care for us is far deeper and wider than we could ever imagine.

~Joyce

"... I'm not trying to win the approval of people, but of God. If pleasing people were my goal, I would not be Christ's servant." Galatians 1:10 (NLT)

When my grandmother (I call her Ammachi) was in her twenties, she did the unthinkable.

She stepped out, all alone, in faith and left her family's traditional church in order to follow Jesus in a way she knew He was calling her to. Those around her questioned and teased her decision, *"Now you won't even have a proper burial."*

Her response: *"I am not worried about my burial. I want a better resurrection."* I think of her wise words often.

It's easy to get caught up with the *"What will others say? I don't want to be all alone"* way of thinking. But my Ammachi's words remind me, my allegiance must be to God first, even if that means stepping out into the unknown ... all alone.

Before David became the David we know, he did something when no one was watching. He killed a lion and a bear with only the sheep cheering him on. But that was okay. His next battle had the audience of two nations, the Israelites and the Philistines.

Moses also spent some time alone. Well, not completely alone ... God was with him. When he came down from his mountaintop experience, his face radiated the glory of God for all to see.

No selfies, no Instagram pics, no 1000 likes for killing the lion...just God and David. God and Moses. God and my Ammachi. I've heard it said, *"God is looking for people who will get private victories in secret places."* Not seeking the audience and the applause of man, but rather the applause of the only one who really matters. Jesus.

My grandmother passed away a couple months ago. Her burial was beautiful. Her resurrection, I can only imagine.

"I'm not trying to win the approval of people, but of God. If pleasing people were my goal, I would not be Christ's servant." (Galatians 1:10 NLT)

~Binu

November 25 ~ Galatians 4-6

"Therefore, as we have opportunity, let us do good to all people, especially to those who belong to the family of believers." Galatians 6:10 (NIV)

We walked out of the sanctuary into our church's main lobby. My husband veered off to the side, his arm around the shoulder of a fellow church member. The two engrossed in deep conversation.

As we drove home, I inquired as to what the conversation was all about. My husband filled me in.

"During the service, I noticed that man's socks. I noticed his socks because of the holes he had in his shoes. I felt a strong nudge from the Holy Spirit to buy the man a pair of shoes. So, I asked the man his shoe size."

We've attended this church for eighteen years. My husband is a giving man, but walking up to a man he has never spoken to before, and asking him his shoe size, that was a first.

Two days later my husband and the man met. There, in the food court, this man began to share his story. A few poor choices had led him to this place. He has a stable job but he still has a long way to go.

"I don't do well with handouts. I accepted your offer because I knew it was God. I have a funeral to attend later on this week. This past Sunday morning when you approached me, I had just looked through my closet to see if I had a pair of shoes decent enough to wear to the funeral. I didn't. I asked God that morning if He could somehow provide a pair of shoes. When you asked my shoe size, I knew God had heard my prayer."

The church isn't simply the building we worship in. *It's you and me.* We are the body of Christ. His hands. His feet. When there is a need, if we can meet it, let's meet it.

Galatians 6:10 tells us, *"Therefore, as we have opportunity, let us do good to all people, especially to those who belong to the family of believers." (NIV)*

Maybe you find yourself alone and in need. Your poor choices may have led you to this place. It doesn't matter. God still hears you. Even those quiet, desperate prayers you pray alone in your closet. God hears.

Our God will drop everything. He will leave the ninety-nine. He will even tug at the hearts of His children, to care for the needs of the one.

~Binu

November 26 ~ Acts 17
"As soon as it was night, the believers sent Paul and Silas away to Berea. ...
they received the message with great eagerness ..." Acts 17:10-11 (NIV)

When my children were babies, I prayerfully decided to leave the workforce and become a stay at home mom. It was the best decision I made, but I quickly realized what a thankless job it is.

Wearing shirts with spit up, constantly cleaning up, changing diapers, having sleepless nights and dealing with temper tantrums was just the beginning. Then, I decided to homeschool and I began dealing with bad attitudes and talking back. Such moments made me wonder ... what was I thinking??

I don't have to think long or hard. There were the cuddles, the hugs, and the kisses. Then, as soon as my children were drawing and writing, I began receiving a plethora of pictures, cards, and letters that expressed their love for me. The moment they began earning money, treasured gifts began filling up my nightstand. There have been many tender moments of my children expressing gratitude and appreciation for what I do, which I am incredibly thankful to God for.

When you set out to do what you are called to do, there is a lot of blood, sweat, and tears involved. What you do may go unnoticed and accolades are few and far between. That's not why you set out to do it but it sure is nice when you receive appreciation for your hard work, isn't it?

We read in Acts 17 that between ministering at Thessalonica and Athens, Paul's teaching of the gospel wasn't well received by all the people. While some were interested, he mostly came across jealous people who created turmoil and those who sneered at him. Being an apostle couldn't have been easy between the time needed to teach and answer questions and to travel from town to town. So, I imagine how refreshing it must have been for Paul when he went to Berea. How nice to be appreciated!

Is there someone in your life who could use a word of appreciation today? Tell them you are grateful for them. Write them a card. Send them flowers. Bless them with a meal. Speak Scripture over them and pray for them: *"And God is able to bless you abundantly, so that in all things at all times, having all that you need, you will abound in every good work." (2 Corinthians 9:8 NIV)*

~Joyce

November 27 ~ 1 Thessalonians 1-5, 2 Thessalonians 1-3
"Rejoice always," 1 Thessalonians 5:16 (ESV)

Have you noticed that saying "Thank you" seems to be a lost art? When you hold the door open someone, they just walk through without any acknowledgement. Or if you let someone get in your lane when you are driving ... no gesture of thanks there either.

It may seem pretty simple but the fact is that a grateful heart can change everything.

My friends know that I am somewhat of a stickler about keeping my house clean (but they would probably remove the word "somewhat"). Thankfully, my husband is neat too but every now and then, things seem to be a bit out of place. Candy wrappers in the couch, multiple pairs of shoes left by the door... and we won't even talk about the toilet seat being left up.

Honestly, it used to drive me crazy. Then, God gently reminded me of how I had waited and prayed to be married. Now, as much as I still want a clean home, these things now serve as reminders of one of the greatest blessings God has ever given to me.

Sometimes our blessings don't look like blessings.

A toddler throwing a tantrum.

A long commute to work.

A pile of laundry.

A to-do list that seems never ending.

Multiple shoes left by the door instead of the closet where they belong.

A toilet seat that is up.

It may be temporarily hidden but the blessing is still there.

Your child. Your job. Your provision. Your purpose. Your family. Your spouse.

My prayer is that God would help me to live my life in constant gratitude. The fact that I can hold the door open for someone means I have arms that are strong enough to do so. If I am on the road, it means that I have a car and a healthy (enough) mind to drive.

And even when the toilet seat is up, I remember how blessed I am ... and then I put it down.

Thank you God for all of it.

"Be thankful in all circumstances, for this is God's will for you who belong to Christ Jesus." (1 Thessalonians 5:18 NLT)

~Anu

"... When Priscilla and Aquila heard him, they invited him to their home and explained to him the way of God more adequately." Acts 18:26 (NIV)

As a married woman, I have believed the lie that "I'm *just* a wife." After all, my husband is the leader of our family and the breadwinner. What could I have to offer that would bring glory to God when my husband was so talented? I didn't understand the fallacy of that thought until I received the revelation of what a godly wife is.

Priscilla's life as seen in the New Testament shows us that a wife is *"one who comes alongside her husband, respecting his God-given leadership in a way that shows respect, yet strength."*[1] Priscilla is seen sharing the same occupation with her husband, Aquila, as a tentmaker. They worked humbly and diligently as unto the Lord. They were also beloved friends to the Apostle Paul and labored with him to win souls for the kingdom of God. As if that wasn't enough, both Priscilla and her husband were loving teachers to Apollos, who wanted to evangelize but had limited knowledge about salvation through the Cross.

Priscilla helped equip others. In other words, she passed on what she learned and knew to be true, in order to help others be the best version of who God created them to be.

You can do the same by being:

- a team player through contributing, encouraging, leading and participating
- a loyal friend
- a gentle, humble teacher

One of the greatest joys of my life has been serving alongside my husband. We have had the privilege of encouraging couples and helping them navigate through the ups and downs of life by sharing our own life experiences.

God has given you a gift to bless others, so pass it on! The seed you plant will cause many to bloom for His glory.

May these lyrics of "Legacy" by Nichole Nordeman inspire you:[2]
"I want to leave a legacy,
How will they remember me?
Did I choose to love?
Did I point to You enough ...?
A child of mercy and grace
Who blessed Your name unapologetically"

~Joyce

November 29 ~ I Corinthians 1-4

"... Let there be no divisions in the church. Rather, be
of one mind, united in thought and purpose."
1 Corinthians 1:10 (NLT)

When I got married, I faced the conflict that is pervasive in many families... where do we spend the holidays?

Thanksgiving is the one time of year that my husband's family comes together- aunts, uncles, cousins once and twice removed. It made the decision easy. We would spend Thanksgiving with them and Christmas with my family.

Our first Thanksgiving came six months into our marriage. Thanksgiving dinner really included the football game *prior* to dinner, dinner and games played *after* dinner. Dinner was a potluck, which meant cooking before I left. Snacks needed to be brought for those of us watching the game. The single meal that I had committed to just became an all-day affair.

Then came the year that my husband coordinated the event. As he began calling his family to invite them and plan for the meal, he started to get some push back. He would ask them to bring a dish, and he would get the response of: *"I don't know how to cook that"* or *"I made that last year. Can I make something else?" "Do we have to do dinner? Can we do lunch instead?" "Your house is so far for us to drive."* My husband was a little surprised. These responses were unexpected. He thought that everyone enjoyed the tradition as much as he did. His excitement turned into frustration.

In this section, Paul is (basically) telling his fellow Christians to quit their whining. They were all unified under the same vision, but several of them were making statements that were dividing the church. In an age without email, social media or even a contemporary postal system, these complaints still managed to reach Paul. It was interfering with the ability to carry out God's plan for the church in Corinthians. Paul does his best to address the issues and encourages them to move forward in their calling.

The problem with entertaining our hang-ups is that they interfere with our ability to accomplish our goals, and they rob us of our joy. They limit our ability to progress and move forward.

God's plan for us does not include whining. Set aside the differences that you may have in the church, at work, or even in your social circles. God has placed you there for a reason, with a mission. Focus on that and let the little things stay little.

~Shiney

November 30 ~ 1 Corinthians 5-8
*"... And even though 'I am allowed to do anything,'
I must not become a slave to anything."
1 Corinthians 6:12 (NLT)*

I have a confession to make. I have an addiction ... to sugar.

You may laugh or even roll your eyes. But to me it's a real struggle. Sometimes, I feel like I am controlled by this craving.

Paul tells us in Corinthians *"You say, 'I am allowed to do anything' - but not everything is good for you. And even though 'I am allowed to do anything,' I must not become a slave to anything." (1 Corinthians 6:12 NLT)*

I have to ask myself, is something mastering me? Does something consume me to the point where I can't say no?

The answer many times is *Yes*.

Paul tells us that our lives and bodies do not belong to us. They belong to God who paid a very high price for us. If I am a slave or servant to anything or anyone, I would rather it be to the one who gave His son's life as a ransom for mine.

Most times this is easier said than done.

The famous entrepreneur and motivational speaker Jim Rohn said *"We must all suffer from one of two pains: the pain of discipline or the pain of regret. The difference is discipline weighs ounces while regret weighs tons."*[1]

Wherever you are in life, you have a choice to make. Neither choice is easy.

I pray that with God's help you and I can choose to honor God with our bodies and choose the pain of discipline today, so that we won't have to face the pain of regret tomorrow.

~Vijoy

December 1 ~ 1 Corinthians 9-11

"You've all been to the stadium and seen the athletes race. Everyone runs; one wins. Run to win. All good athletes train hard. They do it for a gold medal that tarnishes and fades. You're after one that's gold eternally. I don't know about you, but I'm running hard for the finish line. I'm giving it everything I've got. No sloppy living for me!" 1 Corinthians 9:24-26 (MSG)

It's quite exciting to watch the Olympic Games and its races, competition, and victories. The athletes make it appear as if their participation is effortless. Yet, becoming familiar with the stories of the athletes clearly indicates that their arrival at the Olympics didn't just happen overnight.

Carl Lewis. Bonnie Blair. Michael Phelps. Gabby Douglas.

These Olympians began training early (some as young as 3 years old!), some even moving away hundreds of miles from home to train with specific coaches, and ultimately training for several hours a day.

In fact, Malcolm Gladwell famously created the "10,000-hour rule"—the belief that becoming a success in any field requires practicing a specific task for 10,000 hours[1]. Many sacrifices were made in order for these athletes to reach this ultimate race.

In the key verse, Paul wrote to Christians familiar with the races run by Greek athletes as he taught them about the Christian race.

Winners of the Christian race weren't born spiritual giants. Great men and women like Charles Spurgeon, Amy Carmichael, D.L. Moody, and Fanny Crosby fought the good fight in spite of overwhelming pressure and struggles with illness and disaster.

In order for you and me to be successful in our race of faith, Scriptures show us we need:

- SELF-DISCIPLINE: the ability to pursue what one thinks is right despite temptations to abandon it[2]
- ENDURANCE: the ability to withstand hardship or adversity especially the ability to sustain a prolonged stressful effort or activity
- LONGEVITY: long continuance[2]
- PERSISTENCE: the quality that allows someone to continue doing something or trying to do something even though it is difficult opposed by other people.[2]

As we are inspired by the athletes in the Olympic games, may our be renewed and strengthened to walk out our godly purpose towards the line. *"I press on toward the goal to win the prize for which God has heavenward in Christ Jesus." (Philippians 3:14 NIV)*

~Joyce

"All of you together are Christ's body, and each of you is a part of it."
1 Corinthians 12:27 (NLT)

We've all felt let down by people. Years ago, my sister gave me a great analogy to help me deal with this.

"People are like shoes. You have different shoes for different needs. One person isn't going to be able to be everything you need."

For an evening out, I could wear my tennis shoes but it wouldn't be the best choice. Working out in my heels is somewhat doable but not recommended. Why? I could get hurt that way.

When I look to a particular person for something he or she just can't deliver, I'm setting myself up to get hurt. It isn't even that they don't want to (which maybe they don't). Sometimes, it's that they really can't. It's just not them.

My sister (the shoe analogy giver) is always willing to help people in need ... a meal, a visit, a place to stay – she does it all.

Well ... almost all.

Don't ask her to help you organize or pack. It's just not her thing. She will happily watch your kids but steers clear of the boxes and packing tape.

On the other hand, the thought of decluttering makes me happy but please don't ask me to watch your kids – that stresses me out.

My husband doesn't like to shop so I am thankful to have a friend that will join me when the shopping bug hits. I don't usually like to watch movies so my 'sband uses that time to hang out with some of his guy friends.

We want people to understand us and why we don't do certain things...
~d to do the same for them. I'm not saying that we shouldn't oblige
'v and friends every now and then. At times, my husband does come
'ith me and then usually ends up buying more stuff than me. (Win-

re different kinds of service, but we serve the same Lord. God works
ays, but it is the same God who does the work in all of us." (1
?:5-6 NLT)

e each one of us different and that is a good thing. Take a
he entire people-are-like-shoes process. Try it on for size and
l fit your situation too (pun totally intended).

336

December 3 ~ 1 Corinthians 15-16

"... stand firm. Let nothing move you. Always give yourselves
fully to the work of the Lord, because you know that your labor
in the Lord is not in vain." 1 Corinthians 15:58 (NIV)

Do you remember how you felt when you landed your first job? Maybe you were like me, idealistic and ready to take on the world. I knew I was doing what God called me to and I could hardly contain my excitement. Business cards were printed with my name on it AND I had my own office ... with a window ... eek! It just couldn't get any better.

Imagine my bubble being burst shortly after realizing that everything wasn't how it seemed. There was a lack of integrity in the environment and such was acceptable. The Holy Spirit was challenging me to not just go with the flow. I had to try to make a difference in correcting the corrupt system.

I quickly learned that this newbie's thoughts were unwelcome. People were unkind as they questioned my character and I felt alone. Doubts hovered as I wondered if I had heard God correctly. The situation became so difficult that I found myself crying and feeling stressed regularly for months and months.

It appeared that the most logical solution was to just quit. I told myself that anything had to be better than that situation. Yet, the more I sought the Lord's counsel, the more I knew I was not being released to just walk away. Yes, it was a trying position but I had to persevere.

The Lord in His infinite mercy gave me the strength to lift my head each day, to keep my eyes fixed on Him, and to work diligently as unto Him. In His time, positive changes were made and I thank God. When I eventually transitioned to another job, I left with peace knowing that I had obeyed God and that I had done my best.

Dear Friend, I don't know what challenging situation you find yourself in today. I understand that when the going gets tough, you may feel tempted to just give up. But what is the Lord telling you to do? If you haven't done so already, seek Him. Wait upon Him. Trust Him. The Lord will direct your steps. When you follow His leading, His perfect peace will cover you.

~Joyce

December 4 ~ 2 Corinthians 1-4

"... Fix our eyes not on what is seen, but on what is unseen, since what is seen is temporary, but what is unseen is eternal." 2 Corinthians 4:18 (NIV)

My twelve-year-old son reminds me of someone I know.

Me.

People say we look alike, we definitely act alike, and we even think alike.

So, I knew, his visit to the orthodontist was not going to be fun. For we also share the same hypersensitive gag reflex, and it was time for him to be fitted for a retainer. The last time we tried this, it took multiple trials and the appointment ended with a frustrated dental assistant and patient.

But this time we had a different assistant. Poor girl, she must have drawn the short end of the stick. I warned her about my son's gag issues. Sure enough, as soon as she put the putty in his mouth to create the mold, the gagging began.

Instead of reaching for a trash can or removing the putty, the assistant asked my son to raise his right leg. My son glanced over in my direction, gave me a confused look, but did as he was told.

And guess what happened? The gagging stopped.

Unfortunately, as soon as his concentration went back to the gunk in his mouth, the gagging began again. But this assistant was on her A game and quickly asked my son to readjust his position and raise his opposite arm as well. His concentration on this unusual task gave her enough time to complete the impression and we were done!

Pure genius! This wise dental assistant knew what a little change in focus could accomplish.

The psalmist advises us to do something similar. No, not raise our right leg or arm, *if only it were that easy*...he advises us to shift our focus from our misery to our Lord.

"Why are you cast down, O my soul? And why are you disquieted within me. Hope in God, for I shall yet praise Him ..." (Psalm 43:5 NKJV)

When addressing the church in Corinth, Paul says it this way. *"... Fix our eyes not on what is seen, but on what is unseen, since what is seen is temporary, but what is unseen is eternal." (2 Cor 4:18 NIV)*

We must intentionally shift our focus, from ourselves and our troubles, to Christ and His greatness. When we choose to do so, we will be amazed at what God can and will accomplish through us.

~Binu

December 5 ~ 2 Corinthians 5-9
"Godly sorrow brings repentance that leads to salvation and leaves no regret, but worldly sorrow brings death." 2 Corinthians 7:10 (NIV)

Every now and then, my daughter likes to walk around in my heels and wear my jewelry. It's amusing to see her shuffling with the shoes, trying to keep her balance.

The other day, I was wearing a sundress, and she asked me if she could have it when she was all grown up. I love that she loves to dress up and that we share that common interest, but most importantly it reminds me of an important lesson: she wants to be like me.

It's actually a humbling thing to realize that my children watch what I wear and what say, even when I don't realize it. It's one thing to say, *"OK, honey, when you get angry, and you want to say mean things, take a deep breath and walk away."* It's another thing to practice what I preach.

How do I respond when I'm running out the door and her brother spills milk on the floor? Does she see a calm mommy who consoles him and wipes up the mess ... or does she see angry mom who scolds him and stomps away?

I want her to know that I make mistakes and I am taking responsibility for my words. I have learned that being honest with my children shows them that I am human, too.

Paul reminds us that *"Godly sorrow brings repentance." (2 Corinthians 7:10 NIV)* While feeling remorseful can send anyone in a downward spiral of condemnation, godly sorrow can lead to restoration. I want my kids to learn that, even at a young age.

I also *do* want to be that mommy who calmly deals with the curveballs so her little eyes can see me walk in grace. I will be one of the most influential people in her life, and I want her to follow in footsteps of character and integrity. I find that when I am strong in my relationship with God, my relationship with my children is strong, as well.

I love the lyrics to a song from Phillips, Craig, and Dean, which say, *"Lord, I want to be just like you, because he wants to be like me ..."*[1]

My prayer is just that: *"Lord, I want to be just like you, because she wants to be like me."*

~Elizabeth

December 6 ~ 2 Corinthians 10-13

"... For I want to use the authority the Lord has given
me to strengthen you, not to tear you down."
2 Corinthians 13:10 (NLT)

I work in a hospital. We are a smaller hospital, but we see our share of hard cases. In the last year, we've had several that have hit close to home. We had a woman who was admitted to the hospital because she kept falling. She ended up being diagnosed with multiple sclerosis. Then, there was an older gentleman who came in because he was dizzy and ended up being moved out to a larger facility overnight. His tests showed that he had a massive stroke.

I would hate to be the one who has to give out these diagnoses. Often times, we come into the room while the family is still processing the news from the doctor. As a physical therapist, I do have knowledge of disease processes and progression, so patients often ask me questions about what the doctor has just told them.

I answer very carefully, knowing that the patient's need for hope should be balanced with an equal portion of reality.

I've taken this approach into my non-professional life as well. The world is always ready, willing, and happy to tell you all of the things that you're doing wrong - your hair, your diet, your clothes, your opinion, your beliefs, anything, and everything. The world wants to give you doubt where you should have faith. It wants to plant insecurity where there should be confidence.

Paul admonishes the Corinthians, but at the end of chapter 13, his intent is very clear. His purpose is to build them up, not to tear them down.

I want to use the authority that God has given me to build people up, not tear them down. We should use our words and our positions to strengthen, not destroy. We need to choose to speak in love, not offering platitudes or false hope, but compassionate truth. That is how we will separate ourselves from the rest of the world. That is how people will know that the love of God lives in us.

~Shiney

December 7 ~ Romans 1-3

*"Or do you show contempt for the riches of his kindness,
forbearance and patience, not realizing that God's kindness is
intended to lead you to repentance?" Romans 2:4 (NIV)*

We can all probably remember working with or studying under a harsh or highly critical teacher or instructor. I still recall being spoken to in a disrespectful way by one of my instructors, and it stung. You know that feeling of wanting to hide in a room or stare in the mirror and think, *"Did that just happen?"*

But I still remember studying under another instructor, my second-grade teacher, Mrs. Amato. She was fabulous. It's hard to believe it, but almost 30 years later, I can still picture how she was dressed, her big Texas hair ... and her kindness.

Those kinds of people are memorable because they bring a special happiness to you, even years later. She obviously made a great impression, not because of anything she *did* for me, but because of her demeanor and disposition to me.

Do you realize that you may never have to *do* anything so grand or great to be memorable, but *caring* for someone and *showing kindness* can create a lifetime of memories? I love the verse that says that *"God's kindness is intended to lead you to repentance." (Romans 2:4 NIV)* I heard a radio personality say it like this: it's not God pointing a finger at me that led me to repentance ... His *kindness* did.

What is kindness? It is a fruit of the Spirit. It is being generous, benevolent, friendly, and considerate[1].

It's letting the guy get in front of you as you're rushing into work.

It's calling a sad or sick friend and listening.

It's speaking gently to your child when you're nearing insanity.

Ephesians 2:7 says that God showed his kindness to us in Christ Jesus (NIV). God is so kind and loving that He sent his son, Jesus, to die for us. What an ultimate show of kindness that no one can match.

We have opportunities to show kindness to the people we come across. When our natural self wants to lash out or get annoyed, remember God's kindness and how we can mirror that to them.

We have all been on the other side of a harsh, stinging word ... and it hurts. We also know the beauty of being the recipient of a kind gesture. It's time to pass that kindness on.

~Elizabeth

December 8 ~ Romans 4-7

"We know that our old sinful selves were crucified with Christ so that sin might lose its power in our lives. We are no longer slaves to sin." Romans 6:6 (NLT)

Romans 6:6 tells us that Christ's death weakened sin's power in our lives so that we are no longer slaves to sin. When I think of being a slave to sin, I think of people addicted to things like pornography or even drugs; someone who craves something "bad" and can't go a day without getting a taste of it.

I have been a slave to sin at times.

Not the flashy sins ... you probably won't read about me being arrested for robbing a bank or because they've found a body buried in my backyard. My sin is much more subtle.

As much as I don't even want to admit it, I often struggle with bitterness or having an unforgiving spirit. Sometimes I hold a grudge. It didn't seem like a big deal until I realized that there was a stronghold in my life from dealing with the same hurt from a friend.

Slavery entails bondage to something or someone. This bitter, grudge-holding creature inside of me began to affect my other relationships as well and I started projecting my hurt on them. When I allowed myself to step back and change perspective, I could see the bondage that I really was entangled in.

Paul very clearly tells us later in the same chapter: *"Do not let sin control the way you live..." (6:12 NLT)* and that *"the wages of sin is death" (6:23 NLT)*. Bitterness was killing my joy, my attitude, and my spirit.

The Holy Spirit cannot dwell where bitterness lives. The only outcome of my sin will be death - death in my relationships. I submitted it to God, and I know that He is working on healing my heart. I know that it is a process and I know that God will complete His work in me.

What is your subtle sin? What is holding you in slavery? Give it to God. Let Him free you.

~Shiney

December 9 ~ Romans 8-10

"Yet in all these things we are more than conquerors and gain an overwhelming victory through Him who loved us [so much that He died for us]." Romans 8:37 (AMP)

Regrets come in all shapes and sizes ... from eating one too many cookies or that bad hair style back in the 80s. I personally have other regrets too – some a bit more serious than frizzy hair. Thankfully, I can also look back on certain things without regret, like when I changed directions in my career and saying "I do" to my husband. No regrets there.

Several years ago, my grandmother moved from India to the United States so my mom could care for her full-time. I already knew my mom was a great mom but now I got to see what a great daughter she was. Anything my grandmother wanted to eat, my mom cooked. Anything she needed, my mom did. Anything she wanted, my mom made sure she had.

After my grandmother's passing, when I would ask my mom how she was doing, her answer came back to one central theme – *"No regrets."*

There's a question I often ask myself: *"If I could do yesterday over again, what would I change?"*

Sometimes it involves more reading and less Facebook scrolling. Other days, it's a little more serious like "I should have reached out to that person" or "I shouldn't have gotten so frustrated in that particular situation."

The more I've asked myself this question, the more I've seen a trend. My answers tend to repeat themselves.

Go ahead – think back to yesterday ... we often don't have to look back any further than that. What would you have done differently?

Maybe, in certain situations, you feel like your window of opportunity has passed. Press on my friend. God doesn't want you holding on to the shame, condemnation or regret.

"With the arrival of Jesus, the Messiah, that fateful dilemma is resolved. Those who enter into Christ's being-here-for-us no longer have to live under a continuous, low-lying black cloud. A new power is in operation. The Spirit of life in Christ, like a strong wind, has magnificently cleared the air, freeing you..." (Romans 8:1-2 MSG)

So, continue asking yourself the question. Then, when possible, do something with the answer. Self-introspection is great but our days and lives are only changed when we put those thoughts into action. Progress happens. Peace comes.

No regrets.

~Anu

December 10~ Romans 11-13
"Rejoice with those who rejoice; mourn with those
who mourn." Romans 12:15 (NIV)

As I watched my younger son sit on the bench, I thought about you.

He sat, he smiled, he cheered his team on. But beneath his happy exterior, I knew he was discouraged and dying to get onto the court.

My son, Caleb, is a gifted basketball player. Okay, so maybe I'm a *little* biased but he does have skill and has been dribbling a ball since he could walk. Nevertheless, I trusted his coach's judgement and more importantly, I trusted his heart towards my son.

For over the years, this coach has proven to be one of Caleb's biggest fans. As much as he wanted to put Caleb in the game, it wouldn't have been wise. It just wasn't the right time.

As I watched Caleb sitting there on that bench, I thought about times where I and those I love, have sat on a different kind of bench. *Life's* bench. We sit, we wait, we smile, we cheer. We throw showers, attend weddings, send our congratulations on the new house, new job or newly fulfilled dream. We sit on that bench and wait for *"it"* to happen for us like *"it"* has happened for them.

Can I encourage you as I encourage myself?

Even more than I trust my son's wonderful coach, I trust my faithful God. I trust His time and I trust His ways ... even when both do not make sense.

So, while you sit on that bench, give your teammate a high five as they score. Let's do as Romans 12:15 instructs us, *"Rejoice with those who rejoice; mourn with those who mourn." (NIV)*

After the game, I reminded my son, *"Sometimes you learn lessons on the bench that you just can't learn on the court."*

It took a few hours for those words to settle in, but before going to bed, he told me he agreed. The bench taught him what the court could not. On the court, we sharpen our skills. On the bench, we sharpen our character.

~Binu

December 11 ~ Romans 14-16
"Greet Priscilla and Aquila, my co-workers in Christ Jesus." Romans 16:3 (NIV)

A few weeks ago, we celebrated a dear friend's 50th birthday. The evening before the big bash, a few of us sat with the guest of honor. There were lots of laughs and lots of tears, each of us expressing how much we loved and appreciated him. As we made our way around the circle, it was his daughter's turn to speak. With a crack in her voice and tears in her eyes, she said, *"Ubuntu."*

Its meaning: *I need you to be all that you are, so I can be all that I am.*

It's a word her father learned while working on a project in Africa. A word he taught his family and then taught us.

Living Ubuntu out keeps you humble and selfless. However, it also makes you extremely vulnerable to people who will take advantage of you, which happens often. In essence, it means, *I can be successful, if you are successful. So, I'm committed to your success.* It ties together humanity and community.

In Romans 16, Paul completes his letter to the Romans. He gives a little shout out to twenty-six people who have been a support to him during his missionary trips. Twenty-six people who were committed to his ministry and to his success.

Paul writes, '*Priscilla and Aquila risked their lives for me, Mary worked hard for me, Andronicus and Junius are outstanding apostles, Urbanus is my fellow worker, my dear friend Stachys, oh...and I can't forget Rufus' mother, she has been a mother to me....*' *(My paraphrase)*

Y'all, if the great apostle Paul needed people, then we need people too ... and more importantly, people need us.

We can't live in isolation. We can't do life alone. We need one another. And we need to be committed to one another's success.

Ubuntu. *You be you, so that I can be me.*

It was all she said but it was all she needed to say.

~Binu

December 12 ~ Acts 20-23
"So guard yourselves and God's people..." Acts 20:28a (NLT)

I have never ever been into sports, but now it is a part of who I am. Between my two boys and my husband, I am outnumbered. I wasn't trying to increase my sports IQ, but because of who surrounds me, I now know the difference between a pick, pick 6 and a pick and roll.

We are all influenced. It just happens.

In Acts 20, Paul is bidding farewell to the Ephesian Elders. He has spent time with them, mentored them, and now, compelled by the Holy Spirit, he must go to Jerusalem. Before leaving, he passionately warns them, *"Guard yourselves and God's people ... I know that false teachers, like vicious wolves, will come in among you after I leave ...Watch out." (NLT)*

Paul understood that even the best of people with the best of intentions can easily be influenced and swayed in the wrong direction.

In Proverbs 13:20, Solomon states, *"Whoever walks with the wise becomes wise, but the companion of fools will suffer harm." (ESV)*

Solomon also warns us to *'guard our hearts'*, and in doing so, we must guard who pours into our hearts.

Why? Because eventually, out of the abundance of our heart, our mouth will speak.

We don't set out to become a gossip or to lower our moral standards, but the enemy is sneaky. Bad company will eventually corrupt good character. If we spend enough time with Negative Nancy or Gossipy Gladys – we may find ourselves always seeing the cup half empty or enjoying those tiny morsels of gossip.

Being influenced isn't always a bad thing. I like being able to participate in conversations going on around me...even when they involve touchdowns and field goals.

So, in the midst of being influenced or being an influencer ... may our spirits always be sensitive to how we can shine God's light. Who knows? Maybe one day, because of our influence, negative Nancy will finally see the glass is actually half full.

~Binu

December 13 ~ Acts 24-26

"Paul answered: 'I am now standing before Caesar's court, where I ought to be tried. I have not done any wrong to the Jews, as you yourself know very well.'" Acts 25:10 (NIV)

Like most kids, I knew my place when it came to adults, especially those in authority over me. I had always been a good student and hadn't really ever gotten in trouble.

Until high school.

I was serving as the "librarian" in our school choir which basically meant, I was in charge of filing the sheet music. Even back then, I liked things organized so it bothered me to see our music library in disarray.

I distinctly remember going back to the choir room during my free period and working in the library. I went through each folder to make sure that the sheet music was properly filed. After many hours alone in that room, I finally had it organized.

So, it came as a complete surprise to me when my choir instructor decided to lecture all of the choir members about not doing their part ... and specifically called me and my co-librarian out in the process.

I was hurt. I knew what she was saying was not true.

As believers, we strive to be as Christ-like as we can. When we think back to the trial of Jesus, He remained silent as His accusers spoke against Him. But just because He handled that situation with silence doesn't mean that is what He always did.

He had challenged the disciples for their lack of faith and called out the Pharisees for their hypocrisy. Jesus wasn't afraid to defend what was right.

In Acts 24-26, Paul is repeatedly telling his story to the authorities. He knew they hadn't handled his case correctly and pursued justice. He was respectful but bold. He also used this as an opportunity to witness.

Sometimes, the Spirit will lead us to keep our mouths shut. Other times, as Jesus even said, He will "*... teach you at that time what needs to be said.*" *(Luke 12:12 NLT)*

For me back in that choir room, as young as I was, I knew I had to say something. I approached her later, when everyone else was gone, and shared what I felt. She then apologized to me for her poor choice of words. I accepted her apology and continued to serve in my role.

Even when we are defending ourselves, we can still be a reflection of Christ. Trust His leading to know if our defense should be with or without words.

~Anu

December 14 ~ Acts 27-28
"...He ... boldly proclaiming the Kingdom of God and
teaching about the Lord Jesus Christ..."
Acts 28:30-31 (NLT)

It's not fair! This is a phrase I hear at least once a week from one of my children. And if I'm completely honest, at least once a week, the phrase describes how I feel as well.

I may not always know why things happen as they do, but in looking at the life of Paul, I can learn to respond to unfair circumstances in a way that points others to Christ.

After Paul's dramatic conversion on the road to Damascus, he became a sold-out, passionate believer in Jesus. Paul spent the remainder of his life sharing the message of the gospel to Jews and Gentiles alike.

But his newfound faith and evangelism did not sit well with the Jews and religious leaders of the day. They viewed Paul's message of Christ as a threat to their current system and the power they wielded as a result of it. Paul was then arrested and imprisoned for sharing his faith in Christ.

As a prisoner, he boarded a ship for Rome to be tried before Caesar. The journey was met with many challenges, included a massive storm that led to Paul and the other travelers being shipwrecked on the island of Malta. Soon after they arrived there, Paul was bitten by a snake, but miraculously did not die. Paul and the ship's crew spend the next 3 months on the island of Malta.

What did Paul do? He spent that time praying for and ministering to the sick and afflicted on the island. And they were healed! Can you picture it? Paul is still a Roman prisoner. And yet, on the ship and on the island, the scripture says that he was ministering to the others.

Even on his way to be tried before Caesar, Paul doesn't waiver in his faith. His encounter with Jesus changed him forever.

The storms, shipwreck, and unjust imprisonment didn't stop Paul from sharing the gospel ... and may it not stop us either.

May we be challenged and inspired by the life of Paul. In the middle of our "prison," I pray we find a way to be a light to those around us. For it is most often in this environment, people will see God glorified in our life and through our story.

~Vijoy

December 15 ~ Colossians 1-4, Philemon 1
"Whatever you do, work at it with all your heart, as working for the Lord..." Colossians 3:23 (NIV)

When I dropped my son off to his first day at work, it felt a lot like dropping him off to his first day at kindergarten. It was hard.

If you are like me, letting go of our children does not come naturally. I do it because I have to. Because I know one day my son *"shall leave his father and mother"* and he needs to know how to survive. (Ephesians 5:31 ESV)

So, before sending my son off to work, my husband and I went over the *basics* with him. In doing so, I couldn't help but re-evaluate my own work ethic. The following basic Biblical principles apply across the board. To those just entering into the workforce, and also to those of us who have been there for a long, long time.

- While at work, you work. That's why it's called work.
- You don't call in sick unless you are sick. It doesn't matter if you have "sick time" to burn. Be thankful for your health and work with the physical strength God has given you. A little runny nose does not warrant a sick day.
- Always give at least 10% of your earnings to the Lord. (No exceptions). The 90% will go farther than the 100% ever would. (Malachi 3:10)

Why such heavy advice to a fifteen-year-old kid just starting his first job as a sacker (aka package clerk)?

Because Solomon, the man who received his wisdom straight from the heart of God, tells us so.

"Do you see a man skillful in his work? He will stand before kings; he will not stand before obscure men." (Proverbs 22:29 ESV) In other words, 'Do the little things right, and see where God will take you.'

My son may think he is simply learning the fine art of sacking groceries: *to double bag the heavy stuff, to not place cans on top of chips, to separate refrigerated items, etc.* But I believe God is teaching him so much more.

I also believe God wants to remind us all, those just getting started and those ready to retire, when we work, we work not for man, but for God.

"Whatever you do, work at it with all your heart, as working for the Lord..." (Colossians 3:23 NIV)

~Binu

December 16 ~ Ephesians 1-6
"Out of respect for Christ, be courteously reverent to one another." Ephesians 5:21 (MSG)

While my husband and I celebrated our anniversary, I started reflecting on significant moments in our journey.

I remember feeling led to leave my career to stay at home and then, venture into homeschooling. Each of those transitions were completely out of my comfort zone. However, I arrived there after praying and feeling the Holy Spirit prompting me to do so.

But I could have never executed on those desires without the support of my husband. I recall how he heard me out and asked me to provide further details on how each would work. He then prayed about it, and ultimately encouraged me to follow through on each one. Such support is not easy when sacrifices have to be made, especially financially.

I am reminded of The Message version of Ephesians 5:25-28 which says, *"Husbands, go all out in your love for your wives, exactly as Christ did for the church—a love marked by giving, not getting. Christ's love makes the church whole. His words evoke her beauty. Everything he does and says is designed to bring the best out of her."* My husband's support has definitely brought out the best in me, to pursue my passions, and to strive towards fulfilling my dreams.

Just as my husband has shown Christ's love towards me, I have learned to honor him as found in verses 22-24 (MSG): *"Wives, understand and support your husbands in ways that show your support for Christ. The husband provides leadership to his wife the way Christ does to his church, not by domineering but by cherishing. So just as the church submits to Christ as he exercises such leadership, wives should likewise submit to their husbands."*

To live out those verses was quite challenging for me, especially when I thought I was right. As I learned to honor with God's help, I have been able to encourage my husband to be the godly man and leader he is called to be. I have also come under my husband's covering and protection when I submit, which truly has freed me to be who God created me to be: a good steward of my time, talent, and treasure.

Among the many teachable moments in our marriage journey, I thank God for showing us the principles of love and respect for one another as He has designed. I pray it encourages you in your journey as well.

~Joyce

December 17 ~ Philippians 1-4

"Don't worry about anything; instead, pray about everything. Tell God what you need, and thank him for all he has done. Then you will experience God's peace, which exceeds anything we can understand. His peace will guard your hearts and minds as you live in Christ Jesus." Philippians 4:6-7 (NLT)

Do you ever get overwhelmed with worry and anxiety? It can be related to something really big, or maybe something small that seems big at the time.

There was a time many years ago that I would break out with hives all over my body whenever I was stressed. I would often wake up in the middle of the night in a panic about all the things I needed to get done.

Thinking back now, I am shocked at how often I would have this physical reaction to stress on my body. It was so common to me that I referred to them as "stress bumps" whenever someone would ask about it.

But something has changed since then. It's been over a decade since I've had stress bumps or have woken up in the middle of the night in a panic.

The workload hasn't changed. The stress level hasn't changed. But I am now able to talk to God very openly about what I am anxious about. And then I feel an unexplainable peace wash over me.

Not only does God grant me peace, but God somehow makes things work out and come together beautifully.

Sometimes that help comes through a sudden thought in my head. I am finally able to solve a problem that I've been unable to figure out for weeks. Other times, it's physical strength to finish what I'm doing, even though my body is exhausted. I've even experienced instances in which God seemed to make time stand still for me and I was able to accomplish far more than I ever thought possible within the day.

I've heard this scripture so many times since I was young... *"Don't worry about anything; instead, pray about everything. Tell God what you need, and thank him for all he has done. Then you will experience God's peace, which exceeds anything we can understand. His peace will guard your hearts and minds as you live in Christ Jesus." (Philippians 4:6-7 NLT)*

It's only now, after all these years, I am seeing how true this scripture is and how God is faithful to His Word.

Whatever you are stressed or worried about today, lean into the Lord. He wants to hear your needs and He is waiting to help you and cover you with His peace.

~Vijoy

December 18 ~ 1 Timothy 1-6
"Do not neglect the gift you have, which was given you..." 1 Timothy 4:14a (ESV)

I like big purses and I cannot lie ...

My husband gawks at how large my purses are but when he wants hand sanitizer, lotion or gum, guess who he turns to?

However, I was feeling a bit insecure about my latest purse purchase. Would people think it was a small carry-on? At a restaurant recently, I was convinced a couple was discussing the size of my purse (because what else would they be talking about??).

I asked my friends for their honest input. They know I like things organized so would a big purse be right for me? One friend is a physical therapist so she was concerned about me carrying it all the time.

Then, they asked the question... *"Do you like it? Do you feel like it will work for you?"* My answer was... *"If I wasn't concerned about what other people thought, this is the purse I would use."*

Why in the world am I telling you about my purse purchase? Because I think a lot of people treat their gifts, talents and calling that way.

We know what is in us. Unfortunately, we just stop ourselves from doing anything with it because of what people may say.

Don't get me wrong – wise counsel is important and we should listen to that. But if we're doing or not doing something based on the random couple at the restaurant and not what God says, then that's another issue.

"Do not neglect the gift you have, which was given you by prophecy when the council of elders laid their hands on you. Practice these things, immerse yourself in them, so that all may see your progress. Keep a close watch on yourself and on the teaching. Persist in this, for by so doing you will save both yourself and your hearers." (1 Timothy 4:14-16 ESV)

Paul encouraged Timothy to embrace the gift that was in him. Paul also reminded him that it could help lead others to salvation. I think the same could be said of all of us as Christ followers. If we can push past our concerns of what others may say, we could give them exactly what they need.

If you weren't concerned about what other people thought, what would you be doing?

~Anu

December 19 ~ Titus 1-3

"Then they can urge the younger women to love their husbands and children, to be self-controlled and pure, to be busy at home, to be kind..." Titus 2:4,5a (NIV)

According to my calculations, it takes less than a minute to clean a toilet and even less time to clean a bathroom sink. You might be wondering where I am going with this...

I have learned over the years, if I do a little bit of housework daily, maintaining a home doesn't have to be exhausting.

In Stormie Omartian's book, "The Power of a Praying Wife," she writes, *"I don't care how liberated you are, when you are married there will always be two areas that will ultimately be your responsibility: home and children. Even if you are working ... you will still be expected to see that the heart of our home is a peaceful sanctuary- a source of contentment, acceptance, rejuvenation, nurturing, rest, and love for your family."* [1]

In Titus 2:5, Paul instructs Titus to have the older women teach the younger women *"to be self-controlled and pure, to be busy at home, to be kind ...."* (NIV)

Sounds like a lot of pressure on us women, but it doesn't have to be. A clean home may begin with you, but it's important to *kindly* recruit all members of your household in the daily maintenance of your home!

When my oldest son was about ten years old, my husband taught him how to vacuum and create those cool lines. When we moved into our new home, my kids were excited to have a larger closet with shelves. My sister, the master organizer, taught them how to fold their clothes properly and make the most of their space. To this day, their closet stays cleaner than mine.

Don't underestimate what your children can do! Even little ones can throw their toys into large bins at the end of each day in order keep their play areas tidy. They just need to be taught.

Stormie Omartian also recommends that you *"Ask God to help you maintain a house that your husband is pleased to come home to and bring his friends. It's not necessary to have expensive furniture or a decorator in order to do that ... It just takes some thought and a little care."*[1]

Let's raise the bar and keep our standards high. If your family helps with the cleaning, chances are, they will take pride in their home and have a desire to keep it clean. The goal is to make a mess an eyesore and cleanliness the norm ... for everyone.

~Binu

"Since by your obedience to the truth you have purified yourselves for
a sincere love of the believers, [see that you] love one another from
the heart [always unselfishly seeking the best for one another]."
1 Peter 1:22 (AMP)

Working in a county hospital, you encounter a lot of things, including crowded elevators.

When you hit the button, you brace yourself to wait. You hit the button again. You pace. You attempt to avoid eye contact with the other people waiting. Then, someone makes a joke about how slow the elevators are. And we all agree followed by awkward silence and more waiting.

Then, it happens. The elevator comes except it's going in the opposite direction.

Then, it happens again. This time, it's headed where you want to go.

The doors open. And it's full. Not packed. But full.

That can only mean one thing. Slowly but purposefully, you move towards the elevator and pray that people start sucking in a little more or adjust their position to make room for you.

Sometimes, they just stare at me like *"Are you really going to try to get on here?"* And I respond with a stare that says *"Yes, I am. Don't believe me? Just watch."*

Other times, it's a completely different scene. A shift happens inside the elevator. People move towards the back or the side, just to make room for a weary waiter. They know how it is.

Isn't that a picture of grace?

Adding one more person to a very full elevator is uncomfortable and it might take some action on our part. Movement that we didn't anticipate having to do.

Grace works like that. When someone is infringing on our world in a way that is different from what we hoped, it is uncomfortable. But grace nudges us to move over and make space for "them". After all, wouldn't we want someone else to do that for us?

After all, haven't we been "them"?

We are never more like Christ than when we show grace. When we have every right to not forgive, be mad or just not move over, the Christ in you compels you to do unto others what has been done to you.

While we were still sinners, Christ showed us the ultimate picture of grace. A perfect man bearing the weight of an imperfect world and making space for her as His bride.

"Each one should use whatever gift he has received to serve others, faithfully administering God's grace in its various forms." (1 Peter 4:10 NIV)

Even in crowded elevators.

~Anu

December 21 ~ Hebrews 1-6

"God also bound himself with an oath, so that those who received the promise could be perfectly sure that he would never change his mind. So God has given both his promise and his oath. These two things are unchangeable because it is impossible for God to lie ..." Hebrews 6:17-18 (NLT)

Have you been disappointed by someone who has lied to you? I know I have. And I'm sure you have too.

But the truth is, there were many times I was not completely honest towards others.

Over and over, the flaws of humanity rear its ugly head in our relationships with each other. But the writer of Hebrews makes a stark contrast when he describes the character of God.

"God also bound himself with an oath, so that those who received the promise could be perfectly sure that he would never change his mind. So God has given both his promise and his oath. These two things are unchangeable because it is impossible for God to lie. Therefore, we who have fled to him for refuge can have great confidence as we hold to the hope that lies before us. This hope is a strong and trustworthy anchor for our souls..." (Hebrews 6:17-19 NLT)

That is so powerful! God CANNOT lie. He can't and He won't.

But people can, and oftentimes we do.

I have come to understand that human beings, including myself, are broken because of the fall in the Garden of Eden. While we may strive for perfection, we will ALWAYS fall short. Therefore, the sacrifice of Christ's life for us holds a greater significance. His death on the cross and the shedding of His blood covers my past, my present, and my future sin.

I am no longer sentenced to death because of my inability to keep all the rules.

I thank God that I do not have to come to a human high priest with the blood of a spotless lamb to cover up my sin. Our high priest, Jesus, has taken His blood and covered our sins once and for all.

Be encouraged. People may disappoint you, but God will not. His son died to prove how much He loved you. Trust in His word. Trust in His promise. He will never lie.

~Vijoy

"... But he has appeared once for all at the culmination of the ages to do away with sin by the sacrifice of himself." Hebrews 9:26 (NIV)

My sister and I were high school students when we had the opportunity to shadow a doctor who was performing a medical procedure. We were thrilled with this chance, but we were *not* prepared to witness the amount of blood lost from the patient.

My stomach felt funny. My sister almost fainted.

Blood phobia is fairly common and some people have a natural reflex reaction at the sight of it.

It's hard to think of blood as a beautiful thing, isn't it? But did you know that your red blood cells carry and transport oxygen throughout your body and remove carbon dioxide from the body? That's pretty amazing.

Without blood, we literally could not survive.

In a spiritual sense, we could not survive without the blood of Jesus.

Ephesians 1:7 ESV says, *"In Him we have redemption through his blood, the forgiveness of our trespasses, according to the riches of His grace."*

The blood of Jesus was *"poured out ... for the forgiveness of sins."* Matthew 26:28 ESV.

It is through the blood of Jesus ... His precious blood ... that saved us from eternal separation from God. He redeemed us from sin's grip *through* His blood.

We read today that it is impossible for the blood of bulls and goats to take away sins. Before Christ came into the world, the people of God relied on such animals for the forgiveness of sins year after year. When Jesus arrived, everything changed. By God's will, *"we have been made holy through the sacrifice of the body of Jesus Christ once for all."*

We will celebrate Christmas soon. Do you think there was a Christmas tree or a wreath set up that first Christmas in the stable? *No.*

That first Christmas, there was a baby born in a manger to save a broken world. That baby would live a perfect life for 33 years and would then shed His precious blood for a broken people.

Jesus Christ was the perfect sacrifice. His blood was shed for *your* redemption. That's why He came. While Christmas is a memorable time with our family and friends, remember that Jesus' blood is the reason we celebrate this special time.

He came to be the sacrifice.

And we could never have survived without His blood.

~Elizabeth

December 23 ~ Hebrews 11-13
*"Faith shows the reality of what we hope for; it is
the evidence of things we cannot see."*
Hebrews 11:1 (NLT)

Some inspiration from Hebrews 11... a verse by verse motivation for you...

1: Faith is the confident assurance that what we hope for is going to [actually] happen.

2: Want some God approval? Buck up your faith.

3: We believe that God created something out of nothing. He can do it again in my situation. He can create something beautiful with my nothing.

4: Abel's sacrifice was a testimony of his faith. What am I willing to sacrifice to build my faith? My time? My comfort?

5-6: *"Anyone who wants to come to Him must believe that there is a God and that he rewards those who sincerely seek him".* I can do that.

7: Noah obeyed, believing in something that had never happened before. *Believe for something in your life that you deem impossible.*

8-10: Abraham went out not knowing where he was even going. *Blind obedience will get you blessings.*

11-12: Sarah laughed at God's promise and it still came true. *God is still God even in my complete disbelief.*

17-19: Abraham was willing to sacrifice Isaac in spite of God's promise that his children would be like the stars in the sky. *Whatever it is, put it on the altar and watch Him give it back to you with exponential growth*

22: Joseph was so confident that God was going to deliver the Israelites out of Egypt that he commanded them to carry his bones when they left! *Have the guts to believe and plan for big things!*

23-29: Moses refused to give in to the identity that the world wanted to give him and held true to who he really was. He saved his people because of it.

30: The people obeyed and walls that were impenetrable came crashing down.

31: A prostitute believed and is in the lineage of Jesus.

We are surrounded by THIS great cloud of witnesses. You are now included in the aforementioned list. Lay aside whatever slows you down - laziness, annoyance, attitude, and run the race that is set before YOU, not someone else's.

How are you going to run your race? Slow and steady or chasing your tail in every direction but the right one? It takes small things to build up our faith, but big things happen when we take these little steps.

~Shiney

December 24 ~ 2 Timothy 1-4

"I remember your genuine faith, for you share the faith that first filled your grandmother Lois and your mother, Eunice. And I know that same faith continues strong in you." 2 Timothy 1:5 (NLT)

Do you ever feel like you've missed your calling because you haven't accomplished something great in your life?

Andy Stanley says *"Your greatest contribution to the kingdom may not be something you do, but someone you raise."*[1]

There's a notable grandmother mentioned in scripture who did just that: Lois, the grandmother of Timothy.

Timothy was a young man who stood out to the apostle Paul when he was ministering in Timothy's hometown. Timothy was highly regarded there but his journey of faith to this point wasn't likely an easy one.

His mother was a devout Jew-turned Christian, but his father was Greek, and thus assumed to be a non-believer. So, how did Timothy become a young man so full of faith that he stood out among those around him?

His grandmother Lois had a big influence on him. You see, Timothy's faith was taught to him since childhood by his grandmother first and then his mother. Because they were such faithful and trustworthy believers, Paul told Timothy that he could trust what he had been taught by them.

We know that Lois made a big impact in Timothy's life because Paul praises the faith of Lois, who passed that faith down to her daughter Eunice, and then onto Timothy.

Timothy's faith and reputation made such an impression on the apostle Paul that he was asked by Paul to join him on his next missionary journey. Timothy went on to minister with Paul to the Galatians, the people of Antioch, and even served the church in Ephesus. He was a lifelong servant of God and eventually dies as a martyr for his faith.

I can't help but think that the godly influence of his grandmother helped solidify his faith in God and provided the boldness and confidence he needed to step out and change the world.

Don't underestimate the power of your influence in the lives of those around you - whether it is a grandchild, a young person at church or a neighbor down the street. You just might be influencing the next world changer.

~Vijoy

"Now to him who is able to keep you from stumbling and to present you blameless before the presence of his glory with great joy," Jude 1:24 (ESV)

Did you know that a covered pot of water boils more quickly than if it was uncovered?

Did you know that placing the lid next to the pot doesn't do anything to help the water boil?

Recently, I did this while I was cooking. I needed the water to rapidly come to a boil so I got out the lid and then proceeded to put it on the ... counter.

Yes, I am getting older and these things do happen. I have looked for my sunglasses only to realize they were on top of my head.

But I'm realizing that this goes beyond lids on pots and eyewear.

I do it with the Word of God too.

I read scripture about putting God first and how I should treat others. I see the red letters and realize that Jesus is telling me not to worry. The list goes on and on. But then I take those verses and leave them where I found it ... and don't actually apply it to my own life

Having a lid for my pots and pans, sunglasses on a sunny day and the Word of God on my nightstand are great. Using them is when we fully realize the value.

"His divine power has granted to us all things that pertain to life and godliness, through the knowledge of him who called us to his own glory and excellence, by which he has granted to us his precious and very great promises..." (2 Peter 1:3-4a ESV)

As believers, we have everything we need given to us by God. The birth of His Son grants us the opportunity for salvation and an eternal life. His promises provide hope for our future. His past faithfulness assures us in our present situations. His perfect love casts out fear of the unknown.

It is all our ours. We just have to believe it, receive it and apply it.

Just a little something to simmer on.

~Anu

"This is love: not that we loved God, but that He loved us ..." (1John 4:10 NIV)

It was almost closing time and a cup of hot soup was calling my name.

After returning from the soup aisle, I sent my technician home for the night. Business was winding down and I was looking forward to a slow uneventful last hour. Just me and my soup.

But the silence was short lived. Within less than two minutes, a young man approached my pharmacy counter. Interestingly enough, I had noticed this man on my way to the soup aisle. He had no cart and no groceries.

"How can I help you?" I asked.

The man looked behind him then looked straight at me. *"Just hanging out."*

Hanging out? Who walks around a grocery store, doesn't buy any groceries then hangs out at the pharmacy? A thousand thoughts filled my mind. None were good.

That's it. I'm being robbed. My heart began to race. His hand reached to the inside pocket of his jacket. Confirming my fears all the more. He proceeded to pull something out.

"Shhhh," he motioned. My brain was in panic mode. Who is this guy, why is he at my counter and why is he 'shhh-ing' me? It took a few seconds for my brain to register what I saw. It was shiny ... but it wasn't a weapon. It was a badge. *A security badge.* This man was working undercover and was there to protect our store ... and me. Boy, did I misjudge this guy!

Have you ever misjudged someone? Have you ever misjudged God?

I know I have.

When things don't go as planned, when doors close in my face, when an unexpected illness arises. A thousand thoughts fill my mind. *Does God care? Has He stopped loving me?*

How many times have I misjudged the heart of God?

In 1 John 4:10, John states, *"This is love: not that we loved God, but that He loved us ..."* (NIV) This same John wrote the famous John 3:16, *"For God so loved the world..."* (NIV)

John, the beloved disciple, wanted to make sure we knew what he knew so well...

God loves you.

However disheartening our circumstances, I pray we never misjudge the heart of the one who watches over us. Even when we doubt His presence, God is there ... working undercover. He is our defender, our protector, our shield.

He is our security.

~Binu

December 27 ~ 2 John 1, 3 John 1
*"because of the truth that abides in us and will
be with us forever" 2 John 1:2 (ESV)*

When we read the scriptures, it's easy to think about how much times have changed.

But when we read these two letters written by John, we see how a lot of things have stayed the same too.

How we should LIVE - We all want our loved ones to be successful in life but John doesn't mention material possessions or status. His delight was seeing the children "... *living according to the truth ...*" (2 John 1:4 NLT). Jesus taught this too. If a man has the world but loses his soul, he hasn't gained anything.

How we should LOVE - The greatest commandment trickles into much of John's writings. Love God by obeying His commands and love people too. (2 John 1:5-6)

How we should THINK - In 2 John 1:7-10, he warns us against people who will attempt to sway us from the truth. They will pick and choose their own doctrine instead of following the Word of God. Does that sound like the 21st century or what?

How we should COMMUNICATE - In both letters, John makes this statement: "*I have much more to say to you, but I don't want to do it with paper and ink. For I hope to visit you soon and talk with you face to face. Then our joy will be complete." (2 John 1:12 NLT)* Imagine what John would say now with emails, texting and social media? As great as technology is, sometimes things are best said in person ... good and bad. The tone, facial gestures, and posture are all a huge part of what we say - none of which can be seen in our written words alone.

How we should CONDUCT ourselves - "*Beloved, do not imitate what is evil, but [imitate] what is good. The one who practices good [exhibiting godly character, moral courage and personal integrity] is of God; the one who practices [or permits or tolerates] evil has not seen God [he has no personal experience with Him and does not know Him at all]." (3 John 1:11 AMP)* No further explanation needed.

The Word of God may have been written long before our time but it is still for our time ... and for the days and years to come.

~Anu

December 28 ~ Revelation 1-5
"Blessed is the one who reads aloud the words of this prophecy,
and blessed are those who hear it and take to heart what is
written in it, because the time is near." Revelation 1:3 (NIV)

We huddle at the end of each work day.

In case you are wondering, I am not a football player. I wouldn't last long on the field.

The "team huddle" is a time at the end of my work day where the team, about 4-5 people, gathers together for about five to ten minutes. We discuss issues that came up during the day and how we can improve on them, but we also prepare for the next day.

It is an important opportunity to get a "sneak peek" into the next day so that we are *truly* prepared.

Do you know who else was part of a "huddle"? John, the disciple, who walked with Jesus as he ministered on this earth.

John was given a glimpse of heaven and a sneak peek at the days approaching that included God's judgement and final victory over the enemy. He recorded this in the book of Revelation.

The book of Revelation can be daunting, even to the most mature Christian but it doesn't have to be! The name of the book, "Revelation" in Greek (Apocalypse) actually refers to an unveiling to the believer of events that *WILL* take place.

Not probably, not most likely, but without a doubt.

Through this book, we get a glimpse of our future home, but also get a glimpse of the judgement for those who have persistently rejected Christ's invitation for a relationship. We also learn about God and Jesus, and we cannot help but fall down in worship because the character of Christ is revealed.

Not only that, but look at this: we are told that we will be blessed if we read this revelation. You will be blessed! It's a promise!

Wouldn't you want to get a blueprint of a house of you are building before you move in? We have one! You are not home yet ... there is so much more than this life here on earth.

Don't be intimidated to flip to the end of your Bible to Revelation. We get a glimpse into what is positively going to happen. Shouldn't we be prepared?

Take your time to absorb it ... just a few verses at a time. With the right resources, you can untangle some of the complexities you come across. By reading this book, your love for Jesus will grow and you will be transformed!

~Elizabeth

December 29 ~ Revelation 6-11

"... And he who sits on the throne will give them shelter. They will never again be hungry or thirsty; they will never be scorched by the heat of the sun. For the Lamb on the throne will be their Shepherd. He will lead them to springs of life-giving water. And God will wipe every tear from their eyes."
Revelation 7:15-17 (NLT)

Congratulations! You are almost done! In just a few short days, you will be finished with your chronological Bible reading plan. What an accomplishment to have read the Bible in a year!

Quite honestly, when I was reading through the Bible in a year, and I got to this portion of scripture, I wanted to quit. I was thrilled by the thought that I was almost done reading the Bible in its entirety, but the gravity of Revelation began to stress me. The literature in this book is at times too much for my earthly brain to comprehend, and I really started to question what this section could hold that would change my life.

Revelation is an enigmatic book. It is a heavy read with allegories and symbolic characters and animals. We have transitioned from the letters that John has written into his vision with chaos, death, and destruction reigning on the earth.

We see a glimpse of the end times. What vivid imagery of the horse, riders and the carnage that they bring! As you toil through the remainder of Revelation, let me give you a joyous, paraphrased reminder from Rev 7:15-17.

The God that you serve will bring you through your time of tribulation. The God who loves you will bring you shelter and will not allow you to hunger or thirst. He will protect you from the scorching sun. He will wipe away every tear from your eye.

That was encouraging enough to press on and continue reading. What a beautiful promise for those who come through the tribulation.

The tribulation has yet to occur, but this promise stands true for every trial that we face. God's word from beginning to the end confesses His love for us. He protects us. He cheers us on and wants the best for us. Whatever trial you may be going through, hold on to these promises.

~Shiney

December 30 ~ Revelation 12-18

"She gave birth to a son, a male child, who 'will rule all the nations with an iron scepter.' And her child was snatched up to God and to his throne." Revelation 12:5 (NIV)

I was in the kitchen with my kids when the children's song, *"He's got the whole world in his hands"[1]*, came on the radio. To ease the anxiety of the morning rush, we will occasionally play music, and it also helps the kids learn songs that we learned as children.

The lyrics of this song that I've heard and sung countless times suddenly took on a new meaning to me and warmed my heart. How *simple* the chorus, yet how *meaningful*!

My God holds the entire world ... the stars ... the itty-bitty baby ... my family ... in His hands.

How do we know that?

Remember when the news of Jesus' birth reached King Herod? He had asked the wise men to search for the child so that he could *"go and worship him."* (Matthew 2:8 NIV) We know the ruthless king had other plans in mind.

The Magi were warned in a dream not to go back to Herod and returned home via another route.

The enemy's plans were thwarted.

Remember the unfair Roman trial that our Jesus endured? He was despised and crucified on a tree despite his innocence. The enemy thought his plan had succeeded.

But Jesus rose again! He conquered death! Jesus' last words to Pilate *before* his crucifixion was, *"You would have no power over me if it were not given to you from above ..."* Only God had final authority, not man.

The enemy's plans were thwarted.

In Revelation 12, John sees an unusual sign in heaven. A pregnant woman and a dragon. Unusual combination, right? Many theologians believe the pregnant woman represents Israel who brought us our Lord and birthed Jesus and the dragon represents Satan. The dragon wanted to devour the child, but the child was immediately taken to God's throne after birth.

Safe ... in the arms of the Father.

The enemy's plans were thwarted.

You are a child of the Most High God! Nothing ... no man, no power, no law will destroy the kingdom of God.

When the situations around you seem lost or hopeless, and you feel that the enemy is stepping into your life, remember this verse: *"no weapon that is fashioned against you shall succeed". (Isaiah 54:17 ESV)*

The enemy's plans WILL be thwarted. Why?

Because God's got *you* in His hands, and He is in control of your situation.

~Elizabeth

December 31 ~ Revelation 19-22

"Look, I am coming soon! My reward is with me, and I will give to each person according to what they have done. I am the Alpha and the Omega, the First and the Last, the Beginning and the End."
Revelation 22:12-13 (NIV)

I still remember it as if it were just yesterday. I was traveling on the city bus when announcements began blaring through the driver's radio. All transportation services were being canceled. The World Trade Center had just been hit by a plane.

I rushed into my office in a panic. I found my co-workers and told them what I had heard. They couldn't believe it. So, we all ran to the local coffee shop and watched the news for ourselves. We were struggling to comprehend what our eyes were seeing. Just miles away from where we worked, hundreds of lives had been tragically taken.

My husband was out of the country for work. Friends were barely making it out alive from the World Trade Center. The footage of the destruction was overwhelming. Fear had set in. Were we going to get home that day? Would we see our loved ones one more time?

As we scrambled from the coffee shop back to the office, we gathered our belongings and headed to get back home somehow. I waited for hours for the train to be running again and when I finally arrived in my town, the typically busy streets were so empty I thought I was watching a western movie. Never had I seen such a sight. All seemed hopeless and desolate.

But the resolve of our country to remain strong and full of hope permeated the nation within days for which I am so grateful.

There are many situations and circumstances surrounding us that are hopeless and full of despair. But I thank God for the blessed hope that we have in Him. There will be a day when there will be no more crying, no more sickness, no more pain. The promise of the Lord is found in the key verse above.

"Amen. Come, Lord Jesus." (Revelation 22:20b NIV)

~Joyce

Bible Translations Used:
AMP, AMPC, BSB, CEV,ESV, ISV, KJV, MSG, NAS, NASB, NHEB, NIV, NKJV, NLT, TLB
Emphasis added by devotional authors

Chronological Reading Plan:
Copyright ©Back to the Bible (www.backtothebible.org) - www.esv.org/biblereadingplans

---

DEVOTION 17

1. Bert Thompson, Ph.D, 1993. apologeticspress.org, Biblical Accuracy and Circumcision on the 8th Day

DEVOTION 23

1. HELPS Word-Studies. Copyright © 1987, 2011 by Helps Ministries, Inc.
2. Hunt, J. 2013. Forgiveness: The Freedom to Let Go. Rose Publishing CA Publication date: 01/28/2013

DEVOTION 24

1. "Peace Prayer of St. Francis of Assisi". Original title: Belle prière à faire pendant la Messe. First published in: La Clochette. December 1912. Language: French

DEVOTION 30

1. Hooper, Jodi. "7. Self-Control (Galatians 5:23)." Bible.org, Bible.org, 19 July 2011, bible.org/seriespage/7-self-control-galatians-523.

DEVOTION 36

1. "Covet." *Merriam-Webster Online*, Merriam-Webster, Inc., 2019.

DEVOTION 40

1. Lucado, M. 2015. Glory Days. Nashville, TN. Thomas Nelson.
2. Welland, Collan. 1981. Movie: Chariots of Fire. Twentieth Century Fox, Allied Stars Ltd., Enigma Productions

DEVOTION 44

1. Bible Project. https://thebibleproject.com/explore/leviticus/

DEVOTION 49

1. Hall, Elvina. 1865. Jesus Paid It All.

DEVOTION 52

1. Weaver, J. 2002. Having a Mary Heart in a Martha World Colorado Springs, Co., Waterbrook Press

DEVOTION 55

1. Daywalt, Drew and Jeffers, Oliver. 2013. The Day the Crayons Quit. New York, NY., Philomel Books.

DEVOTION 57

1. Dictionary.com 2019

DEVOTION 59

1. Lucado, M. 2015. Glory Days. Nashville, TN. Thomas Nelson.

DEVOTION 60

1. Stuart, Ben. February 5, 2017. Sermon: Don't Waste Your Family. Passion City Church.

DEVOTION 67

1. Helser, Jonathan., Case, Joel., Johnson, Brian. (2015) No Longer Slaves. On *We Will Not Be Shaken* [live recording]. Bethel Music.

DEVOTION 74

1. Author Anonymous

DEVOTION 78

1. Chapman, Gary. (2010). *The Five Love Languages: The Secret to Love that Lasts.* Chicago, IL: Northfield Publishers.

DEVOTION 79

1. Piper, John. November 11, 2016. Episode 970. https://www.desiringgod.org/interviews/which-old-testament-promises-apply-to-me.

DEVOTION 83

1. Lucado, M. 2015. Glory Days. Nashville, TN. Thomas Nelson.

DEVOTION 100

1. Warren, R. February 1, 2007. The Purpose Driven Life: What on Earth am I Here For? Zondervan Publishing Company. Original work published 2002.

DEVOTION 115

1. HELPS Word-Studies. Copyright © 1987, 2011 by Helps Ministries, Inc.

DEVOTION 123

1. Craig Groeschel Sermon: Authenticity #struggles. LifeChurch.tv, Oklahoma

DEVOTION 127

1. "Worship." *Websters Dictionary.* 1828. http://webstersdictionary1828.com/Dictionary/worship

DEVOTION 131

1. Oxford Living Dictionaries. 2018. https://en.oxforddictionaries.com/definition/assumption

DEVOTION 141

1. Redman, M., Myrin, J. & Ingram, J. (2011). Never Once. https://genius. com/Matt-redman-never-once-lyrics

DEVOTION 146

1. Graham, Billy. 2018. Sermonquotes.com

DEVOTION 148

1. Burnett, Mark, creator. Shark Tank. Mark Burnett Productions, 2009–2011.
2. Lambert, Stephen, creator. Undercover Boss. Studio Lambert, 2010-2014.

DEVOTION 154

1. Oxford Living Dictionaries. 2018. https://en.oxforddictionaries.com/ definition/wisdom

DEVOTION 155

1. *A Bug's Life*. Directed by John Lasseter, performances by Dave Foley, Kevin Spacey, and Julia Louis-Dreyfus, Walt Disney Pictures Pixar Animation Studios, 1998.

DEVOTION 159

1. HELPS Word-Studies. Copyright © 1987, 2011 by Helps Ministries, Inc.

DEVOTION 166

1. Stanfill, Kristian. (2011) Always on *Mountains Move*

DEVOTION 173

1. Collins English Dictionary. 2018. https://www.collinsdictionary.com/ dictionary/english/kindness
2. Smith, Emily E. (2014, June 12). *Masters of Love*. https://www. theatlantic.com/health/archive/2014/06/happily-ever-after/372573/

DEVOTION 186

    1.   Hodges, C. October 17, 2017. The Daniel Dilemma. Thomas Nelson

DEVOTION 196

    1.   Kestler, M. 2018. To Every Man an Answer

DEVOTION 205

    1.   Kuzmic, Kristina. May 11, 2013. Yeah, but ... . http://kristinakuzmic.com/yeah-but

DEVOTION 207

    1.   Keane, Bil. *The Family Circus.* August 31, 1994.

DEVOTION 208

    1.   Lucado, Max. 2017. Anxious for Nothing. Nashville, TN. Thomas Nelson.

DEVOTION 210

    1.   Kimmel, Tim. (2004). *Grace Based Parenting.* Nashville, TN: W. Publishing Group.

DEVOTION 217

    1.   Piper, John. January 3, 2018. Episode 1141. Deep Bible Reading Strategies for the Tired and Busy. www.desiringgod.org

DEVOTION 218

    1.   Hillman, Os. (2000). *Today God Is First.* Shippensburg, PA: Destiny Image Publishers, Inc.

DEVOTION 219

1. Chambers, Oswald. (1982). *My Utmost for His Highest.* Grand Rapids, MI: Oswald Chambers Publications Association, Ltd. Original work published 1935.
2. Warren, Rick. 2019 quotefancy.com

DEVOTION 222

1. Asbury, Cory. (2018) Reckless Love on *Reckless Love.*

DEVOTION 239

1. John Henry Sammis. "Trust and Obey." 1919. https://www.hymnal.net/en/hymn/h/582

DEVOTION 249

1. Editors of Encyclopedia Britannica. (1998). Sheep. In Encyclopedia Britannica: retrieved from www.britannica.com
2. Goats. Retrieved from www.nationalzoosi.edu.

DEVOTION 254

1. Mother Theresa. Goodreads.com

DEVOTION 260

1. Bevere, Lisa. *Fast Forward: The Untapped Catalyst to Spiritual Growth.* 2019. E-book.
2. Stephen Hayes Sermon: Best Practices: Prayer. Covenant Church, Carrollton, Texas.

DEVOTION 261

1. Television Show: The Office. Episode no: Season 9; Episode 24/25. Original air date: May 16, 2013. NBC.
2. Sumlin, Shea. July 9, 2011. Sermon: Kingdom Perspective. The Village Church.

DEVOTION 266

1. Taylor, J. Hudson. Quotefancy.com (1875) Source: <u>Dr. & Mrs. Howard Taylor, Hudson Taylor and the China Inland Mission; The Growth of a Work of God, Chapter 19</u>

DEVOTION 275

1. Sheryl Sandberg. June 3,2015. Facebook.com post.

DEVOTION 283

1. Christian Community Church Arklow, Ireland. *Peacemakers, Not Peacekeepers Part 1*. https://christiancommunitychurcharklow.hdpm.org/peacemakers-not-peacekeepers-part-1/

DEVOTION 290

1. Sande, K. The Peacemaker: A Biblical Guide to Resolving Conflict. Baker Books. January 1,2004. Original publication October 1,1990.
2. Pastor Steven Furtick. Quote on Twitter. November 15, 2015.

DEVOTION 301

1. Hillsong UNITED. (2013). Oceans. On *Zion*.

DEVOTION 307

1. TerKeurst, Lysa. (2010). *Made to Crave*. Brentwood, TN: Fedd & Company, Inc.

DEVOTION 308

1. Einstein, Albert. https://www.azquotes.com/quote/1345367
2. <u>www.gotquestions.org</u>

DEVOTION 310

1. Lewis, C. 1952. Mere Christianity. New York, New York. HarperCollins Publishers.

DEVOTION 318

1. www.instagram.com/thenexusinitiative. Accessed July 15, 2018.
   Mathews, James.

DEVOTION 320

1. Chambers, O. 1935. My Utmost for His Highest. America. Dodd,
   Mead & Co.

DEVOTION 332

1. Ashley McIllwain. www.foundationrestoration.org
2. Nichole Nordeman. "Legacy", *Woven and Spun,* 2002.

DEVOTION 334

1. Rohn, Jim. October 15, 2018. https://www.jimrohn.com/success-
   is-a-personal-choice/

DEVOTION 335

1. Gladwell, Malcolm. Outliers: The Story Of Success. New York: Back
   Bay Books, 2011. Print.
2. *Merriam-Webster Online*, Merriam-Webster, Inc., 2017.

DEVOTION 339

1. Phillips, Craig, and Dean. (1994). I Want To Be Just Like You on *Lifeline*

DEVOTION 341

1. www.dictionary.com

DEVOTION 353

1. Omartian, Stormie. 1997. The Power of A Praying Wife. Eugene, Oregon.
   Harvest House Publishers

DEVOTION 358

1. Stanley, Andy. April 17, 2013. Twitter.

DEVOTION 364

1. London, Laurie. (1957). He's Got the Whole World in His Hands. First published in *Spirituals Triumphant, Old and New* in 1927

CPSIA information can be obtained
at www.ICGtesting.com
Printed in the USA
BVHW081526210221
600526BV00002B/14